YOUR KNOWLEDGE HAS VALUE

We will publish your bachelor's and master's thesis, essays and papers

- Your own eBook and book -
  sold worldwide in all relevant shops

- Earn money with each sale

Upload your text at www.GRIN.com
and publish for free

Eliza Claudia Filimon

Worlds in Collision - Angela Carter's Heterotopia

GRIN Verlag

Bibliografische Information der Deutschen Nationalbibliothek:

Die Deutsche Bibliothek verzeichnet diese Publikation in der Deutschen National-
bibliografie; detaillierte bibliografische Daten sind im Internet über http://dnb.d-
nb.de/ abrufbar.

Dieses Werk sowie alle darin enthaltenen einzelnen Beiträge und Abbildungen
sind urheberrechtlich geschützt. Jede Verwertung, die nicht ausdrücklich vom
Urheberrechtsschutz zugelassen ist, bedarf der vorherigen Zustimmung des Verla-
ges. Das gilt insbesondere für Vervielfältigungen, Bearbeitungen, Übersetzungen,
Mikroverfilmungen, Auswertungen durch Datenbanken und für die Einspeicherung
und Verarbeitung in elektronische Systeme. Alle Rechte, auch die des auszugsweisen
Nachdrucks, der fotomechanischen Wiedergabe (einschließlich Mikrokopie) sowie
der Auswertung durch Datenbanken oder ähnliche Einrichtungen, vorbehalten.

Imprint:

Copyright © 2009 GRIN Verlag GmbH
Druck und Bindung: Books on Demand GmbH, Norderstedt Germany
ISBN: 978-3-656-50763-5

UNIVERSITY OF WINCHESTER

UNIVERSITY OF WINCHESTER
LIBRARY

This book at GRIN:

http://www.grin.com/en/e-book/262543/worlds-in-collision-angela-carter-s-hetero-
topia

GRIN - Your knowledge has value

Der GRIN Verlag publiziert seit 1998 wissenschaftliche Arbeiten von Studenten, Hochschullehrern und anderen Akademikern als eBook und gedrucktes Buch. Die Verlagswebsite www.grin.com ist die ideale Plattform zur Veröffentlichung von Hausarbeiten, Abschlussarbeiten, wissenschaftlichen Aufsätzen, Dissertationen und Fachbüchern.

Visit us on the internet:

http://www.grin.com/

http://www.facebook.com/grincom

http://www.twitter.com/grin_com

Eliza Claudia FILIMON

WORLDS IN COLLISION-
ANGELA CARTER'S HETEROTOPIA

TABLE OF CONTENTS

Abbreviations

Shadow Dance (1966) - SD

The Magic Toyshop (1967) - TMT

Several Perceptions (1968) - SP

Heroes and Villains (1969) - HV

Love (1971)- L

The Infernal Desire Machines of Doctor Hoffman (1972) - IDM

The Passion of New Eve (1977) - PNE

Nights at the Circus (1984) - NC

Wise Children (1991) – WC

'The Erl-King'- EK

'The Lady of the House of Love' –LHL

'The Loves of Lady Purple' – LLP

The Bloody Chamber and Other Stories (1996)- BB

The Sadeian Woman: An Exercise in Cultural History (1979)- *SW*

Nothing Sacred: Selected Writings (1982)- *NS*

Expletives Deleted (1992)- *ED*

Shaking A Leg: Collected Journalism and Writings (1997)- *SL*

INTRODUCTION

Angela Carter's work is a bewildering welter of discourses that work towards changing our perception regarding such issues as identity construction, marginality, myth as foundation of ideology, fluidity of boundaries. Her playful intertextual allusions to literature, psychology, politics and popular culture are infused with irony and wit, while components of discordant genres glitter in the ensuing narrative layers. Her fiction and non-fiction, as well as her experiments in screen and radio adaptation have been universally acclaimed, but the challenge of finding a critical framework complex and accurate enough by which to study her work has remained, since no classification seems to do her justice.

My solution in this thesis is to move away from the urge to approach her works according to literary frames, to a discussion informed by a different metaphor, denoting enigmatic spaces, conterdiscourses, borders of otherness – **heterotopia.** The various interpretations given to the term, that I have relied on in my study, are rooted in its designation of otherness in terms of spatial position, provided by Foucault (1966). Displacement gives voice to Angela Carter's characters, and the spaces they inhabit display melting borders. Heterotopia are shaped by the antagonistic relations operating within these ambiguous spaces, by strategies of resistance, such as performance and telling stories. Space is a language that can be employed to articulate social relationships, with realms of multiple discourses and fluctuating centres mirroring the stages of identity formation (Lefebvre, 1991:132): "Every language is located in a space. Every discourse says something about a space; and every discourse is emitted from a space".

Previous studies of Carter's work have made little use of theories of space in relation to her major themes, so my decision to resort to a spatial metaphor has been reinforced by the prospect of a relevant and, most of all, fresh perspective. My growing interest in Angela Carter's fiction has also been spurred by my nine-year professional involvement in film studies, and the opportunity to approach the two movie adaptations of her writings from an academic perspective. After having read her entire work, I have selected the novels and short stories that best serve my purpose of proving that the complexity of Angela Carter's narrative and cinematic investigation can be subsumed under an equally fluid concept, appropriated from cultural geography, **heterotopia**. The works discussed in my study are: *The Magic Toyshop* (1967), *The Infernal Desire Machines of Doctor Hoffman* (1972), *The Passion of New Eve* (1977), *Nights at the Circus* (1984), *Wise Children* (1991), 'The Loves of Lady Purple' (*Fireworks*, 1974), and 'The Erl-King', 'Lady of the House of Love', 'The Company of Wolves' (*The Bloody Chamber and Other Stories*, 1979).

The two movie adaptations I have also selected for my critical endeavour, one of her novel *The Magic Toyshop* and one inspired by her short stories 'The Company of Wolves' and 'Wolf-Alice', will, first of all, help students in media studies better understand the process of page to screen adaptation, and will, secondly, offer avid readers the complete picture of Carter's cross-cultural approach. Apart from the above mentioned novels and short stories, which form the kernel of my study, there are references to her early novels and other short stories, as they complement the development of my argument. I have also included quotations from her philosophical and journalistic texts, *The Sadeian Woman: An Exercise in Cultural History* (1979), *Nothing Sacred: Selected Writings* (1982), *Expletives Deleted* (1992), *Shaking A Leg: Collected Journalism and Writings* (1997), since they share the same thematic concerns, and provide clues to the interpretation of her seemingly conflicting fictional statements.

The first chapter of my study is divided into two sections, the first providing an overview of Carter's themes in the context of various stages of her critical international reception, while the second clarifies the concept of **heterotopia,** from its etymology to its scientific and metaphorical usage, and outlines the theoretical grid of my study. The purpose of the former section is two-fold, as it introduces readers to Angela Carter's concerns and their literary expression, on the one hand, and justifies the novelty of my argument, that spatiality is a chief dimension of her work, on the other hand. The latter section further underscores the inseparability of spatiality and the major dynamic sites I have subsequently termed **heterotopia**.

In the second chapter I have turned to public and domestic zones of confinement and to the crevices between them, explored by characters in their struggle to negotiate their subjectivity, via movement or the lack of it. The division I have operated separates areas of the outside from interior topographies and illustrates the formation of heterotopia in *The Passion of New Eve, The Infernal Desire Machines of Doctor Hoffman, Nights at the Circus ,* 'The Erl-King', using Brian McHale's means of spatial construction, as well as strategies of resistance to confinement inspired by Michel Foucault, Julia Kristeva, and Mihail Bakhtin.

6

Multiple masculinities and femininities are unravelled in the third chapter which deals with the negotiation of boundaries and the meaning of heterotopia as conflicting relationships rooted in sites of patriarchal ideology in *The Passion of New Eve*, *The Infernal Desire Machines of Doctor Hoffman*, *Wise Children*, 'The Erl-King', 'Lady of the House of Love', 'The Loves of Lady Purple'. I have employed Rosemary Jackson and Catherine Belsey's ideas about desire, Foucault's opinions on violence and Laura Mulvey's theories on the gaze, to support Hetherington's definition of heterotopia. The articulation of the subject's desire requires transgression of myths and symbols, while the experience ranges from arousing to grotesque.

The satirical and sometimes irreverent approach of patriarchy under the guise of performance is the focus of the fourth chapter, in which heterotopia denote sites of performative and theatrical transgressions, following Foucault's definition. Dona Haraway's view on the female body, Bakhtin's theories on the grotesque laughter, Kristeva's thetic and abject zones are the main components of the theoretical grid of the chapter, while the corpus of analysis is represented by *The Passion of New Eve* and *Wise Children*. Gender and sexuality become fluid, as impersonation and monstrosity develop into strategies that may ensure secure zones for the formation of the subject.

The acts and artifice of storytelling form the core of the fifth chapter, in which I follow Carter's experiments with cinema in textual and visual forms, and her tricks of linguistic and cinematic focalizations in *The Magic Toyshop*, *The Passion of New Eve*, *Nights at the Circus*, *Wise Children*, 'The Company of Wolves'. Heterotopia arise as an effect of ambiguity generated by discourse, in accordance with Edward Soja's opinion, while Bakhtin's theories on narrative discourse are linked to Grant's strategy of manipulating time schemes and Mulvey, Judith Mayne and Mary Ann Doane's debates on power in film studies. I argue that Carter's politics of appropriation and transformation allows her to confront tradition, leading to heteroglossia and dialogism as means of breaking the narrative frames and paving the reader's way to other spaces.

With my selection of Angela Carter's selection of works, filtered through **heterotopia** as physical, metaphorical or literary spaces, this study invites the reader to follow the lines of one reader's path through a fascinating body of fiction combining fantasy, parody, magical realism, and the angle which shaped them.

7

1. CONVERGING ECHOES

1.1. INTRODUCING ANGELA CARTER

Angela Carter's work is a collage of almost any conceivable genre: nine novels, essays, reviews, lectures, fairy-tales, short stories, poetry, screenplays, radio plays, and a libretto. No wonder that the legacy of a writer who "realised that there were no limitations to what one could do in fiction" (1997:35) defies attempts to an orderly classification, so that hesitancy about using labels in conjunction with her work must be contextualized.

Carter's work addresses as early as the seventies and the beginning of the eighties the specific themes that, in the late eighties and nineties, have become central to mainstream postfeminism. She worked with postmodern conventions before they were widely accepted, at a time when Anglo-American feminism privileged realism. It was not until the mid-to-late eighties that feminist theorists began to consider what had once been an oxymoron, that feminism and postmodernism could be regarded as allies rather than enemies. She is most frequently mentioned in connection to feminism and postmodernism, as long as the border between them is viewed as fluid because she uses both postmodernist techniques and feminist politics in such a way that it is not possible to reduce her to either. Before appropriating the term **heterotopia** as the overarching label of Carter's work, I consider it important to point out some defining features her writings share with both literary developments.

Postmodernism can be defined easily in relation to the ideologies of the Enlightenment and Modernity. Postmodern thinkers reject the idea of the unity of reason, which leads to hostility towards such concepts as the autonomy of the individual or the use of Reason in pursuit of happiness. Metanarratives are held in contempt and the monolithic discourses of Western civilizations are superseded by multiple local narratives. These seem to represent a point of intersection between postmodernism and feminism, with the latter's emphasis on women's voices. The similarity is superficial, however, if we consider that feminism does not reject the values and goals modernity has inherited from the Enlightenment, such as truth, justice or equality. As a result, feminism remains a revisionist movement within modernity, attempting to accomplish its goals here and now, while competing with the postmodern vision of the death of universal values. Feminists have constantly searched for female stereotypes in fiction, and the critical categories used to shape them. Carter shares the feminist view that the whole patriarchal culture on all its levels, from mythology to narrative fiction, is overloaded with false images of women. She lets the stereotypes explode, and reassembles them into seductive, comic or grotesque forms. She also aims at turning the existing social order upside down, attracted perhaps by the Enlightenment promise that arbitrary authority would cease to exist.

Postmodern literature advocates the impossibility of grasping and re-forming 'objective reality'. It is built on the conviction that literature and criticism are dead, and exposes its own weakness and artificiality at every step, by recycling motifs and techniques. Thus, a postmodern text exists in relation to other texts imitated or parodied, as a vanity fair where uninitiated readers are lost. Carter also uses symbols of Western culture, combines them at will, in order to expose their petrified meanings and lack of depth. Her feminist aims to alter our way of thinking about gender roles are reached through postmodern strategies of writing, playing with myth, deconstructing fairy-tales. She remains in intimate relationship with the discourses she attempts to overthrow, both by assuming the form of accepted literary genres and by apparently revitalizing archetypes, symbols or topoi.

According to Margaret Atwood (1992:61), Carter was "born subversive", while the title of Carter's own collection of essays, *Nothing Sacred* (1982), describes her attitude towards everything—literature, culture, society, sexuality, religion, philosophy, and feminism—nothing is exempt, including those things she loves. This ironical mode is described by Carter herself as "to think on my feet" (*SL* 24). She likes to "present a number of propositions in a variety of different ways," thereby leaving the reader "to construct her own fiction for herself from the elements of my fictions" (*SL* 24). As a result, it is often difficult to determine where, ultimately, Carter stands, and this is what can be so troubling for many readers, especially for feminists who want to read her work as prescriptive or consider the protagonists in her stories as role models. This has led to different and sometimes contradictory interpretations of her work, especially in terms of its potential subversiveness and also in terms of her positioning within both postmodernism and feminism.

Her narrative works as a site of mediation, a mode of inquiry, a place to negotiate a number of poststructuralist theories and to combine them imaginatively in a fictional narrative, giving them a new life of their own.

A brief survey of the critical work on Carter reveals a continual attempt to address the subversiveness of her forms, her intentions and their ultimate execution. The congregation of themes that have occupied critics include her place within both postmodernism and feminism, her use of various genres, and her representations of women, concentrating on female agency, sexuality, femininity and most problematic of all, pornography.

It is possible to consider four different periods of criticism with regard to her work: the first two, which exhibit some overlap, existed during her lifetime, in an engagement and response to the work as it was published, with a tremendous increase following the publishing of *Nights at the Circus* (1984), marking the line between the first two periods; the third took shape in 1992 immediately after her death, when it became possible to assess her work as a whole; and then a fourth period has emerged in the late nineties, allowing for a little more historical and critical distance.

Early criticism was concerned with the limitations and patriarchal nature of the genres Carter employed—especially the fairy tale—and her work's pornographic elements, throwing her subversive style and feminism into question. For example, Robert Clark (1987) disparages 'The Company of Wolves', a rewriting of the *Little Red Riding Hood* story, as "old chauvinism in new clothing" while Andrea Dworkin (1981) criticizes Carter for not adequately revising the form of fairy-tales. Patricia Duncker (1984) goes even further in her assessment of the genre itself as hopelessly patriarchal, and reinforcing the pornographic situation of woman as a willing victim. A clear line is drawn between her early and late fiction, where the early novels are considered to contain the seeds for what is developed later into more fully formed incarnations, usually with the assumption that the earlier work is inferior.

One critical practice that emerged in the second period, after the publication of *Nights at the Circus*, was the tendency to employ a hermeneutic of progression with regard to her fiction. Critics dissatisfied with the representation of women in Carter's earlier works were happier with the later ones; they considered those women strong personalities rather than victims, they appreciated Carter's treatment of heterosexual taboos, and the general opinion was that Carter's cynical pessimism is eased by laughter and the comedic (Palmer [1987], Jordan [1990], Duncker [1984]). In the third and fourth periods, there has been an increasing tendency to use the non-fictional work *The Sadeian Woman* as a focal point to explain not only aspects in *The Bloody Chamber* but also problematic representations in the later works, especially in *The Infernal Desire Machines of Doctor Hoffman* and *Nights at the Circus*.

Between 1997 and 1998, three full-length studies of Carter's work were published, Aidan Day's (1998), Sarah Gamble's (1997), Linden Peach's (1998), and a collection of essays edited by Lindsay Tucker (1998), displaying a lack of consensus about where to place Carter. Day reads Carter as a rationalist; Gamble as a feminist interested in dramatizing the liminal, Peach as an English writer strongly influenced by American culture, while Tucker's volume comprises a series of challenging and sometimes conflicting interpretations, with an inconclusive overview. The approaches are either chronological or thematic, providing a general basis for further study. Elaine Jordan (1992), an important critic in Carter studies, has argued that the fairy-tales, along with the rest of Carter's work, represent an exploration of the complex nature of what it is to be a heterosexual woman in a patriarchal society. Meanwhile, Merja Makinen (1992) joins with Jordan and counters Duncker, pointing out that when writers employ ironic strategies of rewriting, as Carter and postcolonial writers do, genres are able to carry new sets of assumptions. Other critics at that time have taken their cue from this more positive reading of her work and have begun to assess her employment of a number of genres. The volume *Flesh and the Mirror,* edited by Carter's friend Lorna Sage (1994), an important critic as regards the biographical aspects of her work, is an excellent example of this trend, as it explores the influence of media, surrealism and science fiction on Carter's writing.

The most recent criticism situates her use of genres within various theories of intertextuality. However, the best analyses demonstrate an awareness of the reading process itself. For example, Lucie Armitt (1997) effectively foregrounds the pleasure involved in the interpretative act itself in her observation that *The Bloody Chamber* holds a great fascination for critics. Further, Armitt indicates that although she agrees with Jordan and Makinen, they do not analyze how Carter rewrites the tale, and she herself begins such work by a brief consideration of the tales in terms of interlocking frames.

It is therefore evident that criticism has evolved as a result of dialogue, but it is also a reflection of changing interests in the general critical climate. For instance, in the early nineties, John Bayley (1992) accused Carter of "political correctness", but it is important to note large critical consideration of Carter's use of postmodernism as subversive. Sally Robinson (1991:78) has also explored how Carter's texts "strategically engage with the theoretical concerns of

11

postmodernism" and she focuses on the preoccupation with the "place of 'woman' in the deconstruction of culture's master narratives".

Criticism continues to focus on what might be labelled postmodern aspects, issues of gender and other related themes of interest to contemporary feminist analyses, such as the body, spectacle, and violence. As Bristow and Broughton (1997:14) note, the most insistent feature in Carter studies is that of "theatricality, spectacle and play-acting", associated with the notion of theory and politics of gender as performance. Despite the fact that Carter did not read Bakhtin's theories until after she had written *Nights at the Circus,* criticism constantly points to these carnival elements to explain her subversion.

Carter is often mentioned in the context of the symbiosis of feminist themes and postmodernist techniques in the essays included in Sage's *Flesh and the Mirror* (1994), or the collection of feminist essays edited by Alison Easton (2000) and Sarah Gamble (2001). *Nights at the Circus* is used as magnifying lens for Carter's array of themes and discourses in Helen Stoddart's book (2007), fairy-tales come under scrutiny in the collection edited by Cristina Bacchilega and Danielle M. Roemer (2001), while countless essays on her work complete anthologies on contemporary British writers (Nicola Pitchford [2002], Sarah Sceats [2005], Julia Simon [2005]).

A less explored aspect of her writing, irony, is vital to understanding her possible subversion and her position regarding both postmodernism and feminism. Linda Hutcheon (1989:160) is well-known for making the link between irony and the feminist postmodern. In *The Politics of Postmodernism,* she argues that parody especially but also the extremely close trope of irony are common postmodern tools that are attractive for many feminists: "I also think postmodernist parody would be among the 'practical strategies' that have become 'strategic practices' in feminist artists' attempt to present new kinds of female pleasure, new articulations of female desire, by offering tactics for deconstruction". However, as Hutcheon herself notes in *Irony's Edge* (1994), there are numerous ways of understanding this trope. Carter's work is extremely allegorical. These allegorical elements, as well as postmodern techniques help to create the multi-layered meanings, the open-endedness and the ground to the irony in her work. I believe that this description is an apt way to describe the particular combination of both the cynical and utopic tendencies in Carter's work, the extreme critique to which she subjects everything, combined with the desire for change. It is the kind of irony Carter herself describes when she talks about presenting "a number of propositions in a variety of different ways" (*SL* 24).

Carter's reference to the role of the reader in relation to her open-ended fictions emphasizes her desire to present positive, creative positions rather than negative, destructive ones. In an attempt to explain her contrasting attitude to some postmodernist issues, she describes her work As belonging to the nineteenth-century because it invites the reader "to take one further step into the fictionality of the narrative, instead of coming out of it and looking at it as though it were an artefact" (Haffenden, 1985:91).

Some have found her work troubling, especially because she has been known to attack particular forms of feminism; for example, either by portraying one character as a mouthpiece for a certain kind of feminism in a gentle caricaturization (Ma Nelson, or Lizzie in *Nights at the Circus*) or in a scathing manner (Mother in *The Passion of New Eve*), a style which is taken by many as a biting critique of the radical feminism of the 1970s. Today, however, she is recognized for anticipating central debates in feminism in the late 1980s and 1990s, for instance, viewing pornography as potentially liberatory and gender as performative.

It is her unique sense of both postmodernism and feminism—and their combination—which largely makes Carter into a kind of chimera. For just as Carter is evasive regarding feminism, so too she expresses resistance to the term postmodernism. In an interview with Haffenden, she equates postmodernism with Borges' metafictional idea of "books about books" (1985:70). In this exchange, she admits to having been interested in this idea in the past, but by the time of the interview, she has reconsidered that this kind of practice is best described as "fun but frivolous" (Haffenden, 1985:79).

There are evidently many reasons why we should hesitate in calling Carter a postmodernist. Yet it is also difficult not to use such a term because it does refer to a certain tradition that engages with concerns and techniques also evident in the work of Carter for which there is no other appropriate label. For instance, many critics cite the overlap between her work and postmodern concerns in terms of her critique of Western patriarchy and representation, the production of "truth" through myth, her use of intertextuality, hybridization and parody, her experimentation with narrative structures, including open-endedness, or her employment of fiction as literary criticism.

One label that Carter has more readily accepted, although with some qualifications, has been 'magic realist'. As Helen Carr (1989:7) has noted, Carter's novels became more acceptable after the discovery of South American magic realism because she could be assigned to an actual genre. This use of the term to describe her continual blurring of the line between realism and fantasy certainly seems appropriate, yet once again, it is the case that she used the genre's techniques before it became popular. Further, although Salman Rushdie is credited with the distinction of being the pioneer of this tradition in the English novel, his friend Carter predated him. Yet, as Peach cautions, the term is more appropriate to Carter's later works than to her earlier ones. As Carter herself points out, the context in which she was involved, "more intellectual than folk", was very different from that of Marquez (Haffenden, 1985: 81).

Other tags she has been given include 'speculative' and 'fantasist', with many critics dividing her work into an early-sixties fusion of realist Gothic and fantasy, and a later post-sixties magic realist, speculative and philosophical phase. One intriguing label that has been used for Carter is that of 'science fiction' writer. In 'New New World Dreams' (1994) Roz Kaveney sheds some light on this designation in her observation that Angela Carter freely made use of tropes derived from this genre.

Like the mainstream postfeminists of the nineties, Carter's work is interested in the themes and limits of female desire and sexuality, in sado-masochism and pornography and their relationship to violence; she is countering the very powerful stereotype of 'woman as victim' by considering masculinity as much as femininity, delighting in popular culture, especially in film, and making humour integral to feminism. Grounded in the carnivalesque and the body, Carter's is the humour of Shakespeare's tragic fools described by Kate Webb (1994:5) as "seriously funny" and by Salman Rushdie (1992) as having a "deadly cheeriness".

Just as postfeminism makes the subject of men and masculinity an important focus, so too, we find these themes in Carter's work. At a time when feminist fiction was interested in promoting strong female characters and the expression of both the female voice and women's experience, much of Carter's work, particularly her early novels, features male protagonists and investigates issues of masculinity. In fact, Sally Robinson's experience of reading *The Infernal Desire Machines of Doctor Hoffman* is that there is "no *place* for a woman reader in this text" (1991:105). But Carter's interest is in investigating the structure of desire itself, along with its implications, both for men and for women. She is one of the first to challenge and to explore what has come to be known as the stereotype of 'the woman as victim', yet her investigation of this theme is more complex. While it remains a focus throughout her novels and short stories, her most sustained analysis appears in the non-fictional *The Sadeian Woman* (1979). This controversial work is known for its challenge to the widespread complicity of women who identify with images of themselves as victims of patriarchal oppression. The book examines the myths surrounding three identities women have in our culture—the virgin, the whore and the mother—and demonstrates the dangers of each, while indicating their similar singular basis; namely, that these identities "have been defined exclusively by men" (*SW* 77). Contrary to the interpretation of a number of critics, Carter does not simply debase the role of the victim and elevate that of the whore; instead, she sees them as two sides of the same coin: "they mutually reflect and compliment one another, like a pair of mirrors" (*SW* 78).

In most of her earlier work, her investigation of desire causes her to create protagonists who are largely female masochists or male sadists. This has been an issue for feminists. Some have addressed this problem by dividing her work into early and late years: Paulina Palmer (1987) considers the later more liberatory than the earlier; Christina Britzolakis defines the early heroines as "puppets of male-controlled scripts" (1995:51) and the later ones as using "theatricality and masquerade to invent and advance themselves" (1995:51); Elaine Jordan considers that "she started out writing as a kind of male impersonator" but later started "writing radically as a woman" (1990:31). There is no question that she does portray strong women, especially in her last two novels, *Nights at the Circus* and *Wise Children.* She confesses that she spent ten years writing *Nights at the Circus* because she had to be "big enough, strong enough, to write about a winged woman"(qtd. in Gamble, 1997:157).

Her love of popular culture and film is demonstrated in the intertextual references throughout her work and her journalism. She was particularly interested in the bad girls of cinema. Unlike postfeminists who seem to privilege this medium above all others, Carter's work is also replete with references from a range of sources—opera, Renaissance drama, philosophy, literature, myth and fairy tales as well as film and television. Thus, rather than understanding the blurring of boundaries between high and low culture in terms of the inclusion of the latter into the former, she turns this postmodern tendency inside out and reads Shakespeare as popular culture, turning high culture into popular culture. For instance, she claims: "I tend to use other people's books, European literature, as though it were that kind of folklore. Our literary heritage as a kind of folklore" (Haffenden, 1985:82). For Carter, then, popular culture is not confined to an understanding of texts that are produced by the mass media, but includes our entire cultural heritage. Performance, looking, and artifice are central to her work, and her work is replete with spaces of theatricality. Her use of carnival allows for transgression and intersects with an underlying examination of gender.

Romanian university curricula have, sadly, shrunk under both national and European constraints, so the study of postmodern literature wavers between a chronological, exhaustive presentation of writers and a thematic, selective approach, dictated by the availability of resources. Two of Angela Carter's novels were translated into Romanian, *The Magic Toyshop* in 2007 (*Magazinul Magic de Jucării*, trans. Adina and Gabriel Rațiu), and *Nights at the Circus* in 2008 (*Nopți la Circ*, trans. Gabriela Grigore), introducing Romanian readers to her intriguing fictional universe. Ileana Botescu Sireteanu's 2007 study, devoted to the fiction of Carter and Winterson represents a necessary addition to the gallery of conference papers written by Romanian academics enchanted by Carter's works (Hanțiu [1999, 2006], Bălănescu [2004], Adăscăliței [1998], Chiper [2002]). My study will hopefully provide an accessible entry to Carter's works and contribute to her inclusion into the local university syllabus.

Fairy-tales, Gothic fiction, a baroque sensibility, feminism, science fiction, magical realism: from this mélange emerges Angela Carter's fiction. A phantasmagorical work framed by the horrific, the erotic, and the humorous, Carter's writing displays her fascination with borders, liminality, and ways of crossing and transgressing limits. I will address these aspects of her work in the following chapters of my study as forms of **heterotopia**, a term I have considered appropriate due to its elastic definitions which I review in the ensuing section.

16

1.2. DEFINING HETEROTOPIA

The term **heterotopia** originally comes from the study of anatomy, where it refers to "parts of the body that are either out of place, missing, extra, or, like tumours, alien" (Hetherington, 1998:72).

Heterotopia as a spatial metaphor derives from the ancient Greek pronoun *heteros* 'other' and the noun *topos* 'place'. Coined by analogy to utopia and dystopia, heterotopia means, quite literally, 'a place of different order' and refers to an actual place conceived as being otherwise and existing outside normative social and political space. The three main places in his work where Foucault refers most explicitly to heterotopia are, firstly, the introduction to *The Order of Things/ Les mots et les choses,* published in 1966, where he discusses Borges' Chinese Encyclopedia (1970/1991:xvff), secondly, in the same year, a radio broadcast as part of a series on the theme of utopia and literature, and thirdly, in a lecture given to a group of architects in 1967, 'Des autres espaces'*,* only released and published unedited shortly before his death, in 1984, and translated into English as *Of Other Spaces* (1986). In all three cases the key issue raised is that of ordering.

> "Utopias afford consolation: although they have no real locality there is nevertheless a fantastic, untroubled region in which they are able to unfold. Heterotopias are disturbing, probably because they make it impossible to name this and that" (Foucault, 1970:xviii)

He gives an inventory of 'other spaces', using a puzzling spectrum of examples, identifying six 'principles' of heterotopology:

Firstly, heterotopia are found in all cultures and epochs. Heterotopia circumscribe rites of passage, "crisis heterotopias", (e.g. schools) and "of deviance" (e.g. prisons). Like elsewhere in the lecture, it isn't clear whether Foucault is talking about kinds of heterotopia or about heterotopia in general.

Secondly, heterotopia have a certain function in relation to 'all' other sites in a 'culture'. They are "absolutely different", and their difference is an effect of the "synchrony of the culture in which [the heterotopia] occur" (1967:241). Thus, their function can change historically.

Thirdly, heterotopia can juxtapose within them heterogeneous elements which are 'in themselves' incompatible. Heterotopia are ambiguous, non-totalisable, contradictory spaces. This third characteristic of heterotopia is the most popular one amongst writers using the word. Edward Soja (1995), in his heterotopologies, concentrates on the holding together of differences within postmodern spaces of Los Angeles. Edward Relph (1991) considers 'postmodernity' to be the generalisation of heterotopia, of the pluralistic coexistence of elements which one would 'normally' think or find apart. Miriam Kahn (1995) writes about the "heterotopic dissonance" resulting from the "displacement" of artefacts and myths in anthropological museums. I will return to the issue of elements being called 'in themselves' incompatible, 'displaced' and 'normally' separate in the second and the fourth chapters of my study.

The forth principle is that heterotopia arise especially through 'heterochrony' or discontinuity in time. They can accumulate the past, as in museums, or stretch out the now, as in carnival and roller-coaster rides. Foucault (1967:242) says tourist destinations combine both, and my focus on performance in chapter four will investigate this principle.

The fifth is that heterotopia operate by demarcation, by territoralization, by a "system of opening and closing" (1967:243). They may be publicly accessible though they curiously do not let the visitor in entirely. "[W]e think we enter where we are, by the very fact that we enter, excluded" (ibid.). The most adequate metaphor to understand a comparable heterotopic place may be the one of the sailing ship, according to Foucault (1984:184-185):

> "the ship is a piece of floating space, a placeless place, that lives by its own devices, that is self-enclosed and, at the same time, delivered over to the boundless expanse of the ocean, and that goes from port to port, from watch to watch, from brothel to brothel, all the way to the colonies in search of the most precious treasures that lie waiting in their gardens, you see why for our civilization, from the sixteenth century up to our time, the ship has been at the same time not only the greatest instrument of economic development, of course, but the greatest reservoir of imagination. The sailing vessel is the heterotopia par excellence. In civilizations without ships the dreams dry up, espionage takes the place of adventure, and the police that of the corsairs".

The last principle refers to the function heterotopia have "in relation to all the space that remains" (1967:243). Foucault is frustratingly vague at the end of his lecture, stating that heterotopia can have two seemingly 'polar' functions to 'the rest' of space. Either they provide 'illusion', making other places in society seem 'still more illusionary' (like brothels do) or they provide 'perfection' (as colonies do). In chapter five I will link this principle to the voices controlling the narrative and manipulating the reader

For Foucault, there are two principal modes of ordering: through resemblance and through similitude. It is the latter that we should associate with heterotopia. The ordering represented by resemblance is a familiar one, social expectations developed over time assume that certain things go together in a certain order. These representations act as signs where what is being signified refers to a known referent. Similitude, however, is all about an ordering that takes place through a juxtaposition of signs that culturally are seen as not going together, either because their relationship is new or because it is unexpected. What is being signified cannot be easily attached to a referent. Foucault (1983) takes the surrealist paintings of Magritte as an illustration of the ordering process of similitude. Similitude is constituted by an unexpected bricolage effect and can be used to challenge the conventions of representation. It is the juxtaposition of things not usually found together and the confusion that such representations create, that mark out heterotopia and give them their significance. This switch from ways of representing through resemblance to similitude is essential to fully grasp the significance of heterotopia for Foucault. As Harkness suggests, in his introduction to the English translation of Foucault's long essay on Magritte 'This is Not a Pipe':

> "Resemblance, says Foucault, 'presumes a primary reference that prescribes and classes' copies on the basis of the rigor of the mimetic relation to itself. Resemblance serves and is dominated by representation. With similitude, on the other hand, the reference 'anchor' is gone. Things are cast adrift, more or less like one another without any of them being able to claim the privileged status or 'model' for the rest. Hierarchy gives way to a series of exclusively lateral relations." (1983:9-10)

For Foucault places of Otherness are spaces, whose existence sets up "unsettling juxtapositions of incommensurate 'objects' which challenge the way we think, especially the way our thinking is ordered" (Hetherington, 1998:42). The surprise effect heterotopia generate results from their different mode of ordering. What defines heterotopia as places of another order is not physical location. The relation of the topos of the 'other' to the topos of the 'same' is determined less by physical position than by the confluence of discourses, institutions, and procedures deployed in a place.

Since Foucault himself was hardly exact and exhaustive on what he meant by heterotopia, his readers have interpreted his lecture in quite different ways. David Harvey (1996:230) says Foucault is talking about "space[s] of liberty outside of social control", whereas Foucault says prisons are heterotopia too (Foucault 1967:240).

Kevin Hetherington's book *The Badlands of Modernity: Heterotopia and Social Ordering* (1998) is more assertive and argues convincingly that heterotopia are the "sites of alternate ordering" in modernity. He qualifies heterotopia as places of "Otherness, whose Otherness is established through a relationship of difference with other sites, such that their presence either provides an unsettling of spatial and social relations or an alternative representation of spatial and social relations" (1998:8). As to the question of what Otherness mans, he describes it as "something without", different to the norm either within a culture or what (Said, 1991) would term between cultures, 'something excessive' or 'something incongruous', a hybrid combination of the incongruous. Angela Carter's female characters in chapter three will serve as arguments of breaking the binary of power, while male ones must find the Other outside the mirror before reaching a deeper understanding of the self. As well as discussing what Foucault had to say about heterotopia, Hetherington looks at the better known term 'utopia', drawing on the work of Louis Marin (1984), and calls attention to Marin's interest not in utopia as imaginary perfect societies, but in the spatial play that is involved in imagining and trying to create these perfect worlds in the spaces that make up the modern world. The term he coins to refer to this spatial play is 'utopics'. For Marin, irreconcilable ambiguity is a necessary requirement for a full understanding of utopia. When Thomas More first coined the term 'Utopia' in his literary satire (1516) of sixteenth-century society, he collapsed two Greek words together: *eu-topia* meaning 'good place' and *ou-topia* meaning 'no-place' or 'nowhere'. His Utopia was a good place that existed nowhere, except in the imagination. Ever since, people have been trying to create utopia, by turning the nowhere into the good place. Marin's aim is, however, to separate the nowhere from the good place, to return utopia to eu-topia and ou-topia and to investigate the zone that opens up between them. That chasm, which Marin calls 'the neutral', is where Hetherington (1998:7) locates Foucault's heterotopia.

"within this in-between space that I call heterotopia. To do that it is in my interest, made possible by Marin, to keep this space-between not quite nowhere, but not as a good space either. Heterotopia do exist, but they only exist in this space-between, in this relationship between

20

spaces, in particular between eu-topia and ou-topia. Heterotopia are not quite spaces of transition—the chasm they represent can never be closed up—but they are spaces of deferral, spaces where ideas and practices that represent the good life can come into being, from nowhere, even if they never actually achieve what they set out to achieve—social order, or control and freedom".

Hetherington's approach, however, is limited, as he relates it to 'utopics' and to 'modernity' alone. Soja (1989), on the other hand, focuses not so much on the difference between heterotopia and the rest of society (heterotopia as counter-sites), but seems to favour the differences (of temporalities, of cultures, of ethnicities, of knowledge) within selected postmodern urban spaces. Soja's *Thirdspace* (1996) centres around what Henri Lefebvre called 'spaces of representation' and Foucault's heterotopias. He argues that, geographically speaking, there have been two conceptualisations of space: what he calls 'Firstspace' is the space of concrete materiality, while 'Secondspace' designates ideas about space. The former is real, the latter imaginary, whereas 'Thirdspace' is real-and-imaginary. It is the result of a fusion between material and mental spaces, but also more than this. Soja suggests that these three spaces can be found in the opening chapter of Lefebvre's *The Production of Space* (1991:33).

Under the influence of both Nietzsche and surrealism, Henri Lefebvre viewed everyday life as a field of political struggle, where the seed of change could grow due to heterogeneous forms and spaces opposing capitalism. He also employs the word heterotopia several times, for he classifies places as 'isotopias' or analogous/ homogenous places, 'utopias' or non-places filled with power and possibility, and 'heterotopias' or contrasting, mutually opposing places (1974/1991:163-164 and 366). Heterotopia, then, always come as a pair. The way I understand it, the heterotopic is not so much a characteristic of one place, as a particular relation between places. Lefebvre advances the idea of a triadic process, which consists of the relationship between 'Spatial Practice', 'Representations of Space', and 'Representational Spaces' (1991:33). Space is viewed as perceived, conceived and lived. The first of these takes space as physical form, space that is generated and used. The second is the space of knowledge and logic, of maps and mathematics. The third space is produced and modified over time, the lived, social space, invested with symbolism and meaning. For Lefebvre, spatial practice is associated with the production of a distinct space by social relations associated with capitalist production and reproduction. Representations of space are linked to the production and conceptualization,

21

the physical form of space. It is Lefebvre's belief that within the capitalist social formation, "its spatial practice is rendered invisible as abstract space by the dominant representations of space, obscuring the social relations of power by which that space is produced" (1998:22). Resistance to the dominant social relations must make this space visible. This resistance takes place through what Lefebvre calls representational spaces. Such spaces are described as "embodying complex symbolisms, sometimes coded, sometimes not, linked to the clandestine or underground side of social life, as also to art" (1991:33). He goes on to suggest that representational spaces are

> "[S]pace as directly lived through its associated images and symbols, and hence the space of 'inhabitants' and 'users', but also of some artists and perhaps of those, such as a few writers and philosophers, who describe and aspire to do no more than describe. This is the dominated—and hence passively experienced—space which the imagination seeks to change and appropriate. It overlays physical space, making symbolic use of its objects." (1991:39)

Representational spaces involve making use of sites that have been left behind or left out as fragments produced by the tensions within the contradictory space of capitalism that lies hidden by its representations of space. The use of sites whose attributed meaning leaves them somewhat ambivalent and uncertain allows for these spaces, according to Lefebvre, to offer a vantage point from which the production of space can be made visible and be critically viewed, exposing thus the social power relations at work. The activities related to the production of representational spaces, are dis-placed, so that marginal groups, and marginal ways of thinking help produce the meaning of the sites. In the 1970s when Lefebvre was writing *The Production of Space* he had in mind the sorts of acts of resistance by students and workers that he had seen in the representational spaces of the campuses and streets of Paris in 1968. Representational spaces are, thus, spaces of freedom.

In her article 'Of other spaces' (2000), Maria Tamboukou presents a Foucauldian genealogy of the disciplinary practices, and the heterotopic relations involved in the emergence of women's colleges in nineteenth century England. 'Heterotopic relations' here refers to the relations shaping women's social life, confined by patriarchy ideologically, and within the college walls, physically. Tamboukou calls these colleges heterotopias, characterized by discontinuous space and time, because they facilitated the blurring of the gendered division between public and private spheres, despite patriarchal surveillance. They are fleeting, plural, wayward, potentially disruptive spaces.

What I have found helpful about Tamboukou's article, is her interest in the voices of those within heterotopia: the women. They managed to transform this lived space from an 'other' space, into an 'own' space, 'isotopic' to a certain degree with other feminine spaces. The women used women's colleges to develop their feminine identities, and struggled to keep patriarchal discipline and pedagogy out.

This struggle over space raises the question of what otherness means. Every space is 'other' for someone – Doreen Massey asks of Foucault, "Surely *all* spaces/places are heterotopias?" (1998: 224). So either we call all spaces/places heterotopias or we call some relations between places 'heterotopic'. All places, then, are heterotopic to certain other places. Woman's body becomes a personal spatial site that she must explore in order to alter her relationship to the surrounding male-dominated cultural and social space, as I illustrate in the second and third chapters of my discussion.

Arun Saldanha, in his article 'Structuralism and the Heterotopic' (2000) refines Foucault's heterotopology, by identifying aspects of the heterotopic that I will relate to Angela Carter's heterotopia: **reciprocality, politics of boundaries, situatedness, multivocality**. Othering is always **reciprocal** and involves the agency of both 'sides' (Saldanha, 2000). Calling the heterotopic relational also means calling it reciprocal. We could say that just as there is no such thing as power, only power relations, so there is no such thing as heterotopia, only heterotopic relations. While spatial othering is a double-sided process, it is possible to say that the means to other, to marginalise, to segregate, are not evenly distributed. One 'side', the 'subordinate' side, is more problematic than the other, 'dominant' side because the latter has more means to confine and define what goes on within the subordinate side. That is to say, a heterotopic relation is also an antagonistic relation (Saldanha, 2000).

Foucault started his discussion of heterotopia and utopia with imagining social relations with a familiar philosophical metaphor: the mirror. Though the metaphor is ego-centric, I take it to be a handy spatialising metaphor for the heterotopic boundary between self and Other, reflexivity, and the workings of the 'virtual' in the 'real' (Foucault 1967: 239-240):

> "The mirror is a utopia after all, since it is a placeless place. In the mirror I see myself where I am not, in an unreal space that opens up virtually behind the surface; I am over there where I am not, a kind of shadow that gives me my own visibility, that enables me to look at myself there

where I am absent ≠ a mirror utopia. But it is also a heterotopia in that the mirror really exists, in that it has a sort of return effect on the place that I occupy. Due to the mirror, I discover myself absent at the place where I am, since I see myself over there. From that gaze which settles on me, as it were, I come back to myself and I begin once more to direct my eyes toward myself and to reconstitute myself there where I am. The mirror functions as a heterotopia in the sense that it makes this place which I occupy at the moment when I look at myself in the glass both utterly real, connected with the entire space surrounding it, and utterly unreal since, to be perceived, it is obliged to go by way of that virtual point which is over there" (Foucault, 1986:179).

In order to realise one's own space and identity, Tamboukou's women students, for instance, had to oppose themselves to the conservative men outside, the virtually present other, the "other side of the glass" (Foucault 1967: 240). Of course, in contrast to Foucault's metaphor, the other behind the glass in Tamboukou's study is not only 'virtual', but men of flesh and blood 'looking back' at women's colleges. When Foucault asserts that the heterotopic "exerts a sort of counteraction to the position I occupy" (1967: 240), his spatial play of presence/absence evokes reciprocality (Saldanha, 2000). The reciprocality of the heterotopic boundary goes beyond segregating self and other, and reflects the antagonism that constitutes and is constituted by that segregation: antagonism between women and men, prisoners and guards, gays and straights.

The second aspect of the heterotopic Saldanha identifies is the **politics of boundaries** and it follows directly from this antagonism. Terms like 'segregation' and 'exclusion' connote processes of spatial othering centred on sharp demarcations between self and other. The heterotopic boundaries between inside and outside are not rigid but fluid, not fixed once and for all, but constantly fought over and negotiated. When speaking about the simultaneous penetratibility and "curious exclusions" of heterotopia, Foucault (1967:243) might have envisaged heterotopic boundaries in the same way:

"Here the heterotopia takes on the qualities of human territoriality, with its surveillance of presence and absence, its demarcation behaviors, its protective definition of the inside and the out. Implicit in this regulation of opening and closing are the workings of power, of disciplinary technologies" (Soja, 1995: 16).

If heterotopias are open-but-closed, accessible but 'sacred' in some way or another, a struggle will emerge between those who want it closed and others who want it open.

24

The third aspect of the heterotopic, **situatedness**, pertains to the way Foucault consistently describes heterotopias as being totally different from all other sites in a society. Foucault's structuralist tendency is to treat every relation as a relation expressing a whole, rather than conforming to a specific time and space. This mistake is evident in Foucault's crucial remark (1967:239) that in heterotopias "all the other real sites that can be found within the culture, are simultaneously represented, contested, and inverted". A major deficiency in Foucault's argument becomes clear: he does not situate the heterotopic relationship (Saldanha, 2000). He seems to believe every element simultaneously relates to all the other elements in perfect "synchrony". In one of the few pieces of writing which is critical of Foucault's 'Of other spaces', Benjamin Genocchio (1995:39) questions Foucault's heterotopology. Genocchio argues that Foucault logically neutralises heterotopia's otherness, for "how is it that heterotopias are "outside" of or are fundamentally different to all other spaces, but also relate to and exist "within" the general social space/order that distinguish their meaning as difference? In short, how can we "tell" these Other spaces/stories?" (Genocchio 1995: 38).

Calling otherness a discursive effect means there must be something to oppose otherness in the first place, so spatial otherness is itself situated, itself relational, itself heterotopic, one might say, to other ways of speaking about space.

Genocchio wishes to redefine 'the heterotopia' not as a discernible actual place, but as a conceptualization of space, thinking space as "polysemous and contestory, made from a woven thread of some still enchanted fabric which must always be questioned, fought over, altered and most of all, unravelled" (1995:43).

The heterotopic must not be defined as 'absolute', as Foucault does, but as *relative*, relative to the way we speak about it. Difference is voiced differently. Hence, the **multivocality** of the heterotopic also implies that every attempt to define it is in some way or the other effective in reality, and therefore political, as I argue in chapter five. This is what Saldanha calls the 'multivocality' (2000) of the heterotopic. It's the fourth principle of heterotopology he brings forth and the fourth critique of Foucault's. Not only do heterotopic relations have different meanings for those involved in them, but also for those analysing them. Other to whom? Counter to what? In geography, it has not gone unnoticed that Foucault writes: "The space in which we live, which draws us out of ourselves, in which the erosion of our lives, our time, and our history occurs, the space that claws and gnaws at us, is also, in itself, a heterogeneous space" (1967: 239). In his work in general, he has had a lot to say about

25

marginalization, entrapment, othering, disjunction, subordination, that is the interaction between space, heterogeneity and relations of power, issues I tackle in chapter three.

Wearing's (1998) heterotopia translates as a place which minority groups find that is liberating: heterotopia designates "space that allows and confines activity" (Wearing, 1998:146). Heterotopic space encourages opportunities for those who have immigrated and resettled "to establish themselves in their new community, restore mind and body, develop friendships and new skills" (Hall and Huyskens, 2002:1). Hall and Huyskens adopt Wearing's definition of heterotopia, based on the latter's study of Foucault (1986), and view the term as a reference to "a liberating leisure site or space" with the potential to provide a place for renewal and enhancement of self-esteem. Hall and Huyskens (2002:2) have identified leisure sites as a key factor in the acculturation of refugee women offering them a site of escape from the difficulties that the new life presents, a space for recovery of pleasure, a zone to assert or reconfigure identity, and an empowering force. The role of heterotopia is deemed to be an essential key in evaluation and understanding because it is a potentially cathartic space in which "rewriting the script of identity" (Wearing, 1998:146) may occur.

Two castles project their shadows over Foucault's (1990) vision of modernity. The first is de Sade's (1785) castle, a space in which the complete freedom of unrestrained, sadistic, male desire is acted out on the bodies of women and children with impunity. The second is Kafka's (1922), although it could also be the labyrinthine space of the law courts in *The Trial* (1925). In either case, it is a space of the absolute irreproachable power of bureaucracy and the law. Both are obligatory points of passage in which freedom and control extend beyond their own limits and mingle with one another. Both spaces are examples of heterotopia. The first is configured as a space of unlimited individual freedom, a freedom that allows unrestrained sexual conduct. If, in this Sadeian vision, freedom is allowed total control, in the second, the Kafkaesque vision, it is social control that is allowed total freedom. Here there are no limits to which surveillance and discipline are exercised:

"The ideal point of penalty today would be an infinite discipline: an interrogation without end." (Foucault, 1977:227)

Perspective cannot be disregarded in either case. For the victims of such spaces, their meanings would be different, because each space is the mirror image of the other. In both, the individual, perpetrator and victim, is defined as a subject. But the point is not just one of perspective: for Foucault at least, the issue is mainly one of the constitution of subjectivity within the uncertain nexus of freedom and control defined by such spaces (1986).

Heterotopia are spaces in which an alternative social ordering is performed, "one that stands in contrast to the taken-for-granted mundane idea of social order that exists within society" (Hetherington, 1988:39). Both of these spaces have an unsettling effect, in their power play on our fears, and leave us in awe. They are spaces of the sublime. Both host a compulsion to order, and that ordering derives from a utopian view of modernity as an exercise in both freedom and control in all its ambivalence. The spaces that de Sade and Kafka conceived are distinctly modern spaces concerned with the issue of social order. They define for us the extremes of modern ways of thinking, from sexual libertinage and the celebration of a libertarian individualism on the one hand, to the absolute liberty given to the bureaucratic apparatus on the other. In both, that modernity is an expression of agency, a coming-into-being of actors through their capacity to make use of their freedom to control others. They come into being as desiring machines (Deleuze and Guattari, 1984) and as judges with absolute authority to define their actions and the actions of others within their own citadels or castles. In so doing they also define themselves and become the subjects of their own control, as I point out in chapter two.

In looking at Foucault's ideas about such spaces it is clear is that there is a strong surrealist theme running though his analysis, notably in his emphasis on similitude and the powers of random juxtaposition in creating alternative perspectives. This is not something just found in the paintings of Magritte, although they are a fine example, but in some of the key surrealist texts and in some of the writings of those who followed the surrealists (notably Antonin Artaud and Georges Bataille). For the surrealists, the surreal product of the imagination had an autonomous existence. Perceived in the manner of the freedom of the imagination, set free through the automatic production of images in meaningless poetry, automatic writing and the painterly representation of the unconscious mind, the world of the surrealist is a world of similitude rather than resemblance in which the wonder of the unconscious is revealed through metonymical juxtaposition of the otherwise incommensurate. Surreality is the affirmation of a world of chance, affect and involuntary memory.

Bataille (1985,1991), for example, favoured the connection of libidinous transgressive 'religious' practices and desires to 'limit-experiences' such as sexuality, madness and death.

27

These heterogeneous experiences, erotic and violent could be enacted as acts of human sacrifice, within a space reminding of de Sade's castle (Bataille, 1989).

Antonin Artaud is another surrealist writer whose concept of space recalls the notion of heterotopia, with his two manifestos on the theatre of cruelty in *The Theatre and Its Double* (1930). To him, theatre had lost contact with life because rationality had drawn it away from emotion, the unconscious and the body, or in a word, with desire. He wanted theatre and life to become one, the emotions of daily life to be reintroduced into theatre, moulding it into a total experience and a shock on the senses of the 'audience'. As a means of rendering desire, Artaud (1977) wished that theatre should become a direct and unmediated situation that employed feeling rather than intellectual analysis, a heterotopic experience, as can be seen from his enthusiasm for Balinese theatre. In his first manifesto, Artaud set out his ideas on what such a theatre might be like. It was to be based on action rather than text and therefore required particular spatial expressions (1977:68). For Artaud, theatre was to be the language of space that "liberates a new lyricism of gestures which because it is distilled and spatially amplified, ends by surpassing the lyricism of words" (1977:70). Such a theatre was to do away with the idea of a text, of a producer and of an audience in the conventional sense:

> "Every show will contain physical, objective elements perceptible to all. Shouts, groans, apparitions, surprise, dramatic moments of all kinds, the magic beauty of all costumes modelled on certain ritualistic patterns, brilliant lighting, vocal incantational beauty, attractive harmonics, rare musical notes, object colours, the physical rhythm of the moves whose build and fall will be wedded to the beat of moves familiar to all, the tangible appearance of new, surprising objects, masks, puppets many feet high, abrupt lighting changes, the physical action of lighting stimulating heat and cold, and so on." (1977:72)

A theatre such as this could lead to the formation of new symbolism through the erasure of grids dividing the stage from auditorium, and a spontaneous approach of the peculiarities of the spatial setting. In practice, such a theatre is a theatre of the body: this is an idea Artaud expresses through his concept of cruelty. With this, Artaud conveys a craving for life in its most passionate and immediate form, as a blind, unmediated form of desire.

Foucault's (1986,1991) analysis of heterotopia parallels Bataille's thoughts on heterogeneity, found most explicitly in the practice of sacrifice, and Artaud's on the transformational possibilities for the body in his theatre of cruelty. Consequently, heterotopia

28

UNIVERSITY OF WINCHESTER LIBRARY

are the sites of limit experiences, connected to the madness, sexual desire and death, in which humans test the limits of their existence and are confronted by its sublime terror. Heterotopic places are sites which rupture the order of things through their different mode of ordering to that which surrounds them. Such sites of limit experience promote acts of resistance and transgression. However, there is another important but related role that heterotopia serve. They were also to act, for Foucault (1986:27) as spaces for the means of alternative ordering through their difference and Otherness. That ordering can be the sadistic ordering of total freedom but it can also be the Kafkaesque ordering of total control:

> "Either their [heterotopia's] role is to create a space of illusion that exposes every real space, all the sites inside of which human life is partitioned, as still more illusory....Or else, on the contrary, their role is to create a space that is other, another real space, as perfect, as meticulous, as well arranged as ours is messy, ill constructed, and jumbled."

Rob Shields in his *Places on the Margin* (1991) has also focused on the relationship between freedom and order in representational spaces. Shields' work draws heavily on that of Lefebvre (1991) and also Victor Turner's (1969) analysis of liminal space. He concentrates on margins in relation to the social construction and production of space, described conceptually as social spatialization, and on the significance of places on the margins within the social production of space. Shields (1991:29-65) develops a social constructionist theory of space, with particular emphasis on the significance of marginal, or liminal places. He is concerned first with the imaginary geography of place and the creation of socially constructed accounts of place or "place myths". His second concern is with places whose meaning are marginal and in transition. He sees the significance of such places as an opening for affective groups, or neo-tribes, engaged particularly in ludic and transgressive practices associated with the creation of new lifestyles. Shields shows how certain places take on a mythological meaning of marginality, which develops an independence from their social construction to become a place myth. The nation is an example of a place myth, but they can be seen to exist at both lower and higher levels of resolution. The body, a room, a house, street, town, city or continent, even the universe, can all be seen as having their own place myths. These are all imagined cultural formations that fit into a symbolic system of placing. Place myths are defined, therefore, not only by their own contested symbolic criteria, but also in relation to other places. Place myths also, according to Shields, form a system of differences. For Shields, margins are always linked in a binary way with centres. Rob Shields notes that places on the margins have "a history of transformations between being markings, near-sacred liminal zones of Otherness, and carnivalesque leisure spaces of ritual inversion of the dominant, authorized culture" (1991:5). They cannot, he argues, be separated from those centres. Rather,

> "their existence is either defined by the centres as all that is excluded from the centre, or as a site of opposition to all that the centre stands for" (1991:276-8). Shields identifies a series of binary oppositions that exist within society: rational and ludic; civilised and nature; centre and periphery; social order and carnivalesque; mundane and liminal (1991:260)

A similar approach to the analysis of margins, associated in this case with the nineteenth-century city, is put forward by Elizabeth Wilson (1991). She has developed a feminist reading of the modern city, aiming to bring out the relationship between women, city space and the construction of their condition of marginality. She attempts to show, through an analysis of the culture of cities, how women have been perceived as the Other of the city, a position which facilitates new opportunities for them. Wilson gives as examples of the Other of the city such figures as the whore or the lesbian, and illustrates how the city comes to be seen as feminine through the promiscuity of crowds, consumption and temptation in male discourse. Woman, for Wilson, is the slippery figure of the Sphinx, who inhabits the other places of the city. As such, the city becomes not so much a place from which women are excluded, but a place whose uncertain spaces offer sites of resistance for women. Wilson's work portrays women as marginalised Others who reside in the interstitial spaces of the metropolis. Again the marginal is somewhat celebrated as a space of freedom, here for women, to explore their identities and their power.

There are other feminist writers, such as Doreen Massey (1994) and Gillian Rose (1993) who have theorized the spatiality of women's resistance through conceptions of Otherness. Rose, in particular, offers a seemingly similar analysis to those identified above, through a concept of what she calls 'paradoxical space'. In her work, however, we begin to see a more complex analysis of the relationship between centres and margins. By paradoxical space she refers to the possibilities of multiple positioning in space that challenge the everyday oppression of women, notably though an objectification by a male gaze in space. By attempting to act differently from social expectations, by "being Other in the territory of sameness" (1993:149), not only do women empower themselves through refusal and constitute for themselves an identity on their own terms, but they also challenge the spatiality of their location, constituting it as an unsettling space. In so doing they create a place for themselves. In contrast to Shields and Wilson, who tend to maintain the separation of centres and margins, Rose wants to think beyond that binary divide. Her concept of paradoxical space is useful in that it suggests that women positioning themselves in ways that resist centrality and marginality offer a way of thinking about space that is not reliant on that neat separation. Paradoxical space creates further interesting paradoxes. It is not just the question of the separation of centres and margins that it puts into doubt, but also the separation of order and resistance to it.

Two main points need to be made about the recent fascination with marginal space. Firstly, when margins are established as distinct sites such as the beach or distinct sites at specific times such as the market, they do not exist as separate spaces with no structure but in relation to other sites, and therefore with some alternate structure and social ordering logic. Secondly, not all marginality or difference is defined by a particular space. Practices that defy the expected, define a site as marginal momentarily because of the unsettling experience one is involved in. It is important to recognize that both marginal space and forms of resistance and transgression are never free from forms of order, it is just that this order is an alternate one, established in relation to another, through the practices in which it is inscribed. This has been convincingly established by anthropologists in their discussions of rites of passage, from where the much used concept of liminality has been taken.

Like the terms carnivalesque, margin, and transgression, the concept of liminality has also featured largely within debates about space within sociology and cultural geography. Again, the emphasis has tended to be on issues of freedom and playfulness rather than order, but liminality is all about the relationship between freedom and order. The term liminality comes from an initial concern with the symbolic ordering properties of the spaces that are associated with rites of passage in small-scale societies (van Gennep, 1960; Turner 1974). Rites of passage are rituals associated with life changes that require the move between different statuses, states, ages or places. Rites of passage are concerned with the ways in which people are socially ordered within society. They involve a process of symbolic transition that van Gennep (1960:11) suggests can be separated, as a process, into three stages: separation, margin and reaggregation. In the first stage, a person who at a particular point in their life is required to move on to another point, such as from childhood to adulthood, or other life stages such as marriage, is required to go through a set of initiation rituals before s/he can take on a new state.

31

S/he is separated physically from the rest of the society and stripped of any previous status and identity. Once this has been achieved, s/he exists in a liminal or marginal phase. Liminality is associated with a transgressive stage of a rite: it is often configured spatially as a threshold, or margin, defined by uncertainty, with a social normative structure temporarily upset. People have to undergo ritualized trials that mark the difference and the in-betweenness of their non-identity. The spaces that they inhabit are also seen as ambivalent and marginal. Magical powers might be attributed to those in the liminal state and to the spaces with which they are associated. In the final stage of a rite of passage, the person is reintegrated into society as a new person. In small-scale societies, liminal rituals, as rites of passage, are an important part of the life of the people. According to Turner, they also exist as a means of self-understanding by a particular society and as a means of renewal of that society through a process of restructuring (1969). Acts of transgression or inversions of everyday, mundane practices define this liminal phase. Turner identifies two particular types of liminal rituals in small-scale societies: rituals of status elevation and cyclical rituals (1969:167). In terms of their relationship with the carnivalesque as a significant form of resistance associated with marginal places, the latter are of significance. Such rituals embody the principles of the world turned upside down, where everything becomes its opposite. For Turner, however, in small-scale societies such rituals embody not only acts of transgression but the means of reintegration and order. As he suggests:

> "Cognitively, nothing underlines regularity so well as absurdity or paradox. Emotionally, nothing satisfies as much as extravagant or temporarily permitted illicit behaviour. Rituals of status reversal accommodate both aspects. By making the low high and high low, they reaffirm the hierarchical principle." (176)

Turner (1982) further differentiates between what he calls liminal rituals and liminoid rituals. Liminoid rituals resemble liminal ones in many structural respects but also have a number of notable differences. First, liminoid rituals are optional rather than attributed; whereas in the liminal rituals of small-scale societies there is no choice involved in rites of passage, in socially differentiated western societies there is. Second, as a consequence of their achieved status, liminoid rituals are weaker as sources of social integration than are liminal ones and do not involve the resolution of a crisis. Liminal rituals involve constraint as well as freedom, liminoid rituals are more ludic in character and are not binding, as liminal rituals are. A third difference lies in the nature of the spaces involved. Liminal spaces are often clearly defined sites that incorporate elements of both the sacred and the profane. They act as a dangerous and polluting margin, as a result of their suspended nature, and as such liminal spaces tend to be clearly demarcated and associated with their own practices. Although profanation may take place, it does so in a symbolically regulated manner. Liminoid spaces are therefore likely to be created out of spaces during particular events or in breachings of the mundane order, effectively what is implied by Rose's (1993) characterization of paradoxical space. Turner associates liminoid space with activities that have a strong carnivalesque element, and relates them to the individualism and personal freedom that such practices aim to achieve. For Turner, one of the most important aspects of liminoid rituals, when freed from the association of liminality with social renewal and regeneration, is their significance as sites for the production of new symbols for new modes of living (1982:33). This is in keeping with his ideas on the duality of structure and anti-structure within a society. In small-scale societies, liminal rituals, as well as being rites of passage for individuals, are also meaningful collectively as means of ordering the social. The structure of a society is symbolically inverted through the transgression of its moral codes, a period of anti-structure, such that a process of renewal and regeneration can occur. Liminality is connected with festivals and ceremonies and passing moments of release.

Mikhail Bakhtin (1973:107), who has described the significant influence of the carnival tradition on literature, identifies the circus as one of "many ancient forms of carnival [that] have been preserved and continue to live and renew themselves". The carnivalesque has been identified as an important feature of magical realist texts by critics such as Wendy Faris (1995) and David Danow (1995), an extremely relevant feature of Angela Carter's works, especially the late ones. The liberating force of the circus ring and the ludic perspective of magical realism sweep the readers across topographies to witness the characters' turmoil in chapters four and five. Magical realism and the circus are both closely related to Bakhtin's idea of the carnivalesque. The circus' influence on magical realism manifests itself as "heterotopia", since the latter are inherently contradictory, polyphonic. One aspect the carnival shares with the circus is the blurring of human-animal boundaries, as it is quite common for people to dress up and embody animal figures. Dressing up for carnival is not simply a matter of wearing funny clothes, but also what Bakhtin calls the "carnivalistic life" (1973:101). This means, as he says, that "its participants live in it, they live according to its laws, as long as those laws are in force". It can indeed be said that the experience of carnival is like living within a different reality

33

altogether. This reality is characterized by the combination of paradoxes. As Bakhtin describes it:

> "[a]ll the things that were closed off, isolated, and separated from one another by the non-carnivalistic hierarchical attitude enter into carnivalistic contacts and combinations. Carnival brings together, unites, weds and combines the sacred with the profane, the lofty with the lowly, the great with the insignificant, the wise with the stupid, etc." (101)

However, unlike the carnival, which is, as Bakhtin says, "the world upside down" (110) within its delimited time-frame, the circus is both the world and the world upside down; it is both the mundane and the extraordinary. The circus not only follows the laws of everyday life and the "outside world", but also incorporates those rules and connects them to illusions and subversive, carnivalesque imagery. As a result, the circus assimilates and combines completely contradictory discourses. Consequently, the seemingly "unbridgeable gap" between humans and animals, running through Western discourses, is blurred in the circus arena, while it is also reinforced by the spatial separation of circus visitors from performing animals in cages. Likewise, circuses promote the idea of equal human-animal partnerships, while simultaneously reinforcing human dominance.

There is thus a dialogic relationship between multiple discourses in the circus, and the same phenomenon occurs in magical realism. Foucault (1991:131) argues in *The Order of Things* that the Linnaean system of taxonomy became a norm for the Europeans to follow in order to systematize the world around them; a foundational narrative of European epistemology. The two kinds of animal spaces within the circus produce an epistemological shift, in Foucault's opinion, and botanical gardens and zoos, for example, were not the result of "a new curiosity about exotic plants and animals", but that the space in which they were represented and perceived had changed."

He writes:

> "To the Renaissance, the strangeness of animals was a spectacle: it was featured in fairs, in tournaments, in fictitious or real combats, in reconstitutions of legends in which the bestiary displayed its ageless fables. The natural history room and the garden, as created in the Classical period, replace the circular procession of the "show" with the arrangement of things in a "table".(ibid)

34

Accordingly, as a fundamentally contradictory and polyphonic space, the circus belongs to the group of spaces which Michel Foucault calls "heterotopia", "counter-sites", in which "all the other real sites that can be found within the culture, are simultaneously represented, contested, and inverted. Places of this kind are outside of all places, even though it may be possible to indicate their location in reality" (1986:24). Foucault names these "counter-sites" "heterotopia" because, as he says, "these places are absolutely different from all the sites that they reflect and speak about".

Both the carnival square and the circus are such heterotopia, and yet the circus is qualitatively different from the carnival. Bakhtin (1973:100–101) stresses that "carnival is a pageant without a stage and without a division into performers and spectators. In the carnival everyone is an active participant, everyone communes in the carnival act". The circus, in contrast, features a marked separation between active performers and a largely passive audience. Moreover, the spectators are usually restricted to those who can afford to pay for the show. In other words, unlike the carnival spectacle with its "human animals", which is free and characterized by the active participation of everyone, the circus showcases animals for profit. Thus, influenced by the circus tradition, magical realism restores the circular spectacle to the text and, incongruously, combines it with taxonomic order. Incongruity, abnormality, eccentricity, extraordinariness inextricably linked with the ordinary and hybridity are the hallmarks of these performative spaces.

Foucault (1977:203) illustrates how the scientific ordering of animals, as manifested by animal display cages, for instance, and the penal system reinforce each other and naturalize the power relations they represent. He compares the royal menagerie at Versailles with Bentham's Panopticon and writes:

> "One finds in the programme of the Panopticon a similar concern with individualizing observation, with characterization and classification, with the analytical arrangement of space. The Panopticon is a royal menagerie; the animal is replaced by man, individual distribution by specific grouping and the king by the machinery of a furtive power. With this exception, the Panopticon also does the work of naturalist."

Bakhtin's utopian conception of the "carnivalesque" is clearly related to heterotopia. In *Rabelais and His World*, Bakhtin (1984:218) explores the writer's description of medieval festivals. The carnivalesque combines laughter and the mocking of authority through the celebration of idleness, extravagance and intemperance. During these festivities, hierarchical distinctions and barriers are disrupted temporarily, norms and customs, official ordering of time and space are suspended. For a short while established order is replaced by a space of freedom and "the self dissolves into a collective spirit" (Webb, 2005:122). Bakhtin's reading of Rabelais has in turn inaugurated much research into popular cultural practices that are said to reveal transgressive, liberatory and utopian features. What ensues seems to be a competition to find the authentic utopian spirit that is sidelined or dissipated by dominant and coercive socioeconomic and political forces.

Heterotopia are not easily located within a system of representation but neither do they exist *sui generis*. Heterotopia do not exist in the order of things, but in the ordering of things. They can be both peripheral and central, associated with both transgressive marginality as well as carceral sites of social control. Heterotopia are sites of all things displaced, marginal, rejected, or ambivalent. Their value derives not from a single centre, but from their relationship to a set of remaining spaces, which may include the immediate surroundings or territories lying at a great distance from a marked site. Furthermore, heterotopia's layers of meaning, that accumulate through our repeated efforts to reconstruct and re-interpret, may make the concept of heterotopia opaque, but the following four chapters will hopefully serve to give Angela Carter's work the glow of transcendence.

2. HETEROTOPIAN ZONES- INNER DEPTHS OF OUTER SPACES

In order to accommodate the spatial concept of heterotopia to Carter' s work I cast a glance to the zone between *eu-topia*, the 'place of good', and *ou-topia*, the 'non-place', and to the resulting neologism *utopia*, which combines both Greek notions in Thomas Moore's (1516) good place, impossible to reach but in our imagination. Utopia leads the way to a better place, yet it only exists as a socially constructed desire. It points to possibilities beyond our reach, to a horizon that escapes us, an ever elusive border. Whereas utopia is an imaginary construction, *heterotopia* constitutes the uncertain local play of social ordering, operating in reality (Hetherington, 1998), a proper shelter for hybrids and paradoxes.

Angela Carter's work is a world in itself, coherent from the inside as far as themes and voices are concerned, puzzling from the outside because of the difficulty one encounters when trying to assign it to a philosophical or literary current. It is rooted in the reality of the writer's times, questioning cultural constructs and answering back to myth, fairy-tale, history and anything taken for granted. It draws on a variety of sources to state a point, mixing registers of language, media, literary criticism and politics. I see her works best characterised by Foucault's (1970: XVIII) words:

> "There is a worse kind of disorder[…], the linking together of things that are inappropriate; I mean the disorder in which fragments of a large number of possible worlds glitter separately[…]without law or geometry…in such a state, thins are "laid", "placed", "arranged" in sites so very different from one another that it is impossible to find a place of residence for them, to define a *common locus* beneath them all'. (qtd. in McHale, 1987:44)

In order to access Angela Carter's work I asked myself the following question: where does everything take place? Can the organisation of space provide any access doors for the interpretation of the novels? Brian McHale (1987:45) remarks that postmodern novels no longer have a 'perceiving subject' around whom space is organised, and he identifies strategies for what is more a deconstruction of space, than its construction. My analysis focuses on the spaces that host the world of Angela Carter's novels. I will resort to the strategies of **superimposition, juxtaposition, interpolation** and **misattribution** mentioned by McHale, and I will unveil the layers of some heterotopian spaces in Angela Carter's following works in particular - *The Magic Toyshop* (1967), *The Infernal Desire Machines of Doctor Hoffman* (1972), *The Passion of New Eve* (1977), *Nights at the Circus* (1984), *Wise Children* (1991), 'The Erl-King', 'The Lady of the House of Love' (1996) - although there are passing references to other short stories and her philosophical and journalistic writings.

I will delve into the "zones" (Mc Hale, 1987) of *the castle, the prison, the cave/the womb* in 2.1. Dismantling Catacombs and *the forest, the desert, the city* in 2.2. Mazes of the Outside, and show the way they are disrupted through the above mentioned techniques, leading to the formation of heterotopia.

Angela Carter's work is a '*bricolage*', she explains, assembled from 'a great scrap-yard' of references to ancient European folklore, eighteen-century fictional devices and nineteenth-century discourses; fundamentally, from "all the elements which are available [...] to do with the margins of the imaginative life, which is in fact what gives reality to our own experience, and in which we measure our own reality" (Haffenden, 1985:92).

I approach heterotopia in her work in close connection to Norman Holland's (1973:151) "potential space": "The most sophisticated cultural experiences go on in a space which is neither inner psychic reality... . they go on in a 'potential space' which both joins and separates the individual and the person or thing he thinks about".

This space is built up from the relics of mythological places that no longer need to be produced, the wonderlands of medieval romance and fairy-tales. Carter then re-arranges them, re-interprets them to suit her subversive intentions.

Before turning to the particular heterotopian spaces I have identified, I should stress once more the importance of the term 'liminal space' in defining ambiguity in contemporary discourse. The French anthropologist Arnold van Gennep (1960) brought the word *limin* (Lat. 'threshold') to the attention of the social sciences, opening a space, the *liminal space*, for future interpretations in the literary discourse. After studying transition rites (marriage, death, puberty, etc.) in primitive societies, he divided transition rituals into three stages, with the middle one as both essential and delicate: rituals of separation (preliminal), rituals of margin (liminal), and rituals of aggregation (postliminal).

It was van Gennep's (1960) attention to the liminal process of transition that caught American anthropologist Victor Turner's (1974, 1982) interest and led him to publish his work popularizing van Gennep's recognition of the symbolic nature of transition rites, especially the middle phase situated in liminal space/time. It is through this work that liminal space has come to mean a place of "in between the margins" in various contexts. Consequently, the term liminal space was created by anthropologists to describe the time and place when/where people went to perform their initiation rites. Here, outside the bounds of their daily cultural conventions, they participated in difficult rituals. When they returned to their communities, they were considered to have undergone a transformation and become something different.

In the postmodern world, as boundaries become increasingly blurred, we all sometimes live on the margins. On entering enter liminal space and time, what we have known is left behind and we face the unknown that lies ahead. In recent years liminal space has turned into a cross-disciplinary trope that denotes a chaotic place of severe ordeal, outside the norms of one's culture. The space no longer needs to be contained by ritual, we do not necessarily go there voluntarily, and often we do not return to our communities after a visit. Cultural theorists (Bhabha, 1994) have referred to liminal space as "hybrid" and speak of border areas where populations mix and where people in societies, who are of mixed race and hold "cross-border" sensibilities, dwell. Social theorists have called liminal space the "badlands," "heterotopia," and "paradoxical" (Hetherington, 1997) and speak of populations outside a city, or travelling carnivals within whose boundaries the breaking of norms is tolerated. Some philosophers have described this space as "smooth" and "nomadic" (Deleuze & Guattari, 1987), running through the creases of a community in a "rhizoidic" fashion, ready to erupt into a sudden riot, where the rules of normality are defied. Richard Schechner (1988:172) described theatre as a "reflection in liminal time during which the transformation of consciousness occurs". In theatre space, we suspend disbelief and enter realities other than our own. We move to understandings that are outside the margins of our personal and cultural experience and include a symbolic realm shared by humanity: a way of thinking that is nonlinear and creative, transpersonal and transcultural. In this interior liminal space, consciousness is altered, and we break the normative rules that have limited our perception. It is here that we access images that were previously outside our capacities and we are able to see new patterns in the chaos.

2. 1. DISMANTLING CATACOMBS

The setting of Angela Carter's novels and stories represents a major obstacle in the characters' quests. It always turns into a labyrinth whose logic is beyond the logic of the heroes and heroines who are crossing it. Despite the shape space takes it most often foregrounds a certain passivity in the characters' relation to it: Desiderio in *The Infernal Desire Machines of Doctor Hoffman* and Eve in *The Passion of New Eve* have to cover large distances in their journeys, whereas the beings in the stories are confined in their own nature. Both categories are led forward down an unpredictable route, populated with surrealistic elements, hallucinations and claustrophobia.

The landscapes are symbolic, illustrative of the stages characters have reached in their peregrinations, taking them deeper down the chambers of the labyrinth. This rite of passage is supposed to help the protagonist change, lose the old self and become different. In Angela Carter's worlds, this magical space of transformation is infused with an air of irony, resulted from the author's subversive mode. The centre of the maze, once uncovered, brings about the harsh realization that there is no mystery hidden there.

There are precise definitions of geographical locations in Angela Carter's novels and stories, such as a Latin American country and Africa in *The Infernal Desire Machines of Doctor Hoffman*, end of nineteenth century London, Petersburg and Siberia in *Nights at the Circus*, twenty-first century USA in *The Passion of New Eve*. However, these realistic indications are used in a symbolical way in order to provide the characters with the necessary space of travel. The topos of the journey appeals to the writer, in that it offers her the possibility to flirt with literary traditions and exploit the dynamic rhythm of the picaresque genre. The exoticism of locations increases the protagonists' sense of alienation and the magical realist dizzying speed that transports them across continents marks the confusion that comes with self-knowledge.

Julia Kristeva suggests in *Strangers to Ourselves* that the abject is part of us alongside the Other: "By recognizing *our* uncanny strangeness we shall neither suffer from it nor enjoy it from the outside. The foreigner is within me, hence we are all foreigners" (1991:58).
Pleasure and pain are aligned in the process of combining opposites – the self/Other, good/evil, - as Angela Carter refuses to privilege one reading or one version. Techniques, genres and

voices mix and generate both attraction and repulsion towards the abject, dangerous other side in terms of character and location.

Myths are exposed as no more than narratives that aim to present women's passivity and men's superiority as natural, whereas fairy-tales evoke the heroines' desire to break free and to rebel against enclosure. The Marquis in 'The Bloody Chamber' and the Erl-King in 'The Erl-King' display a fatal attraction for female subjects. Their irresistible force pulls their victims towards confining spaces. The Erl-King's gaze threatens to reduce the protagonist to a caged bird whereas the Marquis' chamber of bloody secrets turns women into trophies. Both masters have an ambiguous vulnerability. They are trapped in their repetitive games, condemned to repeat the same story and the same violent acts, as the vampire lady in 'The Lady of the House of Love'.

The appeal the myth of the labyrinth holds for the literary imagination is grounded first of all in its multitude of associations. It may be, first of all, an empirical space and a space of estrangement at once. It can be the prison-like maze of mythology, which confines the characters, or the challenging path to self-knowledge. In both cases, the more difficult its intricacies and the obstacles the heroes have to surpass, the more valuable their triumph.

Secondly, we should consider the human mind as the primary source of the labyrinth, a symbol of the ability to use reason in order to overcome fear of the unknown. Ignorance combined with superstition should not prevail over the Enlightenment reason. The purpose of Angela Carter's use of myth seems to be the final revelation of it being nothing more than an arbitrary construction. The labyrinth is simultaneously a structure of circumscribed and boundless possibilities; it refuses the existence of a bird's-eye view hovering above history or outside discourse, but offers interminable passageways and countless journeys within its walls. Furthermore, unlike conventional models of travel, paradigms of departure and return which valorize the origin, travel inside the labyrinth is never completed: there is neither exit nor centre.

2.1.1. THE CASTLE

The castle contributes to an aura of unease and tension, situating Angela Carter's settings within the context of Gothic fiction. Its function is to provide a gloomy atmosphere of isolation, necessary for the presentation of the characters who, as it happens in Gothic novels, are defined by the building they inhabit.

Foucault's discussion of the spatiality of Bentham's design for the panopticon in his *Discipline and Punish* (1977) has received more attention than his comments on heterotopia. The panoptical design of the carceral institutions as total institutions has its origin in the systematic rational organization of space for the purposes of discipline and surveillance of categories of people constituted as criminal, sick or mad (Foucault, 1977). The panopticon was a mode of ordering that was different from the accepted modes of ordering the criminal and insane at the time. It was indeed an example of a heterotopic space associated with the alternate ordering of deviance, in contrast to earlier regimes of incarceration and punishment. However, places of Otherness have more often been envisaged as examples of sites of an ambiguous spatiality associated with identity formation in relation to acts of resistance, rather than panoptical ordering and social control. In general, the term has been used to try and capture something of the significance of sites of marginality that act as postmodern spaces for resistance and transgression—treating them in many ways as liminal spaces. The paradox is that heterotopia can be either or indeed both. Spaces of total freedom and spaces of total control, are a paradox the symbol of the castle embraces.

Behind Michel Foucault's vision of modernity lie the shadowy images of two castles. The first is de Sade's castle in his *One Hundred and Twenty Days of Sodom* (1785), a space in which the complete freedom of unrestrained, sadistic, male desire is acted out on the bodies of women and children with impunity. The second is Kafka's in *The Castle* (1922), although it could also be the labyrinthine space of the law courts in *The Trial* (1925). In either case, it is a space of the absolute irreproachable power of bureaucracy and the law. Both are obligatory points of passage in which freedom and control extend beyond their own limits and mingle with one another. Both spaces are examples of heterotopia. In the first we find a space of unlimited individual freedom, a freedom that pays no heed to moral sanctions over one's sexual conduct, a freedom that endlessly has to outdo itself in its severity and absolutism. This is a freedom that is defined by its desire to totally control its victims. If, in this Sadeian vision, freedom is allowed total control, in the second, the Kafkaesque vision, it is social control that is allowed total freedom. There are no limits to which surveillance and discipline cannot be exercised:

> "The ideal point of penalty today would be an infinite discipline: an interrogation without end, an investigation that would be extended without limit to a meticulous and ever more analytical observation, a judgement that would at the same time be the constitution of a file that was never closed, the calculated leniency of a penalty that would be interlaced with the ruthless curiosity of examination, a procedure that would be at the same time a permanent measure of a gap in a relation to an inaccessible norm and the asymptomic movement that strives to meet in infinity."
> (Foucault, 1977:227)

Angela Carter is interested in the cultural potential of this secluded place, the castle. It is a space of absolute freedom, but it is exercised beyond limits and eventually leads to abnormality, turning into a prison or torture chamber. The castle is a construct of murderous erotic fantasies, more often male. The castle of the Vampire in 'The Lady of the House of Love', the grotesque Mansion of Midnight and the temple of sadism of the House of Anonymity in *The Infernal Desire Machines of Doctor Hoffman*, Tristessa's glass mausoleum in *The Passion of New Eve*, Uncle Phillip's toyshop in *The Magic Toyshop*, all point to Angela Carter's predilection for isolated dwellings and reflect her passion for overthrowing myths. Her subversive intentions are apparent if we take into account the fact that all the sinister buildings tumble down in the end, signaling the collapse of the cultural formula of the victimization of women. The castle is never a shelter; there is no warmth and no harmony. The atmosphere is one of decadence and claustrophobia, and the sense of confinement is ever present.

According to McHale (1987), **superimposition**, implies the existence of two familiar spaces that are placed on top of one another, giving birth to a third one, a hybrid. The main characters inhabit one and are drawn to one of the other two. Brian McHale (1987:77) also observes that in the confrontation of worlds there is usually "a dose of resistance of normality against the paranormal" which may be dramatised or turned into a struggle.

The Infernal Desire Machines of Doctor Hoffman takes the reader into a war of two possible worlds, as the title given to the novel in America, *The War of the Worlds*, indicates. In the Minister's world things have names and identities, dreams are separated from reality, while

43

Hoffman's world is totally different, as rivers can run backwards and clocks can 'tell everybody what time they like' (IDM 3). The name Angela Carter chose for the Doctor is suggestive of the flight of the imagination if one recognises the name Hoffman as that of the inventor of the LSD drug. Everyday reality is at war with Dr. Hoffman's assaults and attempts to project his unrealities into each aspect of life:

> "Since mirrors offer alternatives, the mirrors had all turned into fissures or crannies in the hitherto hard-edge world of here and now and through these fissures came slithering sideways all manner of amorphous spooks. And these spooks were Dr. Hoffman's guerrillas, his soldiers in disguise who, though absolutely unreal, nevertheless, were." (IDM 6)

Desiderio describes the city as overwhelmed by unreality once the siege of Dr. Hoffman has started. The Minister tries to distinguish unreality from reality but it is an impossible approach because of Dr. Hoffman's refusal to allow it to be differentiated. Travelling shows appear in each fantastic novel of Angela Carter as agents of space disruption, as the boundary between the two worlds and the source of knowledge in the novel under discussion. Desiderio learns about the doctor's world view from the peep-show proprietor who keeps changing the pictures he exhibits in his show according to a random principle, since he is blind. The peep-show and the travelling fair are metaphors of the world which is governed by lack of rules and dissolving boundaries between real and constructed, in accordance to Dr.Hoffman's principle that "everything that is possible to imagine can also exist" (IDM 97). The peep-show proprietor looks forward to the instauration of the 'Nebulous Time' which will be "a period of absolute mutability" (IDM 99) if the Doctor's plan succeeds. The two worlds are united through the main character sent by the Minister to kill the Doctor. He is rational and certain that he is immune to the dangers of imagination but he is wrong. Under the Hoffman effect Desiderio falls prey to the manifestations of his deepest and most uncontrollable desires. One of them is Albertina, who appears to him in various disguises – a ghost in his dreams, a mother-like figure, the manservant of the Count, the Madame of a brothel – before appearing as she really is to tell him "all the time you have known me, I've been maintained in my various appearances only by the power of your desire" (IDM 204).

In his journeys through several worlds, many of the happenings are generated by his own imaginative power or longings, some of them displaying violence and cruelty. In the penultimate chapter, *Lost in Nebulous Time*, Desiderio and Albertina arrive at the society of the centaurs, whose leader rapes Albertina. Desiderio becomes somehow aware that he bears responsibility for the event, a conviction strongly held by Albertina herself:

> "She was convinced that even though every male in the village had obtained carnal knowledge of her, the beasts were still only emanations of her own desires, dredged up and objectively reified from the dark abysses of the unconscious. And she told me that, according to her father's theory, all the subjects and objects we had encountered in the loose grammar on Nebulous Time were derived from a similar source – my desires; or hers." (IDM 186)

The Doctor and the Minister are the most illustrative example of how inaccurate the delimitations of the two worlds are. The former has no imagination and is a dull totalitarian, while the latter, despite being "the most rational man in the world" (IDM 24), had "all the Faustian desires" (IDM 28).

In the words of Brian McHale (1987:144), "what had been posed as a polar opposition proves to be a complex and paradoxical interpenetration." Desiderio goes against Dr.Hoffman's plan and against his desires, killing both the Doctor and Albertina, because, in the chaos that has been let loose by his actualized desires, there is too much violence, both physical and spiritual.

The castle is identified with its owner and serves the purpose of presenting him as massive and threatening. Doctor Hoffman regards his castle as a symbol of his invincibility, but the mythical character is lost as soon as Desiderio arrives:

> "The castle stood with its back up against a cliff. The battlements hinted at Hoffman's Teutonic heritage; he had built himself a Wagnerian castle like a romantic memory in stone…it was not really a castle, only a country house built after the style of a castle."(IDM 196)

Moreover, the edifice of reason, surrounded by the garden in Disneyland style, full of artificiality, does not even collapse once its owner is destroyed.

Tristessa's hideaway in the desert of *The Passion of New Eve*, on the other hand, appears to be only a house embodying the Hollywood dream, although its meaning is more profound. With the mausoleum of shadows built in the middle of the desert, Angela Carter alludes to the motif of the Revolving Castle in the Celtic legends, which was situated in the other world. It had no entrance and it was spinning so fast that even the boldest found it impossible to enter. Wine was gushing out its numerous fountains and death or illness were unknown concepts. When Zero and his harem invade the house in the dead of night, it takes its revenge spinning faster and faster, so that they cannot exit and Zero is buried underneath. The same image of the destruction of a castle appears in *The Infernal Desire Machines of Doctor Hoffman*, as Desiderio and the Count flee the House of Anonymity, the temple of sado-masochism, and they see it "had turned to earth and fire in the awesome, elemental transmutation" (IDM 139). Although this image bears associations with the biblical story of the annihilation of Sodom and Gomorrah, it also suggests the end of the myth of domination.

Inside, the castles are Gothic, with gloomy rooms and 'drawing rooms with worn Persian rugs on the floor and walls hung with a once crimson brocaded paper...now faded and figured with damp and mould' (IDM 52). They look deserted: "The gaping doors and broken windows let the wind in everywhere...all the furniture was under dust sheets, the chandeliers bundled up in cloth, pictures taken from their hooks" ('TB' 160). The state of dereliction may also be perceived as Angela Carter's way of subverting the fairy-tale tradition, where interiors are rich, shiny and opulent. There is no fresh air in Angela Carter's castles, no light, they are spheres of chaos that stifle all the senses and, in the extreme case, life.

Tristessa's house, the "spinning, transparent labyrinth" (PNE 116), with a hall of coffins containing waxworks of Hollywood movie stars, is a prison guarded by reflecting devices.

There is an overabundance of language in the paragraphs describing the exteriors and interiors of the castles. Angela Carter's syntax represents a labyrinthine journey we, readers, undertake. It is complex and sophisticated, rife with rare vocabulary, a game of images and styles that she plays.

Interpolation implies the "introduction of an alien space within a familiar one" (McHale, 1987:46). The difference between this method and **superimposition** is that the former does not lead to the formation of a third space. Carter's early novels form a trilogy since they all mix realism with fantasy and are filled with a sense of meaninglessness. The two worlds that interpolate are the real and the imaginary. As far as the real is concerned, Angela Carter insisted that the British slums and smelly streets concerned "a perfectly real area of the city in which I lived" (Haffenden,1985:800), a period of change in the economic and social life. The paragraph is illustrative of the writer's technique of offering one position and turning around its apparent opposite, as Lorna Sage observes:

"The entire space [of the sixties] was sustained by a buoyant economy; everybody was so very, very rich, you see, due to sponging off the state or, I don't know, cornering the market in tie-syed underpants or cover versions of aged Mississippi-blue singers or patchouli-scented candles. But at that time Britain was a low rent, cheap food country with relatively low wages and high taxes – most people I knew lived on very, very little. We were early into recycling." (Sage,1994:16)

Melanie in *The Magic Toyshop* lives in a kind of Eden, in a big house with an apple tree near her window. She experiences intense horror in the garden on climbing the tree and ripping apart her mother's wedding-dress, as she imagines she is guilty for her parents' deaths and her guilt is transposed onto an incapacity to bear the immensity of the sky. She wanders at night in a desolate garden, an alienating space anticipating the hunting space of the Vampire Lady in the short story 'The Lady of the House of Love':

> "On moonless nights, her keeper lets her out into the garden. This garden, an exceedingly sombre place, bears a strong resemblance to a burial ground and all the roses her dead mother planted have grown up into a huge, spiked wall that incarcerates her in the castle of her inheritance." (LHL 197)

There is danger outside and inside houses as well. Her parents' house resembles the castle of the Vampire Lady in the short story, as the building seems to have taken over the inhabitants' freedom to act:

"The castle is mostly given over to ghostly occupants but she herself has her own suite of drawing room and bedroom"(LHL 195).

Melanie in *The Magic Toyshop* has to cope with an inhibiting reality and the imagination of a blossoming woman. The confining space in which the two worlds collide is Uncle Philip's toyshop, nothing like as cosy as a new home that the girl dreams of.

The institution of the family diminishes female authority through the limitations it imposes on women's lives. The family is associated with a danger of submission and suppression, with the help of Gothic topographies and terrorizing imagery:

> "Between a failed , boarded-up jeweller's and a grocer's displaying a windowful of sunshine cornflakes was a dark cavern of a shop, so dimly lit she did not at first notice it as it bowed its head under the tenement above." (TMT 42)

The ambience is Dickensian and it suggests the psychological trauma that threatens from underneath a dilapidated surface. Frightening and rotten, the place is set in contrast to the former luxurious house in which Melanie lived. In Angela Carter's early novels the topos is recurrent – the 'camp on several levels' in *Heroes and Villains* (1972:44), where the Barbarians live, or the chaotic student squats of Bristol Annabel faces when she comes to live with the brothers Buzz and Lee in *Love*. Another patriarchal symbol is the Victorian wrought iron gate of the shop. The girl feels trapped inside it, having to bear the terrorizing ticking of the cuckoo clock and a constant darkness of a five o'clock winter evening, measuring a static world:

> "There is too much,' she repeated. This crazy world whirled about her, men and women dwarfed by toys and puppets, where even the birds were mechanical and the few human figures went masked." (TMT 68)

The image of the gruesome building establishes the fictional convention of the 'gothic enclosure' (Jackson, 1981:47), casting terror on the women characters. Isolation equals powerlessness, especially due to the fact that there is no chance of running away.

> "She felt lonely and chilled, walking alone along the brown passages, passing secret doors, shut tight. Bluebeard's castle. Melanie felt a shudder of dread as she went by every door, in case it opened and something, some clockwork terror rolling hugely on small wheels, some terrifying hideous novelty, emerged to put her courage to the test. And now she was entirely alone, brother and sister both lost to her, Jonathon upstairs, Victoria downstairs and Melanie treading the dangerous route between them, connected to neither." (TMT 82)

'The Lady of the House of Love' is a rather loose adaptation of Perrault's 'Sleeping Beauty' and can also be seen as the ironic parody of Stoker's *Dracula*. The lady vampire in the story suffers from immortality which feeds on humanity. When she is transformed into a mortal woman, she becomes a dying human subject. The lady leads the soldier passing by her village to her bedroom to conduct her fatal ceremony. The young cyclist notices how unhappy she seems with the part she plays as Dracula's descendant:

"Everything about this beautiful and ghastly lady is as it should be, queen of night, queen of terror – except her horrible reluctance for her role." (LHL 195)

This fearless traveller in 'The Lady of the House of Love' experiences the same chilling sensation upon entering the vampire's castle: "the young man stepped over the threshold of Nosferatu's castle and did not shiver in the blast of cold air, as from the mouth of a grave, that emanated from the lightless, cavernous interior." (LHL 201)

> "He was surprised to find how ruinous the interior of the house was -- cobwebs, worm-eaten beams, crumbling plaster; but the mute crone resolutely wound him on the reel of her lantern

down endless corridors, up winding staircases, through the galleries where the painted eyes of family portraits briefly flickered as they passed, eyes that belonged, he noticed to faces, one and all, of a quite memorable beastliness." (LHL 202)

She cuts her thumb in the pieces of broken glass and when he kisses the wound she dies. This is her doom, which takes place at the edge of an unconsummated sexual experience. Her state of inner discontent makes her ready for transformation. The power of the cyclist's virginity enables him to break the spell and let her become human, though at the price of her death.

Growing accustomed to the fear inside the toyshop, Melanie in *he Magic Toyshop* looks for safety at the door to the outside world. But she displays a regressive reaction towards the people she meets in London, projecting her emotions onto them as if they had been external objects, because of her intense way of seeing things as suggested in the image of Aunt Margaret's coal fire that is 'rendered more fierce by the confines of the small, black-leaded grate' (TMT 41). She is fighting with the confines of Uncle Phillip's flat. She is not overwhelmed by madness yet, but the new home makes her feel 'withered and diminished' (TMT 43), "forever grey, a shadow...in an empty space at the end of the world" (TMT 77). This feeling of monotony extends to the world outside, which she observes from the toyshop window, a geographic space of deconstruction: a "weatherless London morning, a mean monotone, sunless, rainless, a cool nothing" (TMT 76)

Apart from the terrorizing function of this environment there is another one implied. The woman in Angela Carter's novels is thus forced to act against her fears, since reality has ceased to be reliable. Angry with and afraid of reality, Melanie in *The Magic Toyshop* resorts to a more comforting world of romantic fantasy. She uses film as a way of coping with the feeling of misery experienced in Uncle Philip's toyshop, dreaming that someone may show up selling popcorn. When she walks with Finn in the ruined garden she imagines they look like a shot from "a new-wave British film" (1981:106) and sees Uncle Philip as an actor. She has no original language to confess her feelings to Finn and to him she sounds "like a woman's magazine" (TMT 155). The patriarchal myth of Eden is revised at the ending of *The Magic Toyshop* as Finn and Melanie watch the house burning. A new beginning is suggested by all the things inside which are burning, paintings, toys, chairs, Edward bear, things that stand for undesirable limitations.

The castle thus displays itself as a spiralling labyrinth whose walls eventually dissipate, in the novels and short stories I have discussed. It turns into a landscape of ambiguous

49

boundaries where art and reality, sanity and insanity, self and other become blurred around the edges of Carter's fictional world.

2. 1.2. THE PRISON

Angela Carter's work has become very popular, some critics affirm, due to misreadings. She was sometimes aware of it herself: "I become mildly irritated when people... ask me about the "mythic" quality work I've written lately...I'm in the demythologising business. I'm interested in myths...just because they are extraordinary lies" (Sage,1994:12)

Angela Carter's display of terror and the desire to disempower the other derives from her reading of de Sade, Foucault, the Grimm brothers and Charles Perrault. In the 'Afterword' to the *Fireworks* collection, she acknowledges E. A. Poe as a major source for the horror tales in her works: "I'd always been fond of Poe, and Hoffman -- Gothic tales, cruel tales, tales of wonder, tales of terror, fabulous narratives that deal directly with the imagery of the unconscious -- mirrors; the externalized self; forsaken castles; haunted forests; forbidden sexual objects."(BB 459)

A combination of realistic details and an excess of symbols illustrates incarceration and physical paralysis. Angela Carter exposes the social configurations of power found in the horror genre as versions of pornography. When asked in an interview with Helen Cagney Watts if she was influenced by Foucault, she responded that the Marquis de Sade was her primary influence: "my reading of Foucault has possibly influenced me to some extent [...] really, though, it had been my reading of the Marquis de Sade that has probably had more impact; it is *the text* on sexuality and power" (1985:170).

In her 'Polemical Preface' to *The Sadeian Woman* Angela Carter writes:

> "All the mythic versions of women, from the myth of the redeeming purity of the virgin to that of the healing, reconciling mother, are consolatory nonsense; and consolatory nonsense seems to me a fair definition of myth, anyway. Mother goddesses are just as silly a notion as father gods. If a revival of the myths of these cults gives women emotional satisfaction, it does so at the price of obscuring the real conditions of life. This is why they were invented in the first place." (*SW*.1)

Carter's point is that myths belong to a system of discourses, the purpose of which is to console women by convincing them that their place in society belongs to a natural order. Acceptance of that natural order results in being controlled by it. Carter rejects any appeal to metaphysical constructs, calling them "consolatory nonsense". Instead, she insists that all discourses are material elements, like language, that have no basis other than the fact of their cultural acceptance, and their will to power.

The Gothicized interiors in Angela Carter's works point to an illegitimate control of women's sexuality and power. A typically Gothic mixture arises, a combination of opposites that allows us to see the cracks and borders, lies and constructions in what we take as stable. Domination is configured spatially in the form of confining interiors in *Nights at the Circus* – Ma Nelson's brothel, the Russian Grand duke's mansion, Christian Rosencreutz's house, Madame Schreck's museum, Countess P.'s prison, all of them examples of heterotopia, as I will argue next.

In *Nights at the Circus*, different voices are heard everywhere. With its allusions to Shakespeare, Milton, Poe, Ibsen, Joyce, and Foucault through the utterances of Fevvers, Walser, Lizzie, the capitalist circus owner Colonel Kearney, and so on, there is a polyphonic interplay of European cultural attitudes and moments (Palmer, 1987:197). Palmer also states that Fevvers, Kearney, Walser, and Lizzie all express different attitudes and ideologies that demonstrate the carnivalesque elements in the novel.

The novel opens as Jack Walser, a young "unfinished" reporter, interviews Sophie Fevvers, a circus performer who claims her wings help her fly in her trapeze act. Walser, a "connoisseur of the tall tale", wants to include his findings in a series entitled "Great Humbugs of the World" (11):

> "Walser is here, ostensibly, to 'puff' her; and, if it is humanly possible, to explode her, either as well as, or instead of. Though do not think the revelation she is a hoax will finish her on the halls; far from it. If she isn't suspect, where's the controversy? What's the news?" (NC 11).

He is an observer who uses his reason, along with his objectifying gaze to put a label on Fevvers. On the other hand, the aerialiste is on a quest of a different kind, that of upsetting the system that has turned her into the "imagined fiction" of patriarchal culture. The effect of her uniqueness is her commodification. All men dream of possessing her sexually, as an exotic exhibit of their collection. Verging between wonder and freak, Fevvers looks for means to recover her value as a human being. As Lizzie, her foster mother observes:

> "the baker can't make a loaf out of your privates, duckie, and that's all you'd have to offer him in exchange for a crust if nature hadn't made you the kind of spectacle people pay good money to

see. All you can do to earn your living is to make a show of yourself. You're doomed to that. You must give pleasure to the eye, or else you're good for nothing. For you, it's always a symbolic exchange in the marketplace; you couldn't say you were engaged in productive labour, now, could you, girl?" (NC 185)

Carter suggests that the first part of a process of liberation and transformation is one of story-telling, whether or not anyone is listening. When women self-consciously reenact traditional feminine gender roles, according to Doane (qtd. in Robinson, 1991:118), they are using the strategy of masquerade, and this strategy has subversive potential. Robinson also quotes Russo herself, who has written that "To put on femininity with a vengeance suggests the power of taking it off" (1991:120). Masquerade, as Robinson explains, "denaturalizes gender," and a woman who uses masquerade has agency because she is the creator of her self-representation (1991:121). Robinson takes Doane's concept of masquerade a step further by claiming that in performing masquerade, a woman is also a spectator to herself "at least metaphorically, if not literally" (121). Carter's protagonist, then, "is both spectacle and spectator" (122).

The novel is populated with a large group of people outside social norms, whose performance, rooted in the corporeal, has exiled them on the margins but has not managed to expel them. The third part of the book, the most picaresque part of the novel, takes us to Siberia, as various characters encounter strange people and situations. As Carter herself admits, the last half of 1984 is intricately plotted like a large huge circus with the ring in the middle (Haffenden, 1985:89).

The clowns, "doomed to stay down below, nailed on the cross of the humiliations of this world' (NC 120), display their degradation in a private dance of abjection, a 'dance of disintegration; and of regression; celebration of the primal slime" (NC 125).

Rabelaisian bodily humor characterizes the occupants of Clown Alley in the novel:

"Clown Alley, the generic name of all lodgings of all clowns, temporarily located in this city in the rotten wooden tenement where damp fell from the walls like dew, was a place where reigned the lugubrious atmosphere of a prison or a mad-house; amongst themselves, the clowns distilled the same kind of mutilated patience one finds amongst inmates of closed institutions, a willed and terrible suspension of being." (NC 116).

The comic grotesque haunts the place. Although Angela Carter has not read Bakhtin's *Rabelais and His World* prior to writing her novel, she has inherited the concept from Swift.

Bakhtin's grotesque is similar to Kristeva's 'abject' in its double nature, both regenerating and degrading, 'contradictory and double-faced' (Bakhtin,1984:23)

The clowns provide a tragic example of Bakhtinian carnival:

> "The festivities associated with carnival are collective and popular; hierarchies are turned on their heads (fools become wise, kings become beggars); opposites are mingled (fact and fantasy, heaven and hell); the sacred is profaned. The "jolly relativity" of all things is proclaimed. Everything authoritative, rigid or serious is subverted, loosened and mocked"
> (NC 4)

Outside the circus ring the dangers of chaos no longer operate, as the very concept of disorder relies on a complicity with the power structure that allows it.

> "The clowns. See them as a band of terrorists. No; that's not right. No terrorists, but irregulars. A band of irregulars, permitted the most ferocious piracies as long as, just so long as, they maintain the bizarrerie of their appearance, so that their violent exposition of manners stays on the safe side of terror, even if we need to learn to laugh at them, and part, at least, of this laughter comes from the successful suppression of fear." (NC 151)

The ensuing show of slapstick horror creates a conflicting discourse of comedy and tragedy to reveal male deformity as sordid behind the glitter of the spectacle.

> "They put the coffin down on the sawdust beside Buffo. They start to put him in it.
>
> "But will he fit? Of course he won't! His legs and arms can't be bent, won't be bent, won't be ordered about! Nobody can lay out *this* force of nature, even if it *is* dead! Pozzo or Bimbo runs off to get an axe to hack bits off him, to cut him down to coffin-size. It turns out the axe is made of rubber.
>
> At long, hilarious last, somehow or other they finally contrive to load him into the box and get the coffin lid on top of him, although it keeps on jerking and tilting because dead Buffo can't and won't lie down.' (NC 117)

Fevvers recollects her childhood in a whorehouse and her experience in a museum of female monstrosities before finding her vocation as an aerial artiste in a travelling circus. She derives several important benefits from posing as a statue in Ma Nelson's brothel. She understands the experience as an educational opportunity, referring to it as an "apprenticeship in *being looked at*" (NC 23). In learning how to pose, Fevvers also learns how to exploit the male gaze to her advantage. She later uses her stage presence to win fame and fortune as the headliner of the circus. Fevvers describes her childhood home, where Ma Nelson oversaw the community of prostitutes, as "one of those old, square, red-brick houses with a plain façade and a graceful, scallop-shaped fanlight over the front door that you may still find in those parts of London so far from the tide of fashion that they were never swept away" (NC 25).

She comments that it was built by the Age of Reason and that it remained, after that age was over, "like the germ of sense left in a drunkard's mind" (NC 26). She characterizes it "a place in which rational desires might be rationally gratified" (ibid).

By posing as Cupid and later as Winged Victory, Fevvers tells Walser, she earned her keep in the house.

In line with the carnivalesque spirit, Palmer (1987:120) shows that Ma Nelson is the "Mistress of the Revels" and that Buffo is "The Lord of Misrule." In telling the story of Nelson's brothel, one of the great heroes of the British Empire is reduced to a figure of fun. In the story, Nelson is an old whore who dresses in men's clothing and who lost one of her eyes in an unheroic encounter. The funniest of all is that she dies after slipping on the "skin of a fruit or dog turd" (NC 43), which is far from being a death of high honour or glorification.

In Ma Nelson's brothel Fevvers plays "the object in the eye of the beholder' (NC 23), an ornamental Cupid in the drawing-room until she is fourteen, while later she poses as Winged Victory, with her hair, face and wings painted white, to exist "only as an object in men's eyes" (NC 39). The result of this apprenticeship is a life in which she would be expected to conform to a number of roles, confining her in a 'sarcophagus of beauty' (NC 39). This does not happen, as she notes that the subordinate position is not for her. Under the "appearance of marble" there lies a different reality: "nothing could have been more vibrant with potentiality than I!" (NC 39). She assumes the position of spectacle in the brothel, but does so self-consciously, and knows that she will not wait to be rescued: "I did *not* await the kiss of a magic prince…With my two eyes, I nightly saw how such a kiss would seal me up in my *appearance* for ever!" (NC 39).

The prostitutes in Ma Nelson's brothel teach her about the complexity of women and the customers teach her about the confines of being Woman. Fevers is not the only one who plays a role in the brothel, as, when Lizzie lets the gentlemen in, all the girls "needs must jump to attention and behave like women" (NC 40). They seem to be just '*damned souls*' intent "to lure men to their dooms" (NC 38), when, in fact they are only working for money, as Fevvers remarks "no woman would turn her belly to the trade unless pricked by economic necessity"

(NC 39). This difference between the interests they follow by day and the pseudo-pleasure they offer by night is summed up again by Fevvers as she recalls Ma Nelson's brothel "a subtext of fertility underwrote the glittering sterility of the pleasure of the flesh available within the academy" (NC 39). As the night falls, the women put aside their books, musical instruments and follow the scripts prescribed to them as objects of desire. This sharp distinction is most apparent when the artifice of the night is exposed, as the brothel is closed down:

"We saw, now, what we had never seen before; how the moth had nibbled the upholstery, the mice had gnawed away the Persian carpets and dust caked all the cornices. The luxury of that place had been nothing but illusion, created by the candles of midnight, and, in the dawn, all was sere, worn-out decay. We saw the stains of damp and mould on ceilings and the damask walls; the gilding on the mirrors was all tarnished and a bloom of dust obscured the glass so that, when we looked within them, there we saw, not the fresh young women that we were, but the hags we would become, and knew that, we too, like pleasures, were mortal." (NC 49)

Because Ma Nelson leaves no will when she dies, the women are forced to leave her house. On their final morning in the house, they are gathered in the parlor when they decide to open the curtains and take a last look at the room. They discover, to their surprise, that "The luxury of the place had been nothing but illusion, created by the candles of midnight, and, in the dawn, all was sere, worn-out decay" (NC 49). As they contemplate this, they begin to understand

"the house had served its turn for [them], for the parlour itself began to waver and dissolve before [their] very eyes. Even the solidity of the sofas seemed called into question for they and the heavy leather armchairs now had the dubious air of furniture carved out of smoke." (NC 49)

They decide to burn the house in order to cheat Ma Nelson's brother, who has laid claim to the house and is evicting them. Fevvers tells Walser, "And so the first chapter of my life went up in flames, sir" (NC 50). Carter here is self-referential because she ends her chapter at the same moment that Fevvers declares she has finished a chapter of her life story.

Fevvers herself experiences the irony of travelling through the alien Siberian wilderness while sitting in a car that reproduces the setting of a brothel: an "Empire drawing-room done up in white lacquer and enough plate-glass mirrors for a mobile bordello" (NC 199). Fevvers comments to herself, "I hate it" (ibid).

In the next dark period of Fevvers' life, we are taken to another prison, Madame

Schreck's museum of women monsters. The gruesome owner, who toured the world as a Living Skeleton, has taken the concept of woman as object underground, and keeps her women prisoners 'in a sort of vault or crypt…with wormy beams overhead and nasty damp flagstones underfoot, and this place was known as "the Abyss"' (NC 61).

In Madame Schreck's museum of women monsters, Angela Carter imagines a female Clown Alley: "the whores of mirth" (NC 119) of the circus ring become here the whores of 'jouissance', the ultimate embodiment of abjection. This "lumber room of femininity" (NC 69) comprises an assembly of boundary creatures: "Dear old Fanny Four-Eyes; and the Sleeping Beauty; and the Wiltshire Wonder, who was not three foot high; and Albert/Albertina, who was bipartite, that is to say, half and half and neither of either; and the girl we called Cobwebs" (NC 60). Further inhabitants of Bakhtin's lower stratum, these "denizens of Down Below" (NC 69) occupy the depths of the female grotesque grouped in the place called 'the Abyss' (NC 61). This prison replicates the tents of the fairground, in which "the dispossessed creatures" (NC 69) are "made to stand in stone niches cut out of the slimy walls", with "little curtains in front"; except for the Sleeping Beauty 'who remained prone, since proneness was her specialty' (NC 61). She exists only in a state of abjection since her slumber is interrupted only to carry out the most basic bodily functions. She plays the "living corpse" (NC 70), prey to bodily pollution, and her beauty is tainted by "death infecting life. Abject" (Kristeva, 1982:4). Madame Schreck's threat: "Shall I open the curtain? Who knows what spectacle of the freakish and the unnatural lies behind it!" (NC 62) lures the 'natural' customers who pay to enjoy the exhibits.

This museum hosts "prodigies of nature" (NC 59) who possess "freakish" (NC 62) physical attributes. These deformities serve as Angela Carter's comment on the cultural constructions of femininity: the Sleeping Beauty stands for extreme passivity, Cobwebs plays patience all day long, the Wiltshire Wonder is so little and insignificant that everybody treats her as a doll. The three of them are not strong enough to survive outside and must be exiled to the world of the eternal feminine. Albert/Albertina the hermaphrodite is "half and half and neither of neither" (NC 59) and Fanny Four-eyes has eyes instead of nipples, embodying the threat of woman as spectator and the undesirable woman who cannot mother, as Fevvers comments: "How can you nourish a baby on salt tears?" (NC 69). The only male spectacle in Madame Schreck's service is a black servant who lacks a mouth and contributes to the thrilling atmosphere in the museum. He is a 'connoisseur of degradation', according to Fevvers, and used to earn a living at fairs. She tells Walser that she has never seen "eyes so full of sorrow as his were, sorrow of exile and abandonment" (NC 57). Toussaint is placed in the feminine position of spectacle, though he is a man, in support of Angela Carter's remark in *The Sadeian Woman* about de Sade's orgies, that 'male means tyrannous and female means martyrised, no matter what the official genders of the male and female beings are' (*SW* 24). Alternately, Madame Schreck is the tyrant controlling what she deems 'freakish', although the white, masculine ideology presented as 'natural' is in fact unnatural, as Toussaint scribbles: "it was those fine gentlemen who paid down their sovereigns to poke and pry at us who were the unnatural ones, not we" (NC 61).

Every Sunday, such a gentleman comes to "worship at [Fevvers'] shrine" (NC 71). His name is Christian Rozencreutz, a fervent opponent of female empowerment in politics, and seeking to restore his manhood and eternal youth with the help of Fevvers, who would be the main ingredient in his '*elixium vitae*' (NC 83). He buys her and plans to possess her body which he both desires and fears, turning the pedestal of worship into an altar for her sacrifice. His conviction is that he can be revived at the cost of transforming Fevvers from living flesh into dead meat. She uses the gilded sword from Ma Nelson's house to defend herself, catching Rozencreutz off guard with her switch from fertility goddess to avenging angel: "He fell back, babbling unfair, unfair...he'd not thought the angel would come armed" (NC 83). Fevvers escapes through the open window, while the other prisoners of the Abyss escape into the night with their due wages after Madame Schreck's disintegration.

In the second section of the novel, which takes place in St. Petersburg, Carter provides us with an example of how Fevvers' apprenticeship in the brothel and the museum has paid off. Fevvers finds herself showered with Parma violets and diamonds from a persistent admirer, the Russian Grand Duke. Blinded by greed, she accepts his dinner invitation hoping to receive a diamond necklace and catch the Trans-Siberian Express leaving at midnight with Colonel Kearney's Circus. The Russian Grand duke has a house decorated with spectacles of all varieties, such as a clockwork orchestra and a slowly melting, life-size ice sculpture of Fevvers. He has also embarked on a quest to uncover the legend of the *aerialiste*, whom he wants to touch, not just to look at. The Grand Duke is another symbol of patriarchal authority taken to extreme. The "fine, masculine smell of leather upholstery" (NC 184) in the coach taking Fevvers to his home is already indicative of her endangered autonomy, that she cannot perceive at this point: "no death in the snow. All she sees is that festive sparkle of the frosty lights that make her think of diamonds" (NC 184). The house appears as "the realm of minerals, of metals of vitrification – of gold, marble and crystal...and a sense of   frigidity, of sterility, almost palpable, almost tangible in the hard, chill surfaces and empty spaces" (NC 186).

With her practical sensibility Fevvers assesses the ostentatious display in the Duke's house in order to determine what price she might demand in exchange for her company. She initially had planned to use her sexuality to receive gifts from him, such as the diamond necklace worn by the statue, but she soon begins to question whether she can emerge safely from the transaction. The first ritual performed under the Law of the Father greatly disturbs Fevvers. The Duke spells her Christian name, Sophia, with full vodka glasses which he then drinks. This act of cannibalisation points to his rejection of any autonomy on Fevvers' part, since the name she uses has been assigned to her by Lizzie outside patriarchal prescription.

Next she is unnerved by his life-sized automaton, depicting a musical trio popping out from the wall at the press of a button. It is comprised of a bird that whistles through its nose, a woman-shaped harp who plays herself, and a gong that rings apparently without being struck. The life size puppets are shaped as half women, half musical instruments, bearing a strong resemblance to Fevvers. The music played has an uncanny effect on Fevvers, it does not seem to be "of this planet but of some remote and freezing elsewhere" (NC 188). Once she understands that the Duke wants her to feel afraid, she refuses to have champagne, for the first time in her life. He is waiting anxiously for the ice statue of Fevvers to melt, as he seeks to annihilate her resistance.

The situation takes a turn for the worse as he takes her through the gallery where he displays his jewelled eggs. This space, designed to display his wealth also reveals the narrative into which he hopes to insert Fevvers. The Duke's collection of eggs presents Fevvers with various versions of herself set within the boundaries the Russian collector has set. His collection of enamelled eggs pay tribute to her 'hatched' beginnings. He plans to trap her physically, to diminish her to minute proportions and preserve her as spectacle within his gallery of eggs in glass cases. Fevers gazes upon an egg of pink enamel unfurling its Russian doll layers

> "to reveal an inner carapace of mother-of-pearl which, in turn opens to reveal a spherical yolk of hollow gold. Inside the yolk, a golden hen. Inside the hen, a golden egg.' The golden egg, to her dismay, discloses 'the tiniest of picture frames, set with minute brilliants. And what should the frame contain but a miniature of the *aerialiste* herself, in full spread, as on the trapeze and yellow of hair, blue of eye as in life" (NC 189).

Fevvers "did not shrink; but was at once aware of the hideous possibility that she might do so" (NC 192), and she flees from the Duke's optical oppression as the melted ice sculpture collapses with a "wet crash and clatter" (NC 192).

The next jade egg discloses flowers made of pearls and diamonds, covering a fruit that splits open to reveal a bird that repeats the song Fevvers sings in her circus act – "only a bird in a gilded cage". However, as mechanically repeated by the bird, it lacks the irony Fevvers has infused into it, so that she turns away from the jade egg with a "sense of imminent and deadly danger" (NC 190). As her ice statue continues to melt, each "squeak, twang, bang and splash" (NC 190) signals her dissolving strength: "she felt more and more vague, less and less her own mistress" (NC 190).

The Duke strips her of clothes and robs her of the hidden sword she relies on for her second escape. The third egg that draws her attention is a miniature of the train she has to catch at midnight, so she enthusiastically chooses it as her due gift. She shrinks and makes her getaway after noticing the golden egg prepared to cage her in the shape of a cage with no bird in it. The prospect of becoming a diminutive idea of the Duke's conception is so unsettling that she bids the diamond necklace goodbye and drops the toy train on the carpet, and, in a magical realist moment, runs "helter-skelter down the platform" (NC 192) in time. Carter's use of magic realism during this crucial moment demands some attention. Fevvers' escape defies all physical laws, and the scene serves as a metaphor for Fevvers' vision and power over space.

In his analysis of Fevvers' flight from the Duke, Brian Finney cites the passage that details the escape: the Duke's orgasm causes a few seconds lapse of his consciousness during which Fevvers runs down the platform and climbs aboard the train. In the next line, Lizzie is commenting on Fevvers' soiled and dishevelled dress. Finney writes:

"Before we as readers have time to protest over the impossibility of such an escape (it defies all the laws of space-time), the new strand of narrative has caught us up and hurried us on into a new self-contained world of fiction that is of course just as reliant on illusion as the last one."(1998:176)

He also contrasts how Fevvers distracts the Duke through "highly physical means," while the escape is "purely fictional" (1998:177). This **juxtaposition** of physicality and textuality suggests the links between the world of fiction and the physical world.

Nights at the Circus marks not only the year the novel was published, but also the publication of a volume of essays on film, in which feminist film theorists Mary Ann Doane, Patricia Mellencamp and Linda Williams approached the panopticon as a defining metaphor for the relationship between 'the gaze' and power. Judith Mayne (2000:117) argues that, "the women-in-prison film thematizes in a very pronounced way the capacity of the cinema not only to objectify the female body, but also to create dramas of surveillance and visibility". She (1991) takes issue with the arguments of Doane, Mellencamp and Williams (1984) and early feminist film theorists that the 'gaze' of the audience and of the panopticon is a male one. Mayne notes that the prison genre is "predicated on the possibility that women observe other women" (117), both in the sense of women looking at and desiring and other, and in the sense of official surveillance as women occupy positions of power in the jail hierarchy. Mayne's approach reflects developments in later feminist analysis that resisted positing a male-centred gaze. The novel has such a woman at the centre of the panopticon watching over her prisoners. Carter shows this panopticism being applied to women who have disrupted the sexual order, by murdering their husbands. The declared purpose of this building is to induce forgiveness and teach the inmates to shoulder their guilt. It hosts women who have murdered their husbands and aims to return them to society.

Countess P. Carter uses the image Bentham's prison, a correctional facility which Michel Foucault sees as an effective method of keeping inmates under control, in *Discipline and Punish: The Birth of the Prison*. Foucault points to the seventeenth century as the period that employed a power mechanism applied throughout the social body. As this "disciplinary society" arose, it depended on "a generalized surveillance," that is, the application of the panoptic mechanism throughout social institutions (1979:209).

In Jeremy Bentham's view such a prison structure allows a strict supervision of each cell from the central tower. Foucault maintains that the purpose of the panopticon is "to induce in the inmate a state of conscious and permanent visibility" that assures the automatic functioning of power:

"So to arrange things, that the surveillance is permanent in its effects, even if it is discontinuous in its action" (1979:201). This system is a lesson in surveillance to all the prisoners. The mechanism of this building, Foucault argues, can be extended to other social systems because it is a "diagram of a mechanism of power reduced to its ideal form" (1979:205). This mechanism

61

"is a type of location of bodies in space, of distribution of individuals in relation to one another, of hierarchical organization, of disposition of centres and channels of power" (1979:205). Countess P.'s prison follows Bentham's design to the letter:

> "It was a panopticon she forced them to build, a hollow circle of cells shaped like a doughnut, the inward-facing wall of which was composed of grids of steel and, in the middle of the roofed, central courtyard, there was a round room surrounded by windows." (NC 210)

The division of space is the key element in the maintenance of discipline, similar to Foucault's example of army barracks or the arrangement of soldiers in military formation, as a way of controlling bodies: "It individualizes bodies by a location that does not give them a fixed position, but distributes them and circulates them in a network of relations" (Foucault, 1979:146).

The monitor in the middle keeps all the inmates under the warden's scrutiny, in complete isolation, as the guards are not allowed to see or touch the prisoners, and contact among them is totally forbidden. They are confined to the cells that have now become their bedrooms.

Sexuality lies at the core of each crime, so that heterosexuality is presented as the recurrent site of violence. The murders, however, are always given a justification:

> "There are many reasons, most of them good ones, why a woman should want to murder her husband; homicide might be the only way for her to preserve a shred of dignity at a time, in a place, where women were deemed to be chattels, or, in the famous analogy of Tolstoy, like wine bottles that might conveniently be smashed when their contents were consumed . . . But for Olga Alexandrovna, who took a hatchet to the drunken carpenter who hit her around once too often, Olga Alexandrovna acted out of a conviction that His eye was on the sparrow and therefore on even such a weak, timorous and unworthy creature as herself, so that the life being beaten out of her was surely worth as much, in the general scheme of things, as the life of the man with the fists –perhaps, since she was a loving mother, more. But it turned out the court thought otherwise than she.. ." (NC 211)

The Countess is the only person watching over the inmates, so her position represents a trap, not a seat of power. She stays in a room in the centre of the prison, from which vantage point she can watch every prisoner. Her eagerness to take on this role suggests her desire for power and for maintaining the social order, but, at the same time, it reflects her fascination with women who act illicitly. By watching the women all day as they occupy their cells, the

62

Countess exhibits a curiosity that goes beyond her stated agenda of the reformation of her prisoners.

> "For the Countess P. had conceived of the idea of a therapy of meditation. The women in the bare cells, in which was neither privacy nor distraction, cells formulated on the principle of those in a nunnery where all was visible to the eye of God, would live alone with the memory of their crime until they acknowledged, not their guilt--most of them had done that, already--but their responsibility. And she was sure that with responsibility would come remorse." (NC 212)

The weakness of the Countess' system lies in her assumption that the prisoners need forgiveness and feel responsible for their acts. None of the women has ever come forward to receive her benediction, since they all regard their deeds as justified self-defence acts. Outside the prison, the state has nevertheless condemned them over their tyrannical spouses, while inside, there are victims of an equally skewed gaze.

Critics have interpreted Carter's panopticon in different ways. Joanne Gass views it as a controlling metaphor for the entire novel because its mechanism operates in the whorehouse and the circus ring. These "defining arenas" serve as confines of elements that society deems disruptive and allow it to categorize them as a way of defusing their threat (IDM 71, 73-74). Gass's argument parallels Foucault's, and my own, by suggesting that panopticism is not limited to literal prisons but instead is dispersed throughout society as a means of protecting the social order. Magali Michael argues that the prisoner who first initiates contact with a guard and begins exchanging notes with her "literally writes herself into subjecthood" (1996:516). Brian Finney makes a similar point, discussing how this communication "enables [the prisoners] to narrate their own lives" (1998:175). As these critics make clear, the Countess' panopticon includes the possibility of agency for the prisoners. They may be the object of the Countess' gaze, but they are never completely objectified because they begin to express themselves. Reclaiming some of their subjectivity, they begin plotting with the guards and eventually escape from her prison, leaving her locked up in the prison of her own devise.

The panopticon fails as prison despite its rigid structure and intense surveillance. Female sexuality cannot be disciplined through strict scrutiny, and the prisoners find loopholes large enough for them to cross and reach one another. It is sufficient for one woman prisoner to look up and meet the eyes of her guard, for the boundaries prisoner-gaoler to dissolve. As Olga first touches Vera's hand, she "knew whoever it was who might truly sit in judgment on her had elected to dismiss the charge" (NC 216). This then triggers a chain reaction:

> "Desire, that electricity transmitted by the charged touch of Olga Alexandrovna and Vera Andreyevna, leapt across the great divide between the guards and the guarded. Or, it was as if a wild seed took root in the cold soil of the prison and, when it bloomed, it scattered seeds around in its turn. The stale air of the House of Corrections lifted and stirred, was moved by currents of anticipation, of expectation, that blew the ripened seeds of love from cell to cell . . Contact was effected, first, by illicit touch and glance, and then by illicit notes, or, if either guard or inmate turned out to be illiterate, by drawings made on all manner of substances, on rags of clothing if paper was not available, in blood, both menstrual and venous, even in excrement, for none of the juices of the bodies that had so long been denied them were alien to them, in their extremity – drawings, as it turned out, crude as graffiti, yet with the effect of clarion calls. And if the guards were all subverted to the inmates' humanity through look, caress, word, image, then so did the inmates wake up to the knowledge that, on either side of their own wedge-shaped cubes of space, lived other women just as vividly alive as themselves. (NC 216–17).

Lesbianism takes on a liberating value after the uprising, as the prisoners and their guards set off to found a republic of free women, episode which parallels the musical community Princess and Mignon form in the Siberian wilderness once they flee the circus.

> "Through the measureless wilderness around them roamed the savage audience for which the women must make a music never before heard on earth although it was not the music of the spheres but of blood, of flesh, of sinew, of the heart.
>
> This music, proclaimed Mignon, they had been born to make. Had been brought together, as women and as lovers, solely to make – music that was at the same time a taming and a not-taming; music that sealed the pact of tranquility between humankind and their wild brethren, their wild sisters, yet left them free." (NC 275)

Love develops in response to each other's humanity. Even if the positions the protagonists occupy reflect an imbalance of power at first, and the setting is ripe for exploitation, the power structures are not just reversed. They are melted as a result of the mixed and contradictory positions the women occupy.

In the novel, Carter playfully lets us know that she is aware of the difficulties of writing a new story of the social using the legible characters of the old. As the prisoners leave the Siberian prison behind them:

"The white world around them looked newly made, a blank sheet of fresh paper on which they could inscribe whatever future they wished" (NC 218).

The quest of the heroine Fevvers to 'rewrite' her own 'happy ending' mirrors the lesbian characters' challenge to devise their new life. It seems that Fevvers can only turn "from a freak into a woman" through the custom of marriage, such transformation being a step down involving collapse into conformity (NC 279–83).

The peripheral institutions Fevvers serves in, the whorehouse, the Museum of women monsters and the circus, treat people as objects to be visually consumed and exploited. She and her fellow inmates are, as Foucault describes the inmates of the panopticon, like actors on the stage, enclosed in "small theatres, in which each actor is alone, perfectly individualized and constantly visible" and which have the effect of inducing "in the inmate a state of consciousness and permanent visibility that assures the automatic functioning of power"(1979:3).

Their excessive physical traits or unusual talents individualise them and condemn them to submissive roles: "one finds in the programme of the Panopticon a...concern with individualizing observation, with characterization and classification, with the analytical arrangement of space" (Foucault, 1979:203).

Within the bounds of the panopticon they can each be used, but the threat they pose to normality is constantly looming.

Foucault notes in *The History of Sexuality*, that society makes room for illegitimate sexuality and madness, in a 'proper' arena for such things.

> "If it was truly necessary to make room for illegitimate sexualities, it was reasoned, let them take their infernal mischief elsewhere: to a place where they could be reintegrated, if not in the circuits of production, at least in those of profit. The brothel and the mental hospital [and in this case, the freak show and the circus] would be those places of tolerance: the prostitute, the client, and the pimp, together with the psychiatrist and the hysteric...seem to have surreptitiously transferred the pleasures that are unspoken into the order of things that are counted. Words and gestures, quietly authorized, could be exchanged there at the going rate. Only in those places would untrammelled sex have a right to (safely insularized) forms of reality, and only to clandestine, circumscribed, and coded types of discourse"(1998:5).

Just as the women prisoners destroy the panopticon of their prison, so does Fevvers break through the panopticons of the whorehouse, the freak show, and the circus. Whenever she stops in such an institution long enough to make a difference, the balance of power is upset.

Ma Nelson's brothel burns down, Madame Schreck dies after trying to sell Fevvers and the inmates of the museum of women monsters are set free, and the circus blows up into the Siberian snows. Her aim to "see the end of cages" (NC 38) can be reached once the panopticon fails and makes room for a new world and a new woman

"And once the old world has turned on its axle so that the new dawn can dawn, then, ah, then! all the women will have wings, the same as I. This young woman in my arms, whom we found tied hand and foot with the grisly bonds of ritual, will suffer no more of it; she will tear off her mind forg'd manacles, will rise up and fly away. The dolls' house doors will open, the brothels will spill forth their prisoners, the cages, gilded or otherwise, all over the world, in every land, will let forth their inmates singing together the dawn chorus of the new, the transformed" (NC 285)

2. 1.3. THE CAVE/THE WOMB

The cave is most often associated with the female space. It also evokes the topos of the journey into the labyrinth, carrying ambiguous meanings, sometimes seen as the entrance to hell, other times representing a soul's return to life. For Plato's cave dweller in *The Republic* it is a space of imprisonment, as he can only see shadows; Freud regarded it as a womb-like enclosure, so that a woman may at some point become "a prisoner of her own nature", according to Gilbert and Gubar (1979:94); Simone de Beauvoir (1989) viewed the cave as a metaphor of the social imprisonment of women.

On the other hand, the cave draws one to its protective enclosure, it is a safe place, womb-like, the source of yearning and pleasure. The journey to the female depths becomes necessary for reaching a deeper understanding of the self. The womb is a liminal space, which must necessarily be crossed to come into the world; as in a rite of passage, this *limen* is ambiguous, it is neither life nor death. Abjection is the recurring, threatening sensation of an incurable instability of the self, that finds expression in the body, in the secretions which exceed it, in its crevices. Sites of expulsion and of incorporation, borderline sites of horror and pleasure, all stand for the critics definition of abjection:

> "We may call it a border: abjection is above all ambiguity. Because, while releasing a hold, it does not radically cut off the subject from what threatens it - on the contrary, abjection acknowledges it to be in perpetual danger. But also, abjection itself is a compromise of judgment and affect, of condemnation and yearning, of signs and drives. Abjection preserves what existed in the archaism of pre-objectal relationship, in the immemorial violence with which the body becomes separated from another body in order to be - maintaining that night in which the outline of the signified vanishes and where only the imponderable affect is carried out" (Kristeva, 1982: 9-10).

Mucus, blood, the wet stickiness of the carnal threshold, create fusion and confusion: they are elements which, in Kristeva's term, we could recognize as belonging to the category of the abject. Because they are secretions, because they are inscribed in a borderline area: between the outside and the inside of the body, between the undefined self and other of the pre-natal dyad. It is an indecent image which exposes a secret everybody knows, the secret of an event everybody has experienced: "The abject is the violence of mourning for an 'object' that has always already been lost. [...] It takes the ego back to its source on the abominable limits from which, in order to be, the ego has broken away - it assigns it a source in the non-ego, drive, and death" (Kristeva, 1982: 15).

Abjection, "one of those violent, dark revolts of being" (Kristeva,1982:1), signals the horror of not knowing the borders of the self, and fuses time and space, just like the pre-natal period. In *The Passion of New Eve*, Eve/lyn is trapped in a red room and tortured by a refrain growing louder and louder in his ears:

> "... other women's voices took up the refrain: NOW YOU ARE AT THE PLACE OF BIRTH, NOW YOU ARE AT THE PLACE OF BIRTH [...] I realised the warm, red place in which I lay was a simulacrum of the womb.
>
> [...]
>
> For in this room lies the focus of darkness. She is the destination of all men, the inaccessible silence, the darkness that glides, at the last moment, always out of reach; the door called orgasm slams in his face, closes fast on the Nirvana of non-being which is gone as soon as it is glimpsed. She, this darkest one, this fleshly extinction, beyond time, beyond imagination, always just beyond, a little way beyond the fingertips of the spirit, the eternally elusive quietus who will free me from being, transform my I into the other and, in doing so, annihilate it." (PNE :52, 58-59)

The scene marks Evelyn's separation from his male persona and his transformation into Eve, as well as his escape from the abjection of the maternal. The space of metamorphosis displays its contradictory nature, as "low, hidden, earthly, dark, material, immanent, visceral" (Russo,1994:1), the 'grotto-esque' and a psychic field, whose insecurity is heightened by its sealed nature, as Punter (1998: 218) notes:

> "the inevitability of seepage, the inglorious but indisputable fact of slime . . . the crypt may seem to enclose and inoculate a condign secret, but it remains only interesting in so far as it can be breached, the secret can be broached; the insides can present themselves for inspection".

Issues of gender difference rise to the surface of ideologies with a closer inspection of spatial shapes. Cillie Rentmeister (in Higonnet, 1994) builds her argument on the observation of the dominance of oval architectural shapes in matriarchal peoples of the Mediterranean before

Greek architecture made its mark and patriarchal voices resounded. Christiane Erlemann (1985:137) builds upon Rentmeister's analysis in her observation of literary forms:

> "women's spatial utopias nowadays lean heavily toward curved forms, and if we want to assume that there is more to them than an outline sketch then they must be rooted in a critique of the dominant shapes, a critique which finds symbolic expression in the circular form."

The curved form, reminiscent of the womb is central to women's conceptualization and actualization of their spatial context Some women writers identify or project curved, female spaces in the external world. Others employ a psychological female space to subvert a male-dominated social structure. Christa Wolf's (1998) heroine is confined to a womb-like basket where her speech is repressed and her sexuality suffocated. The internal space of the womb poses a threat to women even if it is symbolically female. Fairy-tale beauties are imprisoned in caves or dungeons so that the male space outside should ensure its distance.

In *The Passion of New Eve* the womb appears as a dystopian space that enslaves women to their "biological iconography" (*SW* 109). Carter seems to indicate that the myth of the womb as patriarchal and matriarchal locus of the subject is equally repressive and empty, so the female subject must cross it to give free vent to her desires somewhere else. The ways in which women articulate their desires, however, accounts for either a radical subversion of the prevailing order or complicity with it. Carter argues for "the secularisation of women", which necessarily involves a demystification of the womb, or "the biological iconography of women", precisely because:

> "To deny the bankrupt enchantments of the womb is to pare a good deal of the
> fraudulent magic from the idea of women, to reveal us as we are, simple creatures of
> flesh and blood whose expectations deviate from biological necessity sufficiently to
> force us to abandon…the deluded priesteshood of a holy reproductive function." (*SW* 109-10)

That reproductive function derives much of its power from myths that elevate motherhood, or the womb, to a sacred status, which illogically is used to justify the subjugation of women: they are viewed as sacred because they possess the womb, yet that "is why they are treated so badly for nothing can defile the sacred" (*SW* 109).

If women dismiss the maternal function and if the womb is merely "an organ like any other organ," relatively useful but not much use at all if one does "not wish to utilize its sole function, that of bearing children" they invite punishment. Women are granted power because they are in possession of a womb, yet this also turns them into slaves to a patriarchal ideology. This is Carter's way to make us question the values that have been invested in motherhood; instead of it being only one of many possible identifications, the female subject has been allowed no other role. Carter is distrustful when it comes to the nostalgic approach of old myths with mother figures or goddesses; assuming "the invocation of hypothetical great goddesses" (*SW* 5) may empower women automatically, is a dangerous illusion that dismisses lived realities.

We might read Evelyn as an example of Julia Kristeva's foreigner, who, by fleeing his origins gains a freedom of mobility in crossing borders, yet remains haunted by or "riveted to the origin" (Kristeva, 1991:29). The foreigner is consumed by love for the lost mother (or lost homeland), a longing for the maternal body that must necessarily remain repressed, at least in the oedipal scene. By freeing oneself from this desire located in the mother's body, one is also freed from sexual taboos; through a "shattering of repression" one is permitted a "sexual frenzy" in which "everything is possible" (30)

For instance, Evelyn believes he has escaped the sexual prohibitions of a stereotypically repressive English society: "Child of a moist, green, gentle island...how could I resist the promise of violence, fear, madness?" (PNE 15).

As an Englishman in a dystopian New York that is rapidly disintegrating into chaos, Evelyn is free to act out on his darkest desires and sexual fantasies. He becomes the kind of Sadeian libertine he had perhaps always aspired to be, but in that freedom from prohibitions, as Kristeva argues, repression ruptures and one is abruptly confronted by that which one desires most. Thus, in the eruption of repressed desires, one does not so much escape the mother's body (or the origin), but rather returns to it as the very source of desire. Ultimately, this enforces a confrontation with oneself, with that unconscious, desiring 'other' within each of us, indicating an alienated interiority in which we come to recognise "the hidden face of our identity" (Kristeva, 1991:1)

The womb-like space of Beulah, a place where contrarieties exist together" (PNE 48) swallows the male Evelyn into a whirl of uncanny experiences, culminating with the sex-change. The entrance to this 'other' space, "down a paved throat of sand into the depths of the earth . . . fathoms deep [down]" (PNE 48) marks it as alien to the character, before it becomes alienating. It is the core of a foreign country, a dark continent, set against the familiar London physically, prior to the disclosure of its cryptic female otherness.

In the first phase of his journey towards a female identity, the function of the underground bunker is a protective one in relation to the protagonist. He is the unborn child in the womb of the mother.

In order to access the intricate topography of the bunker, after the sex-change, Eve undergoes a backward birth, he has to "slide into the living rock all alone" (PNE 179), face an "ordeal" (PNE 181), before confronting Mother. When she crawls 'into the interstice of rock', Eve experiences physical and psychological discomfort caused by a claustrophobic atmosphere:

> "I went...the freezing little stream, my skin scored and grazed by the cruel embrace of the rock...every movement necessitated the most extreme exertion; I was soon drenched with sweat. The passage was choked, airless, dank, and a faint reek of rotten eggs hovered above the sulphurated streamlet" (PNE 180).

Eve's wandering through the system of the caves, to "the living rock...to rendezvous with my maker" (PNE 179), gives Carter the chance to parody the topos of the mythical journey to the Underworld (Peach, 1998:128). The divide between birth and death is no longer clear and past, present and future are conflated:

> "Men long for it and fear it; the womb, that comfortably elastic organ, is a fleshly link
> between past and future, the physical location of an everlasting present tense than can
> usefully serve as a symbol of eternity, a concept that has always presented some difficulties in
> visualization. The hypothetical dream-time of the foetus seems to be the best that we can do."
> (SW 107-8)

The womb as "the First and Last Place, earth, the greatest mother of them all, from whom we come, to whom we go" (SW 108) is an illusion which "gets in the way of the experience, and obscures it completely" (SW 108). Eve's travel through this site of revelation and initiation marks an alienating temporal suspension until "Time no longer passed" (PNE 184).

The first cave recedes into a smaller cave, and yet another cave within that, revealing a "highly complex system" (idem: 181). Carter intends for this image of a network of caves to indicate both the complex mythology that has been elaborated around the womb, as well as the complexity of women's bodies and desires, which that mythology attempts to suppress.

The womb is often figured as a "devouring mouth" in the masculine imaginary because it "is never thought of as the primal place in which we become body" (Irigaray,1992:41).

By depicting the cave as a bodily space, "the extensible realm sited in the penetrable flesh" (*SW* 107), Carter avoids the definition of the womb as a sacred space; she underlines the biological function of reproductive bodies rather than the mythical one.

Eve's profound disillusionment with the emptiness of myth pushes her forward, into a larger cave and a "wider and lower' corridor, where she has to "crawl against the gentle current of the stream", animated by the fear of "death by pressing, death by drowning!" (PNE 181)

This most interior of the caves is explicitly figured as a womb going into labour: the cave walls "shuddered and sighed", and as its "pulsations exert greater and greater pressure", this movement develops into a "visceral yet perfectly rhythmic agitation", rippling its walls of "meat and slimy velvet", which at first seem to ingest Eve in one last inward pull before shoving her out "into the amniotic sea" (PNE 186).

The final enclosure Eve reaches is more spacious, which offers her the chance to act human, "not creep like a spider or splash like an amphibian" (PNE 184). But the cave undergoes a surrealistic metamorphosis, as it turns into a pulsating womb:

> "This new passage…grew warmer and warmer: the walls dripped with a moisture more viscid, more clinging than water…. My hand stretched before me was drenched…with bloody dew.
>
> The rock has softened and changed is substance; the textures under my enquiring fingers were soft and yielding….Now the dew felt like slime; this slime coated me. The walls of this passage shuddered and sighed at first almost imperceptibly, so that I mistook it for my own breathing. But their pulsation exert greater and greater pressure on me, draw me inward.
>
> Walls of meat and slimy velvet.
>
> Inward.
>
> A visceral yet perfectly rhythmic agitation ripples the walls, which ingest me." (PNE 184)

The womb seems to turn into a reproductive organ, according to the description given. But Eve feels trapped, as the shift in the grammatical tenses also indicates. Thus the organ of birth threatens to annihilate the heroine, it is an insatiable carnivorous monster that frightens Eve but cannot affect her reasoning. Ultimately, the womb is depicted here in all its messy reality, the flesh and blood of the maternal body. That body does indeed become a suffocating space, at least at the point of its expulsion of the child. Thus, according to the biological accuracy of this scene, Carter refutes the masculine imaginary that insists on figuring the womb as a devouring mouth. Just as Eve is expelled from the cave, so too is the infant once the womb no longer provides the room in which it needs to further develop and grow. To take this one

UNIVERSITY OF WINCHESTER LIBRARY

step further, Carter indicates how each of us needs to be expelled from the womb as a fantasized, mythological space.

Although the womb is "the domain of futurity in which the embryo forms itself from the flesh and blood of its mother" (*SW* 107), it is more than a passive receptacle of neonatal growth. It appears lively and aggressive in its formation of Eve, who has to adopt an uncomfortable position at the end of her journey, as she makes her way out of the claustrophobic space.

"The rocks between which I am pressed as between the pages of a book seem to me to be composed of silence; I am pressed between the leaves of a book of silence." (PNE 180)

The cave by the sea is another centre of the labyrinth, a place where "time is running back on itself" (PNE 183), where Eve expects to find the true meaning of her new self.

Even if Carter claims she does not reject the idea of 'mother earth', she indicates how problematic our tendency to equate 'mother' with nurturance is. In her interview with Lisa Appignanesi she points out that 'mother earth' is not benign just as Mother, the grotesque matriarch.

"She has retired to a cave by the sea" (PNE 174), a regression "beyond consciousness" (PNE 184), as Carter herself suggests in *The Sadeian Woman*: "the unguessable reaches of the sea are a symbol of it, and so are caves, those dark sequestered places where initiation and revelation take place" (*SW* 107).

"The goddess is dead. And, with the imaginary construct of the goddess, dies the notion of eternity, whose place on this earth was her womb... We are confronted with mortality, as if for the first time. There is no way out of time."(*SW* 110)

The heroine's subsequent 'lowering of the spirits' (PNE 180) cannot prevent her from noticing ironically "Mother has inserted herself in the most hermetic of fall-out shelters. She clearly plotted to survive the holocaust" (PNE 180). The romanticism of her journey is obviously diluted as a result of her comments. The shrine loses its mythical character as she keeps on removing layers of traditional make-up from a place that is absolutely empty: "however hard I push against the rock, I seem to get no closer to Mother" (PNE 180).

Lacan believed there is a stage in development when the child looks into a mirror and acquires a feeling of completeness. Mirrors, by providing self-knowledge, may bring about freedom. Leilah can escape one life to return to another via the mirror: "She brought into being a Leilah who lived only in the not-world of the mirror and then became her own reflection" (PNE 28).

73

Tristessa constantly renews the mirror stage of recognition as a female by living in a world of mirrors, which can bring him close to his mother and the world of women. The mirror image is an important element of Eve's journey into the simulated womb, at the end of the novel:

> "The womb is an imaginative locale and has an imaginative location far away from my belly, beyond my flesh, beyond my house, beyond this city, this society, this economic structure – it lies in an area of psychic metaphysiology suggesting such an anterior primacy of the womb that our poor dissecting tools of reason blunt on its magnitude." (*SW* 109)

The mirror into which she looks is shattered. It represents a symbolic return to a phase before the recognition of the self, and it means that she loses the initial concept of being male.

> "There was a mirror propped against the rugged wall, a fine mirror in a curly, gilt frame; but the glass was broken, cracked right across many times so that it reflected nothing, was a bewilderment of splinters and I could not see myself nor any portion of myself in it." (PNE 142)

In this second cave, a simulacrum of the womb, "filled with a familiar, dim, red light" (PNE 181), Eve finds three objects that remind her of the past: "a glossy publicity still of Tristessa at the height of her beauty", "a glass flask of 'a strange, swan-necked shape'" similar to that in Baroslav's lab, and "the ingot of alchemical gold I'd given Leilah in the darkness and confusion of the city" (PNE 183).

The psychological effect of the three objects is not consolation, as expected, but grief and sorrow, topped by anger over lost love and friendship. Yet they have some magical qualities that subversively offer some reconciliation. As she rips Tristessa's photo, Eve observes "a red stain, blood…on the cloth the photograph had been" (PNE 184). The bottle contains "a sweet, clean scent of pine", the smell of a remote past which enables the reversal of time. There is no God-like metaphysical being, however, but relics of historical past. The pendant fails to trap Eve in the mythical order of things, as she ironically keeps it to pay her trip back.

For Carter, it is above all women's desire for maternal power that poses the greatest danger when attempting to assert their identities. Mother is just as much an hypothesis as father, as she illustrates later on in *Wise Children*. As we see with Eve, when she calls out for Mother to appear, as absolute proof of her existence, and only receives an empty reply of silence, we realize that "Mother is a figure of speech" (PNE 184, 186). The mother's body is itself rendered redundant, at least in its ability to provide the female subject with a secure, autonomous identity; and perhaps one of the text's greatest ironies is that Eve is the prodigal son turned daughter, forced to return to the womb. "Yet in the end that return is impossible" (Armitt, 1996: 175-6).

So long as the womb remains figured according to a masculine imaginary, to which matriarchal myths contribute and help reinforce, then, as Carter insists: "Only men are privileged to return, even if only partially and intermittently, to this place of fleshly extinction" (*SW* 108-9). Eve is no longer a man, and must negotiate her relationship to the maternal body from an alternative feminine positioning since she is now the bearer of that symbolic place of fleshly extinction, as she herself admits: "I have come home. The destination of all journeys is their beginning. I have not come home" (PNE 186).

Overall, Carter invokes the mother's power only to denounce her potency (Armitt, 1996:177-8, 172) and the myth of matriarchal power is proven "artificial", "infertile", "useless". Eve has descended into "the depths of the earth" (PNE 49) to be reborn, "down an inscrutable series of circular, intertwining, always descending corridors" (PNE 57) to find his/her moment of birth "I could not run away from it but would always be running towards it" (PNE 83), but s/he finds nothing. Like the spirals in Tristessa's glass house, giving the illusion of freedom, the cave hides nothing. This is Carter's response to myth, "Mother goddesses are just as silly a notion as father gods" (*SW* 5-6).

As her journey has reached its final point, and Eve has undergone the mysterious ritual by the sea, she understands eventually that "speech figure see later and has retired to a cave beyond consciousness"(PNE 184). She underlines the metaphorical and the linguistic character of human interpretation of experience, and we should thus understand that knowledge is relative and open to interpretation. As she finds herself at the edge of the Pacific Ocean, she is literally allowed no further room for evasion. The remaining part of her journey positions Eve as the witness to the birth of the American continent. The cave changes into a round screen on which she can see how "rivers neatly roll up on themselves like spools of film and turn in on their own sources. The drops of the Mississippi, the Ohio, the Hudson, tremble on a blade of grass" (PNE 185). As time stops its backwards flow and everything returns into the amniotic sea, Eve is given birth again:

> "The walls of meat expelled me. Without a cry, I fell into a darkness like the antithesis of light, an immensity of darkness, the final cave through which now marched, animating the darkness, the parade of the great apes, which wound me back on the spool of time that now wound up. ...

I have forgotten how I picked up a stone and shattered a nut with it. The sound of the sea becomes omnipresent, the sea, which washes away all memory and retains it." (PNE 186)

In spite of her regained freedom, Eve feels trapped, this time by the cave inside, since she may be pregnant by Tristessa. The novel ends ambiguously because we can take "Ocean, ocean, mother of mysteries, bear me to the place of birth" (PNE 191) as referring to Eve's giving birth or her being reborn . Eve/lyn's perpetual desire to flee from his/her origins, initially prompted by the desire to repress the (m)other, is a movement that has inevitably brought him/her back to a suffocating maternal space. This womb-like space not only threatens to consume his/her identity, but as an instance of the return of the repressed, also reveals his/her violent relation to and desire for the 'feminine', which s/he has attempted to keep concealed in both him/herself and others. Eve can read into the cultural symbols that have contributed to her creation, so she is able to escape from the labyrinth of Beulah, "I knew the plan of the labyrinth now" (PNE 81) and continue her experience in order to be born again.

When Eve finally emerges from the caves/womb, she acknowledges: "I did not want my old self back" (PNE 188), clearly embracing rather than repressing the 'feminine', both within herself and the 'other'. However, the moment Eve realizes she does not want to go back to being her old (male) self, she also admits: "I began to wonder if I might not in some way escape" (PNE 188). She still desires some form of escape, left "on the beach of elsewhere" (PNE 190), in a highly ambiguous space, as Eve offers a final incantation: "Ocean, ocean, mother of mysteries, bear me to the place of birth" (PNE 191). The transparent message conveys the necessity of finding a new female subjectivity, one that would no longer locate itself exclusively in the womb or maternal body. Eve is trapped inside the claustrophobic system of the caves when she finally understands the need to step outside this mythically-laden zone towards an different space that would provide the female subject more room to shape her identity.

76

2. 2. MAZES OF THE OUTSIDE

2. 2.1 THE FOREST

Traditionally, the forest stands for the female principle and equals darkness, mystery, isolation, the unconscious. It isolates and hides, displaying an ambiguous nature. Evil forces under various guises may take shelter under the cover of darkness in the woods. The forest becomes a place of initiation in Angela Carter's works, as the magical permeates the real. The ritual of initiation is made up of several stages, such as facing obstacles, shattering illusions and gaining maturity. Angela Carter's forest is always populated with wild or evil forces. The characters that enter the forest find themselves trapped within a magic circle of confusion. No matter how desperate their situation is, there is also a stronger fascination the forest displays, which they find impossible to resist. They are drawn deeper into the core of the woods, putting their lives at risk in search of the forbidden fruit.

It seems that the aura of the forest is irresistible, because the characters ignore warning signs and give in to the lure of a nightmarish universe. The forest paradoxically seduces and threatens both the characters and the accompanying reader. The journey into the forest has sexual connotations most of the times. Travellers are on the verge of puberty – in 'Penetrating to the Heart of the Forest', 'Master', 'The Company of Wolves' – or at the moment of mid-life crisis – 'The Erl-King', 'Reflections'. The atmosphere is claustrophobic, as in the cave and the desert, and death takes the form of a sexual predator that has to be annihilated, be it an internal demon or an external evil force. The forest becomes a sexual battlefield, where the woman is positioned as the victim. Taboos must be   broken to ensure survival and dispel the evil, mythical wilderness.

Goethe's ballad *ErlKönig* serves as the intertext for the short story 'The Erl-King'. A little boy dies in his father's arms after complaining in terror that he can see a frightening spirit and hear his seductive voice threatening to take him away. The third-person narrator in 'The Erl-King' concludes the story by describing the possible but not real event of the Erl-King's murder. Correspondingly, 'The Erl-King' begins long before its first lines. The narrator's opening description suggests that the ancient woods are laden with significance, their past and multiple histories vaguely discernible but ultimately lost in the overgrowth: The story occurs entirely within the space of the woods, no possibility of exit ever being articulated. However, this labyrinth is not built of stone; it is animate and in flux. The narrator's description of lost pathways, "withered blackberries" and the "blackish water [which] thickens, now, to ice" creates a sense of mutability (EK 186).

The space of the forest is weaved as boundless and confining, at the same time. The complicated structure of the leafy labyrinth opens paths for characters to follow and stray away, with the chance to resist the burden of claustrophobic bowers. The mixture of flexibility and inescapability of the woods mirrors Foucault's concept of the inextricability of power. In *The History of Sexuality* Michel Foucault (1998:2), destabilizes conventional formulations of power as "a group of institutions and mechanisms that ensure the subservience of the citizens of a given state" by viewing it as an unstable and shifting network of force relations "produced from one moment to the next . . . Power is everywhere; not because it embraces everything, but because it comes from everywhere" (93). Further, Foucault's formulation of power as omnipresent and unstable locates resistance as its inseparable companion. He writes that "Where there is power, there is resistance, and yet, or rather consequently, this resistance is never in a position of exteriority in relation to power" (95).

In the short story power lies in the omnipresence of the seducing spirit, so that the girl is under threat upon stepping in the woods. The same effect is achieved discursively, as we, the readers, get lost once we become part of the story's plot. The means of resistance for both the reader and the protagonist are physical movement and articulation of a subject position. The girl narrator must find a voice to match the fluid tones of the Erl-King's chants.

The difficulty the reader encounters when trying to provide a coherent summary of 'The Erl-King' signals the notion of the reader as lost. The story opens with the voice of a third-person narrator describing a woodland scene, a description which sets the tone for the ensuing moments of intertextuality within the tale. As the narrator remarks, this wood is removed from the time and space of quotidian existence: "You step between the fir trees and then you are no longer in the open air; the wood swallows you up" (EK 186). Liminally situated between autumn and winter, the tale is set in a kind of no-time, teetering on the brink of death:

"Now the stark elders have an anorexic look; there is not much in the autumn wood to make you smile but it is not yet, not quite yet, the saddest time of the year. Only, there is the haunting sense of the imminent cessation of being; the year, in turning, turns in on itself" (EK 186)

The effects of this opening are multiple. First, the reader is given a sense of being outside, or separated, from the social. As the first-person narrator later comments: "I thought that nobody was in the wood but me" (EK 187). Further, danger accompanies this sense of isolation, as the narrator pictures the rustling trees as "taffeta skirts of women who have lost themselves. . .and hunt round hopelessly for the way out" (EK 186), producing a sense of inescapable entrapment. The traveller appears simultaneously outside and inside the space of power that cannot be transgressed physically, as the first-person narrator comments in her initial account of walking through the woods: "The trees threaded a cat's cradle of half-stripped branches over me so that I felt I was in a house of nets" (EK 187). Power is anonymous and ubiquitous and its force acquires particular significance as the reader struggles to make sense of the narrative. On one level, 'The Erl-King' is a familiar narrative of a young girl's journey into sexuality and her struggle for subjectivity. And, like many of Carter's tales in *The Bloody Chamber*, this character's voyage is portrayed as similar to the experiences of fairy-tale heroines. As the third-person narrator articulates early on, however, these familiar narrative threads do not provide the reader with verifiable interpretive clues:

"A young girl would go into the wood as trustingly as Red Riding Hood to her granny's house but this light admits no ambiguities and, here, she will be trapped in her own illusion because everything in the wood is exactly as it seems" (EK 186).

The Erl-King retains a dangerously powerful position in his sexual relationship with the protagonist, a situation illustrated in the girl's assertion that the "Erl-King will do you grievous harm" (EK 187). Perhaps the most significant explanation for this power imbalance is her alien status: she is not at home. The Erl-King, conversely, is cozily situated at his hearth in the heart of his birthplace. Juxtaposed against the rapidity with which she loses herself is the Erl-King's intimate knowledge of the woods. The narrator's belief that he himself "came alive from the desire of the woods" establishes a link between the Erl-King's location "at home" and his command of the environment (EK 188). He knows the secrets of the wood. Able to distinguish "which of the frilled, blotched, rotted fungi are fit to eat" from the brambles "he will not touch

79

[because] the Devil spits on them at Michaelmas," the Erl-King clearly belongs (EK 188) to a different world.

This characterization of the Erl-King as comprehending the language of the woods, a language which the girl-narrator does not possess, suggests the structure of the Lacanian Symbolic. As she proceeds into the sexual relationship, the narrator also enters the realm of signification and language and discovers her status as foreigner. According to Lacan's formulation, the Symbolic, the Imaginary and the Real are separate and distinct realms.

However, as I argued at the beginning of this section, Carter positions both the reader and the girl as always already inside the woods: a distinct moment of entrance into signification does not exist. In troubling Lacan's structuralist divisions, Carter emphasizes Woman's differential relation to, not her exclusion from, language. While the Erl-King can read the secret signs of the wood, the third-person narrator remarks that for the interloper "there is no clue to guide you through in perfect safety" (EK 186).

The forest in 'The Erl-King' is described as a normal forest "of late October when withered blackberries dangled like their own dour spooks on the discoloured brambles" (EK 186). It becomes more gloomy as its life forms are presented in a state of agony:
"Now the stark elders have an anorexic look; there is not much in the autumn wood to make you smile but it is not yet, not quite yet, the saddest time of the year. Only, there is a haunting sense of the imminent cessation of being" (EK 186).

The description of decay and bitter cold of winter reinforces the frozen atmosphere of 'introspective weather, a sickroom hush' (EK 186). "All will fall still, all lapse" (EK 186) anticipates the atmosphere of stasis and death.

The reader is lured into a confining space governed by mysterious rules:
"The woods enclose. You step between the fir trees and then you are no longer in the open air; the wood swallows you up. There is no way through the wood any more, this wood has reverted to its original privacy. Once you are inside it, you must stay there until it lets you out again" (EK 186).

The emphasis on the confining aspect of the landscape is paralleled by a shift in narrative perspective: "A young girl would go into the wood as trustingly as Red Riding Hood to her granny's house .... I thought that nobody was in the wood but me" (EK 187).

Although the girl-narrator is introduced as the 'would-be' victim, the shift in reference from 'she' to 'you' has an unsettling effect. "It is easy to lose yourself" (EK 188) opens a paragraph in which the girl's perspective prevails: she has answered the call of the woods and feels the forest has "threaded a cat's cradle over me" (EK 187). There is a warning line repeated in the story with a change of the pronoun, placing the reader in the position of the threatened one: "Erl-King will do you grievous harm" (EK 187).

The forest is a 'subtle labyrinth', 'a house of nets' that confuses the lost travellers, but the self-reflexive aspect of the text is obvious in the hint made at the reader as traveller: "there is no clue to guide you through in perfect safety."

> "The woods enclose and then enclose again, like a system of Chinese boxes opening one into another; the intimate perspectives of the wood changed endlessly around the interloper, the imaginary traveller walking towards an invented distance that perpetually receded before me. It is easy to lose yourself in these woods." (EK 187)

The journey into the woods involves disorientation for both character and reader, as the conventional boundaries of the speaking subject's identity break down.

The identity of the speaking subject becomes impossible to establish as the voices of the narrator and character merge and destabilize the narrative perspective. The journey into the dangerous forest becomes a magical one, into a world that is other.

In another of her stories, in the *Black Venus* volume, 'Overture and Incidental Music for *A Midsummer Night's Dream*', we read of the woods populated by "grave, hideous and elemental beings" in Shakespearean texts, opposed to the image of the modern forest. The latter has been "disinfected", freed from savage beasts Superstitions no longer shape its discourse. In the dark forests fueling the nineteenth-century nostalgia it is possible to "be abandoned by the light, to lose yourself utterly with no guarantee you will either find yourself or else be found, to be committed against your will – or, worse, of your own desire – to a perpetual absence from humanity, an existential catastrophe, for the forest is as infinitely boundless as the human heart" (BB 274). The girl/ narrator or the girl and the narrator in 'The Erl-King' step into this haunted universe, drawn by the force of their desire. The exterior space is internalized as the narrator perceives herself trapped within her own illusions, "because everything in the wood is exactly as it seems" (EK 186). The forest turns into a labyrinth that threatens to imprison the girl and silence her. The journey is in fact not an aimless stroll but an imaginary quest for identity, as the use of the modal auxiliary suggests.

Reaching the core of the forest leads characters to sexual awakening or maturity. The labyrinth of the forest not only hosts the conflict of powers, it is an ever-changing heterotopia that suits the characters' dynamism and their inexhaustible taste for metamorphosis which eventually dissolves polarization.

2. 2.2. THE DESERT

The desert is a place of death and simulation, similar to Baudrillard's metaphor for America, a dream factory from which Eve in *The Passion of New Eve* hopes to escape: "Because you are delivered from all depth there – a brilliant, mobile, superficial neutrality, a challenge to meaning and profundity, a challenge to nature and culture, an outer hyperspace, with no origin, no reference points"(1988:5).

The journey to another realm appears as the antidote to the character's alienation in the novel: "I would go to the desert...there I thought I might find the most elusive of chimeras, myself" (PNE 38).

Sterility becomes a motif in the following episode of Evelyn's wanderings: "I reached the desert, the abode of enforced sterility, the dehydrated sea of infertility" (PNE 40). He has given sterility to Leilah and now feels it as a part of himself "I have found a landscape that matches the landscape of my heart" (PNE 41).

Evelyn himself believes the desert, "peopled only with echoes" (PNE 41), a "sublime form that banishes all sociality, all sentimentality, all sexuality" (Baudrillard, 1988:71) can make him repress violent memories and find himself anew in a different place. This suspension of memory is not only a further denial of one's relation to the 'other', but also, a refusal to his alienated desires. Evelyn certainly is reborn in the desert, but as a woman, Eve, and ironically the desert is figured as nothing more than "the abode of enforced sterility, the dehydrated sea of infertility, the post-menopausal part of the earth" (PNE 40). The desert is also representative of Leilah's enforced sterility, since Evelyn has escaped from the overwhelming sensuality of her flesh "at the price of her womb" (PNE 34).

Evelyn's attempt to escape the inescapable by changing the setting ultimately proves futile, since he is merely "speeding towards the very enigma [he] had left behind – the dark room, the mirror, the woman" (PNE 39).

The empty space he is speeding towards is a "landscape that matches the landscape of [his] heart" (PNE 41), populated with the embodiment of his deepest fears of the feminine. Evelyn fails to perceive that the monstrous Mother represents the horrid force of a society which reinforces the structure of a patriarchal order.

83

The fictional presentation of America appears close to the hyperreality Baudrillard has ascribed to postmodern America. The place where Evelyn's transformation occurs is the desert area of America, a symbolic landscape used by Baudrillard to mark the disappearance of the real and the invasion of the simulacra in postmodern society. In the novel's American desert, models of the real are executed as the real as the sadistic poet Zero and the matriarchal Mother of Beulah enact myths as the real thing. The Gothic depiction of New York shows the chaotic side of a society that is losing its grasp of the real. New York is seen through Evelyn's eyes, originally built as 'a city of reason' as having turned into "a cauldron of chaos" (PNE 11). The reason for this, as Baroslav the alchemist declares, is that "the age of reason is over" (PNE 13). The result is 'an alchemical city', in which the genuine and the artificial appear in the same order of things. Baroslav's gold ingot indicates a successful mutation of essences achieved with an alchemical trick. He makes the gold ingot from mercury and gives it to Evelyn who then gives it to Leilah when they are in the alchemical city of New York. After Eve/lyn's transsexual adventure in the desert, Leilah gives it back to Eve but eventually it ends in Mother's hands as she asks for it from Eve as an exchange for her coffin-boat. From its exchange in different hands we understand how its owners have gone through the 'alchemical change' of their sexual identities. The metaphor of alchemy brings the episodes of the novel together in an allegorical way while pointing to the argument of the fictional text. Elaine Jordan (1992:122) observes that Carter makes her narrative argument using "intertextual dialogues", exploiting the patriarchal this discourse she contests to make her opposition point. Talking about her novel, Carter observes:

> "one of the snags is that I do put everything in an novel to be *read*- read in the way allegory was intended to be read... on as many levels as you can comfortably cope with at the time... As a medievalist, I was trained to read books as having many layers. Using of the word 'allegory' may make it all too concrete."(Haffenden, 1985, 86-7)

While Carter's narrative contains multiple layers of meaning with an internal correspondence among them, this signifying activity occurs on the intertextual level of the novel, which links her style to Craig Owens's theory of postmodernism. According to Owens,

> "allegory occurs whenever one text is doubled by another...the allegorical work tends to prescribe the direction of its own commentary... In allegorical structure, then, one text is read through another... the paradigm for the allegorical work is thus the palimpsest... Allegorical imagery is appropriated imagery; the allegorist does not invent images but confiscates them. He

lays claim to the culturally significant, poses as its interpreter. And in his hands the image becomes something other... He does not restore an original meaning... rather, he adds another meaning to the image... the allegorical meaning supplants an antecedent one; it is a supplement." (WC54)

Eve/lyn's journey through the labyrinth of the desert becomes a pilgrimage from male ignorance to female self-consciousness.

> "I would go the desert, to the waste heart of that vast country, the desert on which they turned their backs for fear.. it would remind them of emptiness – the desert, the arid zone, there to find, chimera of chimeras, there, in the ocean of sand, among the bleached rocks, of the untenanted part of the world. I thought I might find that most elusive of all chimeras, myself. And so, in the end I did, although this self was a perfect stranger to me." (PNE 38)

This is what Evelyn says on leaving the city of rape and decay, New York. The desert is seen as a symbol of emptiness, a space of memory, enigmatic and ambiguous in its opportunity for both exile and escape. Evelyn perceives the threat implicit in his journey to the desert but regards it as a space of hope, with its 'pure air and cleanliness', 'primordial light' which "would purify"(PNE 38) him. He needs to heal his guilty conscience and the memory of bleeding Leilah as well as to restore his sense of balance, affected by the madness of the city. The desert is a land of miracles and also a breeder of hallucinations and insanity. Evelyn's journey takes place not only in the empirical space of the desert, the sphere of death, as he calls it, 'the abode of enforced sterility, the dehydrated sea of infertility' (PNE 40), but also inside his ego where he has to confront his fears:

> "Descend lower, descend the diminishing spirals of being that restore us to our source. Descend lower; while the world, in time, goes forward and so presents us with the illusion of motion, though all our lives we move through the curvilinear galleries of the brain toward the core of the labyrinth within us." (PNE 39)

The paradoxical nature of the desert is apparent as we read into its array of significations. On entering it, Evelyn feels estranged, as if he opened the gates to hell:

> "I am hopelessly lost in the middle of the desert, without map or guide or compass. The landscape unfurls around me like an old fan that has lost all its painted silk and left only the

bare, yellowed sticks of antique ivory in a world which, since I am alive, I have no business. The earth has been scalpelled, flayed; it is populated only with echoes." (PNE 41)

The opposition between the energetic protagonist and the static atmosphere of the desert foreshadows the price one has to pay to gain access to its secrets. Evelyn's movement towards the heart of the desert equals loss of life and the transition to the realm of hallucination: "the air dries out my lungs. I gasp. There is no one, no one" (PNE 41). The repetition of these rhythmical last words marks the beginning of Evelyn's journey within himself, casting doubts, at the same time, as to whether the ensuing experiences are real or a product of his hallucinations. Besides, the surrealistic atmosphere and appearance of the desert, 'the insane land of ...erratic structures', also suggest Evelyn's interior landscape, as he observes: "I have found the landscape that matches the landscape of my heart" (PNE 41).

The symbolic character of the desert is further emphasized through the insistence on its antiquity, "this ancient and terrible place", "the architectless town" under "unfamiliar stars" (PNE 42-43), although this symbolism disguises the author's parodic intentions in relation to the format of the Bildungsroman.

The desert represents the passage from the outside Evelyn has rejected to the inside of the maze, and it constantly faces him with its vastness that paradoxically generates claustrophobia. Dangers and surprises alternate and Evelyn undergoes many trials before he is granted access to the Californian cave by the sea. His upcoming castration is foreshadowed in his reference to the desert as an infertile land. There are no animals, no plants as far as he can see. The only sign of life is a dying albatross that has no place there. The question arises once more: is Evelyn dreaming of it or is it real? Angela Carter seems to stretch our belief to the limit by placing the albatross in the desert. She uses the symbol ironically for us, readers, to recognize the allusion to Coleridge. In *The Rime of the Ancient Mariner* the killing of the albatross brings about a curse on the crew of the ship. Consequently, we should be able to predict an unhappy ending for the feminist guerrilla, which in the end turns to dust.

The desert also appears to be a space of intellectual trial and alienation. The insane experiments conducted by Mother in the heart of the waste land need the seclusion at hand to create the ideal woman that in fact embodies the Platonic idea of androgyny.

The town in the desert, Beulah, represents victory over the phallogocentric culture. As Evelyn arrives he notices in horror that the emblem is 'a broken column', "broken off clean in the middle" (1982 47). The underground feminists have waged war against male dominance from this place where their twisted "philosophy has dominion over the rocks" (PNE 47).

It turns out to be a virtual space possible to define in relation to magical concepts, similar to those in alchemy:

> "Beulah is a profane place…its blueprint is a state of mind, has an unimpeachable quality of realism. But it is a triumph of science and hardly anything about it is natural, as if magic, there, masquerades as surgery in order to gain credence in a secular age" (PNE 48).

Evelyn's failing memory is the key in the interpretation of Beulah more as an embodiment of a mythical rather than a real place: "I am not sure I do not exaggerate its technological marvels…or my shell-shocked memory has invented most of them, in order to soften the mythic vengeance on me there." (PNE 50)

The artificial character of Beulah and its paradoxical character may also stem from the fact that it mirrors the image of its ruler, it is an expansion of "Holy Mother whose fingers are scalpels…a chthonic deity, a presence always present in the shaping structure of a dream." (PNE 47)

Beulah represents the centre of the desert, and the numerous comparisons to a womb stand as illustrations to this. However, it is a mock centre, as it fails to resolve the enigma of the desert's definition as source of life. This false centre proves to be just a technological marvel animated by indoctrinating, repetitive slogans, designed by a grotesque being. The inhuman aspect of Beulah reminds us of Huxley's remark on the dystopian vision in *The Brave New World*, a book about 'the advancement of science as it affects human individuals' (Foreword, 1987:8). Beulah remains in the end a space of imprisonment and claustrophobia, which Evelyn manages to escape after his transformation. It cannot represent a myth come true in spite of its mechanical perfection. It is only a parody of the forces of nature, rendered grotesque by its striking artificiality. The room in which Evelyn wakes up as Eve "was quite round, as if it had been blown out, like bubble gum, inflated under the earth, its walls were of tough, synthetic integument with an unnatural sheen upon it that troubled me to see, it was so slick, so lifeless" (PNE 49). It is an alien space that deepens Eve's feeling of estrangement: "the cool, clean room with its hygienically enforced tranquillity invited me to panic because I'd grown used to disorder and feared order as much as it were inimical" (PNE 51). The place is infused with the imminence of evil or death, as "the darkness and silence around me were as intense as a lapse of being" (PNE 51).

As Evelyn's terror overcomes him, the setting gradually changes from 'very cool' (PNE 50) to "the temperature increased until it was at blood heat" (PNE 52). This psychological torture chamber defies categories so that Evelyn finds it harder and harder to

"hold on to these threads of reason; yet however hard I struggled to reconcile this strangeness with those more familiar to me, the synthetic apparatus of mystery that dominated this place...inexorably exerted upon me all the compulsion of authentic mystery."(PNE 57)

His journey forward is further described as a descent into "the labyrinth of the inner year", "a tracing of the mazes of the brain itself", "the deepest eye of the spiral" (PNE 57). It takes thus the form of a trip to the centre of the mad Mother's brain, where Evelyn feels like "Ariadne in the maze" (PNE 57).

The desert represents, after all, a mirror image of Evelyn's state of mind and a space for a subverted male obsession, in which Zero turns from master of a harem into the victim of female cruelty. Beulah stands therefore more for the symbolic womb hiding Evelyn's deepest fears than for the headquarters of women's guerrilla. His imprisonment in the female space is meant to foreshadow his later imprisonment in the female body.

The Passion of New Eve is a speculative novel, because Eve and Tristessa's experience could never be maintained 'in reality'. They need to transpose their actualised desires into the real world. The desert, as in *Nights at the Circus*, provides them with a geographical and historical *tabula rasa* onto which they may inscribe a new vision of gender, sexuality and love. This setting 'speaks of the otherness of race, sex and class' (Gamble, 1997:58), but it also brings it to life, asking, nevertheless, for a price. They have a choice between dying of emaciation, or being discovered ad saved by the others, who stand for the reality that would not accept their reinvented selves. Reality comes to rescue them, undesired and unexpected, in the form of a children's crusade, and kills Tristessa.

Nights at the Circus takes the reader from Fevvers's dressing-room in London to Petersburg accompanying the circus and even further to Siberia. This increase in distance juxtaposes not only three settings, but also the realms of the real and the fictional. The further characters move in space, the thinner the logical link of events becomes. Fevvers's mysterious nature is reflected in the image of her dressing-room, which has "nothing to give her away…The only bits of herself she'd impressed on her surroundings were those few blonde hairs striating the cake of Pears transparent soap in the cracked saucer on the deal washstand."(NC 14)

Before the train derailment, as Fevvers is watching the icy desert of Siberia out of the train window she is "seized with such an anguish of the void' around her "all white with snow as if under dustsheets, as if laid away eternally as soon as brought back from the shop, never to be used or touched. Horrors!" (NC 197)

There is no origin, no end, so existence has no structure and life is overwhelmed by the nightmare of chaos. Space becomes uncertain accompanied by the deconstruction of time, whose metaphor is that of the vertigo.

Zero and his harem in *The Passion of New Eve* are destroyed and precipitated into space through a similar circular movement to that of Tristessa's revolving mansion in the desert. It is a fall from logic, from grace or from history. Buffo, the clown in *Nights at the Circus*, dances a death dance accompanied by a dizzying circular movement, terrifying to the eye of the beholder:

> "His face becomes contorted by the most hideous grimaces, as if it were trying to shake off the very wet white with which it is coated: shake! shake!shake out his teeth, shake off his nose, shake away the eyeballs, let all go flying off in a convulsive self-dismemberment." (NC 117)

Buffo's clown colleagues follow their master's example, mixing real and imaginary history with the future:

> "They danced the whirling apart of everything, the end of love, the end of hope; they danced tomorrows into yesterdays; they danced the exhaustion of the implacable present; they danced the deadly dance of the past perfect which fixes everything fast so it can't move again." (NC 243)

The prisoners of Countess P's horrific asylum "set off hand in hand, and soon started to sing for joy" (NC 218), heading for the desert to form a utopian female community. The Siberian wilderness becomes their shelter and they discover that "the white world around them looked newly made, a blank sheet of fresh paper on which they could inscribe any future they wished" (ibid.), anticipating Walser's transformation, whose mind has become "a perfect blank" (NC 222) in preparation for the reconstruction of his self. As the train is blown up with the crash "which shatters identity as well as time and space" (Carroll, 2000:191) and derailed, the world of the unconscious permeates the narrative.

The first step to the desert takes Carter's protagonists from the outside into the inside, into a maze of self-knowledge. It stands for a mirror image of the characters' states of mind and a proper space for the dissociation of sex from gender, and the arbitrary rearrangement of basic bodily constituents. Both the sphere of death and rebirth and a space of memory, the desert renders transformation easy, almost infinitely possible.

2. 2.3. THE CITY

Twentieth century literature exploits the topos of the city as a labyrinthine space, in response to the mythical city of nineteenth century literature. The city belongs to the category of confined spaces with no way out, a prison, crowded and cramped, a territory of chaos. It turns thus into an unfriendly, dangerous, even inhuman organism. Characters wander along narrow streets, dirty sewers and squares that contribute to their alienation. Contemporary cities lack the centre, so these journeys characters embark on are futile.

Angela Carter's cities conform to McLuhan's description of postmodern urban space, of the "city as a total field of inclusive awareness" (1965:166). Protagonists enter cities in decay, are trapped in ongoing wars and confined to spheres of despair.

Although there are barricaded houses ('Elegy for a Freelance', the Minister's cabinet in *The Infernal Desire Machines of Doctor Hoffman*) or locked doors in *The Passion of New Eve*, offering the illusion of protection, the protagonists either have to leave them and confront the violent world outside, like Desiderio and Evelyn, or violence creeps into the false oases of peace.

Juxtaposition refers to the overlapping of spaces that are "noncotiguous and unrelated" (McHale, 1987:45) so that their mere association renders them alienating. According to McHale, the American space is reconstructed in postmodern fiction taking as an inspiration source Frank Baum's *The Wizard of Oz* (1990). His explanation for this choice is that Oz is a fantastic world which comprises different realms, open to possibilities. It is the Oz version of America that recurs throughout postmodernist writing about America. The American zone is the 'Zone of the interior' as "its strangeness and liminality are foregrounded by its being located not on the edges of the continent, but at its center" (Mc Hale, 1987:50). *The Passion of New Eve* takes the hero/heroine to a strange America in view of a life-transforming experience.

At the beginning of the novel the boundaries between dream and flesh are dissolving, as Evelyn watches a film starring the feminine object of his fantasies, Tristessa: "the dream itself made flesh although the flesh I knew her in was not flesh itself but only a moving picture of flesh, real but not substantial" (PNE 7-8). He is sure about his capacity to distinguish between reality and fantasy before the cinema screen, which itself functions as the locus of the intersection of the realms.

"I thought I was bidding a last goodbye to the iconography of adolescence; tomorrow, I would fly to a new place, another country, and I never imagined I might find her there, waiting for revivification, for the kiss of a lover who would rouse her from her perpetual reverie, she, fleshy synthesis of the dream, both dreamed and dreamer. I never imagined, never." (PNE 8)

Eve/lyn travels from East to West across an America devastated by wars and arrives to an America of fantasy and nightmare "I found, instead of hard edges and clean colours, a lurid Gothic darkness that enclosed my head entirely and became my world" (PNE 10), which he still regards as an outsider in a cinema hall, failing to notice, as Desiderio, that his journey has begun and he is no longer a spectator, but a performer.

Towards the end of her/his journey, when s/he has pieced the puzzle together, s/he reflects on having "Lived in systems which operated within a self-perpetuating reality; a series of enormous solipsisms, a tribute to the existential freedom of the land of free enterprise."(PNE 167)

In *The Infernal Desire Machines of Doctor Hoffman,* doctor Hoffman begins his Reality War in the capital. The first chapter of the novel, "The City Under the Siege" shows a city beyond understanding, "as an existential crossword puzzle" (IDM 25). Initially, it is "a solid, drab, yet not unfriendly city" (IDM 15), with a Cathedral as its centre. The changes that affect it turn it into 'the arbitrary realm of dream', a triumph of surrealistic imagination and anarchy: "Hardly anything remained the same for more than one second and the city was no longer the conscious production of humanity" (IDM 18).

The actual fall of the city is caused by the Doctor's detonation of the Cathedral, which "expired in a blaze of melodious fireworks" (IDM 29). Chaos follows and the city becomes a surrealistic work of art with direct allusions to paintings by Max Ernst, a virtual reality made up of illusions and shadows. This ontological instability robs the city of any sense of direction, giving rise to a hellish prison that overwhelms the senses. On the other hand, the city represents the centre itself, as Desiderio after killing the doctor, comes back to "the smoking ruins of a familiar city" (IDM 221).

An Englishman, who by the end of the first chapter has landed in New York City, Eve/lyn finds the American landscape foreign to his Englishness, and remarks "nothing in my experience had prepared me for the city" (PNE 10). This America in the midst of a civil war, sometime in the 'near-future' intensifies Eve/lyn sense of disorientation. It is both the place, the American city, and the time, of war and social upheaval that are foreign to this "tender little milk-fed English lamb" (PNE 9).

Eve/lyn, in the midst of social chaos, finds that "all about me was mined; I learned to trust nothing and nobody" (PNE 15). The foreignness in the land, reflected against the Englishness of the main character, is sharpened by the surrounding society that finds itself ever separated.

The lure of the "clean, hard, bright city" of New York, "where the ghosts who haunt the cities of Europe could have found no cobweb corners to roost in" (PNE 10) is irresistible to Evelyn and prompts him to reject claustrophobic London. The surprise this city of "visible reason" (PNE 16) holds in store for the hero is the coexistence of two spaces, a masculine, logical one that in fact attracts him, but also a feminine one, of "lurid, Gothic darkness" (PNE 10-12). The latter is populated with militant groups of women and 'blacks' threatening uprisings, mirroring the dystopian New York of the seventies Carter perceived as torn in the contexts of the Vietnam War protests and the Civil Rights and women's movements.

The omnipresent decadence changes New York into a city of chaos and a tomb "that closed over my head entirely and became my world" (PNE 11). The irony of having this city designed by the human mind as a utopian model of harmony underscores the contradictory nature of the city: "It was, then, an alchemical city. It was chaos, dissolution, nigredo, night" (PNE 16).

The most noticeable feature is the lack of light, seconded by the powerful smell of decay. It resembles a jungle, where danger lurks freely. This New York of suffocation, where no human feelings are present, becomes a labyrinth of death, with Leilah as harbinger: "So she led me deep into the geometric labyrinth of the heart of the city, into an arid world of ruins and abandoned construction sites, the metropolitan heart that did not beat any more." (PNE 21)

The streets face the protagonists with danger at every step. They are routes of alienation, metaphoric projections of the characters' sense of isolation in both foreign and familiar surroundings. The city is a negative space where it is easy to lose one's self. This alchemical New York becomes a suitable stage to perform gender, as Evelyn submits to the urban chaotic space of decadence and morbidity. Once positioned in the middle of the deteriorating city, the incapacity to comprehend the space creates a sense of confusion in Evelyn's mind. In addition to his bodily displacement, he experiences decomposition and re-composition, as suggested by the alchemical experiment that anticipates Evelyn's transformation.

New York draws out the worst in Evelyn, as he becomes the extreme example of desire turning women's bodies into objects. His exotic sexual fulfillment objectifies Leilah's body, which becomes an emblem of victimization after her abortion and sterilization. Angela Carter's urban dimension appears as an alchemical space mapping out human nature, both male and female, not only squeezed into a narrow present reality, but projected towards a possible future, either utopian or dystopian. As a metaphor, therefore, the city occupies a crucial juncture in Carter's imagination and tends to become, as in *Nights at the Circus*, "a city built of hybrids, imagination and desire, as we are ourselves, as we ought to be" (NC 12).

The city represents a reflection of the self, as Evelyn behaves as a male as he wanders the streets, but becomes a woman after leaving its space. He has to strip off the male aspect to develop another subject position. Sexes could be combined in androgyny, so hybridization is the only possible solution. The urban landscape turns into a carnivalized space, a mixture in which every ingredient maintains its own characteristics even while becoming part of a new whole. Before creating gold from steel before Eve/lyn's eyes, Baroslav, the beggar turned magician, gives an accurate description of New York's urban space:

> "Chaos, the primordial substance.... Chaos, the earliest state of disorganized creation, blindly impelled toward the creation of a new order of phenomena of hidden meanings. The fructifying chaos of anteriority, the state before the beginning of the beginning" (PNE 14)

Deconstruction operates at every corner, shaping what Barbara Ward defines as the "unintended city" (1976:29): a city with no memories and no future, a labyrinth with no exit, a closed system.

Entropy affects not only the physical and social universe, but also its linguistic translation (Vallorani, 1994). If London is the romantic style of nostalgia fading in the irony of memory, New York is grotesque, a hybrid, a postmodern and self-reflective metropolis, a whirling universe with no logic and no meaning. The claustrophobic nature of New York is further sustained by its lack of colour. The low-key atmosphere is depicted through the colours of decay, "black," "acid yellow," "mineral green". Dark shades seep into the   physical surroundings as well as psychological states of characters: "a lurid, Gothic darkness that closed over my head entirely and became my world" (PNE 10).

There is no centre of the city, no depth to the seemingly logical topographical organization. In a way, Eve/lyn can perceive, or rather imagine, the original project: "a city of visible reason—that had been the intention" (PNE 16).

Built apparently with no planning, New York city may be disassembled and re-assembled without running the risk of being unable to trace the original design. New York is, therefore, pure image, the slide of a city "as if cut out of dark paper and stuck against the sky," says Eve/lyn, "were the negative perspectives of the skyscrapers" (PNE 30).

Beulah, the city in the desert, is an example of Carter's reverse urban space, the locus of a feminist utopia whose systems prove eventually as rigid as the city of "chauvinist nightmares" (PNE 148). The name of the female community itself defines Carter's satiric intention.

To John Bunyan, Beulah is a place "upon the border of Heaven" through which "pilgrims pass on to eternal life" (1678:155). In Blake's mythology, Beulah denotes one of four states of being, the feminine state which Harold Bloom defines as an ambivalent one, while the "daughters of Beulah" are the Muses inspiring the poet:

> "Of Blake's four states of being – innocence, or Beulah; experience , or Generation; organised higher innocence, or Eden; and the Hell of rational self-absorption or Ulro – it s the lower, unorganised innocence, or Beulah, about which he has most to say. For Beulah is the most ambiguous state. Its innocence dwells dangerously near to ignorance, its creativity is allied to destructiveness, its beauty to terror." (Bloom, 1963:17)

Mother's eulogy of space and eternity as against time and death is derived from William Blake's observation in 'A Vision of the Last Judgement' that 'Time is a Man, Space is a Woman, and her Masculine Portion is Death' (Keynes, 1966:614, in Day). In the matriarchal city this view is changed to:

> "Proposition one: time is a man, space is a woman.
>
> Proposition two: time is a killer.
>
> Proposition three: kill time and live forever." (PNE 53)

Having borrowed the name from the patriarchal tradition, Carter plays with meanings and symbols in order to shape a paradoxical female community.

From a topographical perspective, the desert is the only access route to the city, a road of sterility, a space lacking structure, the exact opposite to the urban landscape Evelyn has left behind. Structurally, the city reflects gender at psychological and physical levels, since it "lies in the interior, in the inward part of the earth" (PNE 47), the ideal place for Evelyn's re-birth. At one point Evelyn refers to this place, Beulah, in a strange slippage of tenses: "It will become the place where I was born" (PNE 47), reflecting on how Beulah is a "place where contrarieties exist together", presided over by a profane goddess who is the incarnation of "a complicated mix of mythology and technology" (PNE 48).

The "lurid darkness" of New York is complemented by the lack of light in Beulah. There are shadows and rays of grey which animate Evelyn's nightmares, indicating to us that the underground space marks the transition to a different realm, away from the patriarchal logic of the American city. The rigidity and separatist nature of the local, homosexual community is anticipated with Evelyn's observation of the structure of Beulah as a "slippage of the differentiation between what is natural and what is artefact" (PNE 60).

Carter's literalization of Freud's myth is suggested not only by Mother's surgical interventions, but also with the emblem representative of the city, the broken statue.

Beulah becomes a dystopian space, operating with as much violence as patriarchal order, which Julia Kristeva warns against in 'Women's Time'. She insists that when confronting the myths or narratives that inform female identity, women need to challenge the place that is "bequeathed to [them] by tradition" (1986:199) and must avoid a repetition of violence located in a patriarchal system, its own violent urge towards the repression of the 'other'. In the topography of Beulah, however, women remain slaves of violence. In the same way as New York, the female community offers Evelyn labyrinthine routes, impossible to escape from while the character uses his reason, as in the geometrical New York. In New York, contradiction is the effect of the dissolution of rationality, while in Beulah it is the structuring principle: "There is a place where contrarieties are equally true. This place is called Beulah" (PNE 48).

Myth and technology operate simultaneously, with the latter gradually fading to the former as Evelyn approaches the theatre of his transformation, as female magic engulfs male rationality.

As Eve/lyn escapes Beulah, s/he is already aware of an irreversible physical change, since the male identity is lost, in biological terms. "I have not yet become a woman, though I possess a woman's shape" (PNE 83) testifies to the hero/ine's self-perception as an empty body, and motivates yet another journey, in search for the lost identity or a new one that may reconcile gender and sex. So Eve/lyn goes back to the desert as a hybrid creature, "a tabula rasa, a blank sheet of paper" (PNE 83), lost in a dry land without memories. The third urban setting s/he has to become part of is Zero's town.

If Beulah stands for the womb and Mother's body, Zero's town represents patriarchal power taken to grotesque extremes, a rigid community mirroring a woman's life in a harem. Zero, the master of all the women in the town, is the tyrant celebrating any form of perversion. His wives seem affected by what Joanna Russ (1978) defines as "idiocy," that is "what happens to those who have been told that it is their god-given mission to mend socks, clean toilets and work in the fields; and nobody will let you make the real decision anyway" (PNE 255).

The topography of the town reflects the dominant traits of the mad poet's iron rule. Contrary to the claustrophobia on New York and the fleshy gloom in Beulah, Zero's town basks in bright sunlight, a metaphor for what is obvious, self-evident, monologic, and linear: in short, what is male (Deleuze , 1988:14ff).

The desert sun shines on the landscape and gives it a ghostlike aura: "The miner's town...looked, in the analytic light of the desert, far older than the rocks on which it was built" (PNE 93).

The town is only a collage of run-down houses, with no center and no history, a town which is old without being ancient. The mad poet Zero lives in a "ranch house in the ghost town" (PNE 85), a space reflecting lost reason. There are numerous references to the slippery border between reality and nightmare, as logic stops operating. In the hands of Zero language itself loses signification: "Zero's rhetoric transformed this world. The ranch house was Solomon's temple; the ghost town was the New Jerusalem" (PNE 100).

"In the ruins of an old chapel," says the narrator, "under a sagging roof of corrugated iron, Zero kept his pigs" (PNE 95). The image of a holy space recalled is annihilated by the reference to pigs, suggesting a blasphemous perspective. The urban spaces of the novel have no ontological status, they are made up through a **juxtaposition** of conflicting elements that may be removed and re-arranged to provide an appropriate setting for the characters' circular journeys "We start from our conclusions" (PNE 191).

In *Nights at the Circus,* the action shifts from London to St Petersburg, which according to Tambling, seems to "impose order", but it is actually "a town of half-crazy people" (2001:14). To most readers, St Petersburg is exotic and different, and therefore serves to defamiliarize. In contrast to London, an unfriendly atmosphere is established. This part of the book tries to build on the contrast between the real, sordid, poverty-stricken life of the city, and the dreams that the city inspires in those who do not really know it. A good example of this is the episode stressing the babushka's futile attempt to tell her grandson Ivan a story about a pig, which is juxtaposed against Walser's lyrical prose about the city. The main focus of this **juxtaposition** is to highlight the fact that Walser's version of the city is a distortion of reality. The babushka's story is very sparse, and consists of only one sentence in very plain language. But Walser, who is a journalist and whose writing should thus be concise and precise, lapses into uncharacteristically purple prose, depicting Russia as a sphinx, St Petersburg, the beautiful smile of her face.

> "Petersburg, loveliest of all hallucinations, the shimmering mirage in the Northern wilderness glimpsed for a breathless second between black forest and the frozen sea. Within the city, the sweet geometry of every prospect; outside, limitless Russia and the approaching storm." (NC 96)

He is supposed to present things in an objective and factual manner. However, the "city precipitated him towards hyperbole; never before had he bandied about so many adjectives" (NC 98). The main aim of the part that is set in St. Petersburg is the transformation of Walser into a circus clown, and the revelation of his love for Fevvers.

The city exposes the clowns as tragic figures, opposing their alienating acts of masquerade. Ivan, the grandson of the poor babushka is fascinated with the new world they present, but cannot understand that their ex-centric position. Buffo explains to Walser that

> "Often, d'you see, we take to clowning when all else fails. Under these impenetrable disguises of wet white, you might find, were you to look, the features of those who were once proud to be visible. You find there, per example, the *aerialiste* whose nerve has failed; the bare-back rider who took one tumble too many; the juggler whose hands shake so, from drink or sorrow, that he can no longer keep his balls in the air. And then what is left but the white mask of poor Pierrot, who invites the laughter that would otherwise come unbidden." (NC 119)

The clowns are exposed as victims of reality: "This giant is the victim of material objects. Things are against him. They wage war on him. When he tries to open a door, the knob comes off in his hand." (NC 116)

Little Ivan sees the clowns as a means of escape from the drudgery of a life lived in poverty with his grandmother. So, he wishes hat he "could terrify, enchant, vandalise, ravage, yet always stay on the safe side of being" (NC 151), that is, act as he likes without facing any consequences. This is why he most admires them – they are "licensed to commit license and yet forbidden to act, so that the babushka back home could go on reddening and blackening the charcoal even if the clowns detonated the entire city around her and nothing would really change" (NC 151). Although this fantasy provided the little boy with an escapist moment, it also proves useless in changing their lives. As a result, once the dust of disintegration has settled, the city is revealed to be exactly as it was. the 'exploded buildings' have gently wafted "to earth again on exactly the same places where they had stood before" (NC 151). As the baboushka kneels before the hearth in a never-ending chore, the clowns entertain the city with their celebration of disintegration and regression.

> "am I this Buffo whom I have created? Or did I, when I made up my face to look like Buffo's, create, *ex nihilo,* another self who is not me? And what am I without my Buffo's face? Why, nobody at all. Take away my make-up and underneath is merely not-Buffo. An absence. A vacancy." (NC 121)

Misattribution is a strategy common to postmodern fiction, signifying the displacement of "automatic associations, parodying the encyclopaedia" (McHale, 1987:47). The readers are intrigued by the connections in Angela Carter's work that seem arbitrary but are not, if one considers the writer's didactical aims. Starting with the first line, *Wise Children* positions the reader next to the narrator, Dora Chance, "on the wrong side of the tracks" (WC1). She remembers events by associating them with places – tram journey to the dancing class, Grandma's going to the pub, the theatre halls, the rooms accommodating family reunions. The concepts of high and low, legitimacy and illegitimacy are constantly under scrutiny, not to be reinforced, but to be deconstructed. Dora's story and summary of the family history of the Chances and the Hazards proves that definitions are unreliable and the values that seem opposite at first glance, may in fact be synonymous.

Perry prefers to pretend it is possible to live outside history, just as Dora herself had lived when she was young. But things have changed and she comments on how, in her old age, at the moment of writing and remembering

> "I understood the thing I'd never grasped back in those days, when I was young, before I lived in history. When I was young I'd wanted to be ephemeral, I'd wanted the moment, to live just the glorious moment, the rush of blood, the applause. Pluck the day. Eat the peach. Tomorrow

never comes. But, oh, yes, tomorrow does come all right, and when it comes it lasts a bloody long time, I can tell you". (WC125)

Now Dora lives in the real world which is not always nice, but at least it is not an illusion, as the world Perry has constructed, evading reality. The two women have always perceived him as "being in constant communication with the angels" (WC87) and have envied his ability to enjoy every moment of his life. On the other hand, Melchior's attachment to legitimacy and 'high culture' is part of a dominant, imperial culture that rejects and represses the 'low' culture which Nora and Dora are associated with. The metaphor for both is Shakespeare. Ranulph and Melchior move in a world guided by the imperial Shakespeare, the elitist reading of his works, while the sisters inhabit the illegitimate side, also celebrated in the realm of gender identities through cross-dressing. Ranulph's wife, Estella plays Hamlet, to respond to cross-dressing in the comedies subverts the masculinity of the tragic genre. The Hazard family is the supporter of the 'high' but contains the illegitimate hybrids of the 'low' in its twisted family tree. This idea is summed up by Kate Webb:

> "Shakespeare may have become the very symbol of legitimate culture, but his work is characterised by bastardy, multiplicity and incest; the Hazard dynasty may represent propriety and tradition, but they, too, are an endlessly orphaned, errant, and promiscuous bunch...
>
> *Wise Children* is like the proverbial Freudian nightmare – aided and abetted by Shakespearian example. Dora's family story is crammed with incestuous love and oedipal hatred: there are sexual relationships between parent and child (where this is not technically so, actor parents marry their theatrical offspring – in two generations of Hazards, Lears marry Cordelias); and between sister and brother (Melchior's children Saskia and Tristram). And there is oedipal hatred between child and parent (Saskia twice tries to poison her father, and she and her twin sister Imogen are guilty either of pushing their mother down a flight of stairs or at least of leaving her there, an invalid, once she has fallen); and between parent and child (All the same, he [Ranulph] loved his boys. He cast them as princes in the tower as soon as they could toddle". (Webb, IDM 282, 292-293)

Melchior sleeps in the cheapest room, the attic, confusing the sound of the sycamores with applause. America is posed in the novel as the colony that has overtaken the power of its 'parent' country, inverting the relation centre-margin. Melchior aspires to the fame and grandeur of his father, Ranulph, whose heroic age coincided with that of the British Empire, but even then America was a threat to stability. It was then that Ranulph lost his ability to discern the real from the fantastic: "By then, Old Ranulph couldn't tell the difference between Shakespeare and living" (WC21).

Melchior insists on demarcating the high and the low but his attempt is fruitless and he lives an illusion. One of its symbols is the 'crown from Lear' (WC20), inherited from his father, which is precious to him, although it is not the original, lost in gambling by his father, but a cardboard copy on which Estella had "dabbed some gold paint" (1992, 20), a fake. American culture is shown to have contributed to this. Melchior goes to Hollywood to take part in making a film of *A Midsummer's Night Dream* , and impose 'high' English culture on the former colony. He instructs the girls to take some earth from Stratford –upon –Avon to sprinkle on the set, but they have to replace it with Californian soil after the cat urinates in it. Melchior's symbolic act becomes compromised. The film of *A Midsummer's Night Dream* is a kitsch and the changes that occur in the Hazard family parallel the decline of the English imperial order. Tristram Hazard becomes the host of a game show, Melchior appears in TV commercials and Dora and Nora are interviewed by Film students about the parts they played in the film of Shakespeare's play. The 'high' comes to court the 'low' eventually. On listening to a recording of Ranulph playing Macbeth, Dora registers the contrast between the last male descendant, Tristram, and the values of his family line:

> "Only a hundred years ago… my own grandfather. Yet it was a voice from before the flood, from another kind of life entirely, so antique-sounding that it scarcely seems possible his granddaughters now sit in silk cami-knickers in the basement of a house in Brixton, drinking tea and watching on television his great-grandson address an invisible audience out of a plastic box, in that between-two-worlds, neither Brit nor Yank, twang of the game-show host." (WC16)

In all the zones brought into focus, as borders melt, time operates in an equally intriguing manner. Since external spaces disintegrate, overlap or mingle, the passing of time is not linear. The real world has clocks ticking but they sometimes measure a frozen time. There is a time of the interior, almost magical, a time of carnival which allows fantasy to disrupt reality. How do characters cope with this intrusion?

In the magical time zone the foundations of self and reality no longer exist. Jack Walser in *Nights at the Circus* hears the bells of Big Ben strike midnight during the interview more than once. He encounters a time-lapse in Fevvers' s dressing-room, feeling as if the room had "without his knowledge, been plucked out of its everyday, temporal continuum, had been held for a while above the spinning world and was now – dropped back into place"(NC 87).

The abandonment of the linear time is a concept that fascinated feminists. Julia Kristeva associates the linearity of time with a patriarchal order in *About Chinese Women*: "There is no time without speech. Therefore no time without the father. That is what the father means: sign and time" (1977:35). The male history has as opposite the feminine, subversive and cyclical time. In Angela Carter's early novels a patriarchal chronology prevails: a "ponderous ticking of the cuckoo clock" (1981:91) marks the authoritarian rule in Uncle Philip's house; a similar cuckoo clock determines the rigid routine on Zero's farm in *The Passion of New Eve*, while time with the Professors in *Heroes and Villains* relentlessly "carved the hours into sculptures of ice' (1972:1). Its impact culminates in the role as the reminder of imprisonment and paralysis in Countess P.'s asylum, where the ticking of the click is that of "another lifetime, another place...the end of hope" (NC 217). The chronological passing of time brings along a sense of temporal and also mental stasis, where change is unimaginable. Yet the abandonment of temporality causes terror in Angela Carter's works, rather than the joy Kristeva predicts as the result of the monumental in 'Women's Time'. The shamanic tribe in *Nights at the Circus* is in a state of 'cultivated indifference' (NC 254), relying on the figure of the Shaman for an understanding of the world, since "time meant nothing to them" (NC 265) and they lack any historical consciousness. They live in a continuous present, sacrificing a bear every year, whose spirit will carry messages to the dead. Where there is no time and no history, Angela Carter sees no future and no possibility for action. Therefore, the feminist call for the deconstruction of time appears more controversial.

Mother in *The Passion of New Eve* is one of the time-destroying mother-goddesses pointing to Angela Carter's skepticism regarding the dangers of female glorification. For Evelyn, she is the representation of the 'cruel and circular logic' of femininity which, although "not operat[ing] in terms of this world" (PNE 48), results in a world as paralysing as that ruled by men. Mother cannot but fail, ending an alcoholic on a lonely beach, after her daughters have left her. Angela Carter rejects both the linear and the circular temporality and suggests a third way, a "curious kind of dreamtime...[where] life passed at a languorous pace, everything was gently untidy, and none of the clocks ever told the right time, although they ticked away busily" ('The Mother Lode' in *NS* 14).

In Ma Nelson's brothel, where Fevvers grew up, they "always kept the blinds pulled down, as if the eyes were closed, as if the house were dreaming its own dream[...], a place that turned a blind eye to the horrors of the outside. " (NC 26)

This type of dreamtime does not destroy the horrid historical reality of the outside world, but ignores it. Ma Nelson's talisman, a gilt clock decorated with a traditional representation of Father Time "with a scythe in one hand and a skull in the other" (29) undermines its task of measuring the day, pointing always to the same hour, 12 o'clock, "the dead centre of the day or night, the shadowless hour of vision and revelation, the still hour in the centre of the storm of time" (NC 29), incidentally the magic hour in Fevers' dressing-room. Lizzie plays tricks on Jack by meddling with the logic of time and space, displaying an almost supernatural power. The loss of the clock puts into question her temporal existence: "we've lost the bloody clock, haven't we... We'll soon lose track of time and then what will become of us?" (NC 226) They cannot imagine life outside rationality and seek to regain hold over temporality.

The two Siberian women prisoners discover the clock in the desert as a "gilded figure of an old man with a scythe that had evidently snapped off a broken box of springs and small brass wheels" (NC 221). The two are able to dispose of it because it has no longer a practical application in a place where ordinary logic doesn't work. They are at home in the desert and they "need no more fathers" (ibid).

The mechanical indicator of the passing of time alludes to a forward movement, linked to the idea of progress. Angela Carter uses the conventions of the picaresque genre where the characters travel through time and space and undergo a psychological evolution. But the progress of the characters is questionable. One complication appears at the level of narration in *The Passion of New Eve*, *The Infernal Desire Machines of Doctor Hoffman* and *Wise Children*, as the method is retrospective and narrators look back on their lives. What is future for the reader is past for the narrator. Another is that in *Nights at the Circus* each character perceives the passing of time in a subjective manner, or that in *The Passion of New Eve* the man Evelyn has turned into a woman, or that in *The Infernal Desire Machines of Doctor Hoffman* the narrator disguises his identity.

There is no functioning clock in the novels. In *Wise Children* time is compressed as the action takes place over one day and Dora Chance revisits over one hundred years of family history. Grandfather's clock, which has always been off by one hour, starts the hours correctly on Dora and Nora's 75th birthday. Dora makes several references to the proximity of death, but the time implied by birthdays is an opportunity to go back in the past and remember it. She is very exact with dates and family events, but there is a fairy tale sense that predominates, since the introductory phrase to Dora's memoirs is 'once upon a time'. Fiction and reality mingle in her story and the its magical time is determined not by clocks, but by performances, the artificial time of the stage. Many settings in the novel look like stage sets. Dora describes Lynde Court as a stage set, Melchior's bedroom as 'self-conscious' (WC 219), and her being accepted into the family as an invitation onto the stage.

***

In my investigation of the hybrid spaces hosting the journeys the protagonists undertake in Angela Carter's selection of works, I have used the term heterotopia in accordance with Holland's 'potential space', one that displays the features of ambiguity, paradoxical nature and elusive character. The complex combination of genres, conventions and literary heritage, that Angela Carter's work is rife with, has served as starting point in my illustration of her subversive method of building puzzling spaces. The concept of liminality, defined as that which is relegated to the margins, applies to both time and space in the works I have chosen, heightening the danger of the unknown the characters need to confront. The danger that lies ahead turns the 'hybrid' (Bhabha, 1994) spaces in the present chapter into heterotopia, or zones.

These settings above the surface or into the depths of the earth- the castle, the prison, the cave, the forest, the desert and the city – constitute major challenges the characters have to overcome in order to complete their quests. I have also noted the irony implied in the description Angela Carter gives to her magical spaces of transformation, as the centre long sought is absent in most of the cases analysed.

The diversity of external spaces is covered by the topos of the journey, in Angela Carter's case the passing from a realm into another. All the main characters travel in space starting with the third novel *The Magic Toyshop*, where Melanie moves from home to the toyshop, Desiderio in *The Infernal Desire Machines of Doctor Hoffman* from the rationalism of the city to the landscapes of the Nebulous Time, Eve/Evelyn in *The Passion of New Eve* to America, then to the underground caves of the Earth in search for a shape. The girl-narrator in 'The Erl-King' has lost herself in the woods, whereas Walser is following Fevvers in *Nights at the Circus* to debunk her, and Dora and Nora in *Wise Children* fly to America in search for a father.

The locations are exotic, increasing the readers' appeal to these works on the one hand, and the characters' sense of alienation, throughout their rites of passage. They cover continents and a complex array of spaces in their quests, just like Angela Carter covers literary traditions in her luring approach. The zones I have turned to are disruptive, unstable and ambiguous, and they all stand for the motif of the labyrinth Angela Carter masterfully deconstructs. It may be, first of all, an empirical space and a space of estrangement at once. It appears as the geographical delineation of the spaces depicted, and the intricate ways of the human mind, struggling with the fear of the unknown. Reason is one means of defence in the face of superstition.

Angela Carter's taste for isolated castles reflects her passion for overthrowing myths. Her subversive intentions are apparent the sinister buildings which tumble down in the end, signaling the breakdown of the cultural formula of the victimization of women. The castle is never a shelter; there is no warmth and no harmony. The atmosphere is one of decadence and claustrophobia, and the sense of confinement is ever present.

Reason and desire clash through **superimposition** in *The Infernal Desire Machines of Doctor Hoffman* and the resulting third space is the real with a haunted Desiderio who has followed his reason but who cannot control his memories and dreams. In *Nights at the Circus* fact and fiction overlap generating an open space, the desert, in which anything can be adjusted, starting from one's name and ending with a philosophy of life. *The Passion of New Eve* juxtaposes the real with the constructed, underlining the thin difference between them with ambivalent characters who fall victims to their convictions. The alien and familiar spaces of **interpolation** are the real and the fantastic in *The Magic Toyshop*, where hallucination or fantasy ask for a price. It is arguable whether or not they find what they look for. One conclusion stands for all, however: on their way they all become prisoners of an enclosed environment, that of the family. To Angela Carter the family is a metaphor of society, imposing its rigours on the individual. The family, situated in a house, a cave, the forest, the city, the brothel, or the stage, is a site of terror mostly because of its members. Melanie is under Uncle Philip's domination, Desiderio looks for a family but what he finds is cannibals or outcasts, Eve is mutilated by the Mother, Fevvers risks her life every time she tries to integrate.

Jacobean revenge tragedy, fairy-tales and the violence, terror and victimization that the Gothic requires are given escape routes through comic and carnivalesque elements. Space can be used to survey, to control, and to veil women's sexuality, in line with Foucault's theory of the implementation of power. I have secondly focused on the realistic details and the symbols illustrative of incarceration and physical paralysis, through the image of the prison. The Gothicized interiors in Angela Carter's works point to an illegitimate control of women's sexuality and power. Domination is configured spatially in the form of confining interiors in *Nights at the Circus* –Ma Nelson's brothel, the Russian Grand duke's mansion, Christian Rosencreutz's house, Madame Schreck's museum, Countess P.'s prison. However, through the failure of the panopticon, Carter suggests that the surveillance of female sexuality is not inescapable, that women can create other possibilities for themselves. Although the human body, and especially the female body, is, as Foucault asserts, "the 'site' at which all forms of repression are ultimately registered," it is also, in *Nights at the Circus,* the locus for another kind of discourse. As David Harvey (1990:6) writes in *The Condition of Postmodernity*, "The only way to 'eliminate the fascism in our heads' is to explore and build upon the open qualities of human discourse, and thereby intervene in the way knowledge is produced and constituted at the particular sites where...power-discourse prevail". In Carter's novel the site is the female body, but that body has wings, and she can fly.

Forever threatened by the frailty of a boundary built on the primordial loss and on the impossible refusal of corporeality, the subject experiences in the feeling of abjection the uncertainty of its identity; the risk - fear and desire - of falling back into that space-time where it grew, which it left in order to be. This happens in the third zone I have explored, the cave-the womb. The womb is a liminal space, neither life nor death, founded on abjection, as the recurring, threatening sensation of an instability of the self. It is uncanny in its familiarity and in its bringing to conscious attention what was and should have remained buried in the unconscious. Space-time which both confuse and produce one and another, questioning that subject/object demarcation on which the delusive stability of the self is founded. Playing with excess, Mother's abjection in *The Passion of New Eve* is at the same time a critique and an overcoming of the situation it also represents. Mother is the negative figure of a feminine reduced to the reproductive function, she is a phrase in a mystifying discourse of power. Yet it is only passing through her hellish uterine realm that the new Eve can be born, to meet in her own body a knowledge capable of surpassing those mean and arrogant partialities. If the womb/cave is a site of initiation and revelation, then Eve's experience of entering this space is figured as a backwards birth, literally climbing back into the womb, as she is forced "to slide into the living rock all alone" (PNE 179). As a deconstructive journey it is explicitly rendered

106

as an "ordeal" (PNE 181). Eve's journey through the caves might also be read as a visionary experience' (Schmidt, 1990:66) since, by the end of Carter's deconstructive process, the text advances the revelation of a new subjectivity, one no longer tied to patriarchal or matriarchal myths. In other words, according to Carter's double meaning, we have to acknowledge the ways in which the womb takes on a life of its own through either myth or fantasy, taking on an imagined existence; and as distinctly removed from our fantasies, its own reproductive biology or reality has very little to do with the myths constructed around women's bodies. Through the process of time reversal operating in the cave, Carter envisions a point of origin located beyond human constructs of time, which might allow for a more fluid subjectivity that is not yet trapped within the confines of a gendered discourse. Such a creature might provide a different model for conceiving a female subjectivity that is multiple, hybrid, and limitlessly free in the articulation of her desires. Carter forces us to return to this imaginary space as the very source of female oppression, as both the beginning and end-destination of the text's journey through the labyrinth of gendered identity.

The forest becomes a place of initiation in Angela Carter's works, as the magical permeates the real. The characters that enter the forest find themselves trapped within a magic circle of confusion. No matter how desperate their situation is, there is also a stronger fascination the forest displays, which they find impossible to resist. They are drawn deeper into the core of the woods, putting their lives at risk in search of the forbidden fruit. The journey into the forest has sexual connotations most of the times. No possibility of exit is ever articulated. The woods operate as a discursive and circumscribing structure; wandering the labyrinth of literary histories and discourses about Woman, women have permanently lost their bearings. Nonetheless, the possibility for resisting and changing these structures exists in the woods' mutability. The combined flexibility and inescapability of these labyrinthine woods invokes the Foucauldian concept of the inextricability of power from resistance and refuses a strictly repressive reading of power. Movement, moreover, is central to the girl's resistance; although confined within the discursive space of the woods, the first-person narrator is mobile. Actively travelling through "the subtle labyrinth" of intertexuality, she navigates multiple representations of Woman and attempts to articulate her own desires.

The desert represents, after all, a mirror image of Evelyn's state of mind and a space for a subverted male obsession. Evelyn certainly is reborn in the desert of America, a symbolic landscape used by Baudrillard to mark the disappearance of the real and the invasion of the simulacra in postmodern society. The desert is seen as a symbol of emptiness, a space of memory, enigmatic and ambiguous in its opportunity for both exile and escape, a heterotopia. The paradoxical nature of the desert is apparent as we read into its array of significations. On entering it, Evelyn feels estranged, as if he opened the gates to hell. The opposition between the energetic protagonist and the static atmosphere of the desert foreshadows the price one has to pay to gain access to its secrets. Evelyn's movement towards the heart of the desert equals loss of life and his transition to the slippery realm of hallucination: The symbolic character of the desert is further emphasized through the insistence on its antiquity, 'this ancient and terrible place', 'the architectless town' under 'unfamiliar stars' (PNE 42-43). The desert represents the passage from the outside Evelyn has rejected to the inside of the maze, and it constantly faces him with its vastness that paradoxically generates claustrophobia.

The city is a territory of chaos. It turns thus into an unfriendly, dangerous, even inhuman organism. **Juxtaposition** (McHale, 1987) is employed in Angela Carter's shaping the city into a surrealistic work of art with direct allusions to paintings by Max Ernst, a virtual reality made up of illusions and shadows. This ontological instability robs the city of any sense of direction, giving rise to a hellish prison that overwhelms the senses of the characters. Although Evelyn insists New York's geometric, logical grid represents "a city of visible reason" (PNE 16), but he neglects the cavernous, labyrinthine depths of Lower Manhattan, and these two aspects of the city are themselves situated as masculine and feminine spaces. The streets face the protagonists with danger at every step. They are routes of alienation, metaphoric projections of the characters' sense of isolation in both foreign and familiar surroundings. New York draws out the worst in Evelyn, as he turns into the extreme example of desire exploiting women's bodies as objects. New York is grotesque, a hybrid, a postmodern and self-reflective metropolis forever hiding the ancient rational project instead of revealing it. Its true identity consists of being able to absorb a whirling universe with no logic and no meaning. Beulah, the second heterotopian city in my discussion is a rigidly homosexual and separatist female community: It becomes the belly of the whale where the rite of death and re-birth will be performed. Rationality, in the male sense of the word, is not its guiding thread: indeed the project of Beulah is conceived to be a radical reversal not only of the structure but also of the meaning of patriarchy. Significantly, an ambiguous relationship to technology as a mainly male concept emerges in the definition of what Mother is: "Beneath this stone sits the Mother in a complicated mix of mythology and technology" (PNE 48). Beulah, therefore, is not anti-technological but perceives technology differently, by considering it similar to mythology. **Juxtaposition** is confirmed as a method of disrupting and subverting traditional semantic borders and the conflict is made more evident by the intrinsic nature of the terms placed side by side: technology and mythology stand for male and female, respectively. The assumed compatibility of both terms is actually an illusion because it is based on phenomena belonging to two different orders that cannot be compared. Myth is neither more nor less reliable than technology. The two terms can however be placed side by side to produce a defamiliarizing effect. Darkness, shadow and light are woven to create an analogy with dream imagery. The frequent repetition of reference to nightmare marks the ultimate breakdown of borders between reality and imagination, which are placed side by side and given exactly the same sort of fictional existence. **Misattribution** brings together the concepts of high and low, legitimacy and illegitimacy in *Wise Children,* not to be reinforced, but to be deconstructed. Dora's story and summary of the family history of the Chances and the Hazards proves that definitions are unreliable and the values that seem opposite at first glance, may in fact be synonymous. The film version of *A Midsummer's Night Dream,* produced in a superficial Hollywood is a kitsch, and the changes that occur in the Hazard family parallel the decline of the English imperial order. The 'high' comes to court the 'low' eventually, America needs no education, the high and the low are empty concepts and history and fiction are no longer separable.

The heterotopian zones under their various guises, the castle, the prison, the cave/womb, the forest, the desert, the city, display a plurality of meanings and an intriguing hybridity. They can only begin to sketch the numerous ways in which Angela Carter borrows, cites, critics, revises an overwhelming heritage to bring to life a haunting and possessing work. Just as travel inside Angela Carter's heterotopia is never completed for her protagonists, whose travels mark the confusion that comes with self-knowledge, we, as readers, are lured to the unstoppable afterlife of her labyrinths of meaning.

3. HETEROTOPIA – REACHING FOR THE OTHER

Heterotopia are places of otherness, a concept that can best be defined through a relationship of difference with other sites. In Foucault's definition of heterotopia as places of another order, physical location is not as important as the confluence of discourses, institutions, and procedures shaping them. Angela Carter's aim is to open our eyes to the falsity of socially accepted representations of woman as Other, which she considers to be "false universals," intertwined with "soothing lies" or "social fictions" that serve to "dull the pain of particular circumstances", the pain of the wound left by the symbolic castration (2000:5, 23, 25).

I have used as starting point in this chapter Hetherington's question about the nature of otherness, and the solution he gives when he defines otherness as something without, something excessive or something incongruous, a hybrid combination of the incongruous.

Elaine Jordan's view of the multitude of meanings to be found in Angela Carter's works emphasizes the hybrid character of Angela Carter's writings, as well as the pleasure derived from her offer to the reader to choose from the possibilities displayed:

> "Angela Carter's writing is impure, penetrated by the theories and practices with which she engages; she abhors utopias and role-models as much as realism – her fiction is not an image of 'what is' or a blueprint of 'what may be', but an unaccommodated space in which the dissatisfied can find some possible openings, some pleasure." (WC 165)

Maria Tamboukou's (2000) heterotopia, are also transitory, ambiguous, deviant, potentially disruptive spaces, populated by women. The hybrid character of these spaces is maintained by the women's struggle to forge an identity by transgressing the boundaries sustained by patriarchal surveillance. Doreen Massey (1998) even regards the woman's body as a spatial site that she must discover in order to alter her relationship to the surrounding male-dominated cultural and social space.

Angela Carter's female characters will serve as arguments of breaking the binary of power, while male ones must find the Other outside the mirror before reaching a deeper understanding of the self.

Othering is always reciprocal and involves the agency of both 'sides', according to Saldanha (2000). The critic also argues that there is no such thing as heterotopia, only heterotopic relations between a subordinate side, and a dominant side. Heterotopic relations are antagonistic relations, between women and men in Angela Carter's case, as section 3.2. Innocent Predators will illustrate.

By attempting to act differently from social expectations, by "being Other in the territory of sameness" (Rose,1993:149), not only do women empower themselves but also challenge the spatiality of their location, constituting it as an unsettling space. Angela Carter's starting point is the reproduction of woman's marginalization as a dramatization of otherness. The more taboos are related to the definition of woman as other, the more dramatic she was in disclosing the confines of those parameters. Her female characters dramatize the differences from within, as they appear as free agents; seen from without their differences appear monstrous. She was interested in the many possible personalities women may assume apart from the roles they are enacting.

In an interview with Haffenden, Angela Carter admitted "my family have always behaved anecdotally, and I perceive every event as having the potential of being retold" (1985:34). Her upbringing under the strong influence of her grandmother allowed her the freedom to express and expose the realities limiting her sex. She used traditional models of femininity and exposed their hideousness. Woman is displayed as an inferior object to be later reshaped into an autonomous subject, which led some critics into accusing Angela Carter of "reinscribing patriarchal attitudes" (Clark, 1987:147). On the contrary, I think her works lead to a re-examination of the issue of sexuality in view of demythologizing the concept of women's experiences.

In 'Notes from the Front Line', Angela Carter compares her experiences as a writer with that of writers marginalized from mainstream literary tradition:

> "I personally feel much more in common with certain Third World writers, both female and male, who are transforming actual fictional forms to both reflect and to precipitate changes in the way people feel about themselves – putting new wine in old bottles and, in some cases, old wine in new bottles." (*SL* 76)

Angela Carter borrowed from the Gothic in order to recover a primitive freedom of imagination. It proved an appropriate medium to allow the transgression from a suppressed group to autonomy. She adopted the artificiality of the gothic to render the artificiality of the definition of woman and allow for the plural manifestations of femininity. Section 3.1. Duplicitous Dolls is concerned with the use of fetishism as a metaphor of exploitation, along

111

that of the woman as automaton.

Women have been taught to consider themselves the weaker sex, and myths are a source of collective dreams and desires. Angela Carter plays with myth as a method of questioning these beliefs. Elaine Jordan notes that "Angela Carter's anti-realistic fiction is a kind of literary criticism, using what is available as a wardrobe and store of props for a satirical performance as demythologizing storyteller" (1992:166). Myth provides false beliefs that maintain a single doctrine, and Angela Carter attacked it by using its power for new ends. The female heroines are the object of myths designed by men to contain them, but they subvert this given identity. They all bear some traits of the Medusa figure, that Cixous (1991) praised. Angela Carter's plural femininity ends the symbolic castration as well as the original symbiotic relation with the mother.

Woman as Other completes the image of the dominating man, but her stories show that power is empty without the woman's masochistic submission. It is the uncanny existence of woman as Other that haunts the masculine psychology. I dwell on the fluidity of borders as far as desire and reason are concerned in the section 3.4. Desired Others. Angela Carter's female characters draw us into the realm of the surreal, seen as a passageway to the unconscious, the site of fear and repression. They are portrayed either as in an intangible or dreamy state, a vacuum, similar to the blank page that men can traditionally write upon, such as Annabel or Emily, the heroines of *Love* and *Shadow Dance*. The invisible power of the father figure in *The Infernal Desire Machines of Doctor Hoffman*, *The Magic Toyshop*, *The Passion of New Eve* creates a sense of anxiety in both the readers and the characters.

Perversion is employed in gothic literature to "unsettle the boundaries between the real and the not-real" (Kaplan, 1991:119). The motif appears in different guises and undermines the boundaries of fantasy and reality in Master, where sadism dominates, takes the shape of voyeurism in *The Magic Toyshop, The Infernal Desire Machines of Doctor Hoffman* , that of lust in 'The Loves of Lady Purple', 'Lady of the House of Love', of rape in *The Passion of New Eve*.

Angela Carter admitted in her middle stage of writing that surrealism is cruel to women and gave it up because of the dominant representation of the female body as distorted and the female mind as blank. She then adopted the style of fantasy as a defamiliarizing technique, a style Jackson relates to desire:

"In expressing desire, fantasy can operate in two ways: it can *tell of*, manifest or show desire...or it can *expel* desire, when this desire is a disturbing element which threatens cultural order and continuity...The fantastic traces the unsaid, and the unseen of culture: that which has been silenced, made invisible, covered and made 'absent'." (1981/1995:3-4)

The writer insisted on bringing up those desires that have been "silenced", testing the imagination and the limits of the readers' response to her experimentation. Elaine Jordan observes that Angela Carter "works with multiple montage and through the power of fantasies, imaginative pleasure and horror, which will differ with different readers" (1992:160).

3.3. Cannibals will bring the facets of Eros and Thanatos into focus and show how the female protagonists cease to be passive impersonators and become involved.

On the surface, Angela Carter's work subverts phallocentrism in a simple role reversal. On closer scrutiny, she calls for the confrontation with the multiplicity of the self that allows the transgression of stereotypes. Male perversity, voyeurism, rape, sadism, are literalized because women's role in them is brought into focus. For Carter, social reality is on the side of fantasy. As Žižek indicates in *The Plague of Fantasies*, fantasy "teaches us how to desire" and provides us with "a schema according to which certain positive objects in reality can function as objects of desire" (1998:7). It is this schema of desire that Carter aims at, in her investigation of the modes a female desiring subject finds appropriate in articulating her own desire, without the curb of patriarchal ideological formations.

Angela Carter's mature style is infused with a combination of gothic and magical realist elements. Mary Ann Doane defines the gothic in *The Desire to Desire* as "a simulacrum of legality constituted by a hyperbolization of the image of the aggressive, punishing, castrating Father – an image which compensates for a precise lack of castration anxiety on the part of the paranoid subject" (1987:145).

The realistic details in her works mingle with the terrors of a primitive imagery in order to give voice to the desires that lie hidden in women. Theo L. D'Haen observes that magical realism attempts to "create an alternative world correcting so-called existing reality, and thus to right the wrongs this 'reality' depends upon. Magical realism thus reveals itself as a ruse to invade and take over dominant discourses" (1995:195).

The fairy-tale tradition also served Angela Carter's purpose of portraying female subordination, due to its "mythic timelessness" (Kaiser,1994:30). In the introduction to *The Old Wives' Fairy Tale Book*, Angela Carter points out the difference between folklore generated by the oral, 'unofficial' culture, and fairy-tales that have a literary, 'official' one. She explains that the former is fluid and results in "stories without known originators that can be remade again and again by every person who tells them, the perennially refreshed entertainment of the poor" (1990:ix), whereas the latter turn an oral tradition into texts that become commodities. The combination of these two strands of narratives parallels Kristeva's notion of intertextuality as "a passage from one signifying system to another" (1984:60).

Harriet Kramer Linkin makes an interesting observation about the stories in *The Bloody Chamber*:

> "balancing desire with aesthetic empowerment is the ultimate feat her characters attempt to perform as they dance across the tightrope of cultural expectations; and the geometric variations that the conflation of desire, aesthetic theory and cultural ideology produces shape the stories" (1994:305).

She states that the Romantic aesthetics assigns women the position of a domestic angel. Angela Carter's volume lacks such an angel, because the binarism associated with the literary representation of women is absent, so as not to deepen the gap between the sexes.

Her intention to connect traditional tales with the "subliterary forms of pornography, ballad and dream" (1996:452) is apparent in the 'Afterword' to *Fireworks: Nine Profane Pieces.* The mystery associated with the female sex takes the form of male's terror, a consequence of the scopic pleasure taken to extremes. In rewriting fairy-tales and folklore, Carter re-imagines the submission of women, contained in the message of traditional fairy-tales. The resulting heroines borrow from the Romantic aesthetics and Freudian feminine psychology. Both Romanticism and Freudianism fall into Angela Carter's criticism of "false universals" (2000:5), which have scripted women's inferiority. She transgresses sexual taboos, that had been stifled in folklore and fairy-tale, and takes mythology to the borders of pornography: "I was using the latent content of those traditional stories. And that latent content is violently sexual" (Goldsworthy, 1985:6).

3.1. DUPLICITOUS DOLLS

The self can be described as a mixture of physical and psychological traits which change their meaning according to historical and cultural contexts. As a result, Angela Carter aims at subverting the traditional concept of a stable world and exposing its pattern of relations. Power operates as a set of negotiations between discourses. Foucault (1979) defines violence and sex as official forms of control in *Discipline and Punish*, raising the question of the difference between natural and constructed, which writers such as Angela Carter try to answer. She is constantly searching for modes of subverting the dominant order, in constructing her female characters.

The Gothic tradition plays a crucial part in her fictional play of sexual identity. Her postmodern celebration of the surface is overlapped with the Gothic space of fear and desire. The Gothic genre offers her the necessary framework, with its exaggerating clichés.

She uses the Gothic in various ways, mostly to parody its theatrics of horror, as she is famous for revisionary writing. But her use of the Gothic goes deeper than parodic rewriting. She gives some hint in the 'Afterword' to *Fireworks*:

> "Though it took me a long time to realise why I like them, I'd always been fond of Poe, and Hoffman.... The Gothic tradition in which Poe writes grandly ignores the value systems of our institutions; it deals entirely with the profane. Its great themes are incest and cannibalism.... Its style will tend to be ornate, unnatural - and thus operate against the perennial human desire to believe the word as fact.... It retains a singular moral function - that of provoking unease." (BB 456)

What is equally revealing is her subsequent comment: "We live in Gothic times" (ibid.). She describes in Gothic terms her experience of the cultural change after her return to England from Japan, and her description illuminates the lurid side of the contemporary world in which the familiar becomes strange and uncanny.

Critics have termed as an internal contradiction of Angela Carter's works her failure to give a coherent perspective to her characters, whose subjectivity becomes problematic. From an external perspective, Angela Carter appears unable to disengage from the attitude keeping women under domination. It seems, though, that this strand of criticism has neglected the contradictions at work in a single text, a feature typical of writing fiction, according to

Bakhtin:

"Instead of the virginal fullness and inexhaustibility of the object itself, the prose writer confronts a multitude of routes, roads and paths that have been laid down in the object by social consciousness. Along with the internal contradictions inside the object itself, the prose writer witnesses as well the unfolding of social heteroglossia surrounding the object" (1981:278).

The more open the reading of the text, the more contradictions it generates. These daring meanings glitter at closer inspection, and have led critics to place Angela Carter on a par with Stephen King:

"both go after the child that inhabits every adult, that sees goblins in the shadows and marvels open-mouthed at fireworks. Both are intensely literary writers, who make no crass assertion that their words mirror real experience, whatever it is" (Kendrick, 1993:68).

He notices Angela Carter's attempt to make the forbidden voice heard, beyond the confines of rationality. The portrayal of the eccentric feminine takes shape in a new literary space populated with male and female protagonists. Angela Carter's female characters cannot be defined as 'normal' according to social norms. She brings to the surface hysterical, obsessive, irrational, beastly women in order to explode the *feminine mystique*. In line with Laura Mulvey's definition of women as object of the male gaze, Leilah in *The Passion of New Eve* is glamorous, the sexual object on display, but also the black, threatening other. Although Evelyn gazes and she is just the object of his gaze, he has no access to her inner self. The more idealized her sexual image becomes, the darker her inner self: "in their traditional exhibitionist role women are simultaneously looked at and displayed, with their appearance coded or strong visual and erotic impact so that they can be said to connote to-be-looked-at-ness" (1989:27).

Patricia Duncker calls her style Queer Gothic since her work "shares many themes and stylistic devices with the literature of the eighteenth century" (1996:58). She underlines the horrific setting that alienates the characters and sets them free from reality at the same time. The grotesque arises from the comic treatment of the subject matter, the combination of horror and ludicrous. The literary parody employed to illustrate gender stereotypes takes the shape of puppetry. For Angela Carter, as for Freud, the living doll stands for the ambiguity of beauty which includes both challenge and threat, but for her it also reflects the attitude towards women as objects in a male dominated culture. The passivity of the living doll feeds masculine fantasies but also deprives any carnal relationship of humanity. The automaton is a grotesque figure, a cross between a living creature and a puppet, an incongruous being that horrifies and amuses. The puppet represents the grotesque form of subordination. Melanie in *The Magic Toyshop* is forced into the role of a living puppet in her uncle's house, against her will, whereas Lady Purple, the oriental Venus, comes to life after draining her old puppeteer of life, and acts out of free will to further re-enact her script.

Although female puppetry may be seen as an uncanny form of woman's otherness, it has been misinterpreted as a reinforcement of the experience of woman as prisoner of patriarchy. Robert Clark misreads Angela Carter as a writer whose works "fall back into reinscribing patriarchal attitudes" (1987:147), and Nanette Altevers sees Angela Carter's writing as "inverted feminism", "often a feminism in male chauvinist drag, a transvestite style" (IDM 18).

However, the puppet women are not entirely helpless. They possess a feminine power although they are owned by men. Linda Hutcheon describes this power as

> "subjectivity represented as something in process, never as fixed and never as autonomous, outside history. It is always a gendered subjectivity, rooted also in class, race, ethnicity, and sexual orientation. And it is usually textual self-reflexivity that paradoxically calls these worldly particularities to out attention by foregrounding the unacknowledged politics behind the dominant representations of the self- and the other – in visual images or in narratives." (1985:39)

This new subjectivity must be read beyond the dominant representations, by adopting the postmodern stance that Hutcheon sees as "self-conscious, self-undermining …wholesale commitment to doubleness, or duplicity" (1985:1).

Fetishism figures prominently in Angela Carter's works. It is a feature targeted at redefining femininity through a critique of male fetishism, as found in the literary canon, and it has earned her Christina Britzolakis' comment: "she writes like an unabashed female fetishist" (1997:46). But Carter is at the same time famous for rewriting literary ancestors' texts. The two features are in fact intertwined, as Britzolakis again suggests:

> "Carter has characterized her stylistic excesses as a species of decadence: 'It's mannerist, you see: closing time in the gardens of the West.' This comment sits uneasily with her expressed belief in her fiction as an instrument of social change and intervention. But it does resonate with

117

the attraction in her work towards the rhetoric and iconography of a prominent, largely male-authored strand of European literary history, which runs from the mid-nineteenth century through Baudelaire, Poe, Sade [sic], much of French symbolism, the Decadent writing of the *fin de siècle* and Surrealism. Carter's readings of these texts unerringly focus on their metaphorization of femininity in its most fetishized and spectacular forms". (1997:49)

Consequently, Angela Carter offers us an example of the way male fetishism transforms woman into an object, a toy seduced by other toys, a living doll. The majority of her tales take up the theme of fetishistic entrapment. We see how women's fate is bound by fetishes: the Beast, in 'The Tiger's Bride', gives the heroine diamond earrings and a sable cloak in the hope to seduce her, the gloved Countess wearing a diamond brooch in 'The Snow Child' is "wrapped in the glittering pelts of black foxes; and she wore high, black, shining boots with scarlet heels, and spurs" (1996:193), while Lady Purple, the prostitute turned puppet turned woman again, is the sum of metonymic substitutes: glass rubies, mother of pearl, enamelled tin, clothes of "vibrating purple" (1996:49). Women are fetishised, turned into inert or living dolls, they are commodities, whose exchange value only matters, as Carter reminds us in the opening line of 'The Tiger's Bride': "My father lost me to The Beast at cards" (1996:51).

'The Erl-King' features an undefined heroine who is lured to her gilded cage by the music played by the Erl-King and, implicitly, by the fascination of the Romantics' image of woman, as suggested by the wealth of hidden quotations from Romantic poetry. The fateful attraction of poetry is indeed exemplified in the very image of the Erl-King and its magic flute. While 'The Erl-King' is a warning against Romantic fetishising, its conclusion does not provide a clear way out of the prison of language. It sets off with the girl victim planning to kill her tormentor: "I shall take two huge handfuls of his rustling hair [...] and [...] I shall strangle him with them". Liberation seems within reach: "Then she will open all the cages and let the birds free; they will change back into young girls [...]" (EK 91), but already the victory is doubtful if we consider the ambiguous agent that results from the playful use of the pronouns. Neither 'I' nor 'she' will have the concluding word, and the personal victory song turns out to be only an impersonal, inhuman lament.

"[...] she will string the old fiddle with five single strings of ash-brown hair. Then it will play discordant music without a hand touching it. The bow will dance over the new strings of its own accord and they will cry out: 'Mother, mother, you have murdered me!'" (EK 91)

118

The most pronounced puppet theme can be found in 'The Loves of Lady Purple' (1974), in which the title heroine, a vampiric marionette, comes to life under the manipulation of the male puppeteer. The uncanny experience is presented as a supernatural event of a doll being transformed into a woman but at the end of the story the supernatural turns ambiguously close to the familiar and becomes uncanny. The tale itself is a rewriting of several literary and psychoanalytical motifs: the fear of a doll coming to life because of its uncanny life-likeness, the threat of its necromantic power, the interchangeable lives of the doll and its creator, and the male fear of female sexuality. Whereas fear and desire are antonymous in Gothic fiction, and the object of disgust holds the hero/ine in enthrallment, these fears in the tale are bound up with a male desire to control the unrestrained female sexuality. The old Asiatic Professor displays an acute desire to define his self through the feared object, Lady Purple, with whom he lives in symbiosis. He creates his doll as a predatory whore enacting dramas of monstrous femininity, such as the show "'The Notorious Amours of Lady Purple'".

Lady Purple is very successful, so that she has "transcended the notion that she was dependent on his hands and appeared wholly real and yet entirely other" (1996:43). Not only is she the simulacra of the living, she becomes the simulacra of the dead. As she sadistically preys on her victims she illustrates a deadly, insatiable eroticism. She cannot be either living or dead, since the dead puppet can become alive at will. Lady Purple looks human, but she is a living dead: "although she was now manifestly a woman, young and extravagantly beautiful, the leprous whiteness of her face gave her the appearance of a corpse animated solely by demonic will" (1996:51). Once the puppet turns into a woman, she is no longer the object of desire, "she was not a true prostitute for she was the object on which men prostituted themselves" (1996:46).

> "The doll seduces and tortures men, squeezes them dry of money and dreams, and in
> taunting their desiccated manhood, forces them to watch her make love with a beggar for
> nothing, and moreover, she does all these compulsively out of a dry desire insatiable and
> unknowable to herself (LLP 46).

In her involuntary monstrosity she ends up "a marionette herself, herself her own replica" (LLP 47), so tells the ancient puppeteer his audience. The puppeteer plays with his doll's metamorphosis between puppet and woman; he claims his doll had once been a woman but now turned into a puppet, "the petrification of a universal whore," for "too much life had negated life itself" (1996:44): "she abrogated her humanity. She became nothing but wood and hair. She became a marionette herself, herself her own replica, the dead yet moving image of the shameless Oriental Venus." (LLP 44)

While monstrous metamorphosis is a recurrent theme in Gothic fiction, it is played here by Angela Carter in a subversive manner. The same scenario of the doll's transfiguration is duplicated in the tale itself in a reversed way; Lady Purple is transfigured from a puppet to a woman and is doomed at the end of the story to re-enact the scenario instilled by the puppet master.

Apart from narrative self-referentiality, there is an intricate exchange of desire and identity implied in the reflexive structure. As Gothic fiction is a fictional discourse of the self in its fantasy world under siege by the Other, the Gothic monster is often an externalization of the self's fear of the threatening Other. Lady Purple, either a puppet or a woman, is always a monster in the Professor's scenario; in fantasizing her as metamorphosed from woman to puppet he has her under his control.

"In her permanent dormant state she is his sleeping beauty his kiss would not waken" (LLP 43). But his script goes awry; one night "[t]he sleeping wood had wakened" by his kiss (LLP 50) and turned from puppet to woman, and sucked him dry of blood and life. The doll becomes a woman, or an automaton. Or a woman with her sexualized body invariably starts as an automaton for she is awakened by his desire which becomes hers. Can she have an inherent desire of her own other than this dry desire that can never be satiated? The scene of her coming to life is a painful process in which the victim and victimizer exchange positions and desires. The exchange seems fantastic, but it produces an uncanny effect, because for the Professor it is the "return of the repressed" (1996:51), and for the doll it is a confirmation of her firm belief that she is authentic.

It seems that even Lady Purple's revenge is questionable. At the end of the story we see the puppet biting back and draining the puppeteer's blood.
Gina Wisker is right in noticing that "Lady Purple embodies both the vengeful vampire and the lifeless marionette. Yet in her determination to stalk into the village, she ultimately returns the horror genre to its own sick source. Brought alive, the living doll at last has her revenge" (1997:130), a questionable one, however, for reasons similar to those pointed in reference to 'The Erl-King', concerning the ontological status of the subject. Lady Purple "might now

UNIVERSITY OF WINCHESTER LIBRARY

perform the forms of life not so much by the skill of another as by her own desire that she did so" (LLP 51); but a paradox remains:

> "had the marionette all the time parodied the living or was she, now, living, to parody her own performance as a marionette? Although she was now manifestly a woman, young and beautiful, the leprous whiteness of her face gave her the appearance of a corpse animated solely by demonic will." (1996:51)

This paradox lies at the core of the feminist debate about femininity as masquerade, but it also reflects the shaping of characters in fiction. For what are characters if not puppets that reading somehow brings to life? The depiction of prostitutes as "mannequins of desire" can be seen to work as a *mise-en-abyme* of the art of building characters in fiction. Their stylised gestures make each one of them "as absolutely circumscribed as a figure in rhetoric" to become "a metaphysical abstraction of the female" (1996:50).

However, Carter's use of the fetish image here is tricky in that there is nothing extraordinary in the first metamorphosis, from woman to puppet, while the most dramatic moment is the reverse transformation into a vampiric woman, mediated by the kiss of life:

> "Her kiss emanated from the dark country where desire is objectified and lives. She gained entry into the world by a mysterious loophole in its metaphysics and, during the kiss, she sucked his breath from his lungs so that her own bosom heaved with it"(1996:50)

His (the creator's) kiss becomes hers (the creature's). This is the paradox of whether a character results from the fetishising of reality or is a fetish returning to reality. Fantasy allows both, and Carter is thus implying that no fiction really comes to life without it.

In the later novels, sexuality and physical oppression are no longer confined to familiar settings, but are projected into exotic environments, such as the Siberian wilderness, the African coast, or a nightmarish America. The illnesses gnawing at contemporary life surface more clearly in a parodied reality, populated by beings on the margins: Fevvers, Eve/lyn, Desiderio. Desiderio in *The Infernal Desire Machines of Dr. Hoffman* is the bastard son of an Indian gypsy prostitute, an origin that gives him a unique and ironic minority standpoint in relation to his post-colonial home. The completion of his assignment to destroy Dr Hoffman's desire machines turns him into a hero, an honour that does not come cheap. The novel reflects the social structures with the various patterns of suffering the protagonist encounters in his journey. Sexuality is the prevailing medium of control and oppression. In keeping with many

121

feminist critiques of psychoanalytic theory, Carter reveals the unconscious to be the repository of patriarchal values. The violent sexual images that make up Desiderio's unrepressed fantasies bear witness to the misogyny of Oedipally constituted sexuality. Through her expositions of the patriarchal structure of the unconscious, Carter establishes her position in the text as a moral pornographer, one who engages in "the total demystification of the flesh and the subsequent revelation, through the infinite modulations of the sexual act, of the real relations of man and his kind" (2000:19).

Desiderio's journey to Dr. Hoffman's castle brings him first to a small seaport town, where he visits a circus peepshow tent on a bleak pier. The peepshow features "THE SEVEN WONDERS OF THE WORLD IN THREE LIFELIKE DIMENSIONS" (IDM 42), a series of tableaux carved in wax that describe women in various violent, sexualized poses:

"Exhibit Four: EVERYONE KNOWS WHAT THE NIGHT IS FOR Here, a wax figure of the headless body of a mutilated woman lay in a pool of painted blood. She wore only the remains of a pair of black stockings and a ripped suspender belt of shiny black rubber. Her arms stuck out stiffly on either side of her and once again I noticed the loving care with which the craftsmen who manufactured her had simulated the growth of underarm hair. The right breast had been partially segmented and hung open to reveal two surfaces of meat as bright and false as the plaster sirloins which hang in toy butcher's shops while her belly was covered with some kind of paint that always contrived to look wet and, from the paint, emerged the handle of an enormous knife which was kept always a-quiver by the action (probably) of a spring. (IDM 46)

Carter's view of such uninhibited sexuality appears dark, as further illustrated in the description of the rest of the "Seven Wonders". As moral pornographer, Carter is concerned with interpreting how the heterosexual male gaze constructs the object of desire. In the universe of Dr. Hoffman, the object of desire is deconstructed through the act of gazing—that is, the image that Desiderio perceives is one whose content reveals the politics underlying its construction. The very title of the "Fourth Wonder" is significant: the phrase "Everyone knows what the night is for" has special resonance for the feminist political sphere. The night challenges women's autonomy, her wholeness—thus Desiderio's unrepressed desire constructs a woman whose wholeness has been irreparably violated: "her breast is sliced open. Her headlessness underscores her lack of subjectivity" (IDM 48).

As Desiderio proceeds through this landscape of unrepressed desire, we find that each chapter of his adventure centers around the brutal sexual subjugation of a woman or group of women.

The "moral" of this succession of increasingly disturbing pornographic images and encounters seems to be that it is only our repressions that separate us from the dictates of a brutal patriarchal unconscious. The ambiguity in the text often makes it impossible for the reader to differentiate between the images of the pre-Hoffman reality and the products of the desire machine.

Each place Desiderio visits shows a negative model of femininity: Mary Anne of the Mansion of Midnight, the child-bride Aoi, the whores of the House of Anonymity, the women centaurs, and the main heroine Albertina. The kaleidoscopic image that emerges is indicative of the faults of a misogynist system. Mary Anne " had the waxen delicacy of a plant bed in a cupboard. She did not look as if blood flowed through her veins" (IDM 53), "her kiss was like a draught of cold water and yet immediately excited my desire for it was full of an anguished yearning" (IDM 56).

Desire is defined in ironic terms, firstly through the dissolution of the male/female binary. Albertina "The white evening dress of a Victorian romantic heroine rustled about Albertina's feet and clung like frost to her amber breasts…" (IDM 201)

The images of Mary Anne and Albertina recall the typical Victorian heroine, whose long white dress and pale complexion stand for passivity. However, Desiderio is attracted to the suffering figures, so that we are made aware of his morbid tastes even from Albertina's first appearance, which he recollects: "I would be visited by a young woman in a negligee…which clung about her but did not conceal her quite transparent flesh, so that the exquisite filigree of her skeleton was revealed quite clearly" (IDM 25).

This transparent female body is monstrous, yet luring, as it is not a symbol of the purity of the Victorian victim, but a reflection of the woman as object. By the end of the novel Albertina reverts the angel-of –the –house stereotype and turns into an 'avenging angel' (IDM 216) who tries to kill Desiderio. It is evident that this portrayal of the women as victims highlights male oppression, because Desiderio experiences a sense of guilt combined with responsibility for the sadistic relation with Mary Anne and for the violent death of her and Abertina: "For it was I who killed her" (IDM 14), "I felt I was in some way instrumental to her death" (IDM 61).

The next grotesque step Desiderio takes is his engagement with Aoi, the child in the River people tribe. The child-bride Aoi "… planted wet, childish kisses on my cheeks and mouth" (IDM 82). She is an example of a sexually trained automaton, a product of customs that have shaped a system "theoretically matrilineal though in practice all decisions developed upon the father" (IDM 80). Like the Amazons, the girls in this tribe are having their genitals manipulated to ensure they perform best within their social context. In the society of the Amazons "...our womenfolk are entirely cold and respond only to cruelty and abuse" (IDM 161), while in that of the Centaurs "...the womenfolk were tattooed all over, even their faces, in order to cause them more suffering, for they believed women were born only to suffer." (IDM 172)

Desiderio's voice guides us into each universe and directs the interpretation of its codes. He is proud of his masculine role most of the time, but still notes the absurdity of Aoi's microcosm, or Mary Anne's status of a "programmed puppet with a floury face who was not the mistress of her own hands" (IDM 92). The sexual lure these women exercise is gradually uncovered as a consequence of paedophilia and incest.

In chapter five, "The Erotic Traveler," Desiderio is given a lift in the carriage of a man who turns out to be a Count of Lithuania. During their travels, the Count, whose autobiography is meant to be a grotesque exaggeration of the life and times of the Marquis De Sade, entertains his guest with exotic tales of sexual conquest, each more bizarre than the last. As the Count observes at the outset of his confessions,

"'The universe itself is not a sufficiently capacious stage on which to mount the grand opera of my passions. From the cradle, I have been a blasphemous libertine, a blood-thirsty debauchee. I travel the world only to discover hitherto unknown methods of treating flesh'" (IDM 126).

The Count brings Desiderio to a whorehouse where, despite the house's name, "The House of Anonymity," they eventually find Albertina—Dr. Hoffman's daughter and the object of Desiderio's desire. Because Albertina has a strong presence both in the non-Hoffman reality of the novel and in Desiderio's unrepressed desires, she sustains the ambiguous nature of the reality status of the scenes in which she appears. Desiderio's description of the denizens of the House of Anonymity paints a grotesque picture of womanhood:

"There were, perhaps, a dozen girls in the cages in the reception room and, posed inside, the girls towered above us like the goddesses of some forgotten theogeny locked up because they were too holy to be touched. Each was as circumscribed as a figure in rhetoric and you could not imagine they had names, for they had been reduced by the rigorous discipline of their vocation to the undifferentiated essence of the idea of the female. This ideational femaleness took amazingly different shapes though its nature was not that of Woman; when I examined them more closely, I saw that none of them were any longer, or might never have been, woman. All, without exception, passed beyond or did not enter the realm of simple humanity. They were sinister, abominable, inverted mutations, part clockwork, part vegetable and part brute." (IDM 132)

In *The Sadeian Woman* (2000), Carter describes the way in which the subjects of the pornographic text are at one and the same time both reduced to the level of graffiti images and elevated to the status of myth. In both cases, the female subject of pornography loses her identity and becomes a vessel that both contains and conveys the idea of feminine sexuality as constructed by the consumer of the pornographic text. In the scene described above, Desiderio discovers, through close examination of the prostitutes arrayed for the fulfilment of the Count's desires, that the women are not really women at all. They represent a grotesque articulation of female sexuality effected by patriarchal desire.

Carter's use of the combined figure of the automaton and the vampire to explore female sexual subjectivity under patriarchy can be seen in another tale 'The Lady of the House of Love' (1979). In the tale it is the female vampire who experiences her sexual life as an automaton. The beautiful vampire, the Countess, is the daughter of Count Nosferatu and the only heiress to the decrepit castle after the patriarch vampire is staked out by a priest of the Orthodox faith. But before his extermination, the father cried, "'Nosferatu is dead; long live Nosferatu!'" (1996:196); and he does live, through the daughter. Here we see one of the satirical twists Angela Carter makes of the conventional vampire script, as the father remains undead, haunting the daughter. The house the daughter inherits is a house of shadows, the ancestors watch and desire through the daughter's eyes from their portraits suspended in the family galleries and her bedroom. The woman vampire, a predator of men, enacts her desire as a puppet of the undead ancestors: "She herself is a haunted house. She does not possess herself; her ancestors sometimes come and peer out of the windows of her eyes and that is very frightening.... The beastly forebears on the walls condemn her to a perpetual repetition of their passions" (1996:197). In her haunted state she is like "a ventriloquist's doll," "a great, ingenious piece of clockwork" whose mechanism is "inexorably running down" and "would leave her lifeless" (1996:204) for she has no real sexual subjectivity. The fatal "queen of night" has no sexual autonomy because this "I" is "only an invention of darkness," an "I" which "vanish[es]" in the morning light" (1996:205), an "I" whose ferocious desire is not just of the other but doubly so as it is the ghost of a ghost, the vampiric father. The woman vampire is offered mirrors which show her monstrous being. The mirror is first provided by the rational eye of the young British officer and then by the shattered dark glasses that make her bleed. The deconstruction of the woman-vampire's sexuality is to be conducted on two fronts.

The figure of the woman vampire has been a heavily invested site of cultural fears of female sexuality; women vampires in conventional vampire fictions connote aggressive female sexuality and excess, or reflect male fear of the threat of the New Woman as conveyed in Bram Stoker's *Dracula*.. Carter's vampire story parodies the male-centred rational discourse with its exorcising power to show that this power is debilitating for women. The Countess stands for the dark space outside rational discourse, haunting men with her dark excess, while the young man, representing the Enlightenment rationality, exorcises her vampiric power with his rational eye. He sees but disbelieves what he sees, for the woman vampire is outside his belief system; what he sees instead is a sick girl confined to a morbid house awaiting his deliverance.

Secondly, the Countess' doll-like vampiric desire reveals the contradictory nature of feminine sexuality, voracious passivity. A shadowy figure in the house, the woman vampire haunts people with her presence. She is a Gothic captive figure, incarcerated in the castle surrounded by spiky roses (1996:195), sick with a vampiric desire for love. She is "the Sleeping Beauty in the wood" waiting for the bridegroom to bring her back to life with a kiss. Her passivity is her source of power, but her power is forever self-annihilating, because she falls victim to romance, which is ironically her rescue. Love reverses her predatory sexuality and sets her free from the monstrous sexual subject, which means death, and she dies in the forbidden self-reflection. But love is never an unproblematic thing in Carter's writing even when it is liberating. The woman vampire falls in love because it is scripted in her identity. She puts on her feminine identity as she puts on her mother's bridal gown, which is "the only dress she has" (1996:197), and she enacts her life with a script from the Tarot cards which prescribes her fate of love and death.

In discussing the significance of Gothic monsters to the postmodern configuration of human subjectivity, Judith Halberstam makes an illuminating observation:

"The postmodern monster is no longer the hideous other.... he makes the peripheral and the marginal part of the center. Monsters within postmodernism are already inside--the house, the body, the head, the skin, the nation--and they work their way out. Accordingly, it is the human, the façade of the normal, that tends to become the place of terror within postmodern Gothic. Postmodernity makes monstrosity a function of consent and a result of habit.... We wear modern monsters like skin, they are us, they are on us and in us.... What were monsters are now facets of identity; the sexual other and the racial other can no longer be safely separated from self " (1995:162-3).

It applies to Carter's fiction, for her depiction of sexual subjectivity is conducted along the line of the uncanny, of regarding what is given as natural, and what is real as culturally mediated and *un*natural (2000:9). The female subject has a problematic relation with her own body, constructed as a body of the other, a doll's body. This is more the monster than the figure of the vampire woman in Carter's works. She wears her sexual identity on her flesh; the female monsters are already in women; their "monstrosity" is shown when the "natural" sexual performance breaks down and is experienced as uncanny, and the body comes to haunt the sexual subject as a thing scripted up for the performance.

The subversive power of Carter's gender performance has constantly come under criticism. Is it possible for the female subject to subvert the patriarchal discourse from an object position without mimicking it? The mirror in which she sees herself displayed, does not reflect a one-way master gaze from the outside, but a complicated visual exchange the subject participates in; and it is the way in which the female subject participates that determines whether her sexual posing is subversive or objectifying. The game of juggling with being can be liberating or self-effacing; the clowns in *Nights at the Circus* illustrate the latter case. They perform various farces of failed manhood in patriarchal terms. Among them, the master clown Buffo, once a great acrobat, now mimics a man who cannot even manage to walk without stumbling over small things, or a patriarch in "the Clown's Funeral," miming a deceased old man who simply would not fit into the coffin and lie dead, jumping out of it persistently to hang on to the living. The traumatic self-deconstruction of the male ego comes when the mock-patriarch Buffo, chasing in a farce after the "Human Chicken", played by Walser, with a castrating knife, is performing a real self-dissolution ending in madness. Buffo's disintegration comes from his failed play of patriarchal image, the son failing to become the Father even when he is placed in the patriarchal position. Behind his mock-play of the failed manly image is nothing, still the play of the failed male image, this mocked face has become his face: "'am I this Buffo whom I have created?.... And what am I without my Buffo's face? Why, nobody at all. Take away my make-up and underneath is merely not-Buffo. An absence. A vacancy'" (IDM 122). He is permitted to play, but with the same patriarchal gaze that sees himself, and he plays the "terror" of man, the clown, and becomes a horror to himself.

Women's voices resound in *Nights at the Circus* as long monologues, associated with subversion and with women who are capable of taking control of their own lives. An example of this is Mignon, whom Jordan (1994:192) describes as bearing an image of Marilyn Monroe. She is presented in a self-mocking attitude as "the Blonde as Clown", Haffenden describes Mignon as one who represents "Europe, the unfortunate, bedraggled orphan – Europe after the war – which is why she carries such a weight of literary and musical references on her frail shoulders" (IDM 87).

Mignon is a born singer and a battered circus wife. Her husband beats her "as though she were a carpet" (NC 115). When they give her a bath, Fevvers and Lizzie find that her skin is "mauvish, greenish, yellowish from beatings" and shows "marks of fresh bruises on fading bruises on faded bruises" (NC 129), which demonstrates how objectified she is by her husband. Palmer asserts that she suffers from the violence "which is rife in a male-dominated culture." (1987:198) Although the novel underscores the oppression of women, it does offer solutions. Mignon, for example, bolstered by encouragement from Fevvers and the musical influence of the Princess, acquires self-confidence and steps beyond her role as "a soiled glove" (NC 155). She pairs up with the Princess to initiate the dancing tigers act, in which the Princess plays the piano and Mignon sings. From simple beginnings, Mignon and the Princess develop a very special kind of friendship that cherishes "in loving privacy the music that was their language, in which they'd found the way to one another" (NC 168). Mignon is strengthened through the music and she believes they "have been brought together, here, as women and as lovers, solely to make" it (NC 275). Fevvers reacts to this by saying that "love, true love has utterly transformed her" (NC 276) in the sense that love has enabled Mignon to become an active subject and discard her vulnerable role as victim.

In the novel, Carter introduces a subversive notion of prostitution by portraying it a positive light. The physical description of the whorehouse is funny, and has a carnivalesque touch. The staircase of the house is described as ascending "with a flourish like, pardon me, a whore's bum" (NC 26) and its drawing room is said to be "snug as a groin" (NC 27). Fevvers further describes the house as having an "air of rectitude and propriety"(NC 26) and as "a place of privilege" in which "rational desires might be rationally gratified" (NC 26), and chooses adjectives that are generally reserved for officially approved institutions. Thus, the novel brings together high and low culture by destabilizing the conventional codes, and launches challenges to the existing rule and order. Fevvers argues passionately that "no woman would turn her belly to the trade unless pricked by economic necessity" (NC 39) because poverty takes away one's choices. Marcus says that people should regard prostitutes "not as some alien and monstrous creature but as a fellow human being" (1964:5).

Nights at the Circus also tries to follow the progress of the prostitutes after they cease to continue their occupation. Most of them do not succumb to death or venereal disease, and some return back to a regular course of life like any 'good' woman. Walser admits that he has known many whores fine enough to be wives. Fevvers' body is a site inscribed with various discourses and social forces, ranging from the monstrous, the grotesque, to the fantastic. She works as an aerial artiste, making a spectacle of her winged body to an audience who wonders about the authenticity of her unusual body. To combat the objectifying male gaze that sees her body as a fetish, Fevvers poses as a fantastic creature playing, not only with her audience but with herself, the game of hesitancy between fact and fiction—"Is she fact or is she fiction?". While the danger of objectification is always there, she manages to escape from it through a parodic strategy. The assumption of identity, as Fevvers is sharply aware, is a "confidence trick," and the identity she assumes for her winged body is a New Woman, free to display her sexual subjectivity. As she laughs joyfully at the end of the novel, saying, "To think I really fooled you!" (NC 195), the "you" is not just Jack Walser her lover, but the reader, and also the gaze she is subject to.

So, sexual subjectivity can be a play, a carnivalesque activity, as Fevvers has exhibited. But Carter has also cautioned about the subversive power of carnival for it is permitted play, a play with limits set. As carnival concludes, the mechanism of power becomes apparent, and Carter's postmodern play fades to the Gothic play of uncanny identity.

3.2. INNOCENT PREDATORS

The love and war between humans and non-humans is an important theme in Carter's a body of fiction which problematizes, interrogates, and expands the boundary between humans and werewolves, vampires, and other monsters to create metaphors for human nature gone awry. All her stories situate both human and non-human characters in a borderland between human consciousness and the consciousness of other species, the realm of the almost/not quite human. The fluidity of boundaries parallels the tension between what Julia Kristeva calls "two modalities, of what is, for us, the same signifying process," the symbolic and the semiotic (1984:24). Angela Carter's rebellious characters are able to understand the parallels between their own existence and that of the non-humans because they are allied with the semiotic, "preceding meaning and signification, mobile, amorphous, but already regulated" (1984:102). This kind of psychic borderland corresponds to Kristeva's description of the thetic, the space between the semiotic field and the symbolic order. The thetic is dangerous, uncertain, and unstable, but it is also the locus of dynamism and creativity; for Kristeva, the thetic is "that crucial place on the basis of which the human being constitutes himself as signifying and/or social" (1984:69). If the thetic cannot be completely expressed in language, it can nevertheless more closely approach articulation in literary language, with its multiplicity of appeals and meanings: "Mimesis and poetic language [...]go through its truth (signification, denotation) [...] to tell the 'truth' about it" (1984:60).

A straightforward reversal of power roles appears in two stories of the volume *Fireworks,* written in the first part of Angela Carter's career, 'The Loves of Lady Purple' and 'Master'. The puppet master in the former has lived within the fairground all his life but the only time he feels at home is when he gives life to his favourite doll, whom he's called Lady Purple. It is a life-size doll, beautifully made of white and delicate leather that makes it look real. She has long nails that look like weapons and a wig of black hair arranged in a complicated way. He lets nobody touch the doll Lady Purple. He brings her to life by pulling her strings, he makes her up by giving her a story to star in.

Lady Purple is moulded into being by what Butler terms reiteration and citation. The Professor cites an already prepared script every night and constructs her only mode of existence. He tells the audience that the doll that plays the role of the prostitute in the show is the evil woman herself, turned to wood. The doll has thus her strings pulled to play herself. It performs her years of youth when she killed her adoptive parents and set fire to her house, her adolescence and her becoming a prostitute who played with men and later murdered them for pleasure. The Professor's invented story ends with the doll's playing Lady Purple's transformation into a wooden doll. Without him she is just an essence of femininity, the *femme fatale*, as the title of the play conveys: "The Loves of Lady Purple. The Notorious Amours of the Dark Oriental Venus...". The sexual identity of the doll is framed in negative terms. She cites myths of femininity and internalises them through performance:

> "gender performativity cannot be theorised apart from the forcible and reiterative practice of regulatory sexual regimes;[...] the materialisation of norms requires those identificatory processes by which norms are assumed or appropriated, and these identifications precede and enable the formation of a subject, but are not, strictly speaking, performed by a subject [...]".
> (Butler, 1993:15)

The practice that brings the doll into being is the play and once she materialises as human it is in order to perform an edited version of what she knows. She wavers between two roles, that of a doll and that of a predator, when she kills him and sets fire to the stage. She does what she had been doing in the play, namely killing her stepfather and setting his house on fire. In killing the puppet master she has performed another form of patricide, after which:

"She walked rapidly past the silent roundabouts, accompanied only by the fluctuating mists, towards the town, making her way like a homing pigeon, out of logical necessity, to the single brothel it contained"(LLP 51).

She seems to know where she is going and the existence of just one brothel reflects the limited direction she may follow. The roundabout is a symbol of repetition and so is her comparison to a homing pigeon. She knows no other way of being. It is true that Lady Purple has no strings attached after the puppet master is dead and that she acts independently, but the strings are still there in absentia. She does "not possess enough equipment to comprehend" and her thoughts cannot go beyond established patterns: "the brain beneath the reviving hair contained only the scantiest notion of the possibilities now open to it" (LLP 51).

Although the options are limited, they still exist. She repeats a repertoire which is "'only a variation upon a theme" (LLP 50), but it is the variation that displaces the script and allows her transgression from one ontological level to another. Butler stresses citation and repetition but she also emphasises the possibility of change:

"The compulsion to repeat an injury is not necessarily the compulsion to repeat the injury in the same way or to stay fully within the traumatic orbit of that injury". (Butler,1994:124)

Lady Purple's kiss of death can also be considered an ironic citation. She eliminates the master by realising his own mythology and opens up a condition of possibility, that of a further deviation from her conditioned course.

'Master' is another story illustrating the force of compulsive repetition. Violence and rape are the first stages of Friday's (the girl's) initiation into the sadistic hunter's world. Her continuous subjection to his abuse gradually begins a process of change in her. The change is not limited to her behaviour or inner reality, but also to the materialisation of her body which becomes marked by all the killing and violence that she suffers, and later performs. She is dehumanised, a beast of the Master's creation. Her metamorphosis reveals a change in conceptions, too. At the beginning Master sees her as an object, "only a piece of curious flesh he had not paid much for" (1996:76), a monstrous other with a Medusa-like hairdo. As long as she remains outside the Western order of things she is condemned to stay separate. When she begins to imitate his behaviour, becoming a hunter, Master's perception of her changes and so does hers. He senses her physical aspect has acquired a beast-like quality, and she witnesses her loss of humanity and metamorphosis into a predator defined by the instinct to kill. She repeats Master's way of being with a difference. Unlike the Master who preys on those weaker than him, she goes for the oppressor. Thanatos is the desire for death, the son of Night and the brother of Sleep in Greek mythology. 'Master' deals with the fatal intensification of a deformed hunting passion into a grotesquely macabre orgy of sex and death.

Degenerating from a tyrannical schoolboy to a sadist in his native country of England, the naturally violent Master searches for colonies to give his thanatic instinct free reign.

> "After he discovered that his vocation was to kill animals [...] the insatiable suns of Africa eroded the pupils of his eyes, bleached his hair and tanned his skin until he no longer looked the thing he had been but its systematic negative; he became that white hunter, [...]. He did not kill for money but for love." (1996:75)

He then specialises in exterminating the "printed beasts", the large spotted cats, until nothing can keep him in the Old World any longer. He exploits the New World as a type of Columbus and Terminator, as an 'English Explorer', a kind of Robinson Crusoe,

".. intending to kill the painted beast, the jaguar, [...] where time runs back [...], the world whose fructifying river is herself a savage woman, the Amazon"(1996:76).

Master's sadism turns eros into thanatos. Friday's development, though, in contrast to hierarchical Western thought and to the Darwinism of the Englishman, is egalitarian and regressive: ".. her cosmogony admitted no essential difference between herself and the beasts and the spirits, it was so sophisticated" (1996:77).

Angela Carter carries her critique of civilisation to the extreme because nature in the short story re-conquers civilisation. The girl in 'Master' evolves from an abstract object into an avenging being. She can only utter the word "master" and lives according to the general beliefs of her tribe that "had taught her to regard herself as a sentient abstraction, an intermediary between the ghosts and the fauna" (1996:77), a non-human other. The master abuses her every night and she experiences a kind of death. He also annihilates the symbolic image of the girl, a member of "the clan of the jaguar" (1996:78), with his hunting obsession.

As the girl accompanies Master in his mad hunt "always more deeply into the forest" (1996:76), leaving behind an Ariadna thread, "a gross trail of carnage" (1996:77), she understands that she belongs with the jaguars:

"While he slept, she flexed her fingers in the darkness that concealed nothing from her and, without surprise, she discovered her fingernails were growing long, curved, hard and sharp. ... the touch of water aroused such an unpleasant sensation on her pelt. ...

She could no longer tolerate cooked meat but must tear it raw between her fingers off the bone before Master saw."(1996:79)

Her otherness is double, as she is a sexual object and the embodiment of the jaguar. She slowly grows into a real jaguar, she dramatizes her otherness and turns against her oppressor: "As she grew more like him, so she began to resent him" (1996:79).

The ghosts of the slaughtered beasts eventually enable the girl to break through the socially imposed taboo of being prey as a woman and as a black.

The two stories suggest that access to the status of subject occurs only through the semiotic realm of our own nature--emotion, sensory experience, instinct--which evades expression in the symbolic and is consequently trivialized or rendered invisible in hegemonic discourse.

The patriarch in *The Magic Toyshop* is representative of a threatening, malevolent deity, yet because his actions are often motivated by fear and insecurity, the status of the father's power is revealed to be extremely unstable. Uncle Philip is a "barely embodied principle", a "grotesquely exaggerated" (Gamble, 1997:71) patriarch, whose tyranny may in fact have very little substance behind the role or artifice. Thus, the text presents patriarchy as menacingly monolithic while simultaneously deflating it, revealing that "its greatest horror and its greatest weakness is that it is sustained by the force of its subjects' belief" (Gamble, 1997:72).

Through the course of the novel, Carter's two protagonists, Melanie and Finn, struggle to break free from Philip's (patriarchy's) oppressive brutality, and it is only by overcoming their own fears of his authority that they are able to gain some measure of freedom from the stranglehold of his law.

Desiderio in *The Infernal Desire Machines of Doctor Hoffman* visits exotic societies that have in common the low social position of women. One such circle is the Amazonian tribe of the River people, where women have the traditional domestic duties of women in patriarchal societies and wear grotesque costumes. These uncomfortable clothes have become a sign of immobility and submission to men, turning women into almost objects whose virtue is passivity. The cosmogony of the River People is a pagan distortion of the biblical myth of Eve and the snake. It is based on the mutilation of disloyal women and is perpetuated in the custom of elongating girls' clitorises from early childhood. Desiderio's position becomes Gulliver-like in the chapter called "Lost in Nebulous Time". He arrives together with Albertina in the society of intelligent centaurs, a clear reference to Swift's Houyhnhnms. The twist is that the rules and myths their social organization is founded on are a grotesque reflection of human society. They believe that "women were born only to suffer" (IDM 172), so they rape Albertina. Angela Carter does not let the episode slip into the realm of fantasy as she defines the centaurs as "not fabulous beasts" but "entirely mythic" (IDM 183). After the centaurs find out that Albertina is Desiderio's mate, that is his "property" (IDM 182), they whip one another to express their apologies.

A more degrading picture of women's social position appears in the description of Zero's harem in *The Passion of New Eve*. This maniacal figure forces his seven wives to occupy a position lower than his pigs. They have had their hair cut and their teeth pulled out, are deprived of speech and spend three months every summer in Los Angeles "peddling their asses…in order to save enough money to keep Zero and his familiar [pigs] throughout the winter" (PNE 98). The entire episode serves as a metaphor of women's sexual and economic

134

exploitation.

The volume *The Bloody Chamber* engages with the violence of destructive masculine desire and explores different expressions of the feminine one. Merja Makinen (2000) has divided the stories in the volume into four groups in order to emphasise the patterns that are repeated, creating multiple possibilities for expressing feminine sexuality and desire: the re-working of *Bluebeard,* the three cat-tales, "three tales of magical beings", and three werewolf stories. Destructive patterns of desire are maintained by the power of the father in the cat stories, while the wolf tales expose the danger of the constraints of the mother. In 'The Bloody Chamber' the mother has to give in to her aggressive instinct and kill the Marquis in order to save her daughter, whereas in the supernatural-beings stories the protagonists' redemption depends on their capacity to refrain from instinctual forces.

In the central stories, desire is shown to be culturally constructed and gendered relations are haunted by patterns of repetition and destruction. The desire of one causes the elimination of the other. The girl in 'The Erl King' kills the mythical figure. The female vampire in 'The Lady of the House of Love' breaks the patterns by not repeating the deathly love act of her ancestors and dies, while the King in 'The Snow Child' is utterly consumed by his own desire, and creates a girl child as an object which only exists to be subjected to his violation. The Count creates an innocent, obedient, pure and silent girl. As long as she is flawless she can survive, because he cannot stand any weakness. She pricks her finger on a rose and dies and the Count ravages her corpse.

'The Lady of the House of Love', this sombre rewrite of *Sleeping Beauty*, opens with the presentation of a village of shadows, overcome with a sense of unease, augmented by a warning against unwise travellers stopping to drink from the fountain with the faucet stuck in the mouth of a lion's head. Any such traveller would become the prisoner of a young woman-vampire living in a decrepit château, in the darkness, in rooms with heavy velvet curtains with moth holes in them, with stains of water on the walls, breathing the heavy layer of dust and sleeping in a coffin from sunrise to sunset. The gaze of her ancestors forms a claustrophobic space of the past in which she exercises her compulsion. She is very beautiful in an animalic way: her nails are extremely sharp, her teeth are like spikes and her gestures are catlike. She is a hunter at night, her daytime companion is a lark that cannot sing which she keeps in a cage, and her sole activity is to deal a pack of old Tarot cards in order to find out who her next human victim is going to be. At night the beautiful and frail woman turns into a ruthless hunter on all fours. But the British officer coming by bike to her castle does not become her victim because he replaces the Tarot card of death with that of the Lovers, introducing a difference.

The cat-stories have as protagonists imprisoned daughters who are unable to explore their desire while they are under the control of the father. They are used as currency in a patriarchal system of exchange. In 'Puss-in-Boots' Pantaleone's young wife is held prisoner in her husband's house with an old hag employed to guard her. Beauty in 'The Courtship of Mr. Lyon' is so self-sacrificing that 'she would have gone to the ends of the earth for her father' (1996:145). A change takes place in the case of the rebellious Beauty in 'The Tiger's Bride', who goes against her role by sending her father a clockwork machine to perform the part of the submissive daughter. Once the daughters have freed themselves from the father they are able to negotiate their own space.

Nothing is fixed, humans start running, and animals end up walking. Instinct as aggression has been annihilated by love and eating turns thus into a social ritual, as illustrated in 'The Courtship of Mr. Lyon' when Beast asks Beauty to join him for dinner. In 'The Lady of the House of Love' hunger cannot be satisfied by sucking the British officer's blood, as the Lady vampire has fallen in love with him. The price is not the consummation of the other, but self-consumption, as she dissolves. The rose replacing her has preserved its beauty although it is a rose of death. Metamorphosis from victim to aggressor in the short stories is not one-sided, because the potential victims change – Beauty turns from an innocent daughter to a loving wife, the blond officer acknowledges the presence of the supernatural.

Dominant predatory characteristics of masculinity are generally illustrated by the animal shapes, but the transformations of women break the pattern in 'The Courtship of Mr. Lyon', 'The Tiger's Bride'. There are possible spaces of in-betweenness where the two genders can meet without the tyranny of the one at the cost of the other. In-betweenness is a term I have appropriated from Homi K. Bhabha's *The Location of Culture* where he uses it in a post-colonial context to mark the space created in the meeting between cultures. As identities are not perceived as fixed, but formed by class, gender and race, culture, the confrontation with the foreign, Bhabha argues, opens up 'cultural interstices' where the self can be reinscribed (IDM 1-9).

In this liminal space, gender differences are not erased, but the notion of a stable gender identity is undermined when gaps in the performance of gender become visible, and differences are re-negotiated.

The last tales of the volume introduce a world of the maternal, locked in a fairy tale logic, in which the abundance of old wives' stories re-creates the feminine subculture of superstitious beliefs. Fear rules this world and its inhabitants are the eaters and the eaten. The grandmothers in 'The Werewolf' and 'The Company of Wolves' have to be removed to make room for the granddaughters. In the former the woman is herself a werewolf who attempts to eat the girl. In the later, the girl removes the grandmother who has a restrictive biblical worldview, and refuses to be the meat for the wolf. The position of the grandmother in 'Wolf Alice' is held by a Mother Superior who wants to civilise the girl and introduce her to religion, but the girl finds refuge in the castle of a werewolf Duke. She is part human, part animal, so she belongs to neither world. The humans have shot her mother and they shoot the Duke. It is her turn to access her nurturing instinct and take care of him, repeating the motherly behaviour. She offers him pity and tenderness without becoming the object of his desire, nor he hers. She is the one who licks him into existence by parodying his role as a carnivorous scavenger in the last scene of the story, which is mediated through the mirror: 'The lucidity of the moonlight lit the mirror propped against the red wall; the rational glass, the master of the visible, impartially recorded the crooning girl' (1996:230). However, any finite reading is undermined as the reflected light of the moon, which is reflected in the mirror, does not suggest lucidity, but the illusion of clarity.

Angela Carter plays with gender roles in 'The Erl-King', having the Erl-King perform domestic roles – "he is an excellent housewife" (EK 188). The Erl-King himself is the most mysterious figure in the story, a lover and perhaps an "innocent" murderer. There is no father in this story, no mother, only the lover, who initiates the narrator into sexuality, into the beauty of the plant and animal kingdoms. He lures the girl with "a goblin feast of fruit for me, such appalling succulence" (EK 189) and his enticing stories about animals and devils. His sexual allure is, however, the hardest to fend off, since it is maintained by two contrary effects, soothing and ravishing.

When the narrator first encounters him, she sees that he is beautiful. He is tall; his eyes are the colour of summer leaves, his abundant mane the colour of autumn foliage. Animals and birds flock to him; birds sit on his arms, bunnies lie at his feet, and "a fox laid its muzzle fearlessly upon his knee" (EK 190).

His embrace is "so lucid and encompassing it might be made of water" that the girl is drawn "back and back to him to have his fingers strip the tattered skin away and clothe me in his dress of water, this garment that drenches me, its slithering odour, its capacity for drowning" (EK 191).

The erotic space in 'The Erl-King' is one of cannibalistic ritual, saturated with fear and suspicion, where the victim offers herself as food and drink to be consumed. The wood is a claustrophobic space described in a language saturated with metaphors of imprisonment. The narrator roams the woods "trapped in her own illusion" (EK 185), which points to the space of her own creation. The Erl-King is her own creation, too. Her comprehension of masculine desire is based on existing cultural constructions, taking Dracula and the wolf in *Red Riding Hood* as role models. She is trapped within her perception of the dichotomy of gender in terms of aggressor and victim. The heroine's sudden awakening takes place as she notices that the Erl-King's eyes represent a "reducing chamber" (EK 190), a trap for her to fall into. The Erl-King is in fact weaving a cage to entrap her and place her next to the other birds in his collection. Were she to accept the position of a victim, she would no longer be different from them. As part of nature, her self-consciousness would vanish and she would be defined by his seductive but at the same time obliterating sexuality:

"His embraces were his enticements and yet, oh, yet! They were the branches of which the trap itself was woven. But in his innocence he never knew how he might be the death of me, although I knew from the first moment I saw him how Erl King would do me grievous harm." (EK 187)

The relations between predator and prey shift. The spirit is initially portrayed smiling in a clearing 'where all the flowers were birds and beasts', so that the fluidity of boundaries affects all the elements in this magical space. Innocence rids him of responsibility, whereas the girl's reason cannot stop her from giving in. The girl listens and learns from him how to cook and make cages from twigs for the "sweetest singers" in the woods which he collects. The Erl-King seduces her but they do not play equal parts in their relationship. She sees him as a "tender butcher who showed me how the price of flesh is love" (EK 189), while his perspective, pointed out in his words denoting aggression, "skin the rabbit" (EK 189), with reference to undressing her, stresses his carnivorous nature.

The girl is not the only other. And what is the other for the girl? Everything in the story shifts its shape. The plants are transformed into food, as is an occasional rabbit. But the plants and animals are also friends and companions, who flock around the Erl-King of their own free will.

The nanny goat serves as a watchdog. The larks and linnets are birds and girls. The Erl-King's cottage is a vortex of tenderness, violence, and change.

The girl weaves her prison herself, a silken cage in which she would only be allowed to sing. The hunter's volatile identity confuses her further – he is masculine, feminine, a god with hair made of leaves that fade and fall, the producer of irresistible music that draws birds into his cages. His touch is compared to the embrace of water and the blood thirst of a vampire with hypnotic eyes. She is aware that her survival depends on his whims and her desire to be possessed is expressed as the wish to be consumed. There is emphasis on food and feeding as a mark of metamorphosis, evident in the unnatural hunger overwhelming the girl after the sexual intercourse.: "The earth supports me only out of complicity with him, because his flesh is of the same substance as those leaves that are slowly turning into earth" (EK 189).

"I should like to grow enormously small, so that you could swallow me, like those queens in fairy tales who conceive when they swallow a grain of corn or a sesame seed. Then I could lodge inside your body and you could bear me" (EK 190).

The fusion of the victim with the aggressor is implied in the girl's ambivalent identification with the Erl-King. If he is her creator, as she desires, he is also her killer.

The Erl-King undresses his mistress and charms her so that she would like to be swallowed and lodge inside him, so she goes back to him. Our knowledge of the conventional fairy-tale reminds us of the existence of a penalty for enjoying a forbidden pleasure. Nothing seems to have changed with the exception of his green eyes compared now to 'dead sea-fruit' (1996:190), eyes of a lycanthrope, eyes with an absorbing force: "I will become as small as my own reflection, I will diminish to a point and vanish. I will be drawn into that black whirlpool and be consumed by you" (1996:191).

The narrator notices an old, unused fiddle with broken strings but it is the linnets and larks, in wicker cages lining the kitchen walls, which fill the hut with music. Little by little the girl concludes that her lover, the "tender butcher", whose lovemaking always begins with a jovial command to "skin the rabbit" (EK 189), will change her into one of these birds: "His touch both consoles and devastates me; I feel my heart pulse, then wither, naked as a stone [...] while the lovely, moony night slides through the window to dapple the flank of this innocent who makes cages to keep the sweet birds in" (EK 190-91).

At the end of the story Angela Carter drops the intimate relation established by the use of 'you/me' and adopts the distant 'he'. The girl strangles the Erl-King with ropes made out of his wonderful hair and sets the birds free so that they could change back into young girls: "she will carve off his great mane with the knife he uses to skin the rabbits; she will string the old fiddle with five single strings of ash-brown hair" (EK 192).

We assume her actions really take place, although the verbs describing them are in the Future Simple, instead of the Present. It is a trick commonly used by the writer in order to create a tension between reality and intention at the linguistic level as well. The power of the woman lies in her potential not just in its manifestation: "she will carve off his great mane with the knife he uses to skin the rabbits; she will string the old fiddle with five single strings of ash-brown hair" (EK 192). Even if the girl seems to take charge of her salvation, the ambiguity of the victim and aggressor roles is maintained. The first person voice appears to address the Erl-King directly "Lay your head on my knee so that I can't see the greenish inward-turning suns of your eyes any more. My hands shake" (EK 192). The split between narrator and character is accompanied by "discordant music" and the answer of who the addressee is in the final line of the story remains open. The song "Mother, mother, you have murdered me!" (EK 192) points to the annihilation of the Erl-King on the one hand, and to the destruction of the girl by the one who has given birth to her. The voices mingle and we cannot solve the puzzle. Is the girl still trapped or free? The closing words give a paradoxical solution, an answer that defies logic. "You have murdered me" (EK 192) is a frustrating ending that opens up more questions than it solves. An animal/plant/human hybrid, the Erl-King happily inhabits the borderland between the symbolic and the semiotic: he meets the narrator within the dangerous, uncertain realm of the thetic. The Erl-King may be a sexual predator, or he may be an innocent predator; there is no way for the narrator to know, and the reader is no wiser.

In Kristeva's analysis, adolescence is a defining moment in human development, the moment when the individual's allegiance finally shifts from the semiotic to the symbolic. In developmental terms, as Kristeva points out, adolescence itself is a "thetic break" (1984:70). At the end of the story, ambivalence gives way to destructiveness, and ambiguity must give way to certainty, however harsh. During the course of the story, the narrator comes to ally herself with the repressive symbolic order, renouncing the energies of the semiotic. For her, the birds in cages are girls, their songs represent the strangled verbalizations of animals who once were human and would be again, while the goblin is only a sinister "natural" force, who will consign her to the same prison after he has taken his pleasure. The adolescent narrator is disturbed by her new awareness of the frontier between childhood and adulthood, and, more frightening perhaps, the thin tissue which separates the symbolic consciousness from the semiotic, verbal language from other ways of knowing, the animal from the human.

3.3. CANNIBALS

The connotations of cannibalism conjure up the primitive, the savage or suggest disintegration of personality and social order. It takes us back to a primary image, that of the suckling child who eats a substance emanating from the breast that psychoanalytic theory tells us is not yet known to be separate from the self. Its most powerful meaning is connected to extreme desire to devour, to incorporate one into the self, reflecting a lust for possession or supremacy. Motivations of power and love turn it into a complex concept.

In Angela Carter's writing it appears in two forms: literal eating of human flesh and a metaphor of desire and narcissistic behaviour. As far as the former category is concerned the motivation needs further consideration. Primitive tribes may be divided into those that eat their enemies to destroy them and those who consume them by way of homage in order to keep alive what is of most value to them or to even transform themselves. Western culture regards cannibalism as insatiable appetite and it is exactly its unappeasable character that turns it into a psychological drive, fuelled by threat and fear. This meaning is regressive, symbolizing an unrealisable longing for that ideal state of wholeness where the self and the other are one, and the eater and the eaten are undifferentiated. The individual becomes aware of difference and manifests a mixture of love and aggression that pushes Angela Carter's characters on the margins of the psyche and the borders of the worlds. Her work displays a fascination with the hidden drives and motivations of psyche and society. The mapping of unconscious processes is obvious in *The Infernal Desire Machines of Doctor Hoffman* and *The Passions of New Eve*, reflecting how the life instinct, Eros, and the death instinct, Thanatos, operate in cannibalistic desire, sometimes emanating from one another.

The connection of food with sex is not a simple one, since the two drives are closely linked, in that they are necessary to sustain the life of the body and must be stimulated and satisfied. In *Three Essays On The Theory Of Sexuality,* Freud advances the idea that sexual instinct is generated out of the child's earliest experiences of eating, so his/her sexual desire later is rooted in the satisfaction of hunger for food:

> "The satisfaction of the erotogenic zone is associated, in the first instance , with the satisfaction of the need for nourishment. To begin with, sexual activity attaches itself to functions serving the purpose of self-preservation and does not become independent of them until later. No one

who has seen a baby sinking back satiated from the breast and falling asleep with flushed cheeks and a blissful smile can escape the reflection that this picture persists as a prototype of the expression of sexual satisfaction in later life. The need for repeating the sexual satisfaction now becomes detached from the need for taking nourishment." (1953, 157)

Nurturing or feeding aspects as manifestations of the maternal instinct are frequently transposed onto substitute figures in Angela Carter's works. As Nicole Ward Jouve observes (1994) natural mothers hardly feature in it but non-biological mothers behave maternally. In *The Magic Toyshop,* Aunt Margaret is able, despite the tyrannical regime imposed by Uncle Phillip, to take solace in her cooking. She welcomes Melanie and the little ones with food which is described in comforting terms: a "steaming and savoury" pie "white bread and brown bread, yellow curls of the best butter, two kinds of jam…and currant cake"(TMT 9). She pours tea from a huge brown teapot and 'presides' over the table with satisfaction. Her metamorphosis from victim to provider is mediated through feeding the loved ones. The giving of food and love are inseparable, as illustrated in her remark on tucking baby Victoria in every night. She scribbles in her notepad "What a fine, plump little girl!" (id 48), reminding of the fairy-tale maternal capacity to devour. Grandma Chance in *Wise Children* is a similar positive non-mother who supports and provides for the twins. She is a vegetarian who educates them to use the vitamins in their food and behave morally. Her attitude to food is cabbage-ridden but she loves birthday cakes, Guinness and crème de menthe. Her figure is placed in opposition to that of cousin Saskia, a carnivore with a predatory nature.

In Western culture the role of the mother is associated with the lack of legitimate power. Aunt Margaret is meant to illustrate disempowerment in her role of mother. But her situation is neither straightforward nor static. She derives obvious pleasures from watching the others eat and from feeding them, thus becoming powerful until her husband returns. Then, her serving function prevails. Patriarchy likes the mother figures benign, but impotent.

The positive, maternal nurturing points out the relation between food and love, from the perspective of the mother. Stephanie Demetrakopulos suggests that the danger of over-feeding flows from this relation:

"Women who force their children to eat, who stuff them with food/love, may be extending their lactation powers and own fulfilment, forcing the child to act as the replete and filled vessel of her gift of nourishment.' this may be the case with men, too, as the saying goes: 'the way to a man's heart is through his stomach". (1982:432)

In Angela Carter's work the profound connection between food and sex is further underlined if we take into account the presentation of eating as an erotic activity, from the preparation of the food to seduction meals and its consumption. The manipulative function of food occurs when women infantilise their husbands, having control over the food and taking advantage of men's subordination to the powerful maternal image of their childhood. Emily cooks for Honeybuzzard in *Shadow Dance*, feeding Morris, too, Nora in *Wise Children* mixes sex, love and learning to cook with her Italian future husband.

Appetite related to the food is present in the image of the cook in 'The Kitchen Child', who is the provider of food. The members of the kitchen staff in the big house of Sir and Madam are very busy once a year, for two weeks, when guests arrive. The guests are ridiculed by the narrator for having superficial taste, as all they want is sandwiches. Nevertheless, the cook wields her influence through the cooking of a lobster soufflé, that one of the guests, a French Duke, orders. She takes her time and is extremely careful when preparing it but, during the process, a man whose face she cannot see creeps into the kitchen behind her back and makes love to her. The consequence is that she drops too much keyenne into the soufflé. The conception of her child takes place while she is cooking, so food and sex have pro-creative forces. The food is presented in sexual terms and the cook's sexuality is inseparable from her gastronomic function.

Social eating acquires positive connotations as an image of solidarity, leading to subversive activities. In Angela Carter's work solidarity is generally of women, which does not mean that men are excluded or that women may not be left out. Traitorous women are most of the times cooks who exploit the dark force of appetite: Saskia in *Wise Children*, or the drunken cook at Madame Schreck's house of freaks in *Nights at the Circus*. The 'freak' women there look out for one another, Fanny feeds Sleeping Beauty and the others when the cook is comatose, and organises their flight. At Ma Nelson's brothel women stay together as a defence against the 'horrors' of the outside, those of masculinity, as the whole population down to the dog and cats is female. It is only after Ma Nelson's death that food is brought into focus. After a slice of fruitcake and a glass of port the women set fire to the house to deprive the brother from inheriting everything. The same type of insurgent solidarity over food occurs in the Siberian

'House of Correction' panopticon, where Olga Alexandrovna touches the gloved hand of the guard who holds her breakfast tray. This is the first step toward breaking the boundary between the guarded and the guards who start exchanging notes, drawings and secrets in bread rolls before arming themselves with bread and sausage to flee and found the republic of free women. The panopticon is watched over not only by the Countess but by a clock adjusted to Moscow time, regulating every second of the time the prisoners spend there, parcelled like the black bread, broth and porridge they are given every morning and evening. As the women rebel, their first act is the destruction of the clock, of order, so that they are free to step into the anonymity of the taiga where time is immeasurable.

However, the predatory connotation of cannibalism is the one prevailing in Angela Carter's novels and short stories. Uncle Phillip in *The Magic Toyshop* is the first hearty eater. Melanie, Victoria and Jonathon find the toyshop a place of contradictory appetites. Any appetite for life is snuffed out by the presence of the puppet-master who controls the finances and everything that moves in his house. He satisfies all his appetites without sharing anything. Aunt Margaret and her brothers Francie and Finn, display a passionate and anarchic zest, evident in their wild red hair, only when he is not around. Aunt Margaret and Francie are hungry for each other and Finn's erotic appetite disturbs Melanie at first. She has to escape from Bluebeard before he devours her.

As Foucault (1995:34) writes in *Discipline and Punish*, "from the point of view of the law that imposes it, public torture and execution must be spectacular, it must be seen by all almost as its triumph".

Uncle Phillip's bullying is inseparable from his relationship to food and its provision. He beats Finn for being late for breakfast and abuses all the members of the household. He is described as somehow draining the flavour from the food and making the dining-room "as cold and cheerless as a room in a commercial traveller's guesthouse" (TMT 124), although he eats hugely so that Melanie can see no resemblance between the real uncle and the one in the picture of her parents' wedding. He derives pleasure from eating the food on the one hand and from depriving others of it on the other hand. Aunt Margaret has to wear her best dress on Sunday afternoons and his wedding present, a silver choker which makes her breathing very difficult. She can hardly sip at a cup of tea and nibble something while her husband cannot have enough:

> "[he] broke the armour if a pink battalion of shrimps and ate them steadily, chewed through a
> loaf of bread spread with half a pound of butter and helped himself to the lion's share of the cake

while gazing at her with expressionless satisfaction, apparently deriving a certain pleasure from her discomfort, or even finding that the sight of it improved his appetite". (TMT 113)

He is the perfect image of the tyrant who enjoys watching his wife in the role of the prisoner, because it is on Sunday evening that he exercises his conjugal rights. He cannot bear to see happiness around him and the major tool of his tyranny is the degradation of the others, culminating in his attempt to drive Finn to rape Melanie. In opposition to his behaviour towards people, Uncle Phillip is extremely tender and careful with his puppets, as they are controllable and unthreatening. With humans he is capable of murder, as illustrated in another of his eating scenes:

"He attacked the defenceless goose so savagely he seemed to want to kill it all over again, perhaps feeling the butcher had been incompetent in the first place....The reeking knife in his hand, he gazed reflectively at Finn..."(TMT 160)

His mean intention translates into serving him just "a mean portion of skin and bone" (TMT 161). When he discovers his wife is having an affair with her brother, he is ready to kill, starting his rage in the kitchen.

Uncle Phillip's appetite is omnivorous, he wants to eat the world. Melanie describes his as "heavy as Saturn" (id 168), Saturn being the god who castrated his father and ate his children to stay in control. The carnivorous nature of the patriarch hides his impotence in fact. He cannot deal with those around him any other way.

The theory of the 'oral' stage, developed by Klein (1975), provides insights into the manifestations of this monster. The oral stage, the first one of libidinal development when nutrition is inseparable from the love relationship with the mother, is saturated with echoes of eating and being eaten. The infant is unaware of anything outside himself, but once he discovers difference, he/she enters the 'cannibalistic' one, characterized by love and aggression towards the person perceived as external. As a defence against anxiety, the love object – the breast - is divided into 'good' and 'bad' according to whether it gratifies or frustrates. The subject desires to either incorporate it (which means destroying it) or sucking it dry.

Sexual power is proportional to the appetite of the women in the novels and short stories. In *The Sadeian Woman* Carter observes that Sade urges women "to fuck as actively as they are able, so that powered by their enormous and hitherto untapped sexual energy they will then be able to fuck their way into history and, in doing so, change it" (*SW* 27).

146

In *Wise Children* life instincts are taken to extreme with the figures of the twins whose libido extends into their old age. Their dedication to show-business is reflected in their sexual conquests and appetite for succulent fried bacon and strong gin.

Saskia is their dark opposite who manipulates male appetite and greed to satisfy her own from a young age. For their twenty-first birthday she cooks a suspect lunch, a 'very bitter' nettle soup, duck vampirically 'swimming in blood', giving Nora an indigestion, while the two fathers compete against each other in eating and praising the cook. Saskia's power manifests itself in the food that upsets people's stomachs and in her incestuous hold over her half-brother Tristram who is much younger and too weak to break up with her, although he loves Tiffany. Dora claims that her influence has something to do with substances she adds in the food, and Tiffany, Saskia's rival, remembers feeling sick during her stay at the latter's villa. Saskia's exploitation of food, sexuality and cruelty is presented in Dora's description of a TV cooking programme, in which Saskia jugs a hare, displaying a sado-masochistic sexuality as well as the sensual quality of cooking:

> "She cut the thing up with slow, voluptuous strokes. "Make sure your blade is up to it!" she husked, running her finger up and down the edge, although the spectacle of Saskia with a cleaver couldn't help but remind me and Nora of how she'd run amok with the cake knife on her twenty-first. Next, she lovingly prepared a bath for the hare, she minced up shallots, garlic, onions, added a bouquet garni and a pint of claret and sat the poor dismembered beast in that for a day and a half. Then she condescended to sauté the parts briskly in a hot pan over a high flame until they singed. Then it all went into the oven for the best part of another day. She sealed the lid of the pot with a flour-and-water paste. 'Don't be a naughty thing and peek!' she warned with a teasing wink. Time to decant at last! The hare had been half-rotted, then cremated, then consumed. If there is a god and she is of the rabbit family, then Saskia will be in deep doodoo on Judgement Day. 'Delicious,' she moaned, dipping her finger in the juice and sucking. She licked her lips, letting her pink tongue-tip linger. 'Mmmm...'" (WC 180-1)

Saskia's power is malign and always motivated by revenge. Dora recalls that Saskia "jugged a hare for Tristram once" and "that cooked his goose" (WC 181). She tries to poison Melchior three times, and kill her school-friend who becomes the third wife of her assumed father. In her, the appetites of the libido combine with the destructive and corrupted energies of the death instincts to appease her lustful nature.

147

On a larger scale, eating becomes a form of colonialism, explored within the confinements of the household in *Heroes and Villains*, turning into an analysis of the drama of three narcissistic egos in *Love*: Annabel, her husband Lee and his brother Buzz. Lorna Sage comments that "they construct themselves, cannibalistically, out of each other, and inscribe their meanings on each other's flesh" (1984:12) . Annabel in *Love* makes Lee tattoo her name on his chest, he takes her home to take care of her after a party, moved by the hunger in her face which he takes to be hunger for food, but is wrong:

> "Annabel ate a little, drank her tea and covered her face with her hands so he could not watch her any more. Her movements were spiky, angular and graceful; how was he to know, since he was so young, that he would become a Spartan boy and she the fox under his jacket, eating his heart out". (L 15)

Annabel's affair with Buzz and their sexual union is described in carnivorous terms "connoisseurs of unreality as they were, they could not bear the crude weight, the rank smell and the ripe taste of real flesh" (L 95). After the disappointing encounter she returns to Lee to seduce him and attacks him like a vampire. He feels her as a sexually predatory succubus whom he wishes dead. So deceptive is her perception of the real world that she hallucinates about Lee being a herbivorous lion, a flesh-eating unicorn or one castrated of his horn. Annabel tells the psychiatrist that she has eaten her wedding ring, Lee tells the fool in the park that she has tried to eat him alive. *Love* is a novel in which sexual desire is seen as a life and death struggle. However, most of Angela Carter's work avoids this explicit conclusion. In *Several Perceptions*, the alienated hero is attracted to his friend's mother, Mrs. Boulder, the first whore in Angela Carter's work. He repeatedly dreams of her and when he sees her in the café he has the sensation of falling through her eyes into the country of a virgin. He then dreams of her as an ice cream, a sign of his cannibalistic desire for her. In his dream she begins to grow as he eats on, so his impression is that he can eat her without destroying her. He is eventually extinguished by the grotesque "polar night of Mr. Boulder's belly" (SP 76). Joseph's simultaneous fear and desire correspond to the responses to the breast in Klein's theory. Both Mr. Boulder and Joseph find satisfaction and are reborn: she finds her black lover from the war, Joseph is hungry for boiled eggs and tea.

The predatory aspect of cannibalism is the one Angela Carter returns to in *Heroes and Villains*, where the principle of 'eat or be eaten' is central. Superstition and ignorance are two

148

of the aspects the two societies, the Professors and the Barbarians, have in common. Cannibalism is sketched as a threat to scare the people. Marianne's nurse warns her that if she is not good the Barbarians will eat her, wrapped in clay, baked in the fire and seasoned with salt, while the Barbarian child Jen tells Marianne of her father's disappearance: "He dressed up and went away and he didn't come back and the P had killed him and baked him and eaten him with salt" (HV 35). Her imagination is haunted by these beliefs during her wedding ceremony, while Donally's blood-mixing ritual takes place, as she says: "I thought he was going to kill me, cut me up, fry me and distribute me in ritual gobbets to the tribe" (HV 76). When Jewel explains to Marianne the purpose of their marriage, after having raped her, the colonial form of cannibalism is illustrated by his words: "I've got to marry you, haven't I? ...Swallow you up and incorporate you, see. Dr. Donnally says. Social psychology" (HV 56). The only way for the tribe to stop seeing Marianne as a threat is to incorporate her. The same mechanism of thinking applies to the tribe of centaurs who look for the best way to digest Desiderio and Albertina. Marianne is in danger and she has to find a way to interact with the Barbarians without being completely subsumed. At first she does not perceive Jewel as existing outside their relationship, and their intimate relation is seen as an alien third thing:

> "This erotic beast...eyeless, formless and equipped with one single mouth. It was amphibious and swam in black, brackish waters, subsisting only upon night and silence...The beast had teeth and claws. It was sometimes an instrument solely of vengefulness, though often its own impetus carried it beyond this function. When it separated out to themselves, again, they woke to the mutual distrust of the morning." (HV 88-89)

Eros is represented as a struggle for power, mixing passion and violence. Marianne barely escapes a pack rape when the brothers direct her toward the bloody table where the carcasses of recently sacrificed animals are still warm. The woman is associated with meat for men's consumption.

The same parallel appears in 'The Bloody Chamber', the first short story of the volume, a first re-working of *Bluebeard*. The Marquis's hunger for his new wife is overlaid with vampiric suggestion, starting with his wet red lips, and hints of cannibalism. The stems of his lilies in water are like severed limbs; his cigar is as "fat as a baby's arm" (BB 12), he serves her lunch including pheasant with hazelnuts and chocolate and a white, 'voluptuous' cheese.

149

The night before their wedding, at the opera, the heroine feels objectified by his gaze: "I saw him watching me in the gilded mirrors with the assessing eye of a connoisseur inspecting horseflesh, or even of a housewife in the market, inspecting cuts on the slab" (ibid 11).

The Marquis is a consumer with perverse appetites. He gives the girl a ruby choker for a wedding present. It has not only the imprisoning and stifling qualities of that in *The Magic Toyshop* which Aunt Margaret receives but that of an omen, prefiguring the cruel ending the Marquis has in store for her. The girl describes his approach as epicurean:

> "He stripped me, gourmand that he was, as if he were stripping the leaves off an artichoke - but do not imagine much finesse about it; this artichoke was no particular treat for the diner nor was he yet in any greedy haste. He approached his familiar treat with a weary appetite…"

and likens herself to the girl in a pornographic etching, "bare as a lamb chop'"(BB 15).

His monstrous appetite is quickened by his bride's delayed approach to the execution:

> "Don't loiter, girl! So you think I shall lose appetite for the meal if you are so long about serving it? No; I shall grow hungrier, more ravenous with each moment, more cruel…run to me, run! I have a place prepared for your exquisite corpse in my display of flesh!" (BB 39)

When he realizes that his wife has visited his chamber and learned his dreadful secret, he seems to be sorry for the necessity of killing her. From this perspective he is comparable to the vampire lady in 'The Lady of the House of Love'. They want to be free of their nature but at the same time know they cannot survive without giving in to their instinct. Murder testifies to the meatiness of human flesh, in a relation regarded in primitive terms between victim and aggressor.

The assertion of matriarchal power in *The Passion of New Eve* takes the form of "terrorism as the desire for power" (Kristeva, 1986:205). The novel demonstrates how this 'feminism as terrorism' hardly grants women access to power. Through its complicity with the underlying violence of patriarchy it is useless in subverting that order. Carter suggests that the only way of freeing oneself from the limitations of both patriarchal and matriarchal myths paradoxically requires a return to their source in order to challenge them more effectively.

Zero in *The Passion of New Eve* eats a lot, while his wives are made to eat in impossible haste or go hungry. He takes sumptuous breakfasts in bed, and enjoys giving his wives only a few moments in which to consume theirs, deriving his pleasure from denying them theirs. The consumption of red meat is a privilege given to Zero and his dog by his wives who sell their bodies in order to feed him. Women are considered primitive and should do without meat. Even if they wanted to consume meat they couldn't do it since Zero has had their front teeth extracted. His vampiristic tendencies are not limited to stealing their food. He feeds off them sexually leaving "the angry marks of love-bites on the exposed flesh of throat and neck" (PNE 88).

Sexual excess in relation to perversion figures mostly in *The Infernal Desire Machines of Doctor Hoffman*. The novel is centred around the release and sublimation of desire but, surprisingly, Desiderio's sexual and gustatory appetites are enmeshed and his sexuality is stimulated through his palate in his intercourse with Mama. The sense of deferred goals, typical of romances, is anticipated by reference to food and eating: he does not have sexual intercourse with his child bride in the river people episode but with her mother in the kitchen, while at the castle of desire he is disappointed by the meal he eats with Albertina and the Doctor, wondering whether their sexual union will be the same. It seems that hunger is better than its satisfaction. But in the novel desire is eventually victorious, as Desiderio, unable to satisfy his appetite, longs for Albertina to his last days.

The death instinct is manifest in the episode involving the sadistic Count. He only lives in order to negate the world. His obliterating selfishness is evident when he eats heavily and leaves almost nothing for Desiderio and Lafleur, when he kills and mutilates to satisfy his sexual appetites, in his habit of not answering questions since he is too self absorbed to notice the one asking them. At the House of Anonymity he chooses a prostitute with a whipped back whom he describes using terms of meat, fire and cannibal feasting. Just as he is on the point of ravishing her, his alter ego, the black pimp, arrives. He is the one the Count most desires and fears, 'my retribution...my twin...my shadow' (ibid 139), 'baleful', 'appalling', like a 'depth of water'. In the chief's brutal society cannibalism is a way of life': the women soldiers are encouraged to eat their firstborn children to keep the society under control.

The deconstruction of the myth of the *bon savage* mirrors the mechanism of domination-annihilation. Angela Carter stresses the obtuse character of the tribesmen with the legend of the Snake and the girl (IDM 89-90) and their cruelty with the ritual designated to cannibalize Desiderio. In *The Sadeian Woman* Angela Carter sees man-eating as the primal form of aggression: "Cannibalism, the most elementary ace of exploitation, that of turning the other directly into a comestible; of seeing the other in the most primitive terms of use" (*SW* 140). The body of the Other is appropriated by the eating subject who seeks to assert his power

151

and assimilate the victim's abilities, as the River People (IDM 91) or gain the physical superiority of the victim, as is the case with the African tribe. In their eyes, Desiderio is the "most abhorred of comestibles" (IDM 159).

In the House of Anonymity, the Gothic brothel, Desiderio meets the prostitutes who lack names. The episode represents Angela Carter's vision of the female body as meat.

> "It was a massive, sprawling edifice in the Gothic style of the late nineteenth century, that poked innumerable turrets like so many upward groping tentacles towards the dull, cloudy sky and was all built in louring, red brick. Every window I could see was tightly shuttered" (IDM 129).

The prostitutes are not just abused or murdered by customers, but also literally dehumanized by having their bodies dismembered into 'appetizing' parts (IDM 132) and rearranged into an impersonal whole. Desire equals injury and the commodification of the weak. Angela Carter exaggerates the effects of sadism using parody and satire.

In the fear of rape, as Angela Carter observed in *The Sadeian Woman*, there is "more than merely physical terror of hurt and humiliation – a fear of psychic disintegration, of an essential dismemberment, a fear of a loss or disruption of the self which is not confined to the victim alone" (*SW* 6) Voyeurism is one of the targets of her satire; inside the brothel there are mirrors which expose the women's naked bodies, cruel images come under scrutiny and violence reigns. The embodiment of sexual deviation is Desiderio's new companion, the sadistic Count, a blend of Dracula and De Sade, who enjoys torturing the prostitutes. The relation aggressor-victim that Angela Carter presents is meant to signal the submission of women under the cover of romantic love, consumption or prostitution. The status of the woman as puppet or automaton backs the writer's controversial statement that "in a world organized by contractual obligations, the whore represents the only possible type of honest woman" (1979:58). The Count feeds on the prostitutes' bodies and absorbs their energies to satisfy his taste for violence. He is a grotesque vampire-like being who wears a ridiculous costume and is completely isolated as a result of his sadistic inclinations. He eventually falls prey to his passion and is eaten by his *alter ego*, the cannibal chief, who wishes to annihilate his will. His destiny is thus similar to that of the "comestible" women in the House of Anonymity. The community of the Centaurs, the last Desiderio visits before arriving at Dr Hoffman's castle, presents women who have their skin covered in tattoos, as a mark of enslavement. The male Centaurs carve the women's bodies and faces following strict religious rituals imposed by the cult of the Sacred

Stallion. They gang rape Albertina out of the sense of duty, without deriving any pleasure. Their society is governed by fanaticism and intolerance, having a lot in common with the Victorian suppression of desire. The sexual tension between Desiderio and Albertina reaches a climax in their final encounter in a way that Sarah Gamble finds troubling: "The undercurrents of sadistic sexuality in this passage are disturbing, containing as they do an echo of the Count's own valorisation of the relationship between predator and prey[...]"(1997,115):

> "She bit me and tore my clothes and I bit her and pummelled her with my fists. I pummelled her breasts until they were as blue as her eyelids but she never let go and I savaged her throat with my teeth as if I were a tiger and she were a trophy I seized in the forests of the night" (IDM 216).

Desiderio witnesses various manifestations of violence in his journey, each generating a dose of self-criticism combined with compassion for the victims. The role reversal is initiated when he undergoes the same atrocities and becomes the subject of humiliation, as in the case of his rape by the nine circus acrobats: "And I could do nothing but watch and suffer with her for I knew from my own experience the pain and the indignity of a rape" (IDM 179). The other instances that add to his status as a passive victim – he becomes the Count's puppet, is positioned as the "meat" of the cannibals- further raise questions in relation to his heroism. Even he admits that it is a consequence of chance: "I became a hero only because I survived" (IDM 11). Desiderio is feminized, since he does not have a stable narrative stance and frequently lends his voice to the women victims. Patriarchal authority is questioned also as a result of his unreliable recollections. Not only does he express self-doubt interrupting the story sequence, he also frustrates the reader with his anti-climatic narrative style that shatters the suspense in the opening pages of the novel. Albertina, on the other hand loses the romantic appeal as she turns into an aggressive "Generalissimo" (IDM 195).

Love-making parodically turns into an act of death and destruction. Not only does Desiderio echo the Count, he even repeats his style. He kills Albertina, a flawed emanation of his desire. Like her father, he is then free to construct her memory as he wishes, without the intrusion of her other role as her father's creation. In his memory, she no longer serves two masters.

The interchangeable roles Desiderio and Albertina undertake signal another mode Angela Carter would employ in her post-Japan volume *The Bloody Chamber* to subvert the fairy-tale representations of gender. The image of the female, good, innocent and naive in most of the traditional fairy-tales is rendered either to have inclinations towards pervert sexual practices or to be violently harmful for the opposite sex. The frame that confines the women to the role of victims and men to that of villains is broken once Angela Carter's wicked women step in.

It is impossible to separate Carter's *The Sadeian Woman*, which is in fact her own reading of Marquis de Sade, from the volume of short stories, in reading and interpreting them. The woman subject is saved from being victimized through the foregrounding of female sexuality. The earlier versions of fairy-tales with their misogynistic message are done away with, as Angela Carter re-imagines the young heroines as active in their own sexual development and experience. In *The Sadeian Woman*, Carter reads Sade in such a way that, she believes he claimed the "rights of free sexuality for women" and created "women as beings of power in his imaginary world"(*SW* 36). She also acknowledges Marquis de Sade's belief that "it would only be through the medium of sexual violence that women might heal themselves of their socially inflicted scars, in a praxis of destruction and sacrilege." (*SW* 26)
Carter concludes the 'Polemical Preface' of The Sadeian Woman by asserting that Sade "put pornography in the service of women, or, perhaps, allowed it to be invaded by an ideology not inimical to women." (*SW* 37)

'Snow Child' is a rewriting of Grimms' fairy-tale. The Count is introduced riding on a grey mare and the Countess on a black one. Carter describes the physical appearance of the Countess in greater detail than the Count's, and the colour black prevails in this depiction: "... she wrapped in the glittering pelts of black foxes; and she wore high, black, shining boots ..." (BB 91). She does not do the needle work while staring outside her window like the queen does in Grimm's story, she is more active and, above all, wicked. In Carter's version the Count is the one who wants a girl as white as snow, as red as blood and as black as raven's feather. He mentions neither her skin, nor her lips and hair. After she appears all of a sudden before them, the Countess hates her, because she feels that she was the child of the Count's desire. He lifts her up and sits her in front of him on his saddle. The evil which has already been attributed to the Countess is aroused in her. She searches for the ways of getting rid of her and orders the girl to bring her diamond brooch back from the ice of the frozen pond. The Count prevents the girl from diving into the pond. But when she orders her to pick a rose for her, the girl's finger bleeds and she dies. He gets off his horse and rapes the dead girl while his wife watches him.

154

In this story Carter creates a female aristocratic voyeur. In the end, she refuses the rose her husband offers her, saying that "it bites." The evil Countess acknowledges the Count's authority. However, she participates in the evil action and evil will. The child who is created to be consumed is a means through which the potential evil in the Countess becomes overt. Furthermore, Elaine Jordan (1998:41) suggests that the death of the virgin girl is the symbol of "killing of masculine representations" not "a killing of women". The presence of evil in the story is no longer implied as a power struggle. The Count and his evil wife plot hand in hand to destroy the innocence through the pervert practice of necrophilia.

Carter attributes unusual and pervert sexuality to the female and creates a possibility for female awakening. The juxtaposition of the female and male evil, within the framework of violent sexuality, brings the female body and voice to the forefront of Carter's fiction.

3.4. DESIRED OTHERS

As an over-determined force in the human psyche, desire in *The Infernal Desire Machines of Doctor Hoffman* is treated with an emphasis on the form it takes as well as the power that accompanies it. Carter's novel analyzes the desired version of reality with the sexual drive as its greatest determining force. In the display of various desired worlds, there looms an erotic force which is not only an egotistic "will to power" to shape the world as it desires, but a will to annihilate the female other.

Angela Carter problematizes the common-sense reality by subverting the long held demarcation between human reason and desire most of all by combining literary genres in her approach. Paradoxically, she uses the fantastic mode to subvert fantasy, both as a psychological activity and as a literary genre. I will refer to Catherine Belsey's analysis of "postmodern" desire and Rosemary Jackson's discussion of fantasy as transgressive mode of subversion in order to approach the intricate relationship between desire, sexuality and cultural conditions in Carter's analysis of desire. The postmodern patchwork that weaves the text of *The Infernal Desire Machines of Doctor Hoffman* provides a fruitful ground for interpretation.

In its multiple rewriting of, or overwriting on the existing narratives two texts come to the fore as we read the story of Dr Hoffman – Marcel Proust's *Remembrance of Things Past* and the *Tales* of E. T. A. Hoffmann. As Susan Rubin Suleiman points out, Hoffmann's *Tales* "are not only alluded to in the novel's title, but provide a structural model for the overall story", and "one finds, pell-mell, echoes of Proust' from the opening sentence "I remember everything" and ' the beloved "lost object" is named Albertina" (IDM 104). Analyzing the structural model for the novel in reference to Hoffmann's *Tales,* Suleiman sums up the model as follows:
"a powerful father with magical powers keeps his beautiful but potentially deadly daughter tantalizingly out of the reach of the desiring young man, a situation that eventually leads to the death of the daughter... or of the young man"(IDM 104).

In discussing *The Infernal Desire Machines of Doctor Hoffman*'s intertexts with Hoffmann's *Tales*, Colin Manlove (1992: 149-150) considers Hoffmann's *The Golden Pot* to be the main story that serves as the overwritten narrative in the relationships among Desiderio, Albertina and Dr Hoffmann.

156

UNIVERSITY OF WINCHESTER LIBRARY

In *The Golden Pot* the structural model is slightly dissimilar and with a happy ending. It is a story of a young woman called Anselmus allured by a magician's daughter called Serpentina, who first reveals herself to the young men in the form of a golden green snake. The young man 'forsakes his former empiricism and his bourgeois betrothed Veronica' (Manlove in Filmer, WC149-150), for the sake of Serpentina, but in the end he is rewarded with a happy union with her and lives forever in the magician's wonderland. It is interesting to note what signifying effects these palimpsest texts may contribute to the surface text of the novel. The story runs that Desiderio, the I-narrator and an aging hero/politician, looks back on his youthful adventures and writes down what he can remember of the past which is to become his country's official history. The 'Great War' he describes is a vehement struggle between two different worlds, one constructed and known to humans reason, the other projected by intense desire as a result of the force released from the 'unconscious'. Desiderio, then a young man with an extraordinary power of metaphysical intuition, works for the rational side represented by the 'Minister of Determination.' The enemy side is commanded by doctor Hoffman, apparently a magician-like figure but more of a crazed puppet master with the great knowledge of science and the power of human desire. His daughter Albertina is his lead puppet to wage the war for him, and a major part of her mission is to lure the prime agent of the Minister, Desiderio, to her father's camp. She comes to Desiderio's dreams in various alluring images and Desiderio, whose mission for the Minister is to annihilate the Doctor, embarks on a love quest for her. But before his final confrontation with her and her father in their high-tech castle home, he is involuntarily involved in a series of adventures in worlds projected under the influence of desire. These adventures have their separate intertextual allusions; one of the important connecting points they present in relation to the overall narrative is their relevance to Desiderio's experience of his own unconscious desire. Throughout his picaresque journey Desiderio alleges his lack of desire for anything except for his beloved Albertina; however, when the ultimate moment comes for him to enter a perpetual sexual union with Albertina in the 'love pen' Dr Hoffman has prepared for them, he suddenly resists violently. In their fierce struggle Desiderion not only kills Dr Hoffman but ferociously bites Albertina on her neck, like a vampire, before he stabs her to death with the knife she carries in her bridal gown. With the death of father and daughter Desiderio easily destroys their 'infernal' machines of desire and ends the fantastic war between reason and desire. For his deeds he is rewarded by his country as a national hero who restored rational order to the world while he himself is tortured forever by his unfulfilled desire for Albertina.

Desire is the overwhelming force lying at the heart of the text, as Albertina's cry suggests: "Oh, Desiderio! Never underestimate the power of that desire for which you are named!" (IDM 167). Desire is everywhere: in the name of the protagonist, in the title of the novel, it is the motor of Desiderio's quest and each episode revolves around various degrees of desire, from love to aggression and obsessive compulsion. If in Proust's text memory functions as a magical light to illuminate the unseen meaning in the corridor of bygone time, then memory in the novel is deeply mixed up with personal and collective desire.

Desiderio, "a man without desires" (IDM 211) at the onset of his quest, lets us know in his Introduction that Albertina is the product of is desire:

"Rather, from beyond the grave, her father has gained a tactical victory over me and forced on me at least the apprehension of an alternate world in which all the objects are the emanations of a single desire. And my desire is, to see Albertina again before I die." (IDM 13)

From the way in which he describes Albertina in the opening pages, "the heroine of my story, the daughter of the magician, the inexpressible woman to whose memory I dedicate these pages, the miraculous Albertina" (IDM 13), he makes it obvious that she is more a product of memory and desire than an objective woman:

"I see her as a series of marvellous shapes formed at random in the kaleidoscope of desire" (IDM 13).

The changes or metamorphoses inflicted on the anonymous city in the novel transform it, as Suleiman (1994) notes, into a surrealist's dream, and formally into a surrealist collage. The surrealist notion of desire was, as Angela Carter notes below, in her essay on surrealism ('The Alchemy of the Word'), about the liberating powers of unconscious desire, and seeing the world as if for the first time, creating it anew by force of desire, hence their embrace of revolutionary desire:

"Surrealism celebrated wonder, the capacity for seeing the world as if for the first time which, in its purest state, is the prerogative of children and madmen, but more than that, it celebrated wonder itself as an essential means of perception .

[...] Surrealism posits poetry as a possible mode, possibly the primary mode, of being. Surrealism was the latest, perhaps the final, explosion of romantic humanism in Western

158

Europe. It demanded the liberation of the human spirit as both the ends and the means of art."
(1997:496)

Albertina clearly stands as illustration of the motif of the Muse as Beloved, a trope that Carter
viewed as explicitly gendered, and commented on in a interview with Kerryn Goldsworthy:

"I think the Muse is a pretty fatuous person. The concept of the Muse is- it's another magic
Other, isn't it, another way of keeping women out of the arena. There's a whole book by Robert
Graves dedicated to the notion that poetic inspiration is female, which is why women don't have
it. It's like haemophilia; they're the transmitters, you understand. But they don't suffer from it
themselves" (1985:12).

Albertina   is not only the artist's other, she is so enigmatic and fragmented that mutability
becomes her definition. Angela Carter's irony takes the shape of literary excess and
literalization in the representation of Albertina as human, inanimate, bestial, or androgynous,
masculine or feminine. She appears first as a hallucination of a transparent woman with a heart
of flames, then as a black swan; later Desiderio sees her in the eyes of Mary-Anne, the
somnambulist and in the decapitated head from the peep-show samples. She then appears
disguised as the masked Madam of the brothel and travels with Desiderio under the disguise of
the sadistic Count's abused boy valet Lafleur. The most complex disguise, however, that which
comprises Albertina's fluidity and triggers Desiderio's fascination, is her appearance as the
Ambassador of the Doctor. Desiderio attributes the Ambassador's appeal to the ontological
ambiguity and the sense of threat he exudes:

"I think he was the most beautiful human being I have ever seen – considered, that is, solely as an
object, a construction of flesh, skin, bone and fabric, and yet, for all his ambiguous sophistication,
indeed, perhaps in its very nature, he hinted at a savagery which had been cunningly tailored to suit
the drawing room. He was a manicured leopard patently in complicity with chaos.
[…]Certainly I had never seen a phantom who looked at that moment more shimmeringly unreal
than the Ambassador, nor one who seemed to throb with more erotic promise" (IDM 32,36).

The desire to penetrate the enigma of the Muse is one aspect of the theme of desire. Angela
Carter's parodical approach surfaces as Desiderio's ambition to "rip away that ruffled shirt and
find out whether the breasts of an authentic woman swelled beneath it" (IDM 40) reveals

nothing but another layer of Albertina's enigma , a "language of signs which utterly bemused me because I could not read them" (IDM 25).

Desiderio's memory is tainted both with his past desire and his present one. But the problem in his desired memory is his insistent claim of his lack of desire until the appearance of the desirable Albertina in his dreams. He is unaware of his passion, "too sardonic...too disaffected" (IDM 12), which makes him the perfect agent to disintegrate the chaos generated by Doctor Hoffman's illusions. The only illusion that does penetrate his indifference is the apparition of the Doctor's daughter.

Critics have presented different readings concerning Desiderio's role and his desire. He can be seen as a character functioning as a narrative device, as Elaine Jordan (1992:161) explains:

> "Formally, Desiderion is not a realistic character, but kin to Gulliver, or the passive of hero of Walter Scott's novels, a double for author and reader in their passage through the story. The episodes he goes through in seeking to destroy Hoffman are also readable as his dream-wrestling with the problems posed, the possibilities of overcoming Reason and Desire as a battleground; dreams of Modern Man".

Colin Manlove notices that "the memories of his journey are his alone: no-one else from the ordered city accompanies him" (1992:152). He questions the male subjective position adopted by Desiderio in the narrative of his heroic deed.

In his quest for Doctor Hoffman, Desiderio comes across "apparent objects that reveal themselves as mere images of the desirable" (Clark, 1987:156), but his libido is kept under control in view of completing his mission at first, and for fear of losing the rational side of himself later, when he understands the world of illusion feeds of eroto-energy.

We can read him and his memoirs, as Colin Manlove (1992:156) points out, in a deconstructive way in which his text subverts his own narrative:

> " we think that he is the detached narrator of all that he sees; the phenomena are outside him... Throughout the narrative he proclaims himself an appropriate hero because of his inherent boredom and indifference before the proliferation of sensible objects. Yet his very name, 'Desiderio' undercuts this; and the extraordinarily powerful desire he comes to feel for Albertina certainly calls it into question... It is perfectly possible to see his journey as one into his own unconscious, into a libido whose existence he strains to deny."

And my reading of Desiderio's character comes closer to Manlove's, for I see Desiderio's denial of desire as actually a contradictory manifestation of his desire. It plays a crucial part in the texture of his narrative. Owing to his ethnic and social background – coming from the lowest stratum of society as the son of a white European prostitute-mother and an unknown Indian customer father – he is doubly marginalized in his society. He is a "very disaffected young man" for he is not unaware of the "disinheritance" (IDM 16) which negates his existence. As an extremely intelligent young man and deprived of any desired object in his situation he can see things 'objectively' for what they are. Desiderio is a hero in the end because of his apathy.

The narrator's own desire emerges unconsciously as a transparent screen between what he remembers and what actually happened in the past. Desiderio's desire stands as an invisible bridge in his memory lane to the vanished past which is filled with flamboyant shows of other people's desires. What he sees as others' fantasies sometimes turns out to be his own or of his own collaboration in spite of strenuous denial of any involvement. As he observes the strange worlds in which he is plunged, worlds projected and brought into being by his and other peoples fantasies, he is caught in an even greater fantastic circle which is the realm of literary fantasy.

Placing Desiderio's ambiguous desire as the implicit focal point of the struggle between a reality set by a reason and the reality desired by desire, I'm also connecting Carter's fantastic text to Rosemary Jackson's (1995:3) theory of fantasy. Fantasy, as she observes, is a literary mode attempting "to compensate for a lack resulting from cultural constraints: it is the literature of desire which seeks that which is experienced as absence and loss." The fantasy world Desiderio and other characters with strong desires find themselves in is not only a world projected by their desires but a world speaking of what has been kept the repressed, unsaid. This is also the fantastic element that has characterized Carter's work as speculative fiction, as her fantastic style is also a serious intellectual exploration into the repressed other side of patriarchal Western culture. Moreover, Jackson employs Freud's theories of the uncanny and the human subject to relate the unconscious desire predominant in ' the modern fantastic' (ibid.: 62-3) to the repressions and taboos in cultural order. Carter's texts pursue the 'strangeness' of the given world, of the given terms that constitute one's sexual identity, and the repressed desire that has arisen from the gap between what has been permitted and what has been forbidden culturally.

However, Carter's fantastic texts are by no means subtle psychological novels. The use of Freudian discourse and fantasy is made with an effect of highlighting the artificiality of psychological activities while exploring the cultural forces that have pervaded, or in a sinister sense, animated all the characters. Almost all her characters are composite figures penetrated through by various cultural narratives and forces, but the acute sense of 'unnaturalness' and strangeness is presented less in the characters' consciousness than in the characterization itself. While the characters are treated as role-players who are not unaware of their own artifice, it is their performance of their artificial self that produces the uncanny effect.

The characters in *The Infernal Desire Machines of Doctor Hoffman* pursue their desires, enact their fantasies as if they were the most natural things to them. This is an important feature in Carter's text which renders her fantasies different from the modern fantastic that Jackson has analyzed in fictions such as Kafka's. In Kafka's work, the grotesque tales of social estrangement are parables of suffering individuals deformed by the forces of modern society. In Carter's fantasies the reality of the world is exposed to be more culture-determined than natural. The fantastic element that marks Carter's fictions reflects an acute sense of coming near the end of the road as Western cultural traditions are seen to head toward dissolution. As Lorna Sage observes, *The Infernal Desire Machines of Doctor Hoffman* and *The Passion of New Eve* are "last–days allegories, reports from the demolition sites, which map out territory for speculation"(Sage, 1994:33).

The characters find themselves already in a fantasy-like world, in which their desired fantasies do not shape the inner yearnings of their souls, they are but a re-play of what has been inscribed on them as desire for that they have experienced as a 'lack' in their existence. The estrangement of this lack is twofold, as exemplified in Desiderio's adventures. And social disinheritance deprives him of his social identity, renders him passive and longing for a static life-form, which is a death-wish psychologically, all he is left is an intellectual power with which to analyze, and jeer at, the imperfect status of the existing world. This destructive death-wish also owes its existence to his prostitute-mother whose fierce female sexuality casts a frightening shadow on his unconscious and generates a blend of hatred and attraction to women in his libido. Almost as if deprived of an object to desire, before Albertina haunts his dreams, his desire is in such a dry, jeering state of negation that he even denies its existence. But several examples can be cited to challenge his assertion of lack of desire. Fantasies such as 'a fat, white owl'(IDM 26) purporting to be his mother and begging for his forgiveness or the

162

turning of all the Opera House's audience, except himself, into crowds of peacocks (16) are also likely to be his own instead of others' as he claims.

Desiderio, who turns his desires into actualities, is continually transforming himself so as to accommodate to the desires of others, as Ricarda Schmidt notices (1989: 57) and he still sees himself as powerless. His dependence on others is so strong that each time he enters a new phase or flees, the experience is similar to a rebirth. The violence inherent in the process of becoming whole is revealed as he runs from the town of S. and he claims that "the moment when my head broke into the fresh air surprised me as much as I were a baby suddenly popped from the womb" (IDM 64-65). After the landslide in which the circus disappears, he has a similar experience, stating: "I turned my back on a whole sub-universe that had been wiped out as if with a huge eraser and on the corpse of yet another of my selves, that of the peep-show proprietor's nephew" (IDM 120).

Desiderio longs for unity and the end of his quest and his regression into the community of the river people is described as a loss of personality:

> "The limited range of feeling and the idea they expressed with such a meagre palette of gesture no longer oppressed me; it gave me, instead, a slight feeling of warm claustrophobia I had learned to identify with the notion, 'home'... Desiderio himself had disappeared because the river people had given him a new name... I was called Kiku". (IDM 77)

Desire for wholeness takes distorted forms of incest and paedophilia, overcoming Desiderio, as revenge is in due course in the form of Aoi's knife and Mama and Papa's cannibalistic wedding feast.

In Hoffman's castle he looks in the mirror and claims: "I had been transformed again. Time and travel had changed me almost beyond my own recognition. Now I was entirely Albertina in the male aspect"(id 199).

In comparison with either the Minister's or the Doctor's intelligence in the reality war, Desiderio's mental vision, like theirs, seems untouched by emotional manipulation. But the Minister's and Doctor's mental power is actually the other side of the will to power. Desiderio's rationality is also in the service of an unconscious desire, different from theirs, one expressed in a negative from. Even if he desires, he lacks a desired object. Thus, until the alluring appearance of Albertina, he tends to negate the magical phenomenal display, no matter how fantastic, which does not answer his desired form categorically. His repressed desire is manifested in something he has in common with the minister, "an admiration for stasis"(IDM 12). His attraction to a perfected static form of existence, such as the one exhibited by "the Ancient Egyptians" who "arrived at and perfected an aesthetically entirely satisfactory pose" (IDM 12), reveals an unconscious wish to cast and freeze people in a tableau-like existence in which generations of individuals are constrained within and repeat the same stereotyped lives of their ancestors. This is a tendency the Indian river people, among whom Desiderio feels most at home, also exhibit and the ancient Indian earthen figurines have signified in their ruined amphitheatre-cemetery (IDM 201-2). Though his wish could be read as a longing to put an order or an end to the chaotic changing world, it is his unconscious desire to control that deserves more scrutiny.

The destructive force of masculine desire is most powerfully illustrated in the woman's appearance only as a fragmented and mutilated object of desire.

The lost mother haunts the hero. In his dream, he remembers a childhood experience of hearing her "grunting like a tiger in the darkness" (IDM 30) and thinking she has turned into a beast. It expresses his "fear of the unknown" (ibid), namely of death and the female sexuality, in the form of Albertina as a black swan. Morris in *Shadow Dance* remembers hearing his mother's "hoarse breathing...like a wolf" (IDM 146), while Buzz's memory of his mother in *Love* has "given him many fears about the physicality of women" (L 94).

Desiderio's narrative produces the image of Albertina as a collage of pre-established roles of femininity. She is the gipsy girl, the prostitute, the cross-dresser. Albertina is caught between two different wills all along: she is both her father's puppet and the object of Desiderio's desire. In the first role she becomes a sacrificial victim. She prostitutes herself as the Count's valet LaFleur, brings Desiderio to the castle and dresses up as a prototype daughter in Victorian lace while serving dinner. In Desiderio's life she occupies a space already defined and framed for her. He has given her a name and shape in his dreams before he even sees her. She is a black swan, who is snakelike and emanates 'mindless evil' (30). Even when she is disguised as the Doctor's ambassador, Desiderio describes her movements as being of 'reptilian liquidity' so that she seemed to move in soft coils" (32). Albertina is defined as the *femme fatale*, animal-like and fatally seductive, a "luring siren" (id 33) who sings a "thrilling, erotic contralto" (ibid). Like the snake in the Garden of Eden, she intrudes on the Minister's city, disrupting the masculine space of power and introducing him to intense emotions so that he 'swayed as if he were about to faint' (IDM 39).

164

The desirable form in which Albertina first appears in his dream is both alluring and mysterious: a silent woman with ' quite transparent flesh' and ' a knot of flames like ribbons' flickering, signifying her passionate heart, while ' her skeleton was revealed quite clearly'. In this sign language, "this visible skeleton, this miraculous bouquet of bone, the formal elements of physicality" (IDM 26) represents the consuming passion a woman has harboured for her lover, waiting for him to pursue and possess her in their elemental sexual union. And the words that accompany the image are meant to urge his unconscious acceptance of this visual form as the materialized object of his desire: "Be amorous!' and 'Don't think! Look", for the desirous form is induced through the eye. The second image Desiderio receives of Albertina in his artificial dreams, artificial since they are invaded by Dr Hoffman's desire machines, is an extremely ugly but magnificent black swan, which has a multiplicity of meanings invested on its image. Its absolute black colour is "as intense as the negation of light", "the color of the extinction of consciousness", and it "flexed its neck like a snake about to strike"(IDM 30-1) before it began to sing, in a female erotic voice, a savage, wordless song. Its voice sounds so mournful that Desiderio knows it is singing its death for love, and this mysterious bird is Albertina, his prime object of desire.

The lover's role Desiderio involuntarily plays in his brief affair with Mary Ane 'the somnambulist' seems to confirm his claim of passivity: He lets others' desire dominate him and plays passively to their fantasies. But Mary Anne is the archetypal princess of passive suffering. In her, Carter combines two classic types of passive femininity, the sleeping beauty and the tragic Ofelia, to emphasize the destructiveness of the passive form of female desire. She has the combined role of living and suffering for love written on her being, as she has been waiting endlessly for the prince to redeem her. Carter gives a wry answer to her waiting in the peep-show: when the princess is awakened from her dream life by the prince's loving kiss, se begins a worse process, that of perishing in the suffocating embrace of her dream prince who becomes the medium of her death. Although in this romantic tragedy it seems that the heroine's desire has activated the love-script and that Desiderio simply falls into her fantasy world to play the prince, the fact that he cooperates indicates his culpability in taking up the role, making love to her 'perfectly aware she was asleep' (id 56). What is also brought to our attention is the destructive potential underlying the negative desire he proclaims for himself. If Ofelia dies of the cyclical love of her tragic hero Hamlet, then Desiderio's emotional numbness in making love to her, 'as cynical as a satyr' (id 57), contributes to Mary Anne's death by drowning no less than the innocent Hamlet to the death of Ofelia. The hero may appear passive in his compliance with other people's desire of him, but his male passivity is different from the feminine one that Mary Anne displays, culturally and psychologically. In his passive posture he does not lose his sexual subjectivity even though he may have lost his social or racial identity; socially anonymous, he still keeps his phallic power intact. His adventure with the Sadeian Count in the brothel 'the House of Anonymity' is indicative of the cultural narratives of sexuality that contribute to his position. In the brothel they are forced to put on a costume that masks their faces, erases their individual features, and highlights only their phallic member as the only source of meaning and power (id:129). He takes up the feminine passive stance to protest against the injustices he has suffered. But in his transgression does not to really give up his male-dominant position, for in his romantic dream of pursuing a mysterious princess, his quest of her implies a kind of sexual hunting. His knife is always there, and when the occasion arises he enacts this negative desire as if it were activated more by others' desire than his own.

My reading of the fantasy of 'Lost in Nebulous Time' tends to treat this fantastic world as mainly occasioned by Desiderio' s unconscious desire after he was given the form through the peep-show samples, specially those with a series of images ' showing a young woman trampled to death by a wild horses'. He is 'particularly struck' by these samples " because the actress bore some resemblance to Dr Hoffman's own daughter" (IDM 107). Although he himself suspects he might be the instigator of the horrible event of Albertina's being gang-raped by the centaurs (180), it never occurs to him that the predominant male desire in the centaurs' world might correspond to his own. His desire as the instigator of this fantasy is further obscured by Albertina's presumption of the role of her desire in activating the horror: "she was convinced that even though every male in the village had obtained carnal knowledge of her, the beasts were still only emanations of her own desires, dredged up and objectively reified from the dark abysses of the unconscious" (IDM 186). But as Hoffman's theory of desire suggests, all the subjects and objects in Nebulous Time "were derived from a similar source – my desires; or hers; or the Count's" (ibid). If Albertina's female desire has a masochistic tendency and corresponds to the general mood of female centaurs' self abnegation, she also has such a strong desire for power as to will the timely appearance of her father's aerial patrols to rescue her. The text itself does not dictate who is the instigator, as desire is mutually induced.

However, judging from the overall textual possibility of meaning, I find the centaurs' world of desire closer to Desiderio's. To argue along this line, I will examine the collective desires of the male centaurs   and compare them with Desiderio's while analyzing his gradual identification with their view of the world. On examining the narrative composition of Nebulous Time, the intertextual allusion to *Gulliver's Travels* is striking. Intense male desire is the central motif of the episode, as the horses embody aggressive brutality in their intense need to violate the female and achieve male assertion. The stamping horses stand for the initial stage of this desire, in a very different picture from that of Swift's Houyhnhnms. In the latter fantastic world, the horses, as we know, exhibit a moral nature far superior to human beings so that their human observer, Gulliver, cannot but admire them and feel ashamed of his humanity. Desiderio shares Gulliver's sense of misanthropy, but the cause of it is different., namely Desiderio's dissatisfaction with his and Albertina's body (IDM 190). The centaurs appear beautiful to him because he equals their sexual potency with the supreme source of power. The wild horses roaming the fields are seen as the embodiment of divine virility which constitutes the fundamental spirit of the centaurs' 'theology', the bi-partite horse-skeleton tree, a sacred live icon they flock to worship (IDM 171), appears to symbolize their intense but 'schizophrenic' desire. The skeleton image in Carter's fiction often represents the clutching intensity of desire which consumes the body to the bone. The 'terrible emaciation' of the Sadeian Count who "wore his dandyism in his very bones" (IDM 122) is an example in point, so the horse-skeleton of the Sacred Stallion, their Saviour, can be read as their consuming desire for virile assertion. The other tree-like element in their desire yearns to have the world frozen static by their virile theology, echoing Desiderio's yearning for a static order. The schizophrenic element does not just occur in their contradictory desire to have the aggressive masculine principle placed at the centre of their religion, it is also revealed in their regressive, sado-masochistic forms of sexuality.

Apart from Carter's sarcastic criticism of their doctrines as 'shit', they also express an ambivalent yearning for Mother. According to their religious myth, Mother betrayed her husband, the Sacred Stallion, by having an affair with 'the Dark Archer', giving birth to the sinful offspring, the centaur (id 185). It is easy to notice here the similarity between the centaurs' 'guilty' sense of being and Desiderio's sense of 'hybrid' existence.

Acting as nothing more than an observer of the centaurs' world, Desiderio reveals a desire too repressed to be recognized. Although he is unaware of his affinity with the centaurs' sadomasochistic sexuality, he is not unconscious of his fear of aggressive female desire and his approval of the centaurs' punishment of the females. The ritual gang-rape of Albertina reveals the double lack in the centaurs' desire, that is, to oppress the female desire, but to assume no erotic pleasure in the sexual ritual. Beside masochistic self-beating, they undertake another painful activity of self-infliction, tattooing the upper part of themselves, the human part, to match the equine image. As tattooing is used as a metaphor for the forceful imposition of cultural archetypes on individual identities in Carter's fiction, the centaurs' action shows how intense and distorted their libidinal desire has become in their attempt to reach the heroic image of sacred masculinity.

His fear of Albertina's desire is intertwined with his desire for a romantic script of love suicide in which the heroine's passion consumes her in self-destructive flames, just as the first image of Albertina in his dreams anticipates. The power of Albertina's desire is, nevertheless, greater than his, and she turns into a desiring Muse. When Albertina assumes ontological solidity as the Doctor's daughter, both the reader and Desiderio face the problem of interpreting her desire. The incident that fist poses it is Albetina's rape by the Centaurs. When Albertina is raped almost to death by the Centaurs she is convinced that the whole event is a result of her desire. Ricarda Schmidt draws attention to Desiderio who has just used *Gulliver's Travels* to teach the river people how to read and write (1989:59). The correlation between the Centaurs and the Houyhnhnms does not seem to be a coincidence. It implies that the rape scene emanates, on a subconscious level, from the way Desiderio's desire cites Swift and generates a misogynistic variation of his text. Desiderio is convinced that he is the instigator of the horrific event, while Albertina is sure that "the beasts were still only emanations of her own desires, dredged up and objectively reified from the dark abysses of the unconscious" (IDM 186). Furthermore, the timely appearance of the Doctor's helicopter saving them from the Centaurs silences Desiderio's objections to the omnipotence of Albertina's desires.

Every time Albertina steps outside her sexual role Desiderio's reaction is one of withdrawal and he ironically tolerates her intellectual capacity: "I did not mind her lecturing me because she was so beautiful" (id 167). He constantly redefines and evaluates her in accordance with sexual desirability, exercising his power to control her, even if he is sometimes unaware of how violent his passions are, and takes them as emanations from others.

She causes their escape by the power of her will, demolishing thus a fantasy world, whose desire Desiderio deeply identifies with. She breaks the romantic plot by reversing their roles in the desire-power game. Instead of the helpless young virgin waiting for his rescue in the Count's fantasy world, she appears more powerful now than Desiderio desires her to be. To his dismay, her formidable power of desire does not consume her to death but destroys instead his masculine fantasy, leaving him feeling "an inexplicable indifference toward her" (IDM 193). To his amazement he later finds her real title in the reality war, 'Generalissimo Hoffman' (192), a figure with tremendous power. What appears inexplicable to himself concerning his feeling toward Albertina is due to his incomprehension of his own desire. His desire is a displaced sexual game for a 'lack' in his male ego, a lack caused by forces seeking substitution in the subjugated female, in the name of love. Her various apparitions contribute to the preservation of her seductive force and her status of desired object. Yet the better Desiderio comes to know her as the living Albertina, the more her bewitching power diminishes. When she is placed within the control of the "reality principle", she loses her appeal and indestructibility: "I felt an inexplicable indifference towards her. Perhaps because she was now yet another she and this she was the absolute antithesis of my dark swan and my bouquet of burning bones" (IDM 193). As Albertina is raped by the barbarians, Desiderio reduces her to a mortal subjugated by men, nothing like his dream ideal, so his indifference is rooted in his own aversion towards her. Angela Carter satirizes the myth of the woman as a virginal ideal who loses her mystique as she steps off the pedestal.

"She wiped the silver from her eyes and the purple dress dropped from the goddess of the cornfields, more savagely and triumphantly beautiful than any imagining, my Platonic other, my necessary extinction, my dream made flesh." (IDM 215).

Albertina becomes the seductress executing her father's orders, when she initiates their sexual consummation. Desiderio no longer regards her as the lover who responds to the call of Eros. He is reluctant to enact his dream as if he knew the Doctor would win.

This can be corroborated in his final confrontation with Albertina. As she, having her father's blessing, offers him the tableau-like pose of lovers' perpetual copulation with her, he refuses to enter it, for Albertina occupies the more powerful position in their relationship. She is the 'Generalissimo', and he is the manipulated puppet in her and her father's game. Another reason is of course her inadvertently showing her close ties with her father than with him. The social deprivation he suffers from his socio-ethnic background sensitizes him to various forms of domination, and the superior socio-economic status of Dr Hoffman and Albertina arouses in him a hostile response after reaching their citadel. The main point I am making is that, if he suffers social discrimination without resistance, since his response is sneer and detachment, he refuses to accept a submissive position in the sexual relationship. Where he suffers from his social 'disinheritance' here he unconsciously wishes to the consoled in his sexual relationship-he will not be disinherited of the dominant sexual role that men have inherited from their long historical traditions. If Albertina's images in his dreams offer his desire on objectified form, this form of desire is not neutral or equal in its power relationship. Its implication of domination and submission in the erotic relationship is not so different from the one displayed in the peep-show proprietor's huge stock of sample desire, though the latter is presented in a more savage way. It is the juxtaposing of the erotic with death, the emphasis of the female as the luring object, and the malicious potential associated with female sexuality projected by the male fear that underlie Desiderio's attraction to the swan-woman. While the two images delineate the form for Desiderio's unformed desire, they also presage the domination struggle that is bound to occur between the lovers. Desiderio kills Albetina to get rid of his desire, the part of himself that he finds difficult to cope with. His indifference is a shield meant to help him to avoid his fear of women.

The power struggle between lovers also appears in E.T.A. Hoffmann's tales, though in very different terms. In *The Golden Pot* the young man Anselmus is first attracted to Serpentina, who assumes the form of a gold-green little snake with 'a pair of blue eyes looking down at him with unspeakable desire', and he feels an instantaneous passion for this mysterious creature, a desire like 'electricity' (1972:18) racing through his body. But the struggle between him and his desired Serpentina is less a struggle for power as analyzed in feminist terms than a Romantic struggle within his psyche between reason (as represented by the rational-minded girl Veronica who tries to win him back) and poetic passion which, seen from the practical rational perspective, dwells on the irrational and verges on the insane. The felicity Anselmus finally achieves by his faith in Serpentina and her magician father confirms the transcendent triumph of poetic passion over the mundane vision of every day life, with Serpentina as the symbolic prize for Anselmus's achievement of the poetic vision of the world.

In contrast, in Carter's text Desiderio's struggle between reason and desire is not just an antithetical struggle between two opposed perspectives; it is more that the clear boundary between reason and desire becomes blurred, erased. The passionate rendering, or 'liberation', of the phenomenal world by Dr Hoffman's poetic vision brings no real liberation of the human 'spirit'; it rather reveals its conditionality by the ready-made cultural forms of desire, or its

170

vulnerability to manipulation by Dr Hoffman's desire machines. In what should be the consummation of his desire in his perpetual sexual ecstasy with Albertina in the 'love pen', Desiderio find the utilitarian, conditional side of the desirous form he has been given and his functional role set by Hoffman and Albertina. Antagonized, he strikes hard to destroy the form in which his passion has been framed. Only in Albertina's death can re-create her in his heart's desire, even if his motive is later justified in the 'history book' as for the common good of humanity.

After the earthquake episode in the chapter 'The Acrobats of Desire' - Desiderio admits he "played through one set of theme and variations upon the subject of an earthquake through the [peep-show] machine"(IDM 107), but he refuses to think that "[he] had anything to do with the landslide" (IDM 118) that later occurs and kills the acrobats who have raped him. – and his encounter with the fantasy world of Nebulous Time are two further examples. In the earthquake episode he has precipitated the disaster with his unconscious will. In Nebulous Time the misogynist, sado-masochistic male world of the centaurs is far more akin to his unconscious than to Albertina's phantasy. Nevertheless, in his recollections he denies any 'wilful' part he might have played in both cases, and perhaps he is right in the sense that he did not consciously want them to happen; he is too rationalistic to understand his own desire.

In Desiderio's negative form of desire what is repressed is the recognition of the interpenetration and interchangeability between desire and reason in his supposedly rationalistic vision of the world; he sees no desire of his own manipulating his representation. He acknowledges the power of desire which could bend the world, but the overlapping of reason and desire escapes him. This cerebral desire figures in Carter's analysis of the intermingling of reason and desire, questioning Desiderio's account of a rational world order threatened by the chaotic forces of desire. He is a despised member of the oppressed, marginalized group in his society, so he seeks to address the world in rational terms, without noticing that his discourse has already been subverted by his desire, which is unresolved.

Catherine Belsey lays emphasis on tracing "the constraints and resistances of desire in their historical discontinuity" (1994:8-9) in her study of desire. Desire is no longer treated as a metaphysical category universal and unchanging in the human psyche, but rather as an experience subject to the changes of social conditions. The key concept in her discussion of desire as a psychosexual drive is derived from Lacan's theory, who regards desire as a structural lack caused by the lost object but refusing to be satisfied by the signifier. She

171

highlights the differential elements of desire in her analysis. In its cultural representation, desire is represented through substitutes but left unsaid because its full presence is always delayed by its sliding, citational mode of speech (1994:16). What I found relevant to Carter's fictional study of desire is that in the writer's text, the deferring aspect of desire accounts for a major part of the driving force that urges the characters to go on their pursuit of the desired satisfaction which can never be fully achieved. According to Belsey, "desire is what is not said, what cannot be said…What is not able to be said is what presses to be given form" (1994:76). The form is where desire can be induced, manipulated and distorted to a different direction, where will to power and sexual domination reside and are invoked.

However, Carter's analysis of desire differs from the poststructuralist discourse in an important aspect. She pays special attention to the effect of sexual politics on the formation of the erotic desire. As desire is elusive and metonymic in delineating itself and has to be formed with an object, it often happens that the form takes over the desiring force, with the patterns of male domination presiding over the circulated images of sexual relationships. On the one hand, the importance of forming an object for desire cannot be more emphatically expressed than in the instructions the peep-show master gives the hero – "To express a desire authentically is to satisfy it categorically" and therefore 'Objectify you desires!' (IDM 110). On the other hand, the implied patterns of sexual domination embedded in the Doctor's sample sets of desire give definite forms to the male desire in its predatory relationship with its female object. To the female are attributed images as prize objects to be hunted or pursued as the final reward for the male quest, while the male is represented as a huge phallus key (IDM 46) whose virility provides the ordering power to the chaotic world. The male is urged to enhance his desire for power while the female is encouraged to cultivate a self-destructive desire to die for love. The point where the libido is repressed makes room for desire to appear, but in its search for gratification, the object cannot be really found except in a series of substitutes. In Carter's fiction the substitutes, the sample sets of desire, come to replace the authentic desire as desire artificial enough can become authentic itself.

The practice of using the female body to reassert the male ego is not restricted to Desiderio; the Sadeian Count, Dr Hoffman and Nao-Kurai (the archetypal figure of the Indian river people) resort to the same practice with less subtlety. In fighting the desire-generated spectacles, the Minister, as the epitome of rationality, believes the chaotic world can be represented in a perfect system of relation object-concept, free of the taint of collective or personal desires. There is however an intense desire behind all his rational thinking. His 'Faustian' (28) desire, as Desiderio observes, is to fit the world into his conceptual pattern. The Count's or Hoffman's drives appear little different, since they all try to assert their supreme male ego by subjugating the world to their desired version, either by rational determination, sexual transgression, or by releasing people's unconscious.

Ironically, Dr Hoffman, the rational irrationalist, is the figure who possesses and applies the 'secret' knowledge of desire that the irrational theoretician Mendoza (a real passionate figure burnt to death by 'fire') has 'discovered'. It is ironical also because he is the figure who conveys a message Carter highlights in several works: the synthetic and cerebral quality of human desire and fantasy possessing the same status a reality. He explains the ideas to Desiderio: "once desire is endowed with synthetic form, it follows inevitably that thought and object operate on the same level" (IDM 208). But most important of all, he is characterized as a 'magician' with tremendous power who instils the scripts of desire into the yearnings of his manipulated heroes and heroines. He is in fact the embodiment of the invisible patriarchal power that comes to release the world from its old repressions. In the name of liberating desire he produces multiple worlds apparently unrepressed, actually still controlled by his own desire: ". .. Doctor Hoffman appeared to me to be proliferating his weaponry of images along the obscure and controversial borderline between the thinkable and the unthinkable" (IDM 22).

But what is the magician's desire? As Desiderio paradoxically comments on this riddle-like figure, he thinks Dr Hoffman "only wanted power" (IDM 209), yet "he seemed to me a man without desires" (IDM 211). Power to manipulate people like puppets and observe them as in a laboratory is indeed what the magician desires, but the greatest source of power, as the fiction ironically indicates through the magician's mouth, is 'eroto-energy' which is capable of producing the greatest fantasy, able to replace whatever the 'real' world may be. Erotic desire may appear as the prime force of the human psyche, but a deeper power structure can be found being inscribed in the desire itself. It is the male desire, as socially constructed, for domination in the sexual relationship that runs through the erotic drive. Dr Hoffmann exemplifies this desire in a most controlled, matter-of-fact way as he treats his beloved dead wife as if she were still alive, though she is an embalmed corpse placed sitting in the parlour like a doll (IDM 198-199). Being dead, she can be whatever he desires her to be, paralleling Desiderio's later treatment of Albertina in his memory. In the full power of the Dr's desire, his fantasy of his wife still being alive becomes as real as it can be fantasized. His cold, controlled erotic desire reveals the same cerebral quality the Sadeian Count shares, only that the latter exhibits it compulsively as a way of the negating the world and asserting his unique male identity. A similar desire can be detected in the erotic exhibits that Desiderio is exposed to when he peeps into the peep-show machines. The erotic scripts he sees provide for his repressed libido a sexual form to react to the lack he has unconsciously experienced both socially and psychologically. The Doctor's appearance stands in contrast to his appalling mind:

> "He was grey-faced, grey-haired and grey-eyed. He wore a handsomely tailored suit and his hands were exquisitely manicured…He was so quiet, so grey, so calm and he had just said something entirely meaningless in a voice of perfect, restrained reason" (IDM 188-9).

The Doctor believes that the liberation of human sexuality would generate enough eroto-energy to annihilate the credibility of reality. Without rationality, civilization would disintegrate. He is also an artist of surrealism, as the reality-modifying machines he operates loosen the rigidity of images.

The consummate image of the desire for realism in the text is the Minister of Determination, whose desire is to determine representation as presence and identity as fixed:

> 'he called his [his philosophy] theory of 'names and functions'. …
>
> "He believed that the city – which he took as a microcosm of the universe – contained a finite set of objects and a finite set of their combinations and therefore a list could be made of all possible distinct forms which were logically viable. These could be counted, organized into a conceptual framework and so form a kind of check list for the verification of all phenomena, instantly available by means of an information retrieval system" (IDM 23-4)

The Minister and Hoffman share the same drive for power and control and the same techniques illustrates that the way they see Desiderio relies on their position, their ideological vision. Representation is to both of them the supreme power, neither denies its force, and both seek to control it. This 'complex and paradoxical interpenetration' (McHale, 1987:144) goes beyond any identification of specific traits that should pertain to one or to the other. The struggle "depends on persistence of vision" (id:114): belief or disbelief.

Desiderio notices that the Minister "had never in all his life felt the slightest quiver of empirical uncertainty. He was the hardest thing that ever existed and never the flicker of a mirage distorted for so much as a fleeting second the austere and intransigent objectivity of his face"

(IDM 116).

The inability to accept mortality is related to the negation of difference. The Count in *The Infernal Desire Machines of Doctor Hoffman* embarks on a journey which is nothing but a desperate flight from death. He runs away from the embodiment of his death drive that simultaneously attracts and repels him: "That man – if man he be – is my retribution… Hold me or I will run into his arms" (IDM 139). Feeling chased by Thanatos, he suppresses his anxiety in an ecstatic celebration of destruction that will eventually become self- destruction.

Sadism is connected with a feeling of impotence and loneliness in Carter's fiction. The sadistic executioner in the story 'The Executioner's Beautiful Daughter' is "locked in the solitary confinements of his power" (1996:40), the 'atrocious loneliness' of the sadistic Marquis in 'The Bloody Chamber' resembles the brutality of Master in 'Master'. Experience does not change these tyrants because they cannot relate to the other as a subject, only as other, as victim. At the same time, Walser and Evelyn undergo a change through suffering.

Buggery is sometimes present, over a cup of coffee – Walser suffers "a sharp dose of buggery in a Bedouin tent beside the Damascus road" (IDM 10), Eve is humiliated by Zero, who also relishes in depriving his wives of their breakfast in *The Passion of New Eve,* Desiderio is raped by the nine deconstructing acrobats of desire before drinking Turkish coffee. The Count represents an exaggerated version of Uncle Phillip. While the former desires love, the latter longs for obliteration and surrenders to Thanatos, seeking union with himself, namely with his shadow. The cannibal chief voices his desire is gustatory terms: "I wish to see if I can suffer, like any other man,. And then I want to learn the savour of my flesh. I wish to taste myself" (IDM 162). The Count's triumph comes as he begins to boil in the cannibals' soup and learns at the moment of death what ordinary pain is. This is the moment that prompts Desiderio to act and save himself and Lafleur, rejecting annihilation in pursuit of his illusive goal of erotic completion that will prove unsatisfactory. The Count is a slave of his desires, no more than a parodic emblem of his type. In contrast to his desire to be unique, he is a stereotypical villain whose nature is revealed in his costume: "I saw his curiously pointed teeth…exactly the fangs with which tradition credits vampires" (IDM 123)

Andrzej Gasiorek proposes a different reading of the novel and sees the Minister as ' a kind of Philosopher-King' who runs the city on 'rational principles', and "the subsequent conflict between Hoffman [as poet] and the Minister, representatives of unfettered desire and disengaged thought respectively, replays the Platonic conflict between the appetitive and the

175

rational parts of the soul" (1995:128). In my opinion there is neither a pure rational mind nor a poetic passion in the novel. I read a highly conceptualized desire – Hoffman's or the Count's- or a rationality wielded by a metonymic desire- Desiderio's or the Minister's. The interchangeability between the seemingly opposed cerebral desire and desired rationality recurs in Carter's fiction. Hoffman, the main figure of desire, exhibits a desire so cerebral for controlled chaos that it overlaps the Minister's longing for controlled order.

On the spectrum of cerebral desires the Count and the Indian river people seem to stand on polarized positions which cannot be farther apart. The Count is a diabolic figure who uses various forms of sexual transgression on the female body to assert his ego and negate the otherness of the world. In contrast, the river people live in a primitive time-frozen community where there is only collective identity, so that personal desire is almost inconceivable. The Count's masculine ego is so strong and his desires so overwhelming, that his fantasies become the 'reality' of other people. The river people's strictly archetypal way of being appears no more real than his as they are confined in their collective fantasies of water-bird existence (id 88). The Count has to negate the world to prove the existence of his supreme self, the river people have to ignore the historical element of existence to secure their collective being, but both maintain their ego myths. That narrative of the Count is as highly pastiched as the other parts of the novel, but the allusions to the Sadeian texts provide a fruitful ground for generating contrastive meaning. The Count is characterized as a Sadeian figure who is, in the words of Albertina, who disguises herself as his valet Lafleur on his erotic journey, "the most metaphysical of libertines. If he had passions, they were as lucid and intellectual as those of a geometrician. He approached the flesh in the manner of one about to give the proof of a theorem" (IDM 167). But in his Sadeian compulsion to use transgressive sex to transcend all the laws that restrain his self, there looms a caricatured desire in his psyche. His desire is that of a Nietzschean superman whose highest manhood is achieved by his willpower to create the world in his image, and, by using his phallic 'pen' on the female body in every conceivable way of ecstasy, he is writing his being on the world that serves him. However, as a connoisseur of desires, Albertina detects a subtle discrepancy in the Count's erotic desires: "his fatal error was to mistake his will for his desire....and so he willed his desires" (IDM 168). While Albertina's comment seems to suggest there is a genuine erotic desire beyond cerebral control, what is ironic in her remark is that her desires are so tightly controlled. She resists Desiderio's sexual desire until the right moment, so that desire and will are no longer distinguishable in her psyche. However, the tiny crack in the Count's willed desires is enough to produce a split self, an ego excited by a watching shadow of himself, the black pimp African chief, set to pursue the object of its masculine desire. This figure embodies the monstrous masculine, the shadowy otherness that turns back on himself, whose ultimate temptation is to hunt himself.

In his all-devouring masculinity the Count/African chief also makes a monstrosity of femininity. As the Count he used to treat women as beasts for the hunter in his erotic journey whereas his double "castrated" (160) the female body to have them respond to cruelty and abuse. This practice seems an opposite way to the River people's effort of elongating the female organ, which seems to masculinize it. Carter's presentation of this primitive practice is pastiched with a mythological representation of female desire with the snake and the doll-motif in E.T.A. Hoffmann's *The Sandman*. In the river people's legend, the elongated clitoris is associated with a myth in which a snake climbs into a girl's body and teaches her the secret of fire which signifies the power of life. The girl's father and brothers, unable to acquire the vital knowledge, kill the girl and eat the snake to take hold of the power. In their customs all the women have their faces painted and look like an automaton in their limited body movement (id 73). On the eve of his wedding, Desiderio finds that there is a knife hidden in the doll of his girl-bride Aoi, and he infers that he will be killed for her folk to eat his meat and obtain his power of writing. While his suspicion may be a valid one, it also reflects a deep fear in him of the aggressiveness of the female sex, which threatens to castrate him. But the river people's custom is not meant to give the females the power he fears, it is exercised in order to homogenize their difference and thus reduce the threat of their power of giving life. Eating the meat is a metaphorical, psychological act of homogenizing the alien. The doll-like element invokes in him a fear of their potential wickedness which may turn out to be either a terrible desire to engulf him or a lifeless female automaton, behind whom a malicious power manipulates her to lure the innocent man. The same fear applies in Albertina's case. Eventually she turns out to be not only a doll-like figure 'programmed' (216) by her father, but also a doll with a knife. When presented with the fulfilment of his desire, the long postponed consummation with Albertina, Desiderio hesitates, because the price is death. Albertina is exchanged for the possibility of becoming the subject of his own narrative. "If narrative is governed by an Oedipal logic, it is because it is situated within the system of exchange instituted by the incest prohibition, where woman functions as both a sign and a value for that exchange" (de Lauretis,1984:140). But the fulfilment of Desiderio's life as narrative leaves him with a sense of disappointment, the text lets him down: "all I know is, I could not transcend myself sufficiently to inherit the universe...When I close my eyes I see her still" (IDM 197). Albertina remains only the object of his unconsummated desire, and Desiderio will end his days in absolute frustration: "there was once a young man named Desiderio who set out upon a journey and very soon lost himself completely. When he thought he had reached his destination, it turned out to be only the beginning of another journey infinitely more hazardous than the first." (IDM 166). He had expected a heroic journey and he laments to the reader: "if you feel a certain sense of anti-climax, how do you think I felt?" (IDM 218). His own narrative traps him in a "coffin" (IDM 221).

The force of Thanatos seems to take over the end of the hero's life. Albertina's death triggers the writing process, Desiderio's ends it: "What a fat book to coffin young Desiderio, who was so thin and supple" (IDM 221). In psychoanalytic terms, melancholia is a metaphorical form of cannibalism. Freud describes melancholia as an aberrant form of mourning which refuses to break attachment to the lost object. This happens to Desiderio. He mourns the loss of Albertina and gives in to depression. She lives on in him and condemns him to live in a "drab, colourless world" (IDM 14), unable to stop thinking of her.

The ending of the novel reinforces the motif of "desire as narrative thematic, desire as native motor, and desire as the very intention of narrative language and the act of telling all seem to stand in close interrelation" (Brooks, 1984:54).

The term desire appears in the title of the novel, evoking the desire to narrate life as meaning. It is "the very motive of narrative", writes Brooks (1984:47), and "once there is text, expression, writing, one becomes subject to the processes of desiring and dying" (1984:53). Desiderio represents a 'desiring machine', as Brooks describes it, he is a

> "representation of the dynamics of the narrative text, connecting beginning and end across the middle and making of that middle – what we read through – a field of force...If the motor of narrative is desire..., the ultimate determinants of meaning lie at the end, and narrative desire is ultimately, inexorably, desire for the end." (Brooks, 1984: 52)

Is Albertina another projection of Desiderio's unconscious desires? Is she raised from the dead only to die again with the final punctuation mark?

Despite his only desire to see Albertina again, Desiderio writes, "I myself had only the one desire. And that was, for everything to stop" (IDM 11). For Desiderio, the desire to narrate life as meaning is countered by his experience of memory:

"and sometimes, when I think of my journey, not only does everything seem to have happened all at once, in some kind of fugue of experience, just as Albertina's father would have devised it, but everything in my life seems to have been of equal value, so that the rose which shook off its petals as if shuddering in ecstasy to hear her voice throws as long a shadow of significance as the extraordinary words she uttered." (IDM 13)

The simultaneous existence of two opposite, even mutually exclusive experiences of history in narrative can best be explained by the insight that history is a product of our desire. Desiderio could tell his story differently. Robinson (1991:116) states that Angela Carter

"systematically disrupts the pleasure of the text by foregrounding the enunciative apparatus behind its inscriptions of desire. If the pleasure of the text is dependent on identification with Desiderio who, after all, has been produced as a 'war hero' by History, that pleasure is continuously disrupted by Angela Carter's insistence on what the official history leaves unspoken: the complicities between desire and domination."

***

Carter's writing is a palimpsest of meanings and each interpretation gives way to another. I have illustrated the way Angela Carter incorporated different literary styles into her work and deconstructed them, to make room for endless interpretations.

Cornel Bonca notes that Angela Carter used

"primitive kinds of narrative space (fairy tale, pornography)...She taps in their basic structural and mythological power as a way of roiling the waters of the unconscious, then proceeds, by means of hyperbole, irony, structural reversals, and the layered development of character, to give those obvious stories thematic complexity and density" (1994:56).

The heroines of her works have gothic features; they are wild, lawless, eccentric, and, most of all different from the conventional mother, daughter, woman. She distanced her female protagonists from tradition by endowing them with an atypical heroism. The result, of course, is the subversion of male heroism, and the challenge to the myth of female passivity.

The recovery of the lost origin will return women to Kristeva's *chora*, "no more than the place where the subject is both generated and negated, the place where his unity succumbs before the process of charges and stases that produce him" (NC 28). Angela Carter's writing is a site of continuous construction and deconstruction, since the production of feminine images involves both the confirmation and negation of woman as subject and object.

Gothic fiction is characterized by an ambivalence of fear and desire, whose terror and horror, as Fred Botting points out (1996:170), "have depended on things not being what they seem." In postmodern times this Gothic metaphysical uncertainty takes a further unsettling turn; Gothic horror, according to Botting, has become the anxiety that "things are not only not what they seem: what they seem is what they are, not a unity of word or image and thing, but words and images without things or as things themselves, effects of narrative form and nothing else" (1996:171). Carter's fiction deals with this kind of horror, as exposes the consequences of power relations by exploiting Gothic devices.

In the section Duplicitous Dolls I pointed out that love poetry is criticised for its fetishising of woman, who may be viewed as a pearl ('The Tiger's Bride'), a flower ('The Lady of the House of Love'), or a bird ('The Erl-King') which is kept in a cage for her song. But the woman is actually a wonderful artefact, a Hoffmann-like puppet, like Lady Purple, "a great, ingenious piece of clockwork" like the heroine of 'The Lady of the House of Love' (1996:102), or "a marvellous machine, the most delicately balanced system of cords and pulleys in the world" as the heroine's maid in 'The Tiger's Bride' (1996:60), a machine eventually made of words, of poetic images.

The heroine of 'The Lady of the House of Love' is doomed because she cannot help being her father's daughter, Nosferatu's daughter, and feeds on the blood of young men lured to her mansion. As such, she is no more than a signifier in the male fetishist's signifying chain. To deconstruct the myth of the fearful power that has been imputed to the female vampire, she haunts because she is haunted. When the young man appears, she falls in love with him as if on cue. Although what follows may seem to celebrate the liberating power of love, the ironic note of its predatory power and the scripted nature of love are never lost. Thus, in the Countess' inner monologues of mourning the young man's imminent death for love we become aware of a satirical note of a ventriloquist speaking in her inner voice even at her most intense moment of love. Her love is death—either the death of herself or her lover. As Carter repeatedly implies, she is the stuff that gothic tales are made of: "a ventriloquist's doll" (1996:102), or better still "a cave full of echoes, [...] a system of repetitions, [...] a closed circuit" (1996:93), forever repeating the same text in "the timeless Gothic eternity of the vampires" (1996:97).

Carter uses the Gothic motifs of physical violence, terror and sadism, victimization of women and stretches them to the point of parody in order to emphasize the absurdity of a

180

gender-biased social structure. Parody is a major feature of Gothic writing; thus her parody of the Gothic is a double play, a postmodern mimicking of Gothic horror which is itself theatrical. The puppet women are a dramatization of the object status of the woman. I have showed that access to subjectivity is granted after cutting loose from the strings of the Other.

A crude representation of the woman's body under male control is offered by the status of Lady Purple, kept under rein by the old Professor. Lady Purple's metamorphosis from woman to puppet to woman may serve as an allegory of characterisation: at one end of the process, characterisation is always dependent on some intimation of real life, but creates a lifeless, abstract, linguistic structure that must be animated. A parallel can also be drawn between the author and the puppeteer who turns his creature into "a monstrous goddess" (1996:96) whose actions are "a distillation and intensification of those of a born woman" (1996:97).

Carter's descriptions of Desiderio's adventures expose a point of view from which we are normally, necessarily, alienated: that of unrepressed desire. In this way, Carter reveals sexuality's roots as a brutal process of Other-ing, of the construction of the feminine as the construction of a grotesque, alien figure. The Women who populate the landscape of Dr. Hoffman's desire-scape are represented as aliens, and Desiderio becomes our guide throughout the phantasmagorical change of a familiar world into a herterotopian territory.

"The interplay between sex and love, freedom and bondage, prey and predation" (Sage, 1994:133) has found a perfect illustration not only in Angela Carter's novels, but in her short fiction writings as well, an issue I have addressed in the section Innocent Predators. Transgression under different aspects is voicing the writer's concern with power relations and the interrogation of the subject's right to exist as whole without the need of a hierarchy.

Postmodernist literature exhibits an awareness of the instability of language, and disillusionment with the grand narratives of religion, science, art, modernism, Marxism and history, all of which make totalizing claims to knowledge and truth. This dissent with the metanarrative of history has led to a loss of a sense of history as a clear sequence of events, and a view of identity as fluid and shifting. In postmodernist literature this is reflected in a disruption of linear narrative, and the presentation of unstable characters that are in a state of flux, merging with or becoming other characters. Her gender performers are not only enthralled with their freedom to create themselves anew, but also haunted by it.

This is illustrated by the game of switching from 'he/she' to 'you/me' in 'The Erl King'. The narrator vacillates between speaking of herself in the third person and owning her story in the first, speaking of the Erl-King in the third person and apostrophizing him in the second, rhetorically involving the reader and self-absorption, present and future tenses. The Erl-King stands between nature and culture, plant and animal, the semiotic and the symbolic.

This uncertainty admits the hope that the thetic border between human and animal can be, in spite of our lust for power and certainty, a flexible, creative space and it allows for the possibility that human beings can somehow temper the existential loneliness of our self-appointed place on top.

The play of appetites is a constant in Carter's complicated representations of power and desire and the challenging of the status quo, as concluded in the section Cannibals.

Eating as a manifestation of vampirism and fairy-tales are closely connected in Angela Carter's work through the symbol of the mouth as organ of both eating and speaking. We should only think of the transmission of fairy-tales at an oral level and of orality as a characteristic of both her novels and short stories. It seems that she places us in the position of a victim while she becomes a 'vampire', literarily speaking. Her intention was to "extract the latent content from traditional stories" (1985:80).

The intertextual characteristics of postmodernism may be regarded as cannibalistic, for postmodern writing devours selected texts and ideas of the past to both assimilate their strength and knowledge, and to digest them critically. Cannibalism as a metaphor includes the paradox of postmodern intertextuality since the pieces chosen are considered valuable enough to consume while the act of devouring them constitutes a violation.

An overwhelming human yearning for oneness is apparent in oral appetites, sexual desire, physical hunger, 'back to the womb' impulses. Eros, the libidinal drive, empowers the mother-substitutes (Aunt Margaret in *The Magic Toyshop*, Uncle Perry in *Wise Children*) and the life-enhancing eaters such as Fevvers in *Nights at the Circus*. Social eating is invested with positive meaning as an image of solidarity, leading women to autonomy in *Wise* Children and *Nights at the Circus*. Erotic appetite almost irresistibly demands completion. But the connection of food and sex assumes an insatiable and sometimes malignant eroticism, so that the predatory quality and the unappeasable nature of appetite suggest not Eros but something deadly. The longing for consummation by negation is manifest in motifs and figures of cannibalism and vampirism in *The Infernal Desire Machines of Doctor Hoffman*. The monstrous appetites of these figures suggest an inner emptiness, fantasies of omnipotence, or a yearning for wholeness impossible to fulfil. In the presentation of Eros as a struggle for power,

182

mixing passion and violence, the woman is associated with meat for men's consumption in *The Bloody Chamber* stories.

The fourth section of my analysis, Desired Others, examines the way male desires have constructed a reality of the world in which female desires are conditioned as if they were automata, animated by an invisible puppet-master. I have analyzed *The Infernal Desire Machines of Doctor Hoffman* as a text of recollections pieced together by Desiderio, a narrator struggling to interpret the past as he intensely desired and to report his adventures filtered through his rational mind. He will discover, in 'nebulous time,' that reality and unreality match his expectations and that the different cultures he gets into contact with hold different versions of reality. As female desire is feared as a potential threat to disrupt the rational order of paternalistic society, it has to be limited through social or religious degradation as well as sadism towards women. I have focused on Carter's feminist strategy of using parody, collage and fantasy to tell a picaresque satirical story of how, in various possible worlds, male desires are manifested in diverse forms to represent the truth.

In postmodern discourse 'seeing is disbelieving'. Whereas "modern aesthetics claimed that vision was superior to the other senses because of its detachment from its objects," (Owens: 1983:70), a belief postmodern works upset. For Desiderio as reader, nothing he sees is believable. Desiderio is both the writer of the narrative and the reader of his own past, of an autobiography composed of different versions of reality. The image of the woman, in the disturbed mind of the melancholic character, combines beauty and horror, femininity and death. Albertina, a doll wearing different guises, takes feminine fluidity to the extremes, culminating with the final words of the novel: "Unbidden she comes" (IDM 221).

Brooks writes "But in the manner of so many fairy tales, the realization of desire comes in sinister forms, destructive of the self" (1984:50). The heterotopic relation between Desire and Reason turns out to be in fact a patriarchal struggle for power which involves us entirely. We are irremediably locked into a position of voyeurism through our consent and complicity with the narrator. Our truth resides only in perspective, as Desiderio observes when he maintains that the beliefs one upholds at a certain point are invalid at another time.

In their quest for the self, all the characters meet the Other, and the desire for oneness need not be either regressive or negative, but fuel the passage to enlightenment. Male characters need to be reborn in a feminine space outside patriarchal time and learn to speak the language of equality. Women are free and whole as long as they give free vent to their instinct, after they have found their voice to fill the universe with their laughter as a liberating manifestation, as evoked by the writer (1985:82) herself in the last *Omnibus* interview: "the inextinguishable, the unappeasable nature of the world, of appetite, of desire…".

4. HETEROTOPIA - DYNAMICS OF PERFORMANCE

Real and fictional worlds come together in every aspect of the theatre, from the overlapping of the actor's appearance with the character s/he plays, to the magical transition from an empty set to the fictional place. The resulting chronotope is the heterotopic world of performance. Theatre, where alternating places form the essence of the stage as a space, is an example of heterotopia (Foucault, 1986), as the manifestations of fictional space in the real one transpose us to the fictional world, and the traditional flow of time is disrupted.

The Passion of New Eve (1967) and *Wise Children* (1991) are under scrutiny in this chapter, as illustrative of various aspects of performance, employed to different ends. Acting becomes a socially transgressive practice (Rose, 1993) that shapes a heterotopia of losing and regaining the self in 4.1. Scenes of Dissemblance, as I will interpret *scenes* as meaning both 'displays' and 'sites' (Thesaurus, 1993) of masquerade. Alchemical figures populate the liminal zones of the former novel, and the bloody stitches of gender performance are exposed as chief ingredients in the now grotesque, now magical act of undermining patriarchal myths in 4.2. Twists of Passion, for I see the term *passion* as an alloy of agony, wrath and ardour.

I will explore the ludic (Shields, 1991) narrative in the latter novel in 4.3. Songs and Dances, as I perceive the novel both as 'a theatrical performance that combines singing and dancing' and 'an elaborate story or explanation intended to deceive or mislead' (Thesaurus, 1993). I will also look for the zone that gives the Chance sisters an empowering force, beyond personal and professional marginality.

Surrealist theatre functions as an experimental in-between space, between consciousness and the unconscious. Antonin Artaud and André Breton saw alchemy as a metaphor for this kind of theatre. Alchemy is appropriate because it combines the material with the spiritual. Gloria Orenstein (1975:25) writes of a new female alchemy whose key figure is the androgyne, a prominent subversive figure in Carter's works. It defies categories and represents a stage one passes through, to the unknown, in terms of gender identity and spirituality. Surrealism includes the revision of time and space, conceiving the two dimensions as part of a continuum. There is no future time, but a present reality that needs to be uncovered.

In an interview for the BBC Omnibus documentary, *Angela Carter's Curious Room,* Lorna Sage observes:

"She took apart the pictures we have of ourselves – blow-ups of ourselves, representations of ourselves, shadows of ourselves through the media, through film and of course through books – a much older medium. But a lot of time our art ignores this fact, but she took it on her and her books introduce people, if you like, to their images, introduce people to their shadows, introduce them to their other selves." (Evans and Carter, 1992: 11)

In her essay 'The Alchemy of the Word' (*ED* 67-73), Carter also expresses her admiration for Surrealism, accepting its celebration of wonder as a means of perception and re-creation of human beings but rejecting its view of woman as the source of mystery and otherness. She takes up the Surrealist struggle changing its terms. Unlike the male Surrealists, whose work is grounded in Freudian psychoanalysis, Carter uses transvestism and transsexuality to undermine psychoanalysis as a model for development. Lacanian psychoanalysis has been useful in developing the idea of the other, which it sees as inherent in the self, so the unconscious "as the discourse of the Other" (Jardine, 1985:106) becomes a space of exploration.

Surrealism, according to Whitney Chadwick (1985:236), aimed at subverting the values associated with the patriarchal and capitalist social organization. The Surrealist revolution:

"sought to liberate the individual from the tyranny of rational thought, economic slavery, and the coercive control exercised by the institutions of family, church and state. The means to this end was through the reintegration of those human values long suppressed by Western civilization: personal freedom and autonomy, intuition, emotion, and the irrational."(1985:220)

Despite their desire for personal liberation, Breton and the other Surrealists' commitment to a spiritual and poetic movement did not give way to a radical revision of contemporary gender values. Rather,

"the art of male Surrealists was shaped by their acceptance of a Freudian unconscious and by their search for the means of effecting the link between the contents of the dream and the unconscious and an exterior reality. The link was often a woman, whose convulsive beauty was sufficiently compelling and disturbing to break through the conscious mind's restrictive control and onto whose image could be projected the secret and often forbidden desires and obsessions lodged in the unconscious." (1985: 186)

In spite of the dichotomy some critics have set up between myth and history, for Carter, being and history are infused with magic. Lorna Sage (1994:3) asserts that Carter "had always taken the line that fantasy was not the shadow side of a binary opposition, but had a real life history. Being was marinated in magic, and imaginary monsters had no separate sphere."

Neither does Elaine Jordan (1990:29) see magic and the material as antithetical, maintaining that her "stories do not replace the realistic experience with literary fantasy, but offer other scenes, other imaginations of what could be made real".

4.1. SCENES OF DISSEMBLANCE

The theatre is used as a mimetic device that undermines patriarchal psychoanalysis through imitation and gender performance. In *The Passion of New Eve*, Carter intertwines the theatrical and the spiritual, using performance to destabilize gender roles and shape a new conception of the self. Theatre becomes a space for self-transformation as well as a way for people to control others in the name of religion. Carter deconstructs patriarchal myths but goes beyond them, rejecting female myths as well. A number of critics have commented on Carter's statement that "all myths are consolatory nonsenses" and have noted that she rejected the redefinition of women as occult priestesses because both redefinition and myth remove women from history: "Mythology" presents us "with ideas about ourselves which don't come out of practice: they come out of theory" (Altevers, 1994:20).

Carter's rejection of myth seems to correspond with her rejection of essentialism in relation to gender. Ricarda Schmidt (1990:67) writes that *The Passion of New Eve* "had deconstructed the conception of the self as an essence and has explored the constitution of the subject in patriarchal society as mediated by the symbols of femininity men have created". Carter displaces these symbols through imitation. At the same time, other critics acknowledge the lure of "unity, wholeness, identity" in the novel as "a possible way out of the patriarchal confines of femininity" (Schmidt, 1990:67). Schmidt considers this a weakness of the text, while Elaine Jordan (1994:199) hails this tension between the desire for wholeness and for multiple identities in Carter, who mocks "modern Romantic fantasies of the restoration of unity and wholeness in the fulfilment of desire" but whose "writing doesn't give up on the romance, the hopefulness of desire. She finds that there is no end to the construction of gender and sexuality, as masquerade, as mimicry and as creative affirmation that can take us by surprise." Connecting gender performance with alterity, Marina Warner writes that Carter's use of

> "double drag scatters certainty about sexual identity...But at the same time it also connects to one form of Carter's utopianism: her dream of synthesis. For the figure of the female impersonator mirrors the hermaphrodite, and this figure of alchemy, wisdom and magic also holds a very potent place in Angela Carter's imagination." (1994:251).

And, notwithstanding Carter's scepticism about religion, out of this gender masquerade comes the space for a new spirituality.

Contemporary work in feminist theory further defines

"female gendered subject as one that is at once inside and outside the ideology of gender; the female subject of feminism is one constructed across a multiplicity of discourses, positions and meanings which are often in conflict with one another and inherently contradictory. A feminist theory of gender, in other words, points to a conception of the subject as multiple, rather than divided or unified, and as excessive or heteronymous vis-á-vis the state ideological apparati and the sociological technologies of gender." (de Lauretis, 1987:x)

The idea of a space accessible to all, a space that transcends gender is similar to the one described by Brian McHale (1987:45), a 'Zone' that is "paradigmatic for the heterotopian space of postmodernist writing". The self cracks, along with the mirrors that have been shaping it. The notion of selfhood becomes fragmented, making identity confusing and defined by multiple selves. The image of metamorphosis often points to the rebirth of the self.

Jackson (1985:186) cites many female writers in her book on fantasy, writers that exploit a genre both thematically and stylistically subversive, with Carter's work as an example in point:

"It is surely no coincidence that so many writers and theorists of fantasy as a countercultural form are women….. Non-realist narrative forms are increasingly important in feminist writing; no breakthrough of cultural structure seems possible until linear narrative is broken or dissolved."

According to Rosemary Jackson (1985) fantasy is subversive and shows that what we regarded as natural is in fact constructed. The Greek *fantasia*, meaning to make visible another order of reality, can be said to voice everything old realist novels have kept quiet. Fantasy shows the underside of realism, so it is not totally divorced from the real world. Fantasy writing produces something new arising from our old world, being rooted in a social context and relating to specific social conditions.

Following Lacan's distinction between the symbolic and the imaginary, Julia Kristeva formulates the pre-semiotic order, the 'language' which erupts into the truly subversive text and takes up a negative position in relation to the symbolic order. The semiotic is an order open to both men and women, but she sees in women's exclusion from logical unity an enforced marginality which allies them to the realm of the 'babble'. Linden Peach (1998:129) discusses this idea in relation to Angela Carter's work:

> "Before the infant child enters the world of symbolic language, it uses pre-linguistic babble, the music of the tongue, learned at its mother's breasts. Since the symbolic language which the child learns involves a separation of the 'I' who speaks from the 'I' that is spoken about, and the voice predominantly expresses a male point of view, rediscovering the music of the tongue is virtually a 'mothering' of the tongue. The initial awareness of the pleasant sounds and the musicality of the tongue Kristeva calls the 'semiotic'. The semiotic is suppressed by the symbolic so that it exists as the shadow or "underworld", capable of disrupting the symbolic (masculine) order."

As far as Kristeva is concerned, representation, in a signifying system in which, according to Lacan, the phallus is the supreme signifier, is intrinsically masculine. For her, femininity is that which cannot be repressed. It is precisely the semiotic world of 'babble', of madness and non-signification, to which women have always been relegated by patriarchy. For Kristeva the subversive lies in the peripheral, and this is part of the attraction of the genre of fantasy.

    Donna Haraway's 1985 essay "A Cyborg Manifesto: Science, Technology, and Socialist-Feminism in the Late Twentieth Century" describes the symbiosis of the female body and technology in the figure of the cyborg that the protagonist of *The Passion of New Eve* accurately represents. Haraway's (1996:152) belief in the liberating potential of technoscience is grounded in her view that technologies that shape the female body confirm the limits of subjectivity as defined by embodiment. Haraway overstates the case that

> "Late twentieth-century machines have made thoroughly ambiguous the difference between natural and artificial, mind and body, self-developing and externally designed, and many other distinctions that used to apply to organisms and machines".

    In *The Passion of New Eve*, Angela Carter filters sex and race categories through technoscience, joining myth, allegory, and the grotesque in the figures of Eve, Mother, and Leilah, who are difficult to place as man, woman, or machine. The encounter between the self and the alien other often reflects the conflict between colonizer and colonized. The production of grotesque bodies reflects the colonizers' anxiety about the fascinating allure of the unknown. The desire for gender role stability is similarly rendered, in the novel, by grotesque metamorphoses which produce alienating bodies.

Carter's grotesque bodies may be interpreted starting from Mikhail Bakhtin's (1984:26) view of the grotesque as an exchange between the body and the surrounding world:

> "[The grotesque body] is not a closed, completed unit; it is unfinished, outgrows itself, transgresses its own limits. The stress is laid on those parts of the body that are open to the outside world, that is,   the parts through which the world enters the body or emerges from it, or through which the body itself goes out to meet the world. This means that the emphasis is on the apertures or the convexities, or on various ramifications and offshoots: the open mouth, the genital organs, the breast, the phallus, the potbelly, the nose. The body discloses its essence as a principle of growth which exceeds its own limits only in copulation, pregnancy, childbirth, the throes of death, eating, drinking, or defecation. This is the ever unfinished, ever creating body"

For Bakhtin, the human body is an entity that exceeds its own apparent limitations. The grotesque body is one that challenges the separation of the body from its environment. In the same way, the grotesque bodies of *The Passion of New Eve* transcend their limits and suffer changes that cast doubt on the stable nature of the body. The means of techno-scientific production and inscription are in the hands of a group of radical feminists. They patch up bodily pieces, and force their technological interventions on Evelyn, to present him with the bitter taste of the link between embodiment and female subjectivity.

Magic and performance are a means of deconstructing gender that opens up a space for other kinds of spirituality. Carter rejects archetypes but her use of alchemy suggests an alternative spirituality, outside the Judeo-Christian framework. She parodies it with the Children's Crusade, an intolerant Christian group wandering through the desert. Alchemy also offers an alternative to the goddess religions, represented by Mother and her priestesses, whom Carter condemns for being autocratic.

In her interview with John Haffenden, Carter puts forward an argument for a type of 'moral curiosity', a kind of cultural investigation that exposes social constructs and opens up new areas of discourse: "I would see it as a moral compunction to explicate and find out about things. I suppose I would regard curiosity as a moral function" (1985:96). It is not the didactic side of writing that comes to the surface, but a process of challenging cultural assumptions, raising questions, and making room for the assertion of things traditionally silenced:

> "it has nothing to do at all with being a 'legislator of mankind' or anything like that; it is to do with the creation of a means of expression for an infinitely greater variety of experience than has been possible heretofore, to say things for which no language previously existed." (1985:75)

She further defines her demythologizing project as the job of
"trying to find out what certain configurations of imagery in our society, in our culture, really stand for, what they mean, underneath the kind of semireligious coating that makes people not particularly want to interfere with them', defining myth both in 'a sort of conventional sense; also in the sense that Roland Barthes uses it in *Mythologies* - ideas, images, stories that we tend to take on trust without thinking what they really mean" (Katsavos, 1994:11-12).

Carter described her writing of *The Passion of New Eve*, in 'Notes from the Front Line', as that of an 'anti-mythical' novel conceived as "a feminist tract about the social creation of femininity" (*SL* 71). Femininity is a social construction imposed on or adopted by women as a masquerade to match the sexual identity prescribed for them by the male discourse.
The narrative strategy Carter prefers to employ, as she once explained that "a narrative is an argument stated in fictional terms" (Sage,1994:50), is a style in which fiction is composed as a kind of literary criticism. The "speculative" (Jordan, 1990) line of her fiction is conducted through the picaresque movement of the narrative, as the issue of sexual and gender identity dominates the hero-turned-heroine's traumatic adventures. The novel is a rewriting of Freud's castration theory, turning it into literal execution. A series of myths of female sexuality centred around the Oedipus myth unfold satirically with Eve/lyn's picaresque adventures in America: woman as *femme fatale,* woman as the castrated other, woman as life-giving mother. The main difference between Carter's works and the Enlightenment narratives is that the faith in universal rationality, the ground in which the latter are secured, is missing in the former. She highlights the end-of–the–world disintegration by questioning stories that have shaped discourses of femininity in the Western culture. If we add concept of a woman writing as a man who then becomes a woman, we are faced with a celebration of fantasy. The world and the characters in the novel present a flight from realistic representation. The Gothic picture of a high-tech civilization is different from reality, as the women's liberation and black power movements animate a chaotic America. This fantastic rewriting of the period reveals Carter's experience of those times. To her 1968 'felt like Year One' (1997:46), as she began to question "the nature of my reality as a woman" (1997:46). She reads the period historically as one of fragmentation. Evelyn leaves London and arrives in America to teach English literature, only to learn that the university system here is in a state of chaos:

"When I presented myself at the university where I had been engaged to teach, the combat-suited blacks who mounted guard with machine guns at Every door and window laughed uproariously at me when they heard my cut-glass vowels and prissy English accent and let me go. So now I had no job; and my reason told me to scurry back, quick as I could, to festering yet familiar London, the devil I knew. But: 'The age of reason is over,' said the old soldier, the Czech who lived on the floor above me. He was, God help us, an alchemist and distilled a demented logic in his attic in

stills of his own devising." (PNE 13)

The landscape of New York represents a symbol of ambiguity and insecurity, while Evelyn himself is frozen in his status of an upper-class academic. Baroslav's science of transformation and his pronouncement of the death of the "age of reason" reflect the instability of the world of the novel, and the displacement that Evelyn feels within that world. Fantasy and reality are blurred starting with the opening scene. As Evelyn watches an adaptation of *Wuthering Heights*, a female partner indulges him in oral sex. His own initial fantasy is to win the same favour from Tristessa, the famous film star.

As Elaine Jordan (1992:122) has pointed out, the structure of the novel follows the alchemical process. Carter uses alchemy as a feminist disrupter of patriarchal language and religions. While Luce Irigary advocates a theory of sexual difference, she sees the components of alchemy as symbolizing

"an unrepresented or latent materiality within phallocentric knowledges, conditioning but unacknowledged by them". She "uses a logic of interactive forces or combinatory 'particles', the 'atoms' of all matter in the universe. Taken together, they indicate a logic, not of being, but of perpetual *becoming*, a world in continuous flux and change" (Grosz, 1989:171).

In Baroslav's room, Evelyn finds

"crucibles and alchemics and strange charts and pictures of bleeding white birds in bottles. There was a seventeenth-century print, tinted by hand, of a hermaphrodite carrying a golden egg that exercised a curious fascination upon me, the dual form with its breast and cock, its calm, comprehensive face" (PNE 13).

The scene foretells the novel's conclusion in which self and other become integrated.

The hybrid figures and doubles in the novel comprise in part the alchemical symbolism Carter employs. The hermaphrodite undermines patriarchal culture because s/he invalidates the male/female binary. Eve/lyn is a figure for the excess of representation and the disruption of fixed identities since a classification according to gender is invalid in his/her case.

Three androgynous figures appear in the novel, supporting the idea of femininity as masquerade. Eve/lyn, Tristessa and Leilah/Lilith are connected by the white bird of Hermes that Eve/lyn finds in the desert, "the bleeding bird of the iconography of the alchemists" (PNE 44). The bird is out of place in the desert, a kind of albatross, a harbinger of apocalypse and also a symbol of aspiration. Jung's folk legend of the spirit in the bottle brings light on the meaning of the bird of Hermes:

> "The bird of Hermes has escaped from the glass cage, and in consequence something has happened which the experienced alchemist wished at all costs to avoid... For if he escapes the whole laborious opus comes to nothing and has to be started all over again' (1967, par.250). Another incarnation of the bird of Hermes, Mercurius is the spiritual essence trapped in matter, a creative element that has cosmic power. Mercurius 'evades every grasp - a real trickster who drove the alchemists to despair" (Jung, 1967:251).

One of Mercurius's aspects is the female serpent-daemon, Lilith. The shifting identities of Mercurius correspond with the characters' shifting identities in the novel, while he retains an essence, just as the characters seek wholeness. The tension resulting is used as a subversive force. If alchemy is subversive of Christian myths, the escaped bird, Mercurius as trickster is subversive of the alchemists. It stands as an intermediary between the self and the other, as manifested in the case of Leilah/Lilith and Tristessa.

Eve/lyn compares Tristessa to the white alchemical bird, a portent of apocalypse:

> "I felt his cheek on my skin and that whispering, tenuous mass of hair settle on my belly like shed feathers of birds, the white wings of a great, dead bird blown by a gale far inland from its ocean, the veritable, Baudelairean albatross" (PNE 147).

Tristessa is the white bird, doomed by Zero's and the Children crusaders' intolerance of gender ambiguity, as well as his own desire to be the woman he most desires (PNE 128-9). Lilith compares Tristessa to the ouroboros, the snake eating its tail, "the perfect circle, the vicious circle, the dead end" (PNE 173) because he is trapped in the stereotype of femininity. Revising

alchemy, Carter breaks the cycle of male–defined femininity. Eve/lyn also compares Tristessa to a unicorn (PNE 147), another magical animal, signifying the synthesis of opposites.

Another alchemical figure, Leilah/Lilith is instrumental in stimulating Eve/lyn's transformation. The black rats that Evelyn sees in New York are the surrealist signs of the repressed desires flaring up the city. In this apocalyptic chaos the city provides him with an incarnation of his twisted desire, the dark Leilah. She represents the first stage of the alchemical work, "a girl all softly black in colour-nigredo, the stage of darkness, when the material in the vessel has broken down to dead matter. Then the matter putrefies. Dissolution. Leilah" (PNE 14). Although Evelyn later admits to seeing Leilah as he wished to see woman, artificial, seductive, irresponsible, he also believes that she has played the most significant feminine role to initiate his quest. Her hybrid nature is connected to gender and seduction,

> "she swayed on shoes so high they took her a little way out of this world; they transformed her into a strange, bird-like creature, plumed with furs, not a flying thing, nor a running thing, nor a creeping thing, not flesh nor fowl, some in-between thing, hovering high above the ground which was, all the same, its reluctant habitat" (PNE 20-21).

The portrayal of Leilah as an intermediate creature makes her difficult for Evelyn to place. She is a hybrid breaking down binaries, pushing the feminine role to extremes to trap Evelyn and deconstruct his conception of woman. The mirror is an important element in her performance. It is a symbol of woman's entrapment in the male gaze and a catalyzing force in alchemy. It serves as a sexual theatre for Leilah and Evelyn. She watches him watching her and

> "she, too, seemed to abandon her self in the mirror, to abandon her self to the mirror, and allowed herself to function only as a fiction of the erotic dream into which the mirror cast me.
> So, together, we entered the same reverie, the self-created, self-perpetuating, solipsistic world of the woman watching herself being watched in a mirror that seemed to have split apart under the strain of supporting her world." (PNE 30)

Evelyn regards Leilah as giving off only reflected light, a light that is part of her mimetic performance:

> "I knew it was my own weakness, my own exhaustion that she had, in some sense, divined and reflected for me that had made her so attractive to m. she was a perfect woman; like the moon, she only gave reflected light. She had mimicked me, she had become the thing I wanted of her, so that she could make me love her and yet she had mimicked me so well she had also

mimicked the total lack in me that meant I was not able to love her because I myself was so unlovable."(PNE 34)

Leilah holds herself up as a mirror to Evelyn, and her emptiness, or appearance of it, reflects his own. But the light she gives is essential to Evelyn's alchemical transformation, just as reflected light helps produce the "alchemical gold" (PNE 150) of Evelyn and Tristessa's union. While the sun is aligned with the masculine, the feminine moon is the real catalyzing element:

> "So many stars! And such moonlight, enough moonlight to let a regiment of alchemists perform the ritual of the dissolution of the contents of the crucible, which, Baroslav, the Czech, had told me, may only be taken in polarized light, that is, light reflected from a mirror, or else by moonlight" (PNE 150).

Leilah takes the prison of the mirror and turns it into a field of possibility, a heterotopia of becoming. When Eve/lyn meets Leilah again later, she is Lilith, the natural daughter of Mother: "Leilah but no longer Leilah; Had she all the time been engaged on guerrilla warfare for her mother? Had that gorgeous piece of flesh and acquiescence been all the time a show, an illusion, an imitation?" (PNE 172). Leilah has played a part, but whether she suffered or just pretended to is left open. As with Tristessa, illusion and reality become blurred. Lilith from the Bible is sketched as a winged serpent, an in-between creature. She inhabits a similarly in-between space for radical transformation, because it destabilizes the terms 'fact' and 'fiction', as Fevvers in *Nights at the Circus*. Lilith plays a double role, explaining that she called herself Leilah in New York

> "in order to conceal the nature of my symbolism. If the temptress displays her nature, the seducee is put on his guard. Lilith, if you remember, was Adam's first wife, on whom he begot the entire race of djini. All my wounds will magically heal. Rape only refreshes my virginity. I am ageless, I will outlive the rocks" (PNE 174).

According to her, the function of such a being is to "interpret and convey messages to the gods from men and to men from the gods, prayers and sacrifices from the one and commands and rewards from the other" (PNE 175). Contrary to her assertion, she is a rebellious figure. Unlike the mythological Lilith and Eve, who were punished for refusing to submit to a man, Carter's women defy this fate by rejecting patriarchal laws and enjoying autonomous positions at the end of the novels.

The ambiguity of Lilith's identity underscores the tension between myth and history. She says that "historicity rendered myth unnecessary" (PNE 173), or

> "when there was a consensus agreement on the nature of the symbolic manifestations of the spirit, no doubt Devine Virgin, Sacred Harlots and Virgin Mothers served a useful function; but the gods are all dead, there's a good deal of redundancy in the spirit world" (PNE 175).

Although she claims to have abandoned myth for history, as an in-between figure, she embodies both. Lilith's magic suggests a spirituality that is not bound by symbols and one that has to be grounded in history. Carter allows a compromise between history and myth through magic. Whereas myth denotes a fixed story, magic has a quality of spontaneity. Carter's preoccupation with religion and her use of religious metaphors points to her intention of replacing established myths with another kind. As gender change is rendered with the help of religious metaphors, Christianity and rigid goddess worship are replaced with alchemy, witchcraft and magic.

The novel moves from the Gothicism of New York to the aridity of the desert, the second phase in the alchemical process. In literature, the desert is a place where one confronts one's inner self, one's temptations and fears. It is the setting for a journey of self-exploration, offering healing possibilities. Whiteness equals spirituality, and in the desert Evelyn is reborn as Eve/lyn. As alchemy is a "process of purification" (Jung, 1967, par. 263), Eve/lyn's longing for an essential self is materialized in his turning into a woman.

Evelyn thinks that he can leave behind a "fatal sickness" on fleeing the city, but he soon notices that he himself is "a carrier of the germ of a universal pandemic of despair. But I wanted to blame my disease upon somebody so I chose Leilah, for she was the nearest thing to myself I had ever met" (PNE 37). He sees her as doubly degraded, through race and sex, but chooses to share this taint. The antidote to despair is spirituality, which Eve/lyn moves towards through sex and gender changes. In the blank desert he looks for and finds "the most elusive of all chimeras, myself. And so, in the end I did, although this self was a perfect stranger to me" (PNE 38).

Having begun his alchemical quest, Evelyn admits that resurrection cannot occur without first dying (PNE 14), but the death of the self is the birth of the other in the self. Evelyn feels the other to be a compelling force within him. In between New York and the desert, he is convinced that

197

"only fatality could have possessed me to go high-tailing off in such troubled times, fatality and the unknowable impulsion of the destination ahead of me, a destination of which I was entirely ignorant although is had chosen me long ago for our destinations choose us, choose us before we are born. And exercise a magnetic attraction upon us, drawing us inexorably towards the source we have forgotten." (PNE 39)

The Beulah section is a literal execution of Freud's theory. New Eve's body is created from Evelyn's castrated body, as part of the plan devised by Mother in order to overthrow patriarchal rule. Mother's power is also subverted by Carter, who renders the relationship to the daughters problematic. The relationship between alchemy and the transformation Evelyn undergoes is compelling. Represented by gold, the alchemist's ultimate aim is a result of antagonistic forces in confrontation. Evelyn describes Beulah as "a place where contrarieties exist together" (PNE 48), 'a crucible', just as an alchemical oven where transformations occur, although Mother's plan is a fabrication.

In the operating room where Evelyn undergoes his change into Eve, he notes that

"Everything in the room had a curiously artificial quality, though nothing seemed unreal, far from it; Beulah, since its blueprint is a state of mind, has an unimpeachable quality of realism. But it is a triumph of science and hardly anything about it is natural, as if magic, there, masquerades as surgery in order to gain credence in a secular age". (PNE 49)

The cult of Beulah revels in woman's status as a vessel of contradictions where "real" women are literally made, not born.

Eve/lyn's metamorphosis consists of two stages, the biological one and the psychological one. After the surgery she learns about dependence, masochism, fear in Zero's harem, about love and sexual pleasure in the desert with Tristessa, and about confronting the Mother in the cave by the sea. Eve/lyn is hardly an example of harmony and serenity, she is more of a grotesque embodiment of the Platonic dichotomy mind-body, with her consciousness of a man in the constructed body of a woman. The resulting hermaphrodite seems at times a deficient man. Carter stresses the idea that sex is a fundamental element in one's identity. The perfection of Eve/lyn's body, however, is not static, but open to becoming. On the one hand, this new body is subjected to constraints by the technology that has activated it, on the other hand it is freed from the constraints of the male body of the past. Technology is but a parody of the alchemy that predicts a new order. The transition from the male body to the female one constitutes a transgression of the border defining gender. The new Eve/lyn is both natural and artificial, as Evelyn's identity disappears along with the significance of sexual differences. Sometimes, Eve/lyn has to get rid of the male inside her as the body follows its own will "the result of my apprenticeship as a woman was, of course, that my manner became a little too emphatically feminine" (PNE 101).

Androgyny, taken to be a combination of the two genders, is seen by Andrea Dworkin (1974) as the abolition of the very notions of masculinity and femininity. Stereotypical representations of gender traditionally take the form of binary oppositions. Carter attempts to write beyond the cultural associations that gender carries, as the problem of how to write about heterosexuality is linked to the problematic images of gender. Gender is linked constantly to the idea and ideal of heterosexual androgyny, a physical appearance combining male and female gender signals. After Evelyn passes through surgery, programming, and hormone treatment, and becomes Eve/lyn, she tells us that the women of Beulah "opened the wall upon the mirror and left me alone with myself" (PNE 74).

At the first sight of his new female body, Eve/lyn admires what s/he sees, calling himself/herself his own 'fantasy'. Carter uses this image in *The Sadeian Woman* to discuss screen icons such as Marilyn Monroe:

> "In herself, this lovely ghost, this zombie, or woman who has never been completely born as a woman, only as a debased cultural idea of a woman, is appreciated only for her decorative value...She is most arousing as a memory or as a masturbatory fantasy. If she perceives herself as something else, the contradictions of her situation will destroy her. This is the Monroe syndrome." (2000:70)

In yet another scene wrought with psychoanalytical symbolisms, Eve/lyn looks into the mirror and reports "But when I looked in the mirror, I saw Eve; I did not see myself. I saw a young woman who, though she was I, I could in no way acknowledge as myself" (PNE 74). When Mother specifically asks Eve/lyn "How do you find yourself?," Eve/lyn replies, "I don't find myself at all" (PNE 75).

When Eve/lyn moves in front of the mirror, wanting to "[touch] the breasts and the mound that were not mine" she sees "white hands in the mirror move, it was as though they were white gloves" (PNE 74). Eve/lyn looks once again, reporting, "I looked again and saw I bore a strong family resemblance to myself" (PNE 74). The process of self-identification is slow and gradual.

To Eve/lyn, her new self seems mask-like, or glove-like, being a false shell. It is this shell that resembles his old self at first. Eve/lyn sees her new hair, her eyes being " a little larger than they had been," a "bee-stung underlip and a fat pout" (PNE 74). Starting from the top of her newly reconstructed self, Eve/lyn works her way down, encountering her new features. After seeing herself as a "*Playboy* centre fold . . [a] object of all the unfocused desires that had ever existed in my own head" Eve/lyn's still masculine mind finds her new image self-erotic as "the cock in [her] head, still, twitched at the sight of [her]self" (PNE 75). It is not a mere change from male to female, but a co-existence with the other who is different.

The androgyne is a stage that Eve/lyn has to pass through. We can say that the hybrid has overtaken the androgyne, evading categories. The hybrid is composed not of masculine and feminine, but of elements such as human and animal, which deconstruct not only gender but also anthropocentrism. The hybrid in Carter has affinities with Deleuze and Guattari's theory of becoming animal. They believe that demonic animals form assemblages that "are neither those of the family nor of religion nor of the State. Instead, they express minority groups, or groups that are oppresses, prohibited, in revolt, or always on the fringe of recognised institutions." (1998: 247)

The hybrid is also a figure that deconstructs the maternal. Sage notes that Carter wanted to demystify motherhood by showing the invention of it (IDM 18). Carter shows fate to be connected with the supernatural and a human made historicity. One has to turn to the sources, Mother, God or other, to eventually expose these sources as constructs. Desiderio, Joseph in *Several Perceptions* and Eve/lyn return to the womb in their quest. The first stage in Evelyn's case is involuntary as he is turned into a woman in Beulah, and is forced to sleep with the 'Mother'. The core of the labyrinth is the self but the self is also other – Evelyn is Eve. Eve/lyn is thus confronted with the female mother/other who exists within himself. He says of Mother: "I did not know her awful patience, the patience of she who'd always been waiting for me, where I'd exiled her, down in the lowest room at the root of my brain" (PNE 58).

The body of the mother is artificial, constructed by technology, as illustrated by the fantastical image of the black Mother who has made herself gigantic and "breasted like a sow" with "two tiers of nipples" (PNE 59) to express fertility. Mother is a mixture of mythology and technology: "Mother has made herself into an incarnated deity; she has quite transformed her flesh, she has undergone a painful metamorphosis of the entire body and become the abstraction of a natural principle" (PNE 49), "the hand-carved figurehead of her own, self-constructed theology" (PNE 58). The divine is thus portrayed as completely manufactured and devoid of spirituality in contrast to alchemy, viewed as fresh. As Keller contends, entities are events rather than substances, the self is "a structure of spontaneity, lacking the sort of solidity that controls self or other" (1986: 200). Ironically, Mother is phallocentric in her desire to create a permanent theology. However, Eve/lyn's experience in Beulah catalyzes the alchemical process, making the spiritual transformation possible after the physical one.

We read in Eve/lyn's metamorphosis the parodied oedipal desire to kill the father and reintegrate with the mother. This forbidden desire to identify with the mother, in Mother of Beulah's mock mythology, is the cause of male predatory behaviour. Roberta Ruberstein (1993:12) observes that

> "Carter's representation of a male-to-female sex change [...] highlights prevailing social constructions of male power and female powerlessness as, literally, extensions of their genitalia [...]. The figure of the transsexual or bisexual is a kind of mediating figure invoked to reconcile symbolically these polarized positions".

Tristessa is another illusory icon of femininity, typified by suffering. He plays the role of woman as victim of sadistic pleasure, a reversal of his former masculine perversion. With the figure of Tristessa several recurring motifs are blended: the automaton-like self-animation of an idea of femininity, the male desire behind the feminine animation, and the simulated authentic passion.

His deconstruction of body as gender is strangely combined with a certain respect for the old order. Tristessa comments on the suffering of women while he seems to enjoy his oppression under patriarchy. Along with other characters in the novel, he combines masculine and feminine qualities without attempting to reconcile the binary. He seems more a transvestite than a truly androgynous figure, suggesting maybe that true androgyny is impossible to achieve in a grim future derived from our present. The descriptions of Tristessa could in fact support fixed gender roles:

> "That was why he had become the perfect man's woman! He had made himself the shrine of his own desires, had made of himself the only woman he could have loved! Tristessa, the sensuous fabrication of the mythology of the flea-pits. How could a real woman ever have been so much a woman as you?" (PNE 128)

Tristessa's air of kitsch dignity almost transcends the gloom of the novel. We are reminded that his true identity was kept secret and that he had requested the operation used on Eve/lyn but was turned down for being too feminine. Tristessa is subversive in foregrounding the element of masquerade in being a woman, but 'her' performance restores the notion of woman as suffering for an essential lack. Moreover, deep in Tristessa's psyche lies a masculine desire that on the surface assumes the feminine spectacle. As Leilah/Lilith tells Eve/lyn near the end of the story, Tristessa, according to Mother's examination of him for transsexual surgery, had "the awfully ineradicable quality of his maleness" (PNE 173).

He becomes the incarnation of his own secret preferences, the perfect woman, sadly just a filmic image.

Eve/lyn and Zero desire Tristessa; Zero and Tristessa are parts of Eve/lyn. They provide the clues for an analysis of the male and female desires in their relationship of predator and prey, as well as a *femme fatale* plot meant to rouse erotic expectation. Both the male predator and the voyeuristically placed reader are duped by feminine dissimulation.

In spite of his male body Tristessa, drag queen and transvestite, is a perfect personification of femininity. Sarah Gamble casts doubt on the reading of Tristessa

"as an emancipatory figure in terms of the gender slippage," for the issue involved is more that kind of woman he personifies than the straightforward gender trespassing. In fact, Tristessa's desire is auto-erotic: "he had become a woman because he had abhorred his most female part – that is, his instrument of mediation between himself and the other…He had made himself the shrine of his own desire, had made of himself the only woman he could have loved' (PNE 128-9).

In the final irony of life, he has 'heterosexual' intercourse with a man in a female body, but is executed for the hint of a homosexual kiss.

The perception of another in terms of one's own desire is a process similar to cannibalism. Eve/lyn in *The Passions of New Eve* identifies it in retrospect as being at work in her relationship, as Evelyn, with Leilah, remembering that the latter had mirrored him too well in his incapacity to love. The opposition Eros/Thanatos turns into a conflict between genders, represented by Zero, a symbol of destruction and sterility, Mother, fertile chaos, and Tristessa, an ambiguous 'essence' of femininity, as the point Angela Carter makes is that such an essence does not really exist.

202

While recounting the event, Eve reflects on her infatuation as an adolescent man:

"The abyss on which you opened was that of my self, Tristessa. You were an illusion in a void. You were the living image of the entire Platonic shadow show, an illusion that could fill my own emptiness with marvellous, imaginary things as long as, just as long as, the movie lasted... To go beyond the boundaries of flesh had been you occupation and so you had become nothing." (PNE 110)

Carter employs words such as 'abyss', 'illusion', 'void', 'nothing' to designate the abstraction of masculine sexuality. As Eve reflects upon it, the void is that of masculine emptiness, since Evelyn desired an illusion supplied by Tristessa. The masculine realm of sexuality and gender is flashed as a screen image in the novel, in an intense blending: "I could not think of him as a man; my confusion was perfect" (PNE 128). Tristessa is "the grand abstraction of desire", has "no ontological status, only an iconographic one" (PNE 129), as she is the feminine born from masculine fantasy. Her femininity is constructed by history, ideology and social forces, and is frozen onto celluloid like her sculptures are fixed by being dropped into the pool, and like the tribe of the river people in *The Infernal Desire Machines of Doctor Hoffman*.

Tristessa's dual nature is outside the rigid gender binarism that Zero is able to control, so he tries to impose his order by organizing the marriage ceremony between Tristessa and Eve/lyn. His intention is countered ironically by Eve/lyn's ambiguous sex/gender. Complete confusion occurs as Tristessa's house goes flying off its axle scattering body parts, suggesting that violence and chaos are necessary to rupture a world order maintained through tyranny and rigidity. A man masquerading as a woman and a woman who used to be a man are forced into marriage by Zero in order to punish and humiliate Tristessa on learning she is a he. They experience a complementary completion in the desert, when they have no water. Eve/lyn is racked with a desire that has not been fulfilled because she craves for the other. Her union with Tristessa is like "the great Platonic hermaphrodite":

"The erotic clock halts all clocks.

Eat me.

Consume me, annihilate me". (PNE 148)

The mock wedding ceremony serves as an illustration of the mystifying character of androgyny. Eve/lyn poses as the groom and Tristessa is the bride. Eve/lyn, seeing herself in "double drag", notes:

> "This masquerade was more than skin deep. Under the mask of maleness I wore another mask of femaleness but a mask that now I would never be able to remove, no matter how hard I tried, although I was a boy disguised as a girl and now disguised as a boy again." (PNE 132)

The women in the harem dress themselves in the glittering costumes in Tristessa's wardrobe and piece together the collection of Hollywood wax figures that Zero broke. The result is a Hall of grotesque, haphazard forms: "Ramon Navaro's head was perched on Jean Harlow's torso and had one arm from John Barrymore Junior, the other from Marilyn Monroe and legs from other donors" (PNE 134). The odd collection of wedding guests is appropriate for a double wedding in which "both were the bride, both the groom" (PNE 135). Carter's grotesque blend of tones – serious, sad, fearful, humorous – captures the air of pure farce the ceremony bears, turning the patriarchal institution of marriage into a parody: "Zero laughed so much when the happy couple kissed he lost the balance he precariously kept upon his wooden leg and tumbled over backwards, letting a resounding fart as he did so" (PNE 136).

The contrast between the beautiful illusion, feminine Tristessa and his actuality is shocking: "He was a mad, old man with long, white hair like Ezekiel" (PNE 145). Eve remarks: "What a satire Tristessa had been upon romanticism!" (PNE 144).

Laughter shapes part of the scene: "He softly bit at my right nipple and began to laugh at the back of his throat" (PNE 147). Still confused about the nature of masculine and feminine, she designates them as 'correlatives' rather than opposites. As they are starving and thirsting in the desert, Eve's remark "the desert would mummify us in the iconic and devastating beauty of our embrace, I nothing but a bracelet of bright hair around his bones" (PNE 151) conveys Carter's vision of the entire female body embracing the male one.

The love affair between Eve/lyn and Tristessa represents a fascinating parody of romantic love. Both of them are each other's hero and heroine. This mockery of gender and sexuality contrasts sharply with Carter's presentation of Eve and Trisessa's passionate lovemaking. Susan Rubin Suleiman describes it as a 'dizzying dance' that is "one of the most extraordinarily sensual and bewildering love scenes in recent literature" (1990:139). They are both making love to each other and to their own reflections. Their desire for each other is so intense and artificial that it is no longer possible to make the distinction between spontaneous passion and simulated love. The love scene is a postmodern subversion of the essentialist view of gender and sexuality, but their performance is haunted by its authenticity as authenticity is haunted by its infinite delay. The lovers are constantly aware of their simulating ready-made romantic motifs.

Eve/lyn's spiritual enlightenment derives from sexual metamorphosis and the union with Tristessa. Eve/lyn still holds on to the terms masculine and feminine, not knowing how to transcend gender altogether. Her retention of these terms and reference to the hermaphrodite she and Tristessa make illustrate a desire for wholeness, which she can only experience in terms of the two gender categories:

> "we had made the great Platonic hermaphrodite together, the whole and perfect being to which he, with an absurd and touching heroism, had, in his own single self, aspired; we bought into being the being who stops time in the self-created eternity of lovers" (PNE 148).

Apocalyptic terms are employed to suggest the end of a cycle and the beginning of another: "Here we were at the beginning or end of the world and I, in my sumptuous flesh, was in myself the fruit of the tree of knowledge; knowledge had made me, I was a man-made masterpiece of skin and bone, the technological Eve/lyn in person" (PNE 146). Eve/lyn exults in playing the feminine role: "I saw myself. I delighted me. I reached out my hand and touched my own foot in a sudden ecstasy of narcissistic gratification at its delicacy and littleness" (PNE 146).

The feminine narcissistic love of her mirror image watched by the male gaze, so feared by Zero as lesbianism, hovers in their love for each other. Eve/lyn feels passionate for Tristessa as she feels herself so desirable: "I thought, how delicious I look! I look like a gingerbread woman. Eat me. Consume me...."(PNE 146). In her passion, she turns Tristessa into a *man* who has been posing as a woman (149)

Despite the fact that the androgynous union of the two characters has been criticized because it promotes a heterosexual union as well as stereotypes of femininity and masculinity (Schmidt, 1990:66), I suggest it is possible to view this alchemical transformation in terms of Deleuzian theory, which equates alchemy with becoming and multiplicity: "a degree of heat can enter into composition with a degree of whiteness or with another degree of heat, to form a third unique individuality distinct from that of the subject." (Deleuze and Guattari, 1988: 253).

But the metamorphosis between the masculine and the feminine isn't just the work of Eve/lyn's female body on Tristessa's male body. Running deep in Tristessa's feminine pose is a male autoerotic desire which can only be satiated by a woman of his own enactment: "He had made himself the shrine of his own desires, had made of himself the only woman he could have loved" (PNE 128-9).

In enacting the woman of his desire, Tristessa, he reveals a desire recalling Zero's, misogynist and sadistic, though expressed in completely contrary terms: "How much he must have both loved and hated women, to let Tristessa be so beautiful and make her suffer so!" (PNE 144). When s/he becomes a male lover for Eve/lyn, his desire is aroused as both a man and woman. Tristessa enacts the autoerotic object of his desire while he also desires Eve/lyn as a synthetic woman desires a synthetic daughter s/he has lost in the movies. The mother-daughter longing looms in their relationship as it constitutes part of their feminine play, substituting the Oedipus complex.

Eve/lyn wants "the swooning, dissolvent woman's pleasure" she has "seen but never experienced" (PNE 147), and she achieves the experience with Tristessa—her body is "defined solely by his" and is lost in the ecstatic ocean-like rhythmic pleasure (PNE 149).

Moreover, Eve/lyn's and Tristessa's role reversal highlights the flexibility of gender roles, and the artificiality of these roles stems from each character's performance of the opposite.

In the erotic relationship between Eve/lyn and Tristessa there is an intricate exchange of desire and sexual identity. The female lack of being is often expressed in the form of female narcissism, through the reflection of the mirror. This female narcissistic loss of being in the mirror is highlighted by the erotic sensation Eve/lyn feels for Tristessa as s/he remembers their first encounter in the glass mausoleum. They fall in love with each other for they are each other's double, "twinned" by their "synthetic life." Eve/lyn loves Tristessa before she knows he is a man: "You were the memory of grief and I fell in love with you the minute I saw you, though I was a woman and you were a woman" (PNE 123).

In order to retain the alchemical metaphor the couple passes through death and produces the perfect child, beyond gender distinctions. Eve/lyn wears the double mask of maleness and femaleness, and compares Tristessa to the "Baudelairean albatross… blown by gale far inland from its ocean" (PNE 147). While Tristessa is absorbed in the fake autobiography made up from film scripts 'she' has played in, so is Eve/lyn engrossed in the experience of romantic love and death in the desert love scene. The reason is the fact that the tears in Tristessa's eyes reflect herself, beautiful, suffering Eve/lyn, vulnerable in a brutal world. As they look into each other's eyes the narcissistic lack of being is made even clearer:

> "Her eyes clear for an instant and direct their dark regard into my own... this ghostly and magnetic woman challenges me in the most overt and explicit manner. The abyss on which her eyes open, ah! It is the abyss of myself, of emptiness, of inward void." (PNE 125)

The scenario of death with the lover heightens Eve/lyn's sense of romantic thrill: "To think we might be dead by morning gave me an exquisite erotic shudder" (PNE 145). Tristessa's tragic death at the hands of the Children's Crusade animates Eve/lyn's dramatic impulse to die together with his body.

Tristessa is a sacrificial figure in Eve/lyn's spiritual quest, the sacrificial act being an integral part of the alchemical process (Jung, 1967, pars 251, 288). The hermaphrodite is eventually a romantic myth that Carter leaves behind by killing Tristessa. Eve/lyn can escape gender stereotypes once Tristessa is sacrificed. Male force and the fear caused by her own inadequacy in the face of male strength have prevented Eve/lyn from demonstrating her anger in any way which is strong enough to help her to accept Tristessa's death. The presence of the mother's womb and the possibility of getting back to her provide her with an escape route for her repressed anger.

As the next phase in her spiritual quest, Eve/lyn's return to her mother in the cave exposes the maternal as a construct. Eve/lyn's femininity, modelled on the old myth of castrated woman and woman as motherhood, renders her 'new' being a 'relic' of the 'old' world. The myth of the Mother is left behind by the tide of history. New Eve is new in her capacity to cross sexual boundaries. Her story ends with a cave allegory of her symbolic rebirth as a woman from the cave-womb arranged by Mother. In her quest for her, deep in the underground caves, she does not find Mother, only hints of what she can be, "a miraculous, seminal, intermediate being" (PNE 185) later embodied by Fevvers in *Nights at the Circus*.

Eve/lyn shows no penis envy, because when it is offered back to her she refuses, laughing. But rebirth as a woman will not fulfil the ideal of wholeness, so Eve/lyn looks for meaning in the cave at the end of the novel. Her symbolic return yields a cracked mirror and an empty echo to her cries, since Mother is absent. Through Eve/lyn's symbolic birth from the cave, the answer to the myth of the Mother is that "Mother is a figure of speech and has retired to a cave beyond consciousness" (PNE 184).

In alchemy, the mother symbolizes nature in her primordial state and the return to the mother is a spiritual experience. Although time reverses in the cave in a process similar to the womb state, Carter disengages the mother metaphor from the biological mother: "I called or my mother but she did not answer me…Speleological apotheosis of Tiresias –Mother, having borne her, now abandons her daughter forever" (PNE 186).

As she moves through the passages in the cave, Eve/lyn finds that words such as 'duration' and 'progression' (PNE 182) are meaningless. The experience in the cave is both historical and ahistorical, the space in between is the compromise site between history and myth. Carter reverses history to show how it is constructed and suggests it is possible to change it. Jordan writes that

> "pre-history, Eve's own and that of humanity, can be replayed like a reel of old film…and that film can be remade. The end of *The Passion of New Eve* looks to an unknown future, one which inevitably includes the possibility of new films, more myth-making. Woman enters history, rewrites herself in it, and tells more stories, as she's always done." (1990: 87)

Mother's ability to sing her own death at the end of the novel, along with Eve/lyn's futile expression of anger in the tearing up Tristessa's photograph challenges the patriarchal male canon:

> "I choked on a sob and a fury gripped me; I seized the photograph and ripped it into four pieces, across, across, and let the fragments drop into the bubbling pool below me, where they floated on the surface like little boats, or white feathers, until the busy current sucked them away, down through the fissure into the lower cave." (PNE 123)

Eve/lyn's discovery of the alchemical gold she had given Leilah suggests that she is undergoing another transformation in the cave, discovering an intermediate creature that reflects Eve/lyn's, Tristessa's and Lilith's intermediate natures:

> "bird and lizard both at once, a being composed of the contradictory elements of air and earth. From its angelic aspect spring the whole family tree of feathered, flying things and from its reptilian or satanic side the saurians, creepy crawlers, crocs, the scaled leaper and the lovely little salamander. The archaeopteryx has feathers on its back but bones in its tail, as well; claws on the tips of its wings; and a fine set of teeth. One of those miraculous, seminal, intermediate beings brushed against a pendant tear of rosin in the odorous and primeval amber forests and left

behind a feather. A miraculous, seminal, intermediate being whose nature I grasped in the desert.

The birds of the air shed all their feathers, which softly fall to the ground; scales now appear on their little bodies. I am inching my way towards the beginning and the end of time." (PNE 185)

The reversal of time leads to this paradoxical creature. Eve/lyn perceives her intermediate nature and understands that her rebirth is not bound to the mother as a biological entity, but one that exists in the binary-disrupting state. The freeing of the birth process from the biological process allows spiritual and psychic rebirth. The concluding part of the novel juxtaposes its deconstructed myths of womanhood. Leilah reveals her other identity as Lilith, Mother regresses to her younger self and Eve/lyn is reborn as a 'natural' woman. Whereas Lilith speaks out the demythologizing message of the novel- "the gods are all dead" (PNE 174), she lays bare her own myth, as Adam's first wife, the temptress, who is ageless and will outlive the rocks, whose wounds will magically heal. But Eve knows her secret, her subversive female power: "she could not abdicate from her mythology as easily as that; she still had a dance to dance, even if it was a new one, even if she performed it with absolute spontaneity" (PNE 179). It is the delicate balance between simulation and dissimulation which keeps Fevvers high in the air, that Eve has to find: "I was preoccupied in watching the complicated aerodynamics of the great, white sea-birds who glided on the turbulent currents of the upper air above the shifting ocean" (PNE 180). She turns what confines her, the coffin, into a lifeboat, that sets her free to mourn for love.

4.2. TWISTS OF PASSION

Carter's writing playfully hovers between postmodernism, feminism and the Gothic. Her experience in Japan sharpened her writing and caused further controversy as her critical eye turned to the issue of women's identity construction. The sharp edge of her writing has come, for a large part, from her use of the Gothic. Her attack of women's discourse of self-victimization, her depiction of violent sexual relationships and of female sexuality as either deadly or monstrously voracious, all indicate affinities with the Gothic. The Gothic tackles these themes in a horrific space while Carter deals with them in a theatrical site, where people cross the boundaries but display an acute awareness of the theatricality of their fear, and the paradox remains, that fear is the more theatrical, the more genuine. So Carter's postmodern play of subjectivity shapes a new space of horror. In this theatrical play, "enjoyment" is affirmed as "the real Thing" (Zizek, 1998:143). Carter's postmodern play is truly subversive, for it is real enjoyment.

The novelist has been fascinated with the 'bloody' way the female body has been scripted by culture as a corporeal-textual site for gender identity. The exploration of the "bloody" textuality is present throughout Carter's work, from her first novel *Shadow Dance* (1966) to her last one, *Wise Children* (1991), favouring the joy more than the horror of play in later fictions. Carter accepts Freud's theory of the unconscious, which has shaped so much of twentieth-century thought, in that it has allowed for problematising the ways in which identities are constructed according to conflicting or contradictory desires within the self. Carter indicates Freud as a core influence on her work, as his theory of the unconscious and dreams were "about life" (Appignanesi,1987). Furthermore, she points out her tendency "to provoke unease" in the way she explores sexuality is inevitable when dealing with the unconscious: "that's what the unconscious is for". The exploration of the unconscious is necessary in exposing the violent drives that fuel desire, and how those desires construct human relationships and identities.

But the greatest problem for Carter and feminism in general is the impact psychoanalysis has had on the notions of masculinity and femininity. Freud's theory of castration, which leaves women as 'lacking' in some fundamental way in relation to the male, is problematic to feminism. Furthermore, Lacan places the phallus as representative of the Father's Law. One enters into language, into the socio-symbolic order whereby identity ensues. Even though French feminist theorists accept this in their explorations of the role of the mother in introducing the child to language, Lacan's scenario raises debate with the implication that subjectivity depends upon identification with the father's law. The child has no connection to the mother's body, leading to a repression of the maternal. If women stand for the threatening 'other' they might begin to subvert the dominant discourse from their marginal position. The French diverge in their views but aim at rethinking the unconscious as a tension between a masculine allegiance to the law and a feminine willingness to disobey it. The same clash between compliance and disobedience of the law runs throughout Carter's texts, which, often speak of the possibilities and limitations of feminine transgressions. Women are capable of disrupting the symbolic order by directly confronting men's repressed desires, by going behind the screen of representation that a patriarchal order imposes upon their bodies. If anything, this might allow for a confrontation with what the symbolic order has always designated as "that unthinkable outside" – the "unthinkable side of femininity" (Clément, Kristeva, 1998/2001:72). Women have the advantage of subversively using their marginal positioning to disrupt phallocentric representations and Carter's novels place women in charge of such subversive performance .

As soon as Evelyn arrives in New York he is already identified as an abuser of women. The intensity of his fantasy world is linked to academic pretension, explicit in the same opening scene. The cultured male expresses his power over popular cinema using sexual language. Even if he experiences some physical enjoyment, he is trapped in the stereotype he has chosen. His level of autonomy will increase with the fluidity of his name. Beyond the fantasy of Tristessa, Evelyn describes his experience in terms that anticipate Zero's: "Sometimes I'd amuse myself by tying a girl to the bed before I copulated with her. Apart from that I was perfectly normal" (PNE 9). As a man, Evelyn violently asserts his masculinity through acts of sexual dominance over women, often taking a sadomasochistic pleasure in their suffering. This "sadistic streak" develops in Evelyn at a very early age, having "acquired an ambivalent attitude towards women" (PNE 9) through his specular fascination with Tristessa. For Evelyn, Tristessa is "necrophilia incarnate" (PNE 7), perfecting the cinematic role of "abused femininity" (PNE 35), since "suffering was her vocation" (PNE 8). Evelyn directly associates the "allure" of her

211

"tragic and absurd heroism" (PNE 7) with his adolescent sexual awakening, "the spectacle of Tristessa's suffering always aroused in me" (PNE 8).

Both Zero and Evelyn have misogynist attitudes and misplaced literary ambitions, both believe that women have deprived them of male fertility. Although Tristessa embodies for Evelyn a supreme image of femininity, she is later revealed to be a transvestite, merely playing a woman in drag. Tristessa represents a masculine ideal of femininity made by and for men, as Eve/lyn himself comes to realise: "*That* was why he [Tristessa] had been the perfect man's woman! He had made himself the shrine of his own desires, he had made of himself the only woman he could have loved!" (PNE 129). This directly reflects back on Evelyn's attitude towards women, before he becomes one himself, desiring them only for the image of suffering femininity that he projects onto their bodies .

Evelyn's misogynistic view of women is made all the more explicit in his relationship with Leilah: "a perfect woman; like the moon, she only gave reflected light" (PNE 34). When Evelyn first meets Leilah, who is "black as the source of shadow" (PNE 18), he projects onto her the role of temptress, leading him against his will into "the geometric labyrinth of the heart of the city" (PNE 21). In a sense, Leilah is leading him into his own heart of darkness, as Evelyn is no longer merely a voyeur taking pleasure in women's pain, as he did with Tristessa, but becomes an active participant in his fantasies of abuse. At one point he believes she is a "succubus", one of the "devils in female form who come by night to seduce the saints", and because of this, he then punishes her by tying her to the bed, beating her, degrading her body, and then defending his acts of sexual violence by claiming she is "a born victim" (PNE 27-8). This scene significantly foreshadows Leilah's reappearance at the end of the novel, and we realise that she has perhaps been determining Eve/lyn's labyrinthine journey throughout the entire text.

Leilah is a projection of Evelyn's desire, as he thinks that "her self seemed to come and go in her body…a visitor in her own flesh" or senses that "duplicity gleamed in her eyes" (PNE 27). She is indeed not what she seems, player of an ambiguous game meant to trick him. Her first appearance is in the form of a "bird-like creature" Evelyn should hunt in the moonlight. Since he sees her as his prey, he naturally "played the hunter" (PNE 20, 25). He treats Leilah as an exotic black nymph guiding him through the chaotic city, while he seems a 'detached' observer. Fear appears as a constituting part of his erotic pleasure, "terror is the most seductive of all drugs", and is felt "as an intensification of the desire that ravaged me" (PNE 15, 24).

The technology of reconstructing the female self is not just conducted on the artificial Eve/lyn; it is also exercised on the "real" women like Mother of Beulah and Leilah. Mother's body is grafted with two tiers of breasts donated by the "daughters" of Beulah, to concretize the mythical essence of woman as fertility. She said to Eve/lyn, "'I am the wound that does not heal,'" and she transgresses against the Father by sleeping with the son Eve/lyn (PNE 64). Leilah, the black girl who seduces Evelyn in the ghetto of New York but later turns out to be Lilith, the seductress of Beulah, transforms herself nightly from a "grubby little bud" into a glamorous sexy girl that exists in the mirror. Leilah's nightly transformation is undertaken by consulting the mirror, which is composed of fashion industry and cultural images of women, and Leilah's labour is to invoke, to become "the formal other" in the mirror. To become herself is to become the formal other because in her female self is inscribed a lack, an imaginary wound : "She was unnatural.... her self seemed to come and go in her body, fretful, wilful, she a visitor in her own flesh" (PNE 27). She, Eve/lyn, and Mother are monstrous for they all wear their flesh of femininity with an open wound.

If the prey-predator metaphor exposes the power relationship between the sexes, the *femme fatale* script suggests the male fear of woman's predatory abilities. Leilah lures Eve/lyn into the labyrinth of the dark city where he feels her power: "I knew how defenceless I was, how much at risk" (PNE 24). Her destructive power is only revealed when she shows her other identity as Lilith luring Eve/lyn to his fate of castration. For now she is only an innocent sex doll, performing a somewhat fatal charm in her narcissistic contemplation in the mirror. Astonished at Leilah's endless desire Evelyn punishes her by tying her to the iron bed during the day. At night, however, as the black whore is set free, she becomes absorbed by her self-image, perceiving herself as other:

> "I used to adore to watch her dressing herself in the evenings... She became absorbed in the contemplation of the figure in the mirror but she did not seem to apprehend the person in the mirror as, in any degree herself. The reflected Leilah had a concrete form and ...we all knew, all three of us in the room, it was another Leilah. Leilah invoked this formal other with a gravity and ritual that recalled witchcraft; she brought into being a Leilah who lived only in the not-world of the mirror and then became her own reflection." (PNE 28)

The mirror Leilah is the incarnation of male desire, although her relation to the mirror self is different from Evelyn's. She is not in love with Evelyn, she is "a born victim" (PNE 28), suffering the abuse of Evelyn the torturer. To him, she represents "a perfect woman, like the moon, she only gave reflected light. She had mimicked me, she had become the thing I wanted of her, so that she could make me love her" (PNE 34). In mimicking what the male desires of her, she double-crosses him.

In *The Sadeian Woman*, Carter argues that "the mutilations our society inflicts upon women" (*SW* 23) are encouraged by the symbolic wound projected onto their bodies, which is derived from the phallocentric view of the female as castrated and thus fundamentally lacking in relation to the male. Evelyn ultimately desires Leilah for "the exquisite negative of her sex" (PNE 27), which allows him control over her. Carter is specifically examining here the ways in which pain and violence are used to control women, when the boundaries between sexuality and violence fade away:

> "The whippings, the beatings, the gouging, the stabbings of erotic violence reawaken the memory of the social fiction of the female wound, the bleeding scar left by her castration, which is a psychic fiction as deeply at the heart of Western culture as the myth of Oedipus, to which it is related in the complex dialectic of imagination and reality that produces culture. Female castration is an imaginary fact that pervades the whole of men's attitudes towards women and our attitude to ourselves, that transforms women from human beings into wounded creatures who were born to bleed". (SW 23)

As Eve/lyn is given the appearance of a woman, he learns the balance of power is tilted to his detriment, as he becomes the feared 'other' of male desires.

Like Leilah, Eve/lyn is repeatedly raped. According to psychoanalytic theory, those fears contribute directly to the making of the male subject, since he defines his identity in relation to the threat of castration. Women represent this threat because they are already 'lacking', and are thus a reminder of what the man might also lose. Furthermore, since women are not afraid of losing what they do not have, they are capable of disrupting the symbolic order. Thus, in order to keep women submissive they themselves need to be convinced they are no more than wounded creatures who are born to bleed, passively suffering the violence inflicted on them. For instance, Evelyn attempts to convince us of Leilah's own masochism, that "she systematically carnalised herself and became dressed meat" (PNE 31), yet Carter does not expect us to accept her as such. Leilah is consciously playing a role of femininity, as Evelyn comes to suspect when he watches her putting on or invoking "this formal other" in the mirror, allowing "herself to function only as a fiction of the erotic dream" that Evelyn projects onto her (PNE 28, 30). Significantly, when Evelyn goes too far in his abuse, Leilah refuses to play her passive part, threatening him with "voodoo threats" of castration: "she told me a chicken would come and snap my cock off" (PNE 32), which of course is what Mother does in order to make Evelyn into a woman.

Evelyn abandons Leilah, fleeing from the degradation and "universal pandemic of despair" that he has found in New York, which he locates in Leila's body, projecting onto her flesh a "corrupt languor" of rotting femininity (PNE 37).
Rather than confront the dark corruption of his own desires, he chooses to blame Leilah for his "disease", claiming: "the slow delirious sickness of her femininity, its passivity, its narcissism, have infected me because of her" (PNE 37). This evasion is, if anything, prompted by his desire to save himself "from that most brutal of all assaults, the siege of the other" (PNE 34). He escapes to the desert, "where there were no ghosts" (PNE 38).

Just as Mother is 'too much', she turns Evelyn into an excessively male version of the 'feminine', modelling her New Eve after a Playboy centrefold (PNE 75), the kind of woman that men are encouraged to desire. Significantly, though, even if Eve/lyn is now technologically altered into an 'unnatural' woman, s/he is hardly a 'feminised' subject.

At first, as Eve/lyn peeks at her new body, she does not undergo any psychological change, merely viewing her external appearance from a masculine perspective: "the cock in my head, still, twitched at the sight of myself" (PNE 75). On one level this indicates a paradoxical split in self-perception, in which the "desiring viewer and the desired object, usually distinct figures, are here confined within the one body." (Johnson, 1997:172) However, Eve/lyn does not think herself as any less male despite all the lessons she is taught. She is shown "non-phallic imagery such as sea-anemones opening and closing; caves, with streams issuing from them; roses opening to admit a bee; the sea, the moon" (PNE 72), images that ironically figure the female body as passive.

Thus, Mother's project of 'feminising' Eve/lyn essentially relies on symbols that a patriarchal order uses to veil women's bodies in mystery. Mother reinforces the patriarchal discourse in her belief that motherhood will provide the supreme proof and triumph of Eve/lyn's femininity. Though Eve/lyn is forced to view reproductions of "Every Virgin and Child that had ever been painted", this absurd attempt "to subliminally instil the maternal instinct itself" (PNE 72) is answered by Eve/lyn when she retorts: "it takes more than identifying with Raphael's Madonna to make a real woman!" (PNE 80).

In spite of Eve/lyn's response, both she and Mother are convinced that "one woman is all women" (PNE 58). For Eve/lyn, that one woman is reduced to the figure of Leilah, the dark temptress luring on the male in order to consume his masculinity: "Leilah had always intended to bring me here, to the deepest cave, to this focus of all darkness that had always been waiting for me" (PNE 58). Though Eve/lyn claims Beulah signifies his/her "journey's end as a man" (PNE 60), as soon as she escapes Beulah, Eve/lyn claims to feel "almost a hero, almost Evelyn, again" (PNE 81). Later, she will realise that she has not in fact "reached the end of the maze yet", and will have to "descend lower", until Leilah brings her to the deepest cave for a final confrontation with Mother and her myths (PNE 49). Fleeing from Beulah, however, embarking on yet another evasion of the 'feminine', Eve/lyn is convinced she is in complete possession of the old Evelyn's "arrogant and still unaltered heart" (PNE 82).

The symbolic castration that a phallocentric discourse projects onto women's bodies, viewing them as 'other' within, turns Eve/lyn into a feminine subject in the end. Women are denied any articulation of their desires, to the extent "where a woman's sexual desire is so repressed that it can only find expression as rape, reflecting a patriarchal misogynist culture which constructs femininity as passive and masochistic." (Johnson, 1997:59). Eve/lyn's 'real' transformation begins with her painful recognition of that 'otherness' within.

The monstrous woman in the novel learns to enjoy her artificial sexuality through the power to play. The bloody process of becoming a woman still torments the performing woman, and the horror is most apparent when performance has replaced nature. Womanhood is monstrous in *The Passion of New Eve* because it involves a process of construction. Eve/lyn is a man turned into a woman, whose body is a collage of metaphor and flesh, to convey the lyrical definition of femininity. Mother and the women of Beulah had carved out her new shape "according to a blueprint taken from a consensus agreement on the physical nature of an ideal woman drawn up from a protracted study of the media" (PNE 78).

Eve/lyn's birth into new Eve is a scene of sexual violence that Carter spices with irony. In the womb-like operating room Eve/lyn is operated on by Mother with a knife, in front of the female spectators "seated in banked seats around the little stage like the spectators of a chamber opera" (PNE 69). The theatrical sense emphasizing the motif of femininity as masquerade is further illustrated by the inculcation of old Hollywood woman's films into new Eve/lyn's head.

Her psycho-programming is fashioned after Tristessa, the kitsch image of womanhood as pain, as well as the Virgin-and-Child icons painted "to instill the maternal instinct" (PNE 72). The ironic point is that the resulting Eve/lyn is "the object of all the unfocused desires that had ever existed in [Evelyn's] head" (PNE 75). The women in Beulah create a theatre around Evelyn's sex-change, which underlines the artificiality of their religion. The theatre becomes a means of both physical and psychological control, as they place him in a womb-like room they call the place of birth. He feels a sense of dread,

> "yet this specifically metaphysical dread...had been created with unscrupulous cunning by ingenious stage-management – a little red light, the sound of a couple of archaic musical instruments. Even my reactions were out of my control, were strictly programmed by the tribe of desert matriarchs" (PNE 52).

They use ritual theatre to indoctrinate Eve: "Sophia must have thrown a switch in the hi-fi for the voice of a vast choir with an organ and a brazen dissension of trumpets burst apart this archetypal hole in which I was lying with a sumptuous prodigality of decibels" (PNE 67). Revising patriarchal Christianity, they tell Eve/lyn he is going to bring forth "the Messiah of the Antithesis"(PNE 67), that she will be a new Eve and the Virgin Mary, that her child will renew the world, "prompt on cue, trumpets and cymbals crashed off-stage" (PNE 77). Spiritual transformation is a matter of staging, which Carter is critical towards, due to its lack of spontaneity. In Beulah, miracles such as the Virgin birth occur with the help of technology, a carefully orchestrated one. On the other hand, the use of magic and the supernatural makes room for the spiritual dimension.

Carter parodies the womb-like caves in 'Familiar panic of entry into the Earth's entrails':

> "Consider the womb, the "inner productive space", the extensible realm sited in the penetrable flesh, most potent matrix of all mysteries. The great, good place; domain of futurity in which the embryo forms itself from the flesh and blood of its mother; the unguessable riches of the sea are a symbol of it, so are the caves, those dark, sequestered place where initiation and revelation take place. Men long for it and fear it; the womb...is a fleshy link between past and future, the physical location of an everlasting present tense that can usefully serve as a symbol of eternity, a concept that has always presented some difficulties in visualization. The hypothetical dream-time of the foetus seems to be the best that we can do." (2000:108)

The theatre is also a space within the psyche where one revises the Oedipal drama. When Sophia says "kill your father! Sleep with your mother! Burst through all the interdictions!" Eve/lyn knows he has arrived "at the place of transgression" (PNE 64). The androgyne breaks the Oedipal model because s/he refuses to identify with one role. The women deconstruct the Oedipal drama, replacing it with their own goddess drama. Eve/lyn has been led to the place where 'I' becomes 'other':

> "When Leilah lured me out of the drug-store, into the night, towards her bed, she had organized the conspiracy of events that involved the desert, the dead bird, the knife, the sacrificial stone…Leilah had always intended to bring me here, to the deepest cave, to this focus of all the darkness that had always been waiting for me in a room with just such close, red walls within me. For in this room lies the focus of darkness. She is the destination of all men, the darkness that glides at the last moment, always out of reach; the door called orgasm slams in his face, closes fast on the Nirvana of non-being which is gone as soon as it is glimpsed. She, this darkest one, this fleshy extinction, beyond time, beyond imagination, always just beyond, a little way beyond the fingertips of the spirit, the eternally elusive quietus who will free me from a being, transform my I into the other and, in doing so, annihilate it." (PNE 58-59)

Elaine Showalter's description of the 'wild zone' uninhabited by patriarchy suggests that women write of freedom and constructed worlds in the wilderness. Eve/lyn describes the place of her birth in similar terms: "I'd lost them by the time I left the desert, the domain of the sun, the arena of metaphysics, the place where I became myself" (PNE 164). Eve understands

> "the slut of Harlem can never have objectively existed, all the time mostly the projection of the lusts and greed and self-loathing of a young man called Evelyn, who does not exist, either. This lucid stranger…seems to offer me disinterested friendship" (PNE 175).

The sexual education that turns Eve/lyn into a 'real' woman is conducted through his/her interaction with another figure, Zero. If Zero and Mother stand for opposed powers of patriarchy and matriarchy, Zero's and Tristessa's sexuality are the allegory of sadism and masochism. Zero is portrayed as a one-eyed, one-legged maniac, who runs a cult of his masculinity with a harem of seven wives as his worshippers. He abuses them and holds them in contempt, treating pigs better. Eve/lyn is tortured as she becomes his eighth wife, and is turned into a 'woman' who cries because of the pain and a "savage woman" (PNE 107, 108), like Mother, who wants to kill her torturer.

Zero's religion is equally artificial and oppressive. He also employs the theatre, giving his version of apocalypse:

> "He'd sung and danced his variation of Gotterdammerung on the bar in the old saloon for them so often they were sure it must be true... I was forced, in the end, to believe they believed it as though it were revealed scripture. Then an awful pity for them overcame me; these poor girls had indeed dedicated themselves, body, heart, and soul, to the Church of Zero' (PNE 99).

Using religion as a manipulative tool, Zero appeals to women's insecurities, providing them with a missing authority figure, and a promise of salvation. Despite the "boredom, the pigs, the toil, the bad food, the fleas, the hard beds, constant beatings, deprived of speech", Eve/lyn, together with Zero's wives endure everything because Zero's rhetoric has transformed their world. "The ranch house was Solomon's Temple; the ghost town was the New Jerusalem; the helicopter his chariot of fire" (PNE 100).

Mixing theatre with pornography, Zero makes them dress and dance in lewd costumes for his poetry recitals, occasions that Eve/lyn dreads

> "for I would remember Leilah watch herself in the mirror and now I sensed all the lure of that narcissistic loss of being, when the face leaks into the looking glass like water into sand. Then Zero would take the centre of the stage, while we supplied him with a sort of visible refrain, and he would dance out the violation and death of Tristessa, followed by the subsequent apotheosis of Zero. This was the unique matter of his drama." (PNE 103-104)

Zero's religion requires woman's loss of self, and it is a loss that comes through performance as sex objects. His goal is to kill Tristessa, the female performer and sex object who has used "various cannibalistic devices" (PNE 104) on him. Although he is unaware of Tristessa's disguise at this point, Zero perceives her as a witch, as a woman in control of her performance. But to him performance is legitimate when he controls it, and religion relies on women as sexual objects. He believes Tristessa to be a lesbian, whom he defines as a woman overacting the feminine role, and later suspects Eve/lyn of it. His hunt of Tristessa is fueled by "the imminence of the apocalypse" (PNE 108), though the consequence reaches far beyond his expectations. In patriarchal culture, a woman has to negotiate a balance, so as not to seem either too masculine or too feminine and undermine gender categories. Eve/lyn says that the "mediation of Zero turned me into a woman" (PNE 107-108), that is, woman defined by male abuse and as male property. Carter undermines woman's forced gender impersonation through mimicry and masquerade. Tristessa subverts femininity by overdoing it, but s/he remains trapped in that role of femininity. In contrast, Eve/lyn becomes a woman but his/her gender remains indeterminate.

Zero and Tristessa possess the qualities of the category of the abject as they "transgress socially established boundaries of gender as written on the body" (Johnson, 1994: 43). So does Eve, as she cannot fit in either sex, as a woman with a man's mind. After undergoing plastic surgery, Eve/lyn is in an abject state and unable to interpret her new identity: "for this one was only a lyrical abstraction of femininity to me, a tinted arrangement of curved lines" (PNE 74). "Psycho-programming" notwithstanding, Eve/lyn's attitude toward the new self is conditioned by the dualism of the phallocratic order. He as Eve/lyn will become the object of Mother's desire as Leilah has been to him.

Zero's sexuality is formed in antithetical terms to Tristessa's screen image. Carter intends to criticize the formation of masculine sexuality in the contemporary media-saturated society. He is 'Masculinity Incarnate' (PNE 104), while Tristessa represents femininity. But Zero's identity is threatened because it centers around Tristessa's authenticity as a woman. The speculation that she may be a lesbian generates his anxiety so he is convinced that he must annihilate her sexual autonomy. He acts out his supremacy in a hysterical dance to the music of Wagner, a dance of "the violation and death of Tristessa, followed by the subsequent apotheosis of Zero" (PNE 103-104). He also negates the other: " I am Zero...the lowest point; vanishing point; nullity" (PNE 102). "Zero,' Elaine Jordan (1992:64) notes, is "the sign for nothing, by which women are represented in graffiti." Zero's obsession with the 'female zero' (PNE 95) shapes his male identity. The predatory relationship between him as aggressor and his victims requires the victims' compliance in order to continue: "he demanded absolute subservience from his women. Although 'subservience' is the wrong word, they gave in to him freely... his myth depended on their conviction... They loved Zero for his air of authority but only their submission had created that" (PNE 100). This relationship of complicity is maintained by the myth of the female space that keeps women passive.

As Carter herself indicates, this education is one that the female subject is often forced to endure, claiming that much of the novel was written as an exploration of "the process of physical pain and degradation that Eve/lyn undergoes in her apprenticeship as a woman." (1997:592)

Zero repeatedly rapes Eve/lyn in order to include him/her into his harem, reminding Evelyn of his previous treatment of Leilah, as s/he acknowledges: "[He] forced me to know myself as a former violator at the moment of my own violation" (PNE 102).

Furthermore, like Leilah, who appeared to be nothing more than "a visitor in her own flesh" (PNE 27), Eve/lyn can only become a woman by pretending to be one; since Zero uses physical appearance to define her femininity, her only means for surviving violence is to act according to the appropriate modes of feminine behaviour that Zero expects of her. Eve/lyn observes the other women in Zero's harem, who also live as 'imitations'. They willingly pretend to be the kind of women that Zero desires: passive, masochistic, and sexually enslaved to his tyrannical rule. Just as he does with Eve/lyn, Zero turns them into 'savage' women, allowing them no other form of communication except to bark like dogs, and locking them up in a room together as if they were a herd of beasts (PNE 87, 97). Zero's farm is yet another dystopian nightmare of the way a patriarchal order operates in its violent oppression of women and Carter exposes a form of female complicity that often sustains it. When Eve/lyn questions how a crippled, mad old man is capable of physically dominating a group of seven strong, healthy young women, she concludes: "his myth depended on their conviction" (PNE 99).

Zero's power is all the more strengthened due to the women's inability, or even unwillingness, to establish a relationship of female commonality amongst themselves. In spite of the fact that they are more than aware they are living double lives, as subhuman for Zero but differently when alone with each other, they continue to behave according to the savagery expected of them. In their struggle for survival, they violently turn on each other, and Eve's arrival is perceived as another source of competition. As a result they brutally beat her, uniting together only through a kind of animal instinct, a pack mentality that fears and rejects any outsider as a direct threat.

The violence inflicted on the women by each other is in part due to their struggle to survive, as Eve/lyn recognises that "perhaps they were fighting for their lives" (PNE 89).

On the one hand this is reflective of how a patriarchal system structures female relationships through fierce competition for male desire. Carter makes us question this form of female survival, exposing the questionable masculine perspective of women in their struggle for control. The end result of conforming to such violence is self-destructive. For instance, when the women eagerly participate in Zero's attempt to kill Tristessa, who is the consummate female impersonator in a mausoleum of wax effigies, they become trapped in Tristessa's glass house. Through their own murderous impulses, exhibited in their desire to please Zero, the house becomes shattered, killing them in its wildly "spinning, transparent labyrinth" (PNE 116). If women play by the rules of violence, they fall into an 'imitation' of femininity, and are destroyed in its transparent labyrinth (PNE 140).

If Zero is a parody of Eve/lyn with his love and hate response to Tristessa, Eve/lyn is also a parody of Zero with the dubious advantage of having suffered female revenge. When Zero rapes Eve/lyn, the mind of the male Eve/lyn looks on the suffering female body, with detachment. The bodily reality of Eve is something Eve/lyn does not get involved in:

"Somewhere in the fear of rape, is a more than merely physical terror of hurt and humiliation – a fear of psychic disintegration, of an essential dismemberment, a fear of the loss or disruption of the self, which is not confined to the victim alone." (Carter,2000:6)

Eve/lyn's repeated rape by Zero constitutes her fall from innocence and her psychic transformation into womanhood. Eve/lyn notes, "although I was a woman, I was now passing for a woman, but, then, many women born spend their whole lives in just such imitations" (PNE 103). Bakhtin's definition of the grotesque body as the "Ever unfinished, ever changing body" describes the contours of woman, who is but a grotesque copy. Eve/lyn's left-behind status as a man produces, as the alchemist draws a pure metal out of a mixture of alloys, the humiliations she suffers as a woman:

"And more than my body, some other yet equally essential part of my being was ravaged by him for, when [Zero] mounted me [. . .] I felt myself to be, not myself but he; and the experience of this crucial lack of self, which always brought with it a shock of introspection, forced me to know myself as a former violator at the moment of my own violation". (PNE 101-102)

Eve/lyn has not only taken on a new sexual identity, but an identity fuelled by a persistent sense of loss. Zero's assault creates further confusion as to the past, as memories merge with the images of a new femininity:

"my new flesh momentarily betrayed me; it swept my memory back to prep school, the smell of fresh sweat, flannel boys' bodies, fresh cut grass…but it was not a real memory, it was like remembering a film I'd seen once whose performances did not concern me. Even my memories no longer fitted me, they were old clothes belonging to somebody else no longer living." (PNE 92)

Both Tristessa and Eve/lyn "embody the feminine passion of suffering" (Ledwon, 1993:32) in Beulah within the process of transsexualization. "Tristessa masquerades as a woman, willingly taking the role of feminine suffering while still a biological man, Eve/lyn experiences bodily pain in the actual body of a woman." (Ledwon, 1993:32). Tristessa is its icon brought to life by the movie industry, and Eve/lyn is a mirrored image.

The myth of the eternal feminine is luring to men, not just because it is created from a male point of view. It is a myth that gives women an ambiguous power reflecting men's Oedipal longing for the mystery, the mother. Tristessa confides to Eve/lyn why she longs to be a woman, pointing out the power of female passivity: "I was seduced by the notion of a woman's being, which is negativity. Passivity, the absence of being. To be everything and nothing" (PNE 137). This confession highlights ironically that women are deprived of social roles, lacking a subject position from which to speak or act. They are vulnerable, as Tristessa in the glass house, confined in the world of shadows.

Eve/lyn, a transsexual who regards her new body as a costume, is aware of her feminine masquerade. She is a woman conscious of her male gaze even if her phallic drive is annihilated by Zero. Before she found out Tristessa was a man, she thought him a woman; later when she learnt he was a man, she 'could not think of him as a man' but a "proud, solitary heroine who now underwent the unimaginable ordeal of a confrontation with the essential aspect of its being" (PNE 128). His/her love for Tristessa appears both feminine- narcissistic and heterosexual since his/her desire for 'her' is predetermined by the masculine sexuality of Eve/lyn.

The impossibility to confine the monstrous, hybrid body resulting from the union of Tristessa and Eve/lyn shatters the pyramid of desire:

"The vengeance of the sex," Eve/lyn remarks as she sets off for the unknown, "is love" (PNE 191). Thus Eve/lyn finally sees her mutilation at the hands of the cult of Beulah not as a simple revenge for the abandonment of their daughter Leilah, but as a gesture of generosity and love. Moreover, Eve/lyn's acceptance of her new status as woman is that it is only in this patched up form that she can achieve the goal of Evelyn; that is, to "find himself." Evelyn could not have found himself because he had not acknowledged any loss or lack, given his privileged position. Through his transformation into a woman, "he" found "himself" through the recognition that "she" has nothing to lose.

In his transformation, Eve/lyn's self as man is annihilated for a new self as woman. Similar to Deleuze and Guattari's use of alchemy as a metaphor for a process of becoming (1988:253), Carter suggests that Eve/lyn's identity as a woman is not the end goal, that her child, whom Schmidt (1990:67) sees as becoming Fevvers in *Nights at the Circus*, will shatter the binary masculine-feminine. Fevvers is "the new symbol of femininity... She is the archaeopteryx Eve/lyn had envisaged". Eve/lyn's journey through the cave at the novel's ending also renders the extinction of the self as time runs backwards, suggesting that Eve as a woman is just as vulnerable to change as Evelyn is, as a man.

The theatre underscores the fluidity of identity. With the doubling of disguises, the terms masculine and feminine become meaningless; gender and sexuality become mixed up. As Judith Butler (1990:140) asserts in *Gender Trouble*, gender is not a stable identity but a variable one constituted "through a stylized repetition of acts", so that the idea of an original gender identity is revealed, through parodic repetition, "to be nothing other than a parody of the idea of the natural and the original" (1990:31). However, Evelyn's transition to Eve suggests finality. Eve can only play at maleness now, and, by the end of the novel, she feels she has found her true identity as a woman by rejecting maleness. In retrospect, nevertheless, Eve/lyn still does not understand gender distinctions:

"Masculine and feminine are correlatives which involve one another. I am sure that the quality and its negation are locked in necessity. But what the nature of masculine and the nature of feminine might be, whether they involve male and female, if they have anything to do with Tristessa's so long neglected apparatus or my own factory fresh incision and engine-turned breasts, that I do not know. Though I have been both man and woman, still I do not know the answer to these questions." (PNE 149-150)

The system of caves at the end of the novel reminds us of the association of the grotesque with the grotto and female anatomy. Eve's remark, "I am inching my way towards the beginning and the end of time" (PNE 185), positions her as the creator of the future, pregnant with the child of the future, born of parents whose gender and sexuality are stripped of traditional dichotomies.

4.3. SONGS AND DANCES

The heterogeneous collection of characters in *Wise Children* marks the novel as carnivalesque, as a site of grotesque realism that, in Bakhtin's (1984:48) words, "discloses the potentiality of an entirely different world". Theatre and performance represent a means of cultural encounter, in which the shift from comedy to tragedy occurs in different styles and registers, and is meant to help us to acknowledge that the past is filtered through clashing discourses, whose values we should question before we adopt.

Carter stressed the significance of Shakespeare's theatre in many interviews, aiming to reclaim him from what she regarded as the confines of high culture, as well as stressing the various ways in which alternative ages and cultures have adapted his work:

> "The extraordinary thing about English literature is that actually our greatest writer is the intellectual equivalent of bubblegum, but can make a 12 year-old cry, can foment revolutions in Africa, can be translated into Japanese and leave not a dry eye in the house." (Sage, 1994:187)

She pays homage to him in her last novel, where he becomes the symbol of capital with his presence on "not just any old bank note but on a high denomination one" (WC 191), and, above all, the subject of interpretation in music-hall, vaudeville, television, advertising and Hollywood productions. The themes of style and theatricality are important in Carter's fictions. Bakhtin states that carnival is an event that liberates participants from social restraints, and stresses the materiality of the body by celebrating a grotesque image. Carnivalesque writing is that which "has taken the carnival spirit into itself and thus reproduces, within its own structures and by its own practice, the characteristic inversions, parodies, and discrownings of carnival proper" (Dentith, 1995:65). The problem for women is that in the model outlined by Bakhtin, the carnival is suited well to masculinity but ill to femininity. Owing to the masquerading nature of femininity, in Carter's view "to be a woman is to be in drag" (Sage,1994:304), so women are already impersonating in the 'real' world. The idea of a transgressive carnival which seems to presuppose "a monistic world" (Webb,1994:304) as its base, is incompatible with the decentred experience of the female gender performance.

The short story 'Puss-in- Boots' celebrates laughter and lust in the style of the *commedia dell'arte*. Puss-in-Boots is described in a short story published posthumously, 'In Pantoland', as

225

"agile, and going on two legs more often than on four to stress his status as intermediary between the world of animals and our world. If he possesses some of the chthonic ambiguity of all dark messengers between different modes of being, nevertheless he is never less than a perfect valet to his master and hops and skips at Dick's bidding" (1996:383).

The story transgresses propriety and revels in the life of the body, with the witty plot of an adulterous wife and a sly, instinctual valet. But Carter's comment on the carnival is illustrative: "The essence of the carnival, the festival, the Feast of Fools, is transience" (1986:386).

Although the carnival is problematic to women with its male-dominated tendency and inherent limits, it is still employed as a major form for subversion in *Wise Children* , a novel structured in five chapters, in a self-conscious nod to its dramatic source.

Dora's Cockney narrative voice is a development of that of the cat-valet Puss in the short story 'Puss in Boots' where "love, sex and desire are demythologized in a hymn to here-and-now common sensual pleasure"(Peach, 1988:131).

In the female cat-like voice Dora joins the carnival of pleasure. In view of Dora's cautioning against the limits of the carnival, Linden Peach (1998:152) reads Dora's narrative voice mainly from the "down stage position" of the "Renaissance stage bastard", emphasizing the theatrical element as the primary writing position in Carter's late fictions:

> "If there is a single position from which Carter writes in *Wise Children* , it is not the carnivalesque *per se* but the theatre. ...she appears to write from the theatre conceived as a location of illegitimate power, pursuing the creative possibilities in the way in which in the Renaissance 'illegitimacy' and 'theatre' were often linked. From this vantage point of view, she is able to explore different sites of illegitimate power associated with the theatre, such as the carnivalesque, the mask, the brothel, and the social margins. Indeed, the source of the carnivalesque element in *Nights at the Circus* and *Wise Children* was undoubtedly Shakespeare rather than Bakhtin..." (Peach, 1998:145)

The source of Carter's carnivalesque is seen as Shakespearean, for the combination of both "the solemn canonical words and the vernacular counterparts" in his plays is also pursued in *Wise Children*: "the interest in the coexistence of two strands – the solemn and the carnivalesque – mirrors the coexistence of the illegitimate with the legitimate" (Peach, 1998:148).

The bastard daughters' story of *Wise Children* is an allegory of how women appropriate the male-centred cultural legacy and find a language to speak their experiences. The result is given a deliberately parodic kitsch effect by Carter with the hybridization of high cultural forms with the popular ones. She also examines the relationship the carnival daughters have with their paternal culture. The figure of Shakespeare as the supreme metaphor for English culture is used to illustrate the tragicomic game of attraction and oppression played by daughters and sons.

Female desire inspires the daughters to participate in the father's carnival and also releases the daughter from the tragic grip of a history troubled by problematic fatherhood. In order to assign meaning to her self, outside the male structure, she has to look for a new basis for personal identification. Being other in a group that is already marginal becomes a means of self-identification.

In *Wise Children* the pairs of identical twins are a key method the female characters exploit to insure the blurring of the self. Once the differences are covered, they have the power to direct the course of events. The mistaken identities, the inversions and the twists that follow as the twins, and their metaphorical equivalents, become better defined in the story, give way to chaos and laughter and spice up the carnivalesque elements of the novel.

> "We're stuck in the period at which we peaked.... All women do. We'd feel mutilated if you made us wipe off our Joan Crawford mouths.... We always make an effort. We paint an inch thick. We put on our faces before we come down to breakfast...." (WC 5-6).:

The Lucky Chances are also metaphorical mirror images of their cousins, Saskia and Imogen. Saskia and Imogen cast their own mother out of her home, and Dora and Nora take her in. While Saskia and Imogen exemplify charming, red-haired English Roses, Dora admits that, in their youth, she and Nora were "more coquette than finishing school. . . . Nymphettes, I suppose they'd call us now. Jail-bait" (WC 70). Saskia and Dora have been rivals since Saskia's childhood, while Imogen's tendency towards dozing off contrasts with Nora's "passion to know about Life [with] all its dirty corners" (WC 81).

The twists and turns in the story that the twins are responsible for stretch the borders of realism, culminating with the distorted reflections of the central image of Dora in various media, from flesh through written fiction, from stage to screen.

First, in the enchanted woods, art and life overlap as Dora confronts her fiancé's ex-wife:

"I saw my double. I saw myself, me, in my Peaseblossom costume, large as life, like looking in a mirror. First off, I thought it was Nora, up to something, but it put its finger to its lips, to shush me, and I got a whiff of Mitsouko and then I saw it was a replica. A hand-made, custom-built replica, a wonder of the plastic surgeon's art . . . .

And after all, she looked very lifelike, I must say, if not, when I looked more closely, not all that much like me, more like a blurred photocopy or an artist's impression. . . ." (WC 155)

The event is clarified later, so we learn that the ex-wife of Dora's fiancé, "Genghis Khan" has transformed herself into an imperfect replica of Dora:

"she'd had her nose bobbed, her tits pruned, her bum elevated, she'd starved and grieved away her middle-age spread. She'd had her back molars out, giving the illusion of cheekbones. Her face was lifted up so far her ears had ended up on the top of her head but, happily, the wig hid them" (WC 155)

However, if we look deeper, we realize that Dora is a simulacrum, because she does not love her fiancé, and his marriage proposal is not spurred by love, either. Nonetheless, the public eye sees them as a loving couple. The ex-wife, on the other hand, has never stopped loving Genghis Khan, so she is his real lover: "Before me stood the exed Mrs. Khan, who loved her man so much she was prepared to turn herself into a rough copy of his beloved for his sake" (WC155).

Carter further alters the definition of woman by distancing her central female characters from the standard roles and stereotypes, especially those of wives and mothers. On a closer examination, the carnivalesque space Dora presents in her narrative is more a feminist parody than an inheritance of the patriarchal carnival of Shakespeare. In Shakespeare's theatre, the comic low is placed alongside the legitimate but it ends up in being reabsorbed into the patriarchal order. Dora's 'vulgar' narrative voice moves the story on mimicking the tones of high culture. Shakespeare's Prospero initiates a wind to disrupt the illegitimate order and re-establish the legitimate one, whereas in Dora's narrative the tempest invoked by Peregrine brings no real change without her intervention. She breaks the patriarchal myth, repeating Gorgeous George's joke about the unfaithful mother to Saskia and Imogen, and changes the tragedy into a comedy, re-crowning the father (WC 226). The bastard daughter abuses the father's legacy, stripping it of any mythological dimension.

228

The spirit of the carnivalesque permeates the novel. And so it is that Dora has absolutely no reverence for the more exalted characters in the novel. The Lady Atlanta Hazard, first wife of Dora's father, Melchior, becomes "Wheelchair" after her daughters try to kill her. And even when Lady Atlanta is at her height of beauty and glory, Dora describes her as "a fair-haired lady with a sheep's profile," (WC 56) and "a sheep in a tiara" (WC 70).

Saskia and Imogen are also described as resembling "sheep with bright red fleece" (WC 74). Dora bluntly refuses to pay homage to her social "superiors", and is more inclined towards taking off their masks: " 'The lovely Hazard girls', they used to call them. Huh. Lovely is as lovely does; if they looked like what they behave like, they'd frighten little children," (WC 7). She is always ready to laugh at the absurd, no matter how elaborate its disguise. In her eyes and consequently in the story, social class divisions make no sense. She brings out everybody's flaws, including her own, backed up by shame and few regrets.

Dora's subversion can be analyzed in two stages, first in her youth and later in her old age. When she was young, she seemed engrossed in performing the sexy dancer role; when she grew old, she learned to see things as Grandma Chance did, coming to the conclusion that "nothing is a matter of life and death except life and death" (WC 215). Her illegitimate, old-hag position gives her a vantage point to see through the theatricality of the tragic pose of the failed father figures. Sharing the same popular cultural space as Shakespeare, the Chance sisters inherit his comic subversion with a sense of alienation. But in this ambiguous state of both inheriting and disinheritance, the overlapping paternal and maternal strands in the family tradition complicate the situation. The family history, reconstructed by Dora, can be traced back to their Victorian grandparents on the paternal side, Ranulph and Estella Hazard, the two most distinguished Shakespearean players of their generation. Their acting career, beginning from the mid-nineteenth century, spans the period of the rise and fall of the British empire. The grandparents represent two distinct performing traditions which sum up Carter's observation of sexual subjects as masqueraders. One is totally identified with the sexual role he/she plays, the other, seeing through the 'make-believe' of the act, played it with laughter.

In the family's theatrical tradition, the maternal Estella stands for the subversive laughter whereas the paternal Ranulph, wearing the mask of the tragic hero, is unable to take it off. "Shakespeare was a kind of god for him' and he thinks, as Dora notes, 'the whole of human life was there" (WC14). His belief in Shakespeare is so intense that the dramatic personae he had played on stage became more real than real life to him while he became a live puppet of them. The tragic scenarios run so deep in his character that they eventually substitute for his life-story.

In contrast, his wife Estella could not help but "giggle" (WC 14) during the tragic scenes, a comic indication of her seeing through its theatrical sense. Ranulph plays heroic, patriarchal roles, while Estella is a gender performer. She can play Hamlet as well as Cordelia. They make up contradictory lines of life as performance in the family's theatrical tradition.

Dora is not the sole female carnival player in the novel. Nora, Daisy Duck (the Hollywood sex star) and Estella feature significantly in the show. If we take their play collectively, we can find a linking point in their separate acts, as they all play out a daughter's transgression against patriarchal rule. The female subversion of the male carnival takes the form of tragedy turned into farce and bawdy. Estella gives her Lear a paper crown to mark his display of royal dignity. Dora, Nora and Daisy Duck share a common symbol for their transgressions – Melchior's Shakespearean casket. It is a container made in the shape of the playwright's bald head, filled with the sacred earth from Stradford-upon-Avon, completely fouled by Daisy's cat, which uses it as a piss-pot. As the Shakespearean pot becomes an empty container, Dora and Nora fill it with Hollywood dirt at Melchior's opening ceremony of his film adaptation of *A Midsummer Night's Dream*. The episode is farcical, pointing out the vulgarization of high art by mass culture, while implying a female satire on the worship of the father figure, Shakespeare.

Dora's reconstruction of the family history in terms of the paternal/maternal, tragic/comic theatricality is a cultural allegory. If in the theatrical family the patriarchal tradition has always been the dominant one, there is a subversive force of boundary-crossing in the figure of Estella, the irrepressible wife murdered by Ranulph. The two directions pass on to their twin sons Melchior and Peregrine, with Melchior continuing his father's tradition, Peregrine the mother's celebration of life as carnival. Following his father's faith in the transcendent greatness of Shakespeare worshipped beyond categories of gender, class and race, Melchior dedicates his life to impersonating Shakespeare's heroes. His identity, like that of his father, is occupied by the theatre's royal figures. In contrast to Melchior's "all for art" Peregrine is "out for fun", "a holy terror and couldn't keep a straight face, just like his mother" (WC 22). Another difference also sets the two brothers apart. Different from Melchior's princely charm, Peregrine is endowed with a charm of "pulp romance" (WC 30) which links him to pop culture. He also continues his mother's talent for sexual transgression and celebration of light comedy in defiance of the tragic hero's death. He is a magician who can summon doves out of handkerchiefs (WC 31), make a full set of china and cutlery disappear after an afternoon picnic (WC 62), snatch a couple of cream buns from Grandma Chance's cleavage (WC 73) or, best of all, extract a scarlet macaw from Melchior's tights.

Perry is like a travelling carnival, turning sudden disappearances into an art. When he finally reappears, he brings fun and revelry with him. It is he who first introduces Dora and Nora, at an early age, to the magic of the phonograph, and the joy of song and dance (WC 33). Yet, beyond his conjuring talents and his ability to raise the spirits of those around him into a celebratory state, events themselves often take up an aura of magic when Perry comes to visit. On one occasion, Perry suggests that they dance: "As I remember it, a band struck up out of nowhere.... Or perhaps it was Perry on his harmonica, all the time, who provided the music, so that we could dance for him"(WC 68). Later, even stranger things ensue:

> "Peregrine spread his arms as wide as wings and gathered up the orphan girls, pressed us so close we crushed against his waistcoat, bruising our cheeks on his braces' buttons. Or perhaps he slipped one of us in each pocket of his jacket. Or he crushed us far inside his shirt, against his soft, warm belly, to be sustained by the thumping comfort of his heart. And then, hup! he did a back-flip out of the window with us, saving us" (WC72).

He is monumental – "the size of a warehouse, bigger, the size of a tower block" (WC206) and as far as he's concerned "life's a carnival"(WC 222). As Dora says, he is "always the lucky one, our Peregrine, even in his memories, which [a]re full of laughter and dancing; he always remember[s] the good times" (WC 18).

Peregrine is apparently presented as the embodiment of male-dominated carnival, but he is also a key figure in showing Dora the fantastic exchange between illusion and reality. He is not the only carnival player, and, more importantly, he is unable to transgress his own sexual role. Dora is the one playing the tigress to seduce him on his centenary birthday as she is the other key carnival player. If carnival is a site of the cultural low subverting the high, the illegitimate other overthrowing the legitimate centre, then Dora's position is closer to the carnivalesque than Peregrine's. He may be the male force mocking patriarchal authority, making his father Melchior jump for the paper crown, but it is Dora who subverts the male carnival as she joins the game.

Carter's critique of the imperialist use of Shakespeare appears in Dora's satirical narration of the Hazard family's ambition to tour and enlighten the world with the Bard's words. The satire is directed at the national cult, not at the dramatist, and Carter's message is that the spreading of the Bard's words has become a family mission paralleling the British imperialistic enterprise. From the novel's feminist point of view, the Hazard's dream of spreading the 'seeds' to the world indicates a patriarchal desire to Anglicize the globe or educate it with great Shakespearean heroes. This great dream is further ridiculed by the performance of Gorgeous George. This comic figure, as Kate Webb observed, "comes in the tradition of the holiday camp entertainer", whose 'punchline' is "a withering attack on a foolishly deluded old patriarch who thinks himself the greatest stud around." (1994:285)

While Gorgeous George's performance exhibits the Shakespearean motifs of male anxiety about paternity, the linking of the imperial posture with clownish anxiety is most striking. Gorgeous George, posing as a rake, wielding his "golf club" as display of his power, finds the father's authority overthrown by cuckoldry. When he goes on to the climatic showing of his body tattooed with the British imperial map he is showered with rosy light, losing his manly authority (WC 65-6). Near the end of the novel, he acts out the disintegration of the masculine masquerade, turning into "some old cove in rags, begging" outside Melchior's centenary birthday party (WC 195).

Dora and Nora's rise to fame includes their participation in *What? You Will?*, a musical revue with crazy numbers, such as the Hamlet sketch, where the twins, dressed as bellhops, question whether a package should be delivered "2b or not 2b". The dazzling collection of sketches mentioned adds to the allure of the production whose title is punctuated differently for virtually each usage in the novel. Secondly, the twins play Peaseblossom and Mustardseed in *The Dream*, a full-fledged, classical-Hollywood production of *A Midsummer Night's Dream*, rife with a water ballet, "kaleidoscope effects", a cascade, all the requisite aspects to turn the work from classical to kitsch. The film is an extravagant example of a shameless commodification of Shakespeare, as Dora's regretful voice suggests:

"What I missed most was illusion. That wood near Athens was too, too solid for me [...] there wasn't the merest whiff about the kind of magic that comes when the theatre darkens, the bottom of the curtain glows." (WC125).

All the Shakespearean-style villainy, comic relief and intricate plot elements are revisioned and re-enacted and they shape a new story, whose love triangles off-set literally blow up the production. The ultimate carnival transgression Dora commits is her and Nora's dressing themselves up as their seventeen-year-old selves when they are seventy-five. They appear at their father's centenary party as female impersonators inviting and defying the public gaze: "we painted the faces that we always used to have on to the faces we have now. From a distance of thirty feet with the light behind us, we looked, at first glance, just like the girl who danced with the Prince of Wales" (WC 192).

Nora's remark shows how femininity and masculinity are both theatrical performance, as well as the anxiety that lies behind the play: "'It's every woman's tragedy that, after a certain age, she looks like a female impersonator,'" and it is "Every man's tragedy" that "'*he* doesn't'" (ibid.).The theatre becomes thus the Lacanian 'scopic field', in which the subject performs for the public gaze. Dora has sex in her father's bedroom, Grandma goes naked in the boarding house, Melchior invokes his father's role.

Peach's observations link the carnivalesque with the theatrical. The carnival always represents a theatrical site for transgression, but the reverse cannot be said about the theatrical, as the Elizabethan theatre was more dominated by the legitimate power. Melchior cannot laugh at the roles he plays, so his performance verges on tragedy. Contrary to his performance is Dora's masquerade, who refuses to play the tragic part of self-annihilation and makes fun of her and Nora's estranged images of "old painted harlots" (WC:229).

No matter how problematic the theatrical tradition is, what the Chance sisters have inherited from their paternal line falls within the popular cultural realm to which Gorgeous George belongs. The site they inhabit is, however, a female one. The power is shown through their legs, linking them to their grandmother , Estella: "'We've got the legs from her', Dora asserted" (WC12) and to her carnival power. As the initiator of the transgressive force of the family, Estella subverts the tragedy performance from within, although her romantic comedy ends tragically in her husband's live performance of the *Othello* plot. The dancing legs link their performative art to their sexual power and desire, in contrast to Gorgeous George's male sexual power figured by his golf club.

The Chances start their subversive activity against the patriarchal hierarchy from the low base of music-hall dancing. Patriarchy is presented as prone to tragedy in its outlook, imbued with the father's fear of the son's challenge and the son's anxiety of how to become a father. There is the funny "2b or not 2b" light comedy of Dora and Nora against the 'son's' tragic soliloquy of "to be or not to be", and Ranulph's "never, never, never..." (WC 53). It may seem a mere coincidence for Melchior to say to Dora "Strange how potent cheap music is" (WC 87) when he first admits to their father-daughter relationship on the Chances seventeenth birthday. The so-called cheap music is the cultural realm the sisters have chosen to live in. It is also significant that the low cultural realm the Chances inherit comes from their Grandma Chance, who presided over a ghetto-area boarding house for chorus boys and girls. The Chance sisters were conceived and born in her house and the first experience they had with the world was the joyful sight of children "dancing and singing" (WC26) in the middle of the Great War. The song they heard was a tragicomic song about Charlie Chaplin, a major figure of modern pop culture who came from the music-hall tradition, with his comic art nurtured by his mother.

The maternal, the low-cultural and the illegitimate are three equal terms in the high cultural realm. In the modernist imagination, female performative art, be it dancing, singing, sewing or cooking, was considered unoriginal. On the other hand, the figure of woman is elevated to the status of the muse, inspiring male artists. This paradoxical approach is exemplified in Dora's relationship with the depressed playwright Irish, a writer whose talent is crippled by his involvement with the Hollywood industry. Coming to him as a muse who made the world look "like a benediction" (WC 120) to him, Dora represents a split image of femininity. She both inspires his writing, the *Hollywood Elegies*, and emerges as a "vulgar", "painted harlot" from his stories. To him, Dora illustrates vulgar mass culture, the Hollywood he "loved to hate". Although Dora's "vulgarity" needs Irish's "philanthropic" (WC13) education in order to find a language and tell her story, she does not allow his vision to substitute for hers. "That California sunshine", portrayed as "insincere" by Irish, is regarded by Dora as "the most democratic thing" (WC 121) shining on everyone.

Dora and Nora, the two perfect dolls on stage, seem absorbed by the forces of mass culture, hitting rock bottom as *Nudes* in vaudeville. They are however able to counter the power of mass culture to objectify their body, and the disdain high art has for their art, with the help of Grandma Chance's lesson in survival "Hope for the best, expect the worst" (WC 168). Whether treated as the inferior other or as the inspirational muse, Dora and Nora choose the vulgar comedy of love, measured in number of lovers, to resist the tragedy of love and death. Music-hall dancing becomes a manifestation of sexual and cultural assertion.

Pop songs are also a site for male chauvinism. The strategy Dora and Nora adopt is to confront the repertoire of Gorgeous George with manifestations of their desire. The pop songs they sing or hear in their youth are used in old age by Dora to assert their wrong-sidedness and satirize the education received from her mentor-lover Irish: "I balked at Proust" (WC:95), expresses the opposite style of remembering her past, the 'unrefined' bawdy style.

Bawdy is an important stylistic element in Dora's narrative, employed as a parodic tool to foreground paternal authority from a sexual or literary point of view. As a literary skill, bawdy, like farce, deflates the high tone of serious art, being a frequent feature employed by Shakespeare. As a comic intrusion into the romantic sexual drama, bawdy is one of the links in Carter's approach of Shakespearean drama as part of the English pop culture. Dora's low style contrasts with Gorgeous George's performance and Uncle Perry's carnivalesque attitude. If Gorgeous George's bawdy enacts a vivid archetype of Shakespearean manhood, it is not a performance that can maintain its vitality. He gradually loses his 'theatre' in today's changing world. This is seen most clearly in his Hollywood performance as he joins Melchior's movie production of *A Midsummer Night's Dream*:

"He was like a fine wine if only in the one respect, he didn't travel. The moment he stepped off his native soil, he stopped being funny. In California, he was not bawdy, he was lewd...he wore a baffled look as if, when nobody laughed, he didn't know what to do with himself" (WC151).

While this type of manhood loses its appeal, the carnivalesque type Peregrine embodies maintains its transgressive power. The carnival side of Shakespeare is, in my opinion, what fascinates Carter, a fascination voiced through Dora as narrator. Dora allows her vision of events to slip even further from the bonds of realism and shift into a magical realist perspective. Anything can, and does happen. And so it is that during the party following the filming of the movie *The Dream*, the set of the Athenian woods can be transformed:

"The tin roof over our head seemed to have cracked open and disappeared, somehow, because there was a real, black sky above us... And I no longer remember that set as a set, but as a real wood, dangerous, uncomfortable, with real, steel spines on the conkers and thorns on the bushes, but looking as if it were unreal and painted, and the bewildering moonlight spilled like milk in this wood, as if Hollywood were the name of the enchanted forest where you lose yourself and find yourself, again; the wood that changes you; the wood where you go mad; the wood where the shadows live longer than you do." (WC 157-8)

Here, we catch a glimpse of the ambivalence of the carnivalesque since the magical aspects of the revelry are also reminders of mortality. The celebration of life may be ongoing, but the individuals are transient. The carnivalesque celebrates the cycle of birth, life, death and transformation, drawing our attention to mortality at the same time. The revelry of the carnivalesque displays its darker side as well. This darker side is as intriguing an aspect as the brighter one, and it fuels the excitement of the protagonists (Danow,1995). The climax of all the wild, surreal celebrations can be found at the end of the novel, during Melchior's 100th birthday celebration, a party jazzed up with monumental laughter. There are shadows of death and betrayal, but also relief, once the reports of both Perry and Tiffany's deaths are invalidated. Dora adopts a comic vision on life, although the tragedy of the two sisters pondering on a childless old age is evident. But she fights off the tragic sense with a comic mask "I refuse point-blank to play in tragedy" (WC 154).

Three-month old twins, "brown as [...] quail[s], round as [...] egg[s]" (WC 226), are presented to Dora and Nora, courtesy of Perry, so that the novel ends with the marvellous, utterly carnivalesque image of the laughing hags, serenading their new babies as they head toward their home on Bard Road.

***

The merging of fictional space and real space, punctuated by ritual activity turns theatre into heterotopia. Located simultaneously in the world of the performance and in the real world, the stage can be one of the border crossings to a hybrid world. Theatre proves to be not only a key site of textual exploration and a cultural institution to be questioned, but also an essential component of Carter's fictional style leading to a profound duality in her work, as Haffenden notes:

"I suppose that someone could approach the fantastic and exotic surface of your fictions and not be able to bridge the gap to the central point that your theatricality is meant to heighten real social attitudes and myths of femininity" (1985:91).

He perceives the overlap of fantasy and reality as an inexplicable paradox:

"You are a committed materialist, I know, and yet your writing unleashes what you've elsewhere called all sorts of 'imaginative gaiety'. So we're left with the paradox that you choose to accentuate the real by writing tall stories in lush locales" (1985:92).

In *The Passion of New Eve*, Carter explores the formation of the subject in relation to desire and gender, as I have argued in Scenes of Dissemblance. The question of how to break the hold of patriarchy is answered within a space of infinite flexibility accessed through fantasy. The notion of the marvellous enables new ways of seeing, revealing the limitations of the traditional, patriarchal ways of knowing. As the art of alchemy is the conversion of the four elements into each other, Carter uses it to dissolve gender categories and patriarchal myths, re-creating the world of the novel. She deconstructs sex and gender distinctions through hybrid figures, a Surrealist technique. The quest of the hero turned heroine combines the material with the spiritual, while the tension between becoming woman and escaping gender categories, and self and other, creates the hybrid figures in the novel. Mythical versions of the female body are laid bare, with the figure of the castrated woman at their heart.

The mirror is an important element in the characters' performance. It is a symbol of woman's entrapment in the male gaze and a catalyzing force in alchemy. It serves as a sexual theatre for Leilah, Tristessa and Eve/lyn. Sexuality appears as a disruptive force, as the bodies, reflected in mirrors, show the splits in the self. The image of metamorphosis often illustrates the rebirth of the self with the notion of selfhood becoming fragmented, making identity confusing and defined by multiple selves. Androgyny is presented in Carter's works as a mystification, but also as necessary for the development of self-knowledge. This exposes the ways in which the social construct of gender and accompanying notions of femininity and masculinity are not dependant on one's sex: these notions, like Tristessa, are "an illusion in a void" (PNE 110), reflected in the mirrors of postmodern plurality.

Heterotopia can be described as places that comprise other places and open upon a breach in traditional time. The end and the beginning of time co-exist in the novel to reinforce the idea of female sexuality as culturally constructed through violence, as I have determined in Twists of Passion. Mimicry becomes an effective means of confrontation with the ways in which a patriarchal order violently constructs gendered identities. Carter refuses to entertain any notion of women as victims. Nanette Altevers asserts that Carter, though accepting Foucault's idea of the construction of sexuality, "does not accept his deconstruction of the subject. She believes in the "self, as autonomous being" (IDM 19). Alchemy bridges the essential and the fragmented subjects, as the infinite combination of the four essential elements also suggests, according to Catherine Keller's (1986:182) theory. Performance empowers the characters of Carter's paradoxical spaces, while magic, as the hybrid figures in the novel imply, shatters the violence of the real creating another possibility. Tristessa and New Eve are two different embodiments of the mythical figure, which cannot be separated, for Eve bears Tristessa's child. Both negation and affirmation are comprised in the definition of carnival the writer follows, in line with Bakhtin:

237

"While carnival lasts, there is no other life outside it. During carnival life is subject only to its laws, that is, the laws of its own freedom. It has a universal spirit; it is a special condition of the entire world, of the world's revival and renewal, in which all take part." (1984:7)

She was drawn to the capacity of drama to activate fantasy and reality simultaneously. Albert Camus describes the struggle of the actor to voice the inner state of the characters he plays:

"He will die in three hours under the mask he has assumed today. Within three hours he must experience and express a whole exceptional life. That is called losing oneself to find oneself. In those three hours he travels the whole course of the dead-end path that the man in the audience takes a lifetime to cover". (1991:80)

Carter directs her characters towards overtly performing environments. But Dora and Carter have consciously chosen to shy away from this subtext to revelry in *Wise Children*, as I have indicated in Songs and Dances. Dora is an actor who knows all her steps and lines by heart, so the novel is an ode to a different kind of celebration, kindled by spectacular moments but thoroughly balanced, at the same time.

Mary Russo (1994:218) takes on the issue of disruption that carnival brings into society:

"The masks and violence of carnival resist, exaggerate, and destabilize the distinctions and boundaries that mark and maintain high culture and organized society. It is as if the carnivalesque body politic has ingested the entire corpus of high culture and, in its bloated and irrepressible state, released it in fits and starts in all manner of recombination, inversion, mockery, and degradation.... Carnival can be seen above all as a site of insurgency, and not merely withdrawal."

Furthermore, Carter is not so much mocking the Shakespearean plot, but locates in Shakespeare those elements that have always belonged to the family romance, the origin of stories. This is not to say that Carter is accusing Shakespeare of perpetuating patriarchal myths. Rather, she finds in him an ally for interrogating these myths, using elements from his own texts that work to disrupt the accepted social order through their exploration of alternative relationships to otherness. She sought to celebrate Shakespeare's plurality rather than his fixity, his endless textual reinvention in the context of different media.

238

Foucault calls places which differ from the systems that they reflect heterotopias. Theatre stands for the heterotopia that stages its spaces and offers them to the spectators at the level of characters, events or to narrative styles. In the two novels I have analysed, Angela Carter allows theatricality to permeate the characters' journeys across continents, to ultimately reveal that identity cannot be separated from performativity. Notwithstanding the author's tight grip, orchestration of theatricality can be made to appear chaotic and wild in *The Passion of New Eve* and *Wise Children*. Although Angela Carter holds sway over her characters and her stories, the air of carnivalesque dazzle is vividly felt.

5. HETEROTOPIA –
THE WARP AND WEFT OF STORYTELLING

The world constructed in and by the literary text refers outside the text to the objective world and to all that it embodies. However, the overlapping and merging between real and fictional planes opposes the realist tradition, and the resulting narrative produces a flickering of worlds, with the author both inside and outside heteroglossia (Bakhtin, 1982). Angela Carter's postmodernist writing strategies foreground the textuality of fiction, force constant reinterpretation, and generate a plurality of worlds for the readers to cross: "I don't mind being called a spell-binder. Telling stories is a perfectly honourable thing to do" (Carter, 1985:82). In her 'Afterword' to *Fireworks*, Carter refers to the rejection of realism in her narratives:

> "The tale does not log everyday experience...[but] interprets everyday experience through a
> system of imagery derived from subterranean areas behind everyday experience, and therefore
> the tale cannot betray its readers into a false knowledge of everyday experience" (BB 459).

Angela Carter's intertextual references keep the reader hovering between distant observer and entangled participant. She draws on a multitude of discourses, ranging from oral to historiographic, keeping the reader alert, on his/her intertextual journey, in line with Sean Hand's (1990:79) vision of an "act of transference which involves creating an intertextual space in which the story changes as it is listened to and worked on... a search for the narrative's forgotten origin is replaced by a recognition of the active process of constructing the narrative".

This chapter addresses the polyphonic aspect of Carter's novels *Nights at the Circus, Wise Children, The Passion of New Eve* and her two cinematic adaptations which she co-scripted, *The Magic Toyshop* and *The Company of Wolves,* as the hidden stitch in her narrative fabric. Her characters are Scheherazades inventing stories, whereas the author spins the threads guiding them through heterotopia of liberty. I will illustrate the importance of *memory* in the creation of the fictional universe of the novels and the two movies, as it appears to be the chief trigger of the instability of the narrative. The discourse is heterotopic since is folds back on itself, opening new perspectives for the readers. There are unstable frames of temporal reference in the stories shaped by narrators whose position we constantly call into question, spurred by the interchangeability of characters and narrators. The writer requires us, the readers, to read through the lenses of other texts, just as she mingles various discourses in her texts, and "turns letters into seductive and harmless weapons" Brînzeu, 1995:13 [my trans.]). Narrative is exposed by Angela Carter as a trickster, as heterodiegetic (Chatman, 1983) ideologies resound, allowing freedom of expression to her characters/narrators. Fiction turns into film beyond the mirror, structured on anachronism, linear narration becomes circular in her heterotopia of the grotesque, where the reader ventures guided by laughing hags weaving threads of significance.

In his essay 'Forms of Time and Chronotope in the Novel', Bakhtin (1982:243) elaborates a study of the chronotope in the history of the novel, stating that "a literary work's unity in relationship to an actual reality is defined by its chronotope" and "in literature and art itself, temporal and spatial determinations are inseparable from one another, always coloured by emotions and values".

He discusses kinds of chronotopes in the novel, using examples such as the road (in *Don Quixote*), the castle (in the Gothic novel) or parlours and salons (in the realist novels of Stendhal and Balzac), to trace the development of the novel. On explaining the chronotope as a particular spatial location that resonates with the passage of time, Bakhtin (1982:250) poses a question:

"What is the significance of all these chronotopes? What is most obvious is their meaning for *narrative*. They are the organising centres for the fundamental narrative events of the novel. The chronotope is the place where the knots of the narrative are tied and united. It can be said without qualification that to them belongs the meaning that shapes narrative... it is precisely the chronotope that provides the ground essential for the showing-forth, the representability of events... Thus the chronotope, functioning as the primary means for materialising time in space, emerges as a centre for concretizing representation, as a force giving body to the entire novel. All the novel's abstract elements... gravitate toward the chronotope and through it take on flesh and blood, permitting the imaging power of art to do its work. Such is the representational significance of the chronotope."

Spinning stories turns into a means of reshaping the world in *Nights at the Circus* and *Wise Children*. The expectations of a novel's structure are upset through the postmodern construction of multiple narratives that defy the conventional logic of plot. Comments related to this structure appear in the novels, mirroring the reflexivity of postmodern fiction. They are meant to demystify the construction of the story, illustrating the profound effect of the multiple

241

narratives on both the characters and the readers. Teresa de Lauretis (1984) argues that strategies of writing and reading are forms of cultural resistance. This can also apply to oral storytelling. By having Fevvers and Dora Chance tell their own stories as they choose, the novels challenge the traditional appropriation of women's lives in Western male-centred culture. Furthermore, both women narrators, Fevvers and Dora Chance deliberately flirt with the boundary between truth and non-truth. Their stories are both autobiographies and fairy-tales, and therefore destabilize male definitions of womanhood.

5.1. THE 'CONFIDENCE TRICK'

The fictional play of sexual identity in *Nights at the Circus* is pursued mainly in the narrative lines of Fevvers and Walser's adventures. The major cause of fantastic hesitancy that drives the multiple narrative strands forward is the spectacle of Fevvers' winged body. With these wings, her identity can hover from the extreme of a biological freak to that of an angelic being. But the meanings that have been associated with her body image are metaphorical readings that have never served the women's cause. Her main problem appears to be how to construct a sexual subject position for her 'unnatural' existence and, speaking from that pose, to fight the forces pinning her down as a goddess or fetish. The sexual identity Fevvers constructs for herself is the image of a New Woman whose power derives from the spectacle of her winged body. She believes her body signifies "the abode of limitless freedom" (NC 41) which will set women free to form a new sexual order. The crucial point in her confidence game is not the belief in a transcendental identity; it is the recognition of the fictional nature of human representations. She gives up the puppet role assumed by her predecessors who act out the scripts that 'write' them. In her invented identity as a New Woman opening a new century, she is engaged in a fictional play, both visual and narrative. As her slogan 'Is she fact or is she fiction?' suggests, her mystery lies in her appearance and in convincing her audience of her status.

Fevvers represents the uncanny other Freud defined as

> "nothing new or alien, but something which is familiar and old-established in the mind and which has become alienated from it only through the process of repression…the uncanny as something which ought to have remained hidden but has come to light" (1998:50).

The bird-woman recalls the animality of the humans, and it is displayed at the physical and psychological levels, simultaneously. She is in control of the commercialization of her animality for the scopic enjoyment of the viewers. She basks in her eccentricity and the mystery of her in-between body:

> "My be-ing, my me-ness, is unique and indivisible. To sell the use of myself for the enjoyment of another is one thing; I might even offer freely, out of gratitude or in the expectation of pleasure – and pleasure alone is my expectation from the young American. But the essence of myself may not be given or taken, or what would be left of me?" (NC 281)

What she sells is her image, not her soul. The bird state is part of her "essence", that not only defines her, but preserves her as a whole. Her wings undermine the patriarchal authority represented by "the circus ring with its hierarchy of male performers, [...], a spirit of competition, a preoccupation with financial profit and an oppressive treatment of subordinates, including women and animals" (Palmer,1987:198).

As Cixous explains,

"Flying is woman's gesture – flying in language and making it fly. We have all learned the art of flying and its numerous techniques; for centuries we've been able to possess anything only by flying; we've lived in flight, stealing away, finding when desired, narrow passageways, hidden crossovers. It's no accident that *voler* has a double meaning, that it plays on each of them and thus throws off the agents of sense. It's no accident: women take after birds and robbers just as robbers take after women and birds". (1997: 356–7)

Constructing Fevvers' image in the icon of Winged Victory and the grotesque New Woman, Carter is engaged in an ongoing dialogue with de Sade's stories about female sexuality pursued in *The Sadeian Woman*. Fevvers' characterization echoes the monstrous Juliette, but her power is based on "the pleasure of the flesh" promoted in Ma Nelson's brothel, and is not an oppressive, threatening weapon. According to Linda Williams (1995:15), Fevvers is "partly the simple symbol of *jouissance*" as "dreams of flying are dreams of sex" and "she might also be the wish-fulfilment of another dream-desire which Freud discusses, to be like a bird." She uses her power to build up relationships.

Another link between Fevvers' and Juliette's female power is their ability to fabricate, which, in Carter's reading of de Sade's satirical stories of sexual relationships, is essential for survival either in a brothel or in a brothel-like culture:

"Juliette's story-telling function is itself part of her whorishness. She is a perfect whore, like the whores in *The Hundred and Twenty Days at Sodom*... These four women survive the ensuing holocaust... because, like Scheherazade, they know how to utilize the power of the word, of narrative, to save their lives.... Juliette, the personification of the whore as story-teller, often breaks off her narrative encounters with her listeners, who are all old friends and occasionally appear as actual actors in it. She leaves a pornographic hole in the text on purpose for them." (2000:81)

244

The stories are not only meant to persuade customers to participate in her sadistic games, but also to destroy the law that confines women to the passive role of suffering. On the other hand, she is objectifying herself. In looking for satisfaction from her customers, she positions herself as object of desire. This type of female predator is present in many tales of Angela Carter where the female victim takes on the male's role to enact the victimizing plot on others as well as on herself. Fevvers, in contrast, uses narratives for a different purpose. She parodies Juliette's pornographic approach and lures her audience into joining her teasing game, inviting them to 'peep at' and speculate about her body, fighting the confining power of the male gaze. Story-telling, in Fevvers' case, is linked to the image of her wings. In the seductive game she plays with her audience, she simulates the fantastic image of an extraordinary woman. She claims authenticity while the spectacle she offers clearly encourages speculation about it. In a broader sense, she raises the question about the validity of the Western tendency to privilege the visual as source of truth.

Craig Owens's (1992:202) discussion of the subversive potential of 'posing' is relevant, I think, in illuminating Fevvers' career as performer. In his analysis of contemporary conceptual arts, he observes that "if these artists all regard sexuality as a pose, it is not in the sense of position or posture, but of imposition, imposture". All along, when Fevvers has been posing for representations of femininity focused on the figure of the winged woman, she has been participating in a show of duplicity. Her simulation is an active act of faking a passive archetype. Since she knows the archetype is fake, she acquires the necessary distance to avoid identification with it and can create a space for making up a subject position: "the freedom that lies behind the mask, within dissimulation, the freedom to juggle with being" (NC 103). Fevvers knows how to use language to play the game of seeing and believing and win it. She mimics the female icons imposed on her with satirical detachment.

A comic text, that asks us to doubt the apparent coherence of realism along with the traditional representation of woman, *Nights at the Circus* has that "ineffable something" (Flieger, 1991:3) that "lends a plural and playful quality" (Flieger, 1991:5) to postmodern texts, something that demonstrates a "tendency to duplicity" (1991:6). Flieger notes "the comic symptom and scene of postmodernity" (1991:xi). In *Nights at the Circus* there is a "recasting of Oedipal drama as a comic play of shifting roles rather than a tragic fate assigned by gender" (Flieger, 1991: ix).

245

Bakhtin identifies the multiple languages that coexist within the same narrative as a fundamental feature of the English comic novel:

"Thus the stratification of literary language, its speech diversity, is an indispensable prerequisite for comic style, whose elements are projected onto different linguistic planes while at the same time the intention of the author, refracted as it passes through these planes, does not wholly give itself up to any of them." (1982:311)

Part I, *London*, centres around Fevvers' narration, with Lizzie's interference. Her birth from an egg places her "outside the Oedipal triangle, outside the Law of the Father" (Schmidt, 1990: 67). The versions of her life-story are designed for public consumption. Fevvers' self-representations invite us to respond with disbelief to the life she shapes as a theatre. She performs her femininity, just as she performs her various roles as 'Winged Victory' (NC 37), 'Cupid' (NC 38), 'Azrael, the Angel of Death' (NC 79), 'Dark angel of many names' (NC 75), 'Queen of ambiguities, goddess of in-between states, being on the borderline of species' (NC 81), 'Scheherazade' (NC 40) and 'the great confidence artiste' (NC 90).

Bakhtin's and Cixous's concepts of the grotesque and laughter stress the connection of the latter to the world of materiality. Bakhtin asserts that

"the medieval culture of laughter was the drama of bodily life which the new ruling class inevitably presented as eternal truths. In the new official culture there prevails a tendency toward the stability and completion of being, toward one single meaning, one single tone of seriousness' (1984:101).

In his final years he declares that "Everything that is truly great must include an element of laughter. Otherwise it becomes threatening, terrible, or pompous; in any case, it is limited" (1986:135). Although Bakhtin does not directly explore the connection between laughter and sexuality, the bodily nature of laughter indicates a link. Carter's humour derives from the grotesque and is a means of resistance to the negative and a celebration of the positive realm of possibilities. The figures of Fevvers and Walser are the vehicles Carter uses to interrogate the authenticity of sexuality and desire. The main question asked at the opening of the novel in regard to the aerialiste – "Is she fact or is she fiction?" recalls Carter's interest in the question of what is real in fiction.

Confronted with Fevvers, Walser struggles to maintain an objective pose, starting from his desperate attempts to answer the question. He stands for the traditional serious reader, determined to 'read' Fevvers and answer the question once and for all. What he finds, however, is a world of distortions, excess and ambivalence that upsets his world of ordered knowledge. His transformation takes him from fear to understanding when faced with the grotesque. Fevers defies the reality within which humans grow wings and fly; in his deluded certainty, Walser is determined to prove her a fraud.

Linda Williams' (1995:102) reading of the fantasies of *Nights at the Circus* places the focus on Walser. Fevvers' story of fantastic appearance is a "process of visual re-education which Walser has to undergo in relation to the impossible". Walser is "our rational reader-in – the-text trying to resolve the mysteries of monsters" (1995:124). He moves from a static world of objectivity into a dynamic world of experience. Early in the novel we witness his confusion regarding Lizzie and Fevvers' stories:

"as the women unfolded the convolutions of their joint stories together, he felt more and more like a kitten tangling up in a ball of wool it had never intended to unravel in the first place; or a sultan faced with not one but two Scheherazades, both intent on impacting a thousand stories into the single night." (NC 40)

To bridge the gap between seeing and believing Walser has to learn how "to hesitate or long enough to believe what he sees, even if what he sees is impossibility" (NC 97).

At least two factors conspire to confuse Walser: his erotic response to Fevvers and the narrative thread spun by the two women. The initial reaction he has comes as a surprise to him:

"Fevvers yawned with prodigious energy, opening a crimson maw the size of a basking shark, [...],and then she stretched herself suddenly and hugely, extending every muscle as a cat does, until she seemed to fill up all the mirror, all the room with her bulk as she raised her arms, Walser, confronted by stubbed, thickly powdered armpits felt faint; God! She could easily crush him to death in her huge arms, although he was a big man with the strength of Californian sunshine distilled in his limbs. A seismic erotic disturbance convulsed him -- ...He scrambled to his feet, suddenly panicking ...If he got out of her room for just one moment, was allowed, however briefly, to stand by himself in the cold, grimy passage away from her presence, if he could fill his lungs just the one time with air that was not choking with 'essence of Fevvers', then he might recover his sense of proportion."(NC 52)

The ambiguity of whether she seems grotesque because he desires her, or he desires her because she is grotesque is beyond solution. In either case, the erotic power of the grotesque is evident.

The scene is a parody of masculine fear of women's power, in Walser's case, Fevvers' apparent power to literally 'crush him to death', but also of his own disturbing desire in the face of her power. He would prefer a "cold, grimy spot" to the 'essence' of Fevvers. Although he manages to overcome the sense of terror, the erotic attraction moves his actions forward.

Walser's desire to rationalise Fevvers, which seems an easy task to one who has exposed such commonplace 'illusions' as the Indian fakirs and the burning coal walkers, is gradually confounded by two areas of the grotesque – Fevvers' body and her narrative.

Confusion and discomfort, both physical and psychological, are new experiences to Walser who has been detached and self-possessed all his life. He has no experience of internal change as a result of shared experiences. A passage of *The Sadeian Woman* addresses the detached and consequently inauthentic nature of the sexual experience in Sade: "Sexual pleasure is an entirely inward experience...sexual pleasure is not experienced as experience; it does not modify the subject. An entirely externally induced phenomenon, its sensation is absolutely personal" (*SW* :144). In her description of Walser, Carter echoes this passage

> "Walser had not experienced his experience *as* experience; ...like the boy in the fairy story who
> does not know how to shiver, Walser did not know *how* to be afraid. So his habitual
> disengagement was involuntary; it was not the result of judgment, since judgment involves the
> positives and negatives of belief" (NC 10).

The irony is that Walser, the most rational human in the novel is the one least connected to others through shared experiences. His desire has been contained in a self-absorbed need to challenge rationally whatever upsets his expectations of the universe. He has tried to circumscribe his world according to rational and wilful certainties. Fevvers, with her grotesque figure, is far from the conventional object of his desires, but will fuel his transformation through her grotesque energy and laughter. The figures Walser meets as he joins the circus and pursues Fevvers represent multiple manifestations of authenticity. His life will become authentic, different from his previous actions built upon the will to limit the object of desire. The nature of the grotesque provides him with new ways of thinking and seeing.

Fevvers will not come under the control of the circus ring, because of her self-confidence. Although she is deviant, she does not perceive herself as monstrous. Her fluid identity blurs the boundary between self and other, while Walser struggles to maintain it using reason.

Becoming a circus clown is a crucial stage to Walser's transformation. Bakhtin speaks of clowns, rogues and fools and their importance to the novel:

> "Essential to these three figures is a distinctive feature that is as well a privilege – the right to be 'other' in this world...They see the underside and the falseness of every situation. Therefore, they can exploit any position they choose, but only as a mask...These figures are laughed at by others, and themselves as well. Their laughter bears the stamp of the public square where the folk gather. They re-establish the public nature of the human figure... in novel texts, they themselves undergo a series of transformations, and they transform certain critical aspects of the novel as well." (1982: 159)

Fevers is the grotesque figure of the New Woman at the threshold of a new century. Her claim to have been "hatched from an egg, not gestated *in utero*" (NC 5) deems her parental origins a mystery: "Who *laid* me is as much a mystery to me, sir, as the nature of my conception, my father and my mother both utterly unknown to me, and, some would say, unknown to nature"(NC 17). Fevvers' emphasis on the double meaning of 'laid' mingles conception and birth with sexuality. Her desire is not confined to the Oedipal triangle, but shaped by her condition as an orphan. Her origins are a mystery she prefers to keep, thus signalling her refusal to engage in the traditional quest for identity. In her study on feminism and postmodernism, Magali Cornier Michael explains that "Fevvers challenges prevailing notions of identity that are grounded in verifiable origins and binary logic" (1996:175). Instead, Fevvers grounds her subject formation socially, in the whorehouse.

She "was reared by these kind women as if I was the common daughter of half-a –dozen mothers" (NC 21), and Lizzie becomes her foster mother.

The fictional game of Fevvers' gender performance is linked to a wider theme of the novel, the writing of the sexual history of a rising new femininity. The historical scene that allows it is located on allegorical places such as the whorehouse, the grotesque museum of woman monsters, the fake séance of female ghosts, and the circus arena. The image and the body of the woman are a commodity in the hands of puppet masters such as Colonel Kearney, the circus owner, and Herr M., the fake séance medium. In their separate show sites Fevvers plays the fantastic angel and Mignon the ghostly angel of the house. They are mimicking a sexual role for the desiring males without identifying with it. Fevvers employs the strategy of masquerading by posing as a living statue, a *tableau vivant* according to the sexual scenarios imposed on her.

The novel includes a collage of twentieth-century feminist discourses mouthed by Lizzie, the activist, the hag whose wisdom accompanies the New Woman to the New Age. As Carter remarked, "the creation of Fevvers necessitated the creation of her foster mother, Lizzie, a gnarled old leftist" (1994:178).

In her role as a foster mother, she gives Fevvers a 'parentless' history as source of identity. As a leftist, her political views differ from those her foster daughter hold, which keeps them united in their difference. According to Mary Russo, in their grotesque image as 'an intergenerational body' of the 'senile hag' and the young female body, Lizzie and Fevvers reconfigure "the pure child of the new century,' the 'new' becomes a possibility that already existed, a part of the aging body in process" (1994:179).

Russo's analysis juxtaposes the two bodies and points to the dialogic interaction of their sometimes discordant discourses. Lizzie's subversive force manifests itself in laughter. The "tiny, wizened, gnome-like apparition", with "tri-coloured hair" and "incipient moustache" (NC 13) laughs at the male sexual games and cackles like a witch. Her presence in the female site gives Fevvers a materialist grounding, protecting her at the same time from going back to the old happy endings of romance. Her position as a whore allows he to use her body to 'preach' to he customers the injustice of the social system, although she deliberately confuses Walser by disguising her habit as a religious one (NC 26-27). Later she becomes the brothel's housekeeper, in charge of keeping the fireplace burning.

This anachronism of clashing discourses opens the heterotopia for the play of masquerade Fevvers represents. It is close to the anachronisms Linda Hutcheon notices in postmodern historiographic fiction. In contrast to Hutcheon's analysis, Carter's anachronism achieves a different purpose. The genre Hutcheon investigates shows "an intense self-consciousness about the act of narrating in the present the events of the past" and "juxtaposes what we think we know of the past" with "an alternate representation that foregrounds the postmodern epistemological questioning of the nature of historical knowledge" (1989:71). The primary concern, in Carter's case, is not with the problematic nature of historical knowledge but with the construction of a line of female history. This history comes into being through the contestation of historical discourses in which women are either silent or spoken for by male voices. The voice is given back to the voiceless women populating an extra-historical site.

Virginia Woolf has first envisioned the strategy, later employed by feminist writers, "it is precisely in the cracks, the slippage between fact and fiction, that Woolf can begin to sight the possibility of the missing woman" (Linda Anderson, 1997:52). Carter's approach of these male representations of the figure of woman is parodic, as the absent female history is made to speak again, in a voice artificially constructed, like Fevvers' narrative voice, "of a fake medium at a séance"(NC 43). The voice that summons the ghost of the female past is also the collective voice of whores, vulgar and cunning, as Fevvers and Lizzie suggest. The French clock they keep with them is "a signifier of Ma Nelson's little private realm," which, with "a figure of Father Time" on it and the time always pointing at 'either midnight or noon,' "the hour of vision and revelation"(NC 29), symbolizes the brothel realm as a primal site of female history. Behind the satirical presentation of Ma Nelson's academy, de Sade's discourse is echoed. As the Sadeian brothel is an arena for men, in Carter's fabulation it is transformed into a site of subversive activities. All the whores are supporters of women's suffrage and use their body as a site for mutual pleasure.

In the presentation of Fevvers there is an overlapping of categories usually kept separate, in line with Kristeva's theory of abjection, concerned with figures that are in a state of transition. The abject is located in a liminal state that is on the margins of two positions. On the first page of the novel the emphasis is laid on the lower region of the body as Fevvers is depicted on "a wall-size poster, souvenir of her Parisian triumphs":

> "The artist had chosen to depict her ascent from behind -- bums aloft, you might say; up she goes, ...shaking out about her those tremendous red and purple pinions, pinions large enough, powerful enough to bear up such a big girl as she. And she was a *big* girl." (NC 7)

It is a body that suggests the possibility of regeneration, the body of the material world, in opposition to the static body constructed as a vision of desire. The grotesque body realigns the mechanisms of desire because it is shaped in accordance with the larger social body. Fevvers' use and creation of her body arise from her desire to make an independent living for herself.
In her presentation of woman as soiled, Angela Carter stresses the positive potential of contamination; contamination as a breakdown of confining categories:

> "The place of the abject is where meaning collapses, the place where I am not. The abject threatens life, it must be radically excluded from the place of the living subject, propelled away from the body and deposited on the other side of an imaginary border which separates the self

251

from that which threatens the self." (Creed, 1993:65)

Kristeva describes one aspect of the abject as 'jouissance' which is a sensation akin to joyousness. It is because of this sensation that "one thus understands why so many victims of the abject are its fascinated victims - if not its submissive and willing ones." (1982 9). Walser's perspective in the first section of the novel presents Fevvers as soiled: her "down-at-heel pink velvet slipper trimmed with grubby swansdown" (NC 41), her "grubby dressing-gown, horribly caked with greasepaint round the neck" (NC 19). He is struck by her unfeminine appearance and voracious appetite, and detects no angelic femininity in Fevvers, raised by "women of the worst class and defiled" (NC 21).

> "She gorged, she stuffed herself, she spilled gravy on herself, she sucked up peas from the knife; she had a gullet to match her size and table manners of the Elizabethan variety. Impressed, Walser waited with the stubborn docility of his profession until at last her enormous appetite was satisfied; she wiped her lips on her sleeve and belched." (NC 22)

Angela Carter draws attention to the final days of a century under patriarchal rule and the irony is apparent: "For we are at the fag-end, the smouldering cigar-butt, of a nineteenth century which is just about to be ground out in the ashtray of history. It is the final, waning, season of the year of Our Lord, eighteen hundred and ninety nine." (NC 11)
She regards Fevvers' selling herself as spectacle or monster as honest, as stated in *The Sadeian Woman*:

> "in a world organized by contractual obligations, the whore represents the only possible type of honest woman. If the world in its present state is indeed a brothel – and the moral difference between selling one's sexual labour and one's manual labour is…an academic one…at least the girl who sells herself with her yes open is not a hypocrite and, in a world with a cash-sale ideology, that is a positive, even a heroic virtue." (2000:57-8)

She provokes Walser's curiosity, presenting herself as the subject of his endless speculation. He wonders "Does she have a navel?" or even if she might be a man. Later in the novel, as Fevvers is "consumed with jealousy", he experiences a similar erotic arousal as that produced by her "prodigious yawn". After Fevvers orders him to kneel "he suffered a sudden access of erotic vertigo" (NC 143). For Walser, desire is realigned in a comical way. He wants to escape the 'essence of Fevvers' consisting of "perfume, sweat, greasepaint and raw, leaking gas that made you feel you breathed the air in Fevvers' dressing–room in lumps" with its final ingredient "a powerful note of stale feet" (NC 8, 9).

She is vulgar, big, "more like a dray mare than an angel", masculine, "it flickered through his mind: Is she really a man?" (NC 35). The initial attraction he feels is generated by her sexual energy: a "seismic erotic disturbance convulsed him" as she yawned with a crimson maw opening "the size of a basking shark" and with her raised arms that "could easily crush him to death", "although he was a big man" (NC 52).

Fevvers makes a spectacle of herself using a body that cannot be readily interpreted and, depending on the point of view, she is either wonder or freak. Not only does the grotesque body reek, it also consumes food in excess. When she eats, Fevvers "gorged, she stuffed herself, she spilled gravy on herself, she sucked up peas from the knife; she had a gullet to match her size and table manners of the Elizabethan variety" and, when done eating "she wiped her lips on the sleeve and belched" (NC 22). It is evident that neither her manners nor her body come close to the high standards of the desired body; they belong to the low regions of the material world.

"The material bodily principle is contained not in the biological individual, but in the people, a people who are continually growing and renewed. This is why all that is bodily becomes grandiose, exaggerated, immeasurable." (Bakhtin, 1984:19)

She symbolizes the almost mystical notion of the grotesque put forward by Bakhtin: "[…]the grotesque body is cosmic and universal. It stresses elements common to the entire cosmos: earth, water, fire, air.[…] It can fill the entire universe." (NC 318)

She manifests an extraordinary appetite for life. The artiste is aware of her being the object of male gaze but has determined to be so on her own terms. Fevvers wants to be desired, thus her appetite may be linked to her erotic power. At the same time, the heroine rejects and resists external constructions. She exhibits herself as the object for the audience's gaze but controls how much of herself the audience can consume.

"Look at me! With a grand, proud, ironic grace, she exhibited herself before the eyes of the audience as if she were a marvelous present too good to be played with. Look, not touch!" (NC 15)

For Fevvers, maintaining her narrative power is a means of surviving as subject. The way she tells her story is so captivating that Jack feels that he "has become a prisoner of her voice" (NC 43). Fevvers' greed manifested in her eating and drinking a lot is paralleled by her generosity. She is also generous with sharing her life story, conscious of the effect it will have on Jack Walser.

Nights at the Circus makes the presence of woman outside masculine creation a fact. Although the winged heroine Fevvers has a remarkable appetite, she refuses to be associated with cannibalistic behaviour. When she describes to Walser the dinner offered at the house of Mr Rosencreutz she points out that, given the option, she will not eat fowl and "play the cannibal". Later, on the train to Russia when the appetite of the circus proprietor, the Colonel, is sharpened by the similarity in taste of human flesh to pork, she gives her 'nasty' veal cutlet to the pig. Her appetite is not predatory and represents the longing for experience. It is the antidote to the frozen one that the cannibal has.

After the narration of Fevvers' early life, the two women start spinning tales of other grotesque bodies. In the joint narration of their history, Fevvers and Lizzie portray Ma Nelson as the matriarch who initiates the strategy of female history-fabulation. As a transvestite herself, she mimics the navy hero Nelson in command of a ship of prostitute warriors and names Fevvers as their guardian angel, 'Victory with Wings' (NC 38), holding a sword as a mockery of male authority. She also creates Fevvers' role as the harbinger of the New Woman in "the New Age in which no woman will be bound to the ground" (NC 25). In her mock celebration of the pleasure of the body in the space of the brothel she displays a 'fake' Titian *Leda and the Swan*, interpreting it as "a demonstration of the blinding access of the grace of flesh" (NC 28). Fevvers incorporates this interpretation in her own myth. She will become, apart from Helen and Leda, a female Zeus-swan. In the brothel she waits to realize her 'self' as she confesses to Walser:

> "I existed only as an object in men's eyes after the night-time knocking on the door began. Such was my apprenticeship for life, since is it not to the mercies of the eyes of others that we commit ourselves on our voyage through the world? I was as if closed up in a shell, for the wet white would harden on my face and torso like a death mask that covered me all over, yet, inside this appearance of marble, nothing could have been more vibrant with potentiality than I! Sealed in this artificial egg, this sarcophagus of beauty, I waited, I waited. . . although I could not have told you for what it was I waited. Except, I assure you, I did *not* await the kiss of a magic prince, sir! With my two eyes, I nightly saw how such a kiss would seal me up in my *appearance* for ever!" (NC 39)

UNIVERSITY OF WINCHESTER LIBRARY

When the repressive regime of Ma Nelson's brother threatens the brothel and its activists, the institution is sacrificed. The whores burn it down after Ma Nelson's sudden death, but carry on her subversion to the public domain.

Lizzie's ex-whore hag figure contrasts strikingly with two different figures, Madame Schreck, a scarecrow hag who exploits women for their deviation from the social norms, and the weak, submissive and senile Russian babushka, crushed by work. Lizzie rebels against any kind of exploitation of women, including romantic love. Fevvers' struggle with the social fictions is fought on a double front, mythical and historical. Her origin alludes to the motif of 'Leda and the Swan'. Female spectacle is fetishized by the discursive forces prevalent at that historical moment, as illustrated by the four spaces Fevvers covers after her apprenticeship at the brothel academy: Madame Schreck's Museum of Female Monsters, Christian Rozencreutz's home, the circus, and the Russian Grande Duke's palace.

In Madame Schreck's Museum Fevvers' body appears as one of the many grotesque commodities at the mercy of male customers. Femininity is structured as an antithesis, with Fevvers' winged image as 'the Angel of Death'. In a tomb-like basement called 'the Down Below' she spreads her wings like the shadow of death over the living corpse of Sleeping Beauty (NC 70). Madame Schreck displays women as monstrosities to be observed, objectified. Foucault tells us that monsters are "etymologically, beings or things to be shown" (1988:70). Fevvers blames the label of monstrosity applied to the women on those coming to view them: "there was no terror in our house customers did not bring with them" (NC 62).

In the episode involving Christian Rozencreutz, Fevvers' winged body is bought to be used as a "fleshy bottle of elixum vitae" (NC 83). Rozencreutz, a politician in Parliament, invokes myths to stop the passing of 'Votes for Women' arguing "how women are of a different soul substance from men,' how 'too pure and rarefied' the female soul is to worry about 'things of this world" (NC 78-9).

In *Petersburg*, the second part of the novel, Angela Carter explores human experience through the figure of the world as a circus. Captain Kearney's circus comprises the world of grotesque characters whom Walser meets without the mediation of the two women's tales, as he becomes the Human Chicken. These figures include the Princess of Abyssinia, a tiger trainer whose "body has, every inch, scarred with claw-marks, as if tattooed" (NC 149); Samson, the Strong Man; the Ape-Man's wife, a chimpanzee; the Professor; Buffo the Great, the master Clown.

255

The circus is the metaphor for life and allows the public display of the self, reflecting both outwards, to life, and inwards, to the desire for completion:

"What a cheap, convenient, expressionist device, this sawdust ring, this little O! round like an eye, with a still vortex in the centre; but give it a little rub as if it were Aladdin's wishing lamp and, instantly, the circus ring turns into that durably metaphoric, uroboric snake with its tail in its mouth, wheel that turns full circle, the wheel whose end is its beginning, the wheel of fortune, the potter's wheel on which our clay is formed, the wheel of life on which we are all broken. O! of wonder; O! of grief." (NC 107)

The clowns are the tragic figures who illustrate the bitter side of comedy, having Buffo as the lead representative. His hunger for the world is fuelled by despair. He has a "tremendous and perpetual thirst", but his prodigious drinking is never satisfied, "as if alcohol were an inadequate substitute for some headier or more substantial intoxicant, as though he would have liked, if he could, to bottle the whole world, tip it down his throat, then piss it against the wall" (NC 118).

Buffo's hunger is cruel, he acts on his cannibalistic and murderous impulses at the expense of Walser. He chases Walser dressed in the Human Chicken, with a carving knife during the Clowns' 'Christmas Diner ' act, ending up symbolically crucified in a straightjacket. But there is no Ascension. Clowns are "doomed to stay down below, nailed on the endless cross of the humiliations of this world" (NC 120). Buffo is a figure of negation who celebrates Lear's threat "*Nothing* will come of nothing… that's the glory of it" (NC 123). The clowns dance for Buffo a requiem of surrender to the forces of negation:

"They danced the perturbed spirit of their master, who came with a great wind and blew cold as death into the marrow of the bones. They danced the whirling apart of everything, the end of love, the end of hope; they danced tomorrows into yesterdays; they danced the exhaustion of the implacable present; they danced the deadly dance of the past perfect which fixes everything fast so it can't move again; they danced the dance of Old Adam who destroys the world because we believe he lives forever". (ibid. 243)

Fevvers, the incarnation of Eros, tells Walser that she hates clowns and regards them as an assault on humanity. She too falls prey to nostalgia, because, according to Lizzie, all wise children want to stay in the womb of their mothers and remain whole. The circus, as the focal stage for masqueraders to 'juggle with being', is not only a play arena of transgression and

256

mockery, but a place highlighted by the exchange of market values. Fevvers is once more the object of the gaze, as a hybrid bird/woman: "A free woman in an unfree society will be a monster" (Carter, 2000:27)

However, Fevvers also says that 'nature' must prevail, and she embraces nature with its mutability. She will not allow the male gaze to objectify her, so her femininity is that of the 'tiger-lady'. It is her turn to objectify Walser who imagines that "the teeth closed on his flesh with the most voluptuous lack of harm" (NC 204).

While Fevvers is using the carnivalesque side of the circus as a façade for her performance, the circus economy is bearing on the self-jugglers. Colonel Kearney, the impresario, is an allegorical figure of American capitalism, promoting 'the Ludic Game' (NC 100). In this combined context of transgression within/against market forces, Fevvers' aerial act is constrained by a recreational value that casts her social function of the provider of spectacle 'to give pleasure to the eye' (NC 185). Nevertheless, the game of self-juggling is tricky. Posing without a primary self behind the mask may lead to the dissolution of the self. Walser's sceptical eye notices her potential crisis in the rehearsal in the circus ring of Petersburg: "She looks wonderful, but she doesn't look *right*...there was an air about her that suggested, whilst convincing others, she herself remained unconvinced about the precise nature of her own illusion" (NC 159). Her crisis of confidence will materialize as the forces of the circus conspire to turn her into a fetish in her rendezvous with the Russian Grand Duke. As a result her confidence is damaged and she is in danger of becoming a fiction to herself.

The existential freedom of flying is performed in a parodic show called 'Only a bird in a gilded cage', in which she mimics a caged bird let out to do a daring trapeze act and outdo the virtuosity of the real area5liste, claiming to be an authentic 'bird woman'. While she masquerades as an 'imitation' mythical creature, she is a real fantastic being who is given a unique status of ambiguity as a commodity. Her value is thus heightened, placing her at risk once the Russian Grand Duke desires her. The Russian Grand Duke episode in St Petersburg satirizes the fetishization of woman in multiple forms, most strikingly as the combination of commodity value with the artistic celebration of the figure of woman. The Russian Duke assumes the dominant position and has the power to subjugate women according to his desires. In his icy-cold palace of 'minerals' he collects "toys –marvellous and unnatural   artifacts", which he desires most passionately. Fevvers' body represents the ultimate object exchangeable with the diamonds meant to lure her, as well as a winged substitute for the missing phallus.

257

Fevvers' toy sword, the Nelsonian heritage, is broken in two by the muscular Duke. Her will is the only thing preventing her from melting like the ice statue in the Duke's house, completed by the strategy the whore-house trained her to apply: she lures the Duke and escapes while he is carried away by erotic ecstasy.

Fevvers' magic flight from the Duke's house and cage into the desolate world of Siberia signifies a leap from a historical zone to another. In the new world, various possibilities of feminist movements open like the rare violets Fevvers and Lizzie find. Olga and her fellow women are trying to build a lesbian society, Mignon rises from the victim position to that of a composer making music 'to tame the tigers' which used to prey on her. Accompanying her is the Princess of Abyssinia, the former tamer of the tigers. All these, together with Fevvers' laughter tend to point to a utopian celebration of woman-centred culture that Paulina Palmer (1987) argues Carter is moving toward in her later fictions.

The second aspect that unbalances Walser's sense of control is the narrative web Fevvers and Lizzie weave. They are Scheherazades inventing stories, evading Walser's desire to 'pen' them as fictional or frauds. As Fevvers starts telling her story in her dressing room, time slowly slides to another realm. At first, Walser is the intelligent, sensitive male victim of the world of enticement. The world he knows reflects a desire for control and dominance, a life that he watches rather than embraces. Laughter, pleasure, love are unknown to him, for he has constructed his life as something he can control and understand. Lizzie makes a first cup of tea and Walser hears Big Ben strike midnight for the second time; she brings in bacon sandwiches and more tea when it strikes again. It is the suspended time of narration, punctuated by eating, drinking and storytelling, the time of the carnival when Walser's certainties are shattered and he starts his quest. He does not eat the eel pies with mash or the sandwiches, reservedly describing English food as 'an acquired taste' and "the eighth wonder of the world" (ibid 22). The tea and the champagne seem to affect him while he watches Fevvers and Lizzie feast. He still occupies a marginal position in their story because his views are supported by scepticism and disbelief.

Time and space also seem to disintegrate at the Clowns' supper. Over the fish soup and black bread Buffo preaches on the nature of the Clown turning the sermon, after a few glasses of vodka , into a dance:

"It seemed that they were dancing the room apart, as the babushka slept, her too, too solid kitchen fell into pieces under the blows of their disorder as if it had been, all the time, an ingenious prop, and the purple Petersburg night inserted jagged wedges into the walls" (NC 124).

The more confused Walser becomes, we see his energy forced into channels utterly unknown to him. The power the two women exercise on him through their storytelling operates in comic ways sometimes, building upon the early image of Walser as a kitten caught in a ball of thread: "Lizzie fixed Walser with her glittering eye and seized the narrative between her teeth". Walser's desire to interrogate Lizzie's narrative is boldly interrupted by Fevvers' narrative: "Fevvers lassoed him with her narrative and dragged him along with her before he'd had a chance to ask Lizzie if – " (NC 32, 60). Such dizzying narrative movement propels Walser into a void of potentialities which animates authentic desire. The ambivalent force of the grotesque absorbs Walser into the whirl of experience and love.

Sandra Gilbert in the "Introduction" to *The Newly Born Woman* (Cixous, Clement, 1986) discusses a narrative combining belief and disbelief, being an evocation of a hysterical and a utopian prophetic mode: "the paradigms of sorceress and hysteric become increasingly convincing when one contextualizes them with contemporary anthropological theory about "sex-gender systems"' (1986:xiii).

Traditional categories of identity and gender are contaminated and, therefore, questioned in the narratives of *Nights at the Circus*'s women. They combine the mute madness assigned to women through traditional representation, with the powerful voice of the prophetess. Fevvers, Lizzie and the rest of the women populating their stories reflect Clement's image of the sorceress, the possessed and the hysteric (1986), in their ways of 'acting out' in order to break the contracting space of their confinement. Cixous, in 'Sorties' further states that:

> "men and women are caught up in a web of age-old cultural determinations that are almost unanalyzable in their complexity. One can no more speak of "woman" than of "man" without being trapped within an ideological theatre where the proliferation of representations, images, reflections, myths, identifications, transform, deform …and invalidate in advance any conceptualization." (1986:83)

A new identity may be established for woman, man, the hysteric, the sorceress. Elaine Jordan refers to the power of myths: "the more veiled they are, the more dangerously perhaps they lie coiled in and around the psyche and behaviour." (1990:23)

Jerry-Aline Flieger is of the opinion that one function of the postmodern text "is to play the role of trickster...exposing the trickery which sustains the myth of the finished literary masterwork, and reactivating the literary game in the bizarre hope of not winning" (1991: 52). Carter adopts a postmodern comic mode in her seduction of the reader, which equals Fevvers' seducing Jack: "those who play the Ludic Game sometimes win but sometimes ...lose" (NC 202).

One confidence trick of narrative is the mirror effect of Realist representation. Catherine Belsey in *Critical Practice* writes that realism is "useful in distinguishing between those terms which tend to efface their own textuality, their existence as discourse, and those which explicitly draw attention to it. Realism offers itself as transparent" (2002:47). Postmodern practice exposes this assumption as a confidence trick. Belsey, in 'Constructing the Subject' describes the assumptions of Realist representation:

> "classic realism offers the reader a position of knowingness which is also a position of identification with the narrative voice. To the extent that the story first constructs, and then depends for its intelligibility, on a set of assumptions shared between narrator and reader, it confirms both the transcendent knowingness of the reader-as-subject and the "obviousness" of the shared truths in question." (2002:664).

The assumption that the Realist novel tells the truth about life is rooted in the belief that the novel "should mirror the world, and through this impersonal mirroring show truth. It is a common Realist sentiment that fiction is to be mistrusted unless it pretends to be something else" (Lee, 1990:11). Angela Carter's magical realist mode draws attention to the constructed nature of the text. The Classic Realist text "instils itself in the space between fact and illusion through the presentation of a simulated reality which is plausible but not real" (Belsey, 2002:672), whereas the magical realist one forces the reader to confront the elements of fiction as language constructs, not real meanings found in the world. Christopher Norris describes *Nights at the Circus* as

> "a book much concerned with the topics of *mimesis*, representation and the non-originality of origins [..] doubling back and forth between naturalistic detail and a 'post-modern' stress on those elements of fabulous narrative contrivance that resist the strong pull toward mimetic illusion." (1988:51)

Angela Carter defeats mimetism by a narrative that lacks authority. The voice telling the story is suspect starting with the first chapter , where there is so much wondering that our belief is tried several times. It sometimes seems that Fevvers is the one filtering the story, other times it appears that Walser is taking control, but a third point of view confuses the planes. The narrative is unbelievable from its onset, the narrator's presence is constantly suggested and his/her objectivity is undercut by Walser's incredulity, signalled in parentheses. As Walser is confronted by Fevvers' "uncomfortable-looking pair of bulges" we read on: "('How does she do that?' pondered the reporter)" (NC 8). As he witnesses her performance in the air, we read: "(But surely, pondered Walser, a *real* bird woman would have too much sense to think of performing a triple somersault in the first place)" (NC 17). Other clues that the point of view is Walser's appear as he first remarks of Fevvers, "such a lump it seems" (NC 16), only to change his opinion as he admits he is "surprised at her wholesome look" (NC 18). All these observations are, however, reported in the third-person. His speech is confused and it further contributes to the preservation of a fragmented perspective of both him and Fevvers. The narrative voice further weakens any objective view of Walser as it characterizes him as a "kaleidoscope equipped with consciousness" (NC 10) and tells of "his habitual disengagement [...] it was not the result of judgement, since judgement involves the positives and negatives of belief" (NC 10).

When it comes to direct address to the reader, the confusion is deeper as to the source of the question "'a touch of sham?'" (NC 8), when Fevvers pops the cork with her teeth. The description of "something fishy about the Cockney Venus -- that underlay the hot, solid composite of perfume, sweat, greasepaint and raw, leaking gas that made you feel you breathed the air in Fevvers' dressing-room in lumps" (NC 8) is followed by seemingly Walser's perspective, "when she got round to it, she might well bottle the smell, and sell it. She never missed a chance" (NC 9). However, Walser hardly knows Fevvers, so he cannot be the one speculating about her love of money. Three pages later the narrative voice reinforces Walser's lack of knowledge: "for Fevvers, the music of the spheres was the jingling of cash registers. Even Walser did not guess that" (NC 12). The point of view of the narrative, much like its subject, is unstable, making the reader uncertain of who is speaking and of what to believe.
We are sometimes uncertain as to the narrator's relation to the narrative. There are numerous shifts between the first and the third person. Fevvers' initial first person discourse is contained between quotation marks as an unnamed third person narrates omnisciently, thus placing a mediating presence between Fevvers and the reader. Right after the opening exclamation, "Lor' love you, sir!" we are told "Fevvers sang out in a voice that clanged like dustbin lids" (NC 7),

and the third person narrative continues, in alternation with Fevvers and Lizie's comments. This extradiegetic narrator is not Walser , because his first impressions of Fevvers as "the Blonde" reflect his limited perception and habit of objectifying the woman. Later, however, Fevvers' first-person discourse becomes the dominant voice as she narrates.

By the same token, the description of Lizzie as "the witch" (NC 60) points to a view the sceptical Walser would hold, rather than Fevvers or Lizzie herself, the only other characters present. In the third part of the novel, however, Fevvers engages in an almost dialogic confrontation with the reader, as she denies adamantly that Lizzie is a witch: "Her household magic, she calls it. What would you think, when you saw the bread rise, if you didn't know what yeast was? Think old Liz was a witch, wouldn't you!"(NC 150).

The act of removing the 'false' eyelashes does not necessarily reveal the 'authentic' ones, because later an unnamed narrator tells us, as Fevvers bats her eyelashes at Walser, that "from the pale length of those eyelashes, a good three inches, he might have thought she had not taken her false ones off had he not been able to see them lolling, hairy as gooseberries, among the formidable refuse of the dressing-table" (NC 40).

Fevvers describes the end of her experience as inhabitant of the whorehouse where she took the title of the 'intacta' Winged Venus. She indicates how narrative constructs reality, but also that all narratives, and thus reality, must come to an end. With this recognition comes the understanding that the future is always embedded in the present:

> "It was the cold light of early dawn and how sadly, how soberly it lit that room which deceitful candles made so gorgeous! We saw, now, what we had never seen before; ...The luxury of that place had been nothing but illusion, created by the candles of midnight, and, in the dawn, all was sere, worn-out decay. ....the gilding on the mirrors was all tarnished and a bloom of dust obscured the glass so that, when we looked within them, there we saw, not the fresh young women that we were, but the hags we would become, and knew that, we too, like pleasures, were mortal." (NC 49).

The multiple narratives in the novel confer upon it an effect of "always conceiving", a hallmark of Bakhtin's grotesque realism (NC 210).

In the *London* section, we have the choice to dismiss the fantastic as a "confidence trick", along with Walser, the main focaliser. As the story sweeps its characters and listeners to *Petersburg*, the situation becomes uncanny, as the unidentified omniscient narrator reports fantastic events affecting Walser, such as the Professor's (an *extremely* educated ape) speech on human physiology or Fevvers' escape magical realist escape from the Duke. The reader is forced to leave aside realist presuppositions as the story becomes increasingly fantastic. The progression of the narrative relies on the ambiguity of meanings, which requires a continuous search. So that we accompany Walser through a grotesque world in terms of both structure and content, struggling to keep up. We also learn, along with Walser, that keeping up is not the point, but the energy and movement prompting us forward.

Carter repeatedly indicates that the constructed narratives, fictions, are reality, but she constantly exposes the absurdity and destructive aspect of investing such constructions with finality. We are reminded of the necessity to invent the story of our lives, for when we stop doing that we become inauthentic in our stasis. In her Introduction to *Expletives Deleted* she speaks of "the strategies writers have devised to cheat the inevitability of closure, to chase away the demons, to keep them away for good" (*ED* 3).

Fevers understands this necessity in her own life, never pausing long enough to allow an invented story to stagnate. In this way her identity is perpetually shifting. Cixous cautions against the stasis of identity in a similar way:

"we have extremely strong identifications, which found our house. An identity card doesn't allow for confusion, torment, or bewilderment... Which is why we live in legalised and general delusion. Fiction takes the place of reality." (1993:51)

Identity cards and the grotesque are incompatible. Fevers refuses an identity card, always moving on to the next narrative. Her ambivalent reaction to the grotesque of the whorehouse and her glimpses of the future propel her into a new phase. As she tells Walser, at the end of chapter one "we, girls...shivered from sorrow at the end of one part of our lives and the exhilaration of our new beginnings... And so the first chapter of my life went up in flames, sir" (NC 50). The next chapter opens with her exclamation "What a long drive it was to Battersea!" (NC 51) and she narrates to Walser her brief career as an ice-cream vendor.

With Walser, she takes control of the narrative and witnesses his transformation from "a sardonic contemplator like Desiderio in *The Infernal Desire Machines of Doctor Hoffman*" (Jordan, 1990:38) to someone who can love. The Duke deprives Fevvers of her knife, so she jumps into the next and last part of the novel, *Siberia*, in the heart of the frozen landscape. However, Fevvers dislikes barren landscapes "I both hate and fear the open country. I do not like where Man is not" (NC 80). As she goes "deeper and deeper into an unknown terrain" (NC

226), Fevvers feels claustrophobic "thrust into the heart of limbo" (NC 225). If there is no Man where she is, there is no gaze to be cast on her to maintain her status as object. This is why her sense of self changes accordingly:

"Day by day she felt herself diminishing, as if the Grand Duke had ordered up another sculpture of ice and now, as his exquisite revenge on her flight, was engaged in melting it very, very slowly, perhaps by the judicious application of lighted cigarette ends. The young American it was who kept the whole story of the old Fevvers in his notebooks; she longed for him to tell her she was true. She longed to see herself reflected in all her remembered splendour in his grey eyes. She longed; she yearned." (NC 273)

Fevvers depends on Walser to confer her an ontological status, but he is also lost in the same landscape. Her existence pales if it is not contained in the narrative discourse.

"The confession unfolds within a power relationship, for one does not confess without the presence of a partner who is not simply the interlocutor but the authority who requires the confession, prescribes and appreciates it, and intervenes in order to judge, punish, forgive, console, and reconcile". (Foucault, 1998:61-62)

Fevvers needs Walser as an amanuensis to whom she can entrust her personal story. The reader and Walser fulfil the role of the confessor, but our narrative satisfaction is diminished by the contradictions arising from Fevvers' dependence on the male gaze as well as her refusal of objectification:

"a twofold process of identification, sustaining two distinct sets of identifying relations. The first set is …the masculine, active, identification with the gaze (the looks of the …male characters) and the passive, feminine identification with the image (body landscape). The second set is implicit in the first as its effect and specification, for it is produced by the apparatus which is the very condition of vision[…]. It consists of the double identification with the figure of narrative movement, the mythical subject, and with the figure of narrative closure, the narrative image. Were it not for this second, figural identification, the woman spectator would be stranded between two incommensurable entities, the gaze and the image. Identification, that is, would be either impossible, split beyond any act of suture, or entirely masculine. The figural identification, on the contrary, is double; both figures can and in fact must be identified with at once, for they are inherent in narrative itself." (De Lauretis 1984:143-144)

The passage helps us to interpret Fevvers' complicity with the gaze. Fevvers is such a figure for the figural identification, contradictory, therefore doubled: she identifies with the active male principle, as she observes herself being built as image of the gaze. Fevvers addresses both Walser and the reader at the end of the novel: "as to questions of whether I am fact or fiction, you must answer that for yourself!"(NC 292).

> "Fevvers needs to see herself mirrored in the eyes of the others. But in contradistinction to the Lacanian constitution of the symbolic 'I', where the mirror image comes first and the symbolic 'I' follows from it, the miraculous Fevvers is the inventor of her own singularity for which she seeks acclaim. She, however, functions as a mirror image for the readers of the novel, representing an image of a freedom which does not yet exist in the non-fictional world."
> (Schmidt, 1990:72)

In *Siberia*, Walser and Fevvers alternate voices. Walser becomes a Shaman and becomes similar to Fevvers, as Schmidt (1990:71) points out; both depend on society's belief in their magic and rely on their magic to ensure food or cash dollars and thus continue their life of dissimulation. The shift in perspective extends to this third part of the novel, as we struggle to determine the origin of the authority of the discourse. A paragraph opens "the giantess found herself trapped" (NC 205) and the following paragraph switches to Fevvers' point of view: "I have broken my right wing" (NC 205) only to conclude with her assertion: "big birds must look after themselves, so I'd better snap out of it sharpish, hadn't I!" (NC 208). The question posed concerns the identity of the addressee of Fevvers' confession. Walser is absent, so we, the readers are the ones hearing it, and should assume the position of authority. She not only tricks the Duke, the Colonel, Walser and Rozencreutz, who want to turn her into an object in the stories of their lives, she tricks the reader with the multiple voices and identities created. The Colonel exploits her tricks for financial purposes, and we cannot miss Angela Carter's irony, directed at us, in the motto she assigns to this character: "the bigger the humbug, the better the public likes it" (NC 147).

Rozencreutz and the Duke see Fevvers as the mythical woman. Fevvers is similar to Albertina from *The Infernal Desire Machines of Doctor Hoffman*, a creature of "dream and abstraction" (NC 30), that is, a fantasy, an object of the male gaze. Her existence seems to depend on her status as object of desire; desire for immortality for Rozencreutz, for pleasure for the Corporal, for power for the Duke, and for truth for Walser, while to the reader she represents desire for meaning. She resists all these forms of objectification, thus "impending the fulfilment of the male's desire, as well as narrative closure" (de Lauretis, NC 142). She uses a knife to defend herself against the threat of Rozencreutz, outdoes the Corporal's appetite at the 'seduction dinner' (NC 171) and escapes as the Corporal "lapsed into a slumber" (NC 171).

The lover's gaze re-establishes the necessary confidence. Fevvers needs Walser's gaze to reflect back to her what she believes she is – a symbol of female freedom and power. The scopic field narrows from the social gaze to the close scrutiny of the lover, meant to acknowledge the subjectivity if its beloved. Walser is willing to see Fevvers' spectacle as a source of wonder and new meanings, not as a site of monstrosity under observation. He believes what he sees, although what he sees is not what is, but an image Fevvers fabricates and needs to see reflected in his eyes. The visual field of the lovers' reciprocal gaze is not only the site of the symbolic exchange of the erotic thrill but a space for the fictional play of the sexual subject. If Fevvers poses to Walser as a spectacle of the only fully-feathered virgin in human history and he believes her story, it does not mean he rescues her from crisis. The 'princess' in the story rescues the 'sleeping prince' from his dream world, more than he saves her.

While Fevvers plays on the paradoxical nature of 'seeing is believing', Walser's problem is that he registers only one side of the game. At first, he only sees but believes nothing; later in the Siberian shaman's world he sees only what he is given to believe. In order to be initiated into her fictional game of juggling with the self, he needs to evolve from his initial skeptical gaze to the illusive vision of the shaman. The fantastic spectacle of Fevvers is the key to his initiation into the fictional game of sexual identity. Walser's story is one of the learning how to play his male sexuality in relation to the changed female sexuality. That grand spectacle has produced in him an erotic challenge to his gender identity because Fevvers represents a femininity which is no longer beautiful or desirable. His adventures with the circus can thus be read as his journey of metamorphosis into a New Man who can give up the masculine mask and join the tigress. His rebirth is conducted in his relation to Fevvers' winged image so he has to undergo a series of somersaults before articulating a new subject position. His initial gaze is more like that of the camera-eye than of the male voyeur, for Walser does not see with desire or belief, having suspended his own subjective being: "yet it was almost as if he himself were an *objet trouvé,* for, subjectively, *himself* he never found, since it was not his *self* which he sought" (NC 4).

His journey is marked by a series of humiliating experiences and loss of certainty, culminating with his job as a clown at the circus. In playing the 'Human Chicken' on the Fool's Christmas

Feast he is threatened by the metaphorically castrating knife Buffo the Lord of clowns chases him with, mad about his own lost manhood. If playing fool is a forced and failed somersault of manhood for Buffo, for Walser is a transitional stage. Walser turns into a clown and his change is perceived with his first tint of make-up: "he looked in the mirror and did not recognise himself. As he contemplated the stranger peering interrogatively back at him out of the glass, he felt the beginnings of a vertiginous sense of freedom" (NC 103).

He is allowed to play with his male ego, ridiculing his masculine image, and mimic a hero who rescues Mignon. His masculine climax at the circus comes at his dancing show with a tigress, a hint at his relationship with Fevvers. The old power relationship between the sexes is reversed and the bridegroom must overcome his fear and match the power of his bride.

The whole process of clowning is, however, humiliating, as Buffo observes. He "started out in life as an acrobat" (NC 118) and is now the object of laughter for his failed manhood. Walser follows the female fictional play, masquerading as a clown playing a "chickened" man and a tigress-tamer. To rise again, he has to be knocked down to a sleep which erases his past. The kiss of Olga, a mother figure who has murdered her husband, wakes him first (NC 222), Fevvers' winged image wakes him the second time. Walser becomes the Sleeping Beauty, the male dreamer waiting for the princess to wake him from the world of believing is seeing, that of the shaman's tribe. He learns how to play the fictional game of identity without suffering the fate of self-dissolution. Buffo could not take off the painted mask; it eventually took over his being, leaving behind the story of madness. Walser, on the other hand, knows how to tell his life story differently (NC 293-4).

Bakhtin recognises that the formation of the self is a linguistic process, which we see enacted through Walser. He reports on for his newspaper, but his style changes when he becomes a clown. At a moment when he has finished a dispatch describing St. Petersburg, we are presented with linguistic evidence of his change:

> "Walser reread his copy. The city precipitated him towards hyperbole; never before had he bandied about so many adjectives. Walser-the-clown, it seemed, could juggle with the dictionary with a zest that would have abashed Walser-the-foreign-correspondent. He chuckled, thinking of his chief's brow wrinkling over the dispatch" (NC 98)

Walser's panic is evident as he tries to rid himself from the unscripted attraction he feels when confronted with the power and abundance of Fevvers. Carter transforms him into someone who,

267

reunited with Fevvers, sees at last that she "indeed appeared to possess no navel" but he is "no longer in the mood to draw definite conclusions from this fact" (NC 292). Walser no longer desires the power of certainty. There is another aspect of his change:

> "He was as much himself again as he ever would be, and yet that "self" would never be the same again for now he knew the meaning of fear as it defines itself in its most violent form, that is, fear of the death of the beloved, of the loss of the beloved, of the loss of .love" (NC 293)

He has metamorphosed into someone who shares, loves, and is profoundly connected to another human. His movement through the grotesque world sweeps him into a territory previously unimaginable, leading a narrative voice to declare at the end of the novel "Walser took himself apart and put himself together again" (NC 294); His transformation results in his falling in love with Fevvers. With Fevvers exclamation "Gawd, I fooled you!" comes his final discovery that she has actually been a fraud. The details of her game are deliberately left unclear. Following this ambiguous revelation, "She laughed so much the bed shook" and "Her laughter spilled out of the window" (NC 294). Walser takes up this laughter at the end of the novel, a laughter that crosses into the New Century:

> "The spiralling tornado of Fevvers' laughter began to twist and shudder across the entire globe, as if a spontaneous response to the giant comedy that endlessly unfolded beneath it, until everything that lived and breathed, everywhere, was laughing. Or so it seemed to the deceived husband, who found himself laughing too, even if he was not quite sure whether or not he might be the butt of the joke." (NC 295)

This all-encompassing laughter resonates with Cixous's declaration that "The world and I are laughing" (1993:125), invoking a desire for the world of others. The novel's laughter also recalls Bakhtin's words about the complexity of carnivalesque laughter:

> "It is, first of all, a festive laughter. Therefore it is not an individual reaction to some isolated comic event. Carnival laughter is the laughter of all the people. Second, it is universal in scope; it is directed at all and everyone, including the carnival's participants. The entire world is seen in its droll aspect, in its gay relativity. Third, this laughter is ambivalent: it is gay, triumphant, and at the same time mocking, deriding. It asserts and denies, it buries and revives. Such is the laughter of the carnival." (NC 12)

This New Year's Eve laughter, while presenting a utopian vision, is nonetheless fraught with ambivalence and irony for the reader, who is well aware of the horrors to come in the twentieth century. Walser's position as possible butt of a joke also supports this ambivalence. Moreover, dark references to the future scattered though the novel indicate the deeper ambivalence of both the reunion between Fevvers and Walser and laughter. Fevvers' ideal vision of the future is counterbalanced by Lizzie's views:

"And once the old world has turned on its axle so that the new dawn can dawn, then, ah, then! all the women will have wings, the same as I. This young woman in my arms, whom we found tied hand and foot with the grisly bonds of ritual, will suffer no more of it; she will tear off her mind forg'd manacles, will rise up and fly away. The dolls' house doors will open, the brothels will spill forth their prisoners, the cages, gilded or otherwise, all over the world, in every land, will let forth their inmates singing together the dawn chorus of the new, the transformed" (NC 285).

The same unpredictable changes occur in the case of Walser's voice. At the end of the novel, Walser's story of his self shifts from an objective perspective to a subjective one, mirroring the novel's ongoing alternation. More narrators do not clarify ambiguities. When Lizzie completes Fevvers' stories, both of them maintain the utter confusion of a realist reader such as Walser by complicating the story even more. Walser "continued to take notes in a mechanical fashion but, [..] he felt more and more like a kitten tangling up in a ball of wool!" (NC 40)

We are offered a possible explanation and understanding of these shifts at the end of the novel as Carter has Walser imagine his own narration of how his experience is linked to the novel's events:

"Jack, Walser, ever an adventurous boy, ran away with the circus for the sake of a blonde in whose hands he was putty since the first moment he saw her. He got himself into scrape upon scrape, danced with a tigress, posed as a roast chicken, finally got himself an apprenticeship in the higher form of the confidence trick, initiated by a wily old pederast who bamboozled him completely. All that seemed to happen to me in the third person as though, most of my life, I watched it but did not live it." (NC 294)

It is possible to speculate from this remark that the novel's third person narration might be Fevvers' or Walser's. The important conclusion drawn from these narrative shifts is

Walser's recognition of his former life as stasis, a life in which he has played the role of the observer, not the participant.

Towards the end of the novel Fevvers loses her appetite for life after she has been separated from Jack. This happens not because she has lost her lover, as it may seem, but because she needs an audience and Jack as reader of her life story:

"The young American it was who kept the whole story of the old Fevvers in his notebooks; she longed for him to tell her it was true."(NC 273)

When they reunite Jack is a reconstructed reader and Fevvers is delighted at discovering the transformation whose architect she has been. Walser's transition from Jack who 'watched' his life to an 'I' who is hatched   summarizes the unbelievable experiences he has undergone in such short a time, and constructs his interpretation of his life-story both past and future:

> "I am Jack Walser, an American citizen. I joined the circus in order to delight my reading public with accounts of few nights at the circus and, as a clown, I performed before the Tsar of All Russians, to great applause.[...] Let me introduce my wife, Sophie Walser who formerly had a successful career on the music hall stage." (NC 293-4)

But this product of patriarchal narrative forms robs Fevvers of both name and career and Fevvers is not satisfied with Jack's approach. His interpretation needs rephrasing:

> "Jack, ever an adventurous boy, ran away with the circus for the sake of a blonde in whose hands he was putty since the first moment he saw her. And now, hatched out of the shell of unknowing, by a combination of a blow on the head and a spasm of erotic ecstasy, I'll have to start all over again."(ibid 294)

He has been alienated from his own experiences but is learning the necessity of involvement with others. To objectify others is also to deny one's own humanity and experience. He has lost his profession as a journalist, become a beaten and abused clown, a Human Chicken in danger of being eaten, a he-Sleeping Beauty, all in order to learn to believe with out seeing.

Fevvers takes over the narration at the end of the novel: "'That's the way to start an interview... Get your pencil and we'll begin!'" (NC 291). The narration begins as the novel's narration ends for us, readers. It extends beyond our gaze, although Fevvers cannot exist other than language on the page. Fevvers is "transformed back into her old self again, without an application of peroxide, even" (NC 293), as she begins her tale anew. This time, we are no longer the ones who confirm her status; the reader is left in the dark, in a state of unknowing, and must construct a new self, just as Walser. Angela Carter suggests that we can lay aside the rules of Realist conventions related to narrative closure.

"Seeing is always a complex and untrustworthy business" (Pearson, 1999:249). Fevvers is an empowered object when she is seen, and an assertive subject when she is heard, so she can fend Walser's questions:

> "I'm not the right one to ask questions of when it comes to what is real and what is not, because, like the duck-billed platypus, half the people who clap eyes on me don't believe what they see and the other half thinks they're seeing things" (NC 244)

If the confidence trick is an analogy of fiction, narrative becomes a kind of exploitation of the reader. The reader suspends disbelief, just as the 'gull' of the confidence trick lays aside incredulity. Like Walser, the narrative prompts us to "contemplate the unimaginable – that is, the absolute suspension of disbelief" (NC 17). Lennard Davis argues that "we seek to locate ourselves in the character and to merge with the character" (1987:136). But if we regard identification as a motivation of reading, then, as readers of *Nights at the Circus* , we have to face our identification with the dupe of narrative.

Just as Walser is deceived by Fevvers' confidence trick, so is the reader a 'gull' of the narrative. The final words of Fevvers to both the readers and Walser suggest that many of us have been fooled although we do not admit it: "To think I really fooled you!... It just goes to show there's nothing like confidence" (NC 295). Our confidence in narrative identities is tried. Since we question this mode of narrative representation, our confidence in the identity of Woman is undermined. As we express confidence in narrative representations, we give in to the experience of reading, which is, according to Walser, a combination of "a little primitive technology and a big dose of the will to believe" (NC 16).

The novel looks like an illusion since it twists Realist narrative conventions in favour of magical realism. Narrative is exposed by Angela Carter as a trickster. I think Carter's shifts in narrative voice demand action on the part of the reader, urging us to make connections, not just read and observe; our experience parallels Walser's, and without participating in this process, the reader misses the transformative force of the novel. Such an experience cannot be gained "via normal channels", but rather through the grotesque narrative that ensures progression, as the old fakir tells Walser: "what would be the point of the illusion if it *looked* like an illusion? For... is not this whole world an illusion? And yet it fools everybody" (NC 16).

271

5.2. EMBROIDERING GENEALOGIES

Life is configured as theatre and play for Dora, the heroine of *Wise Children*, a novel which parallels Shakespeare's domestic five-act comedies, with its five chapters. The metaphor of life as a theatre is crucial to the novel, revealing also Carter's vision and concerns with reality and illusion. She magnifies this vision by constructing the novel as drama, populating it with a variety of stage performers and scattering theatrical references throughout. *"Wise Children* moves in and out of present and past moments in a deliberately non-chronological order" (Sanders, 2002:7).

The Cockney guise is the base to contest the cultural establishment, as it represents a banished voice in English culture. Carter uses this vulgar voice to question the high centre of culture, symbolized by Shakespeare. In her reflection on the lack of great female writers with a literary stature matching Shakespeare's, she conceded in 'Notes from the Front Line', "So there hasn't been a female Shakespeare" (1997:48). She seems to be saying that English women writers, alienated from the privileged centre, are able to see through the theatricality of the family show and make a carnival out of the patriarchal drama. *Wise Children* is a woman's dialogue with the great legacy. The space the female narrator, Dora Chance, occupies is set ironically in the low realm of popular culture, spoken with a Cockney accent.

I will unveil the strategy used by the female narrator in the construction of her voice. One device under scrutiny will be Carter's parodic use of popular culture to subvert the centre, represented by the Shakespearean discourse; the second slant I focus on is the problematic dialogue between father and daughter in terms of cultural identity; the third is the use of carnivalesque transgression in bringing down the patriarchal rule to give volume to the female voice.

In *Wise Children* the dialogue with the Shakespearean discourse can be approached from two directions: the cultural significance of the historical theatre, and the critique of the imperial use of its legacy. The novel does not deal with the historical theme directly, but re-deploys Shakespearean theatrical practice on the life-stage in Britain. The popular cultural element in Shakespeare's theatre, long obscured in its canonizing process, is conjured up. As the classical discourse tends to privilege tragedy over comedy, Shakespeare's criticism reflects this differentiation. Dora Chance remarks about the theatre-life she had been part of: "tragedy, eternally more class than comedy. How could mere song-and-dance girls aspire so high? We were destined, from birth, to be the lovely ephemera of the theatre" (WC58).

The link of low comedy with popular culture is indicative of the carnival power that popular culture possesses in shifting the perspective on the edifice of Shakespeare. In an interview with Lorna Sage, Carter remarked "Shakespeare just isn't an intellectual" and intellectuals are "still reluctant to treat him as popular culture" (WC186), and she observed,

> "Shakespeare, like Picasso, is one of the great hinge-figures that sum up the past – one of the great Janus-figures that sum up the past as well as opening all the doors towards the future…I like *A Midsummer Night's Dream* almost beyond reason, because it's beautiful and funny and camp – and glamorous, and cynical…English popular culture is very odd, it's got some very odd and unreconstructed elements in it. There's no other country in the world where you have pantomime with men dressed as women and women dressed as men…It's part of the great tradition of British art, is all that 'smut' and transvestism and so on." (WC187)

Treating Shakespeare in the category of popular culture does not only release the father figure from its altar, it also highlights the comic force of his theatre, neglected by critical attempts to make him serious. Lorna Sage points out that for Carter "perhaps today's equivalent to the old oral tradition was to be found in the soap opera and the dirty joke - genres *Wise Children* also celebrates" (1994:56).

The reproduction of Shakespeare in the mass cultural realm is observed in a paradoxical way in the novel – it can be subversive as a pop cultural form, or it can be utterly commercialized and lose its critical force. The dominant side of culture is declining, along with its claimed universal truths, supported by elements of class and sexuality. Dora's narrative springs from the wrong side of the mainstream, the illegitimate one. The low cultural space the Chances inhabit is impregnated with subversive potential and cultural trash. As music-hall song-and-dance girls, the Chances' catchphrase "what a joy it is to dance and sing!" illustrates their carnivalesque opposition to high art's view of their art as tragic and vulgar.

In the narrative string of Shakespearean motifs, Carter's tendency to associate the legitimate Hazard dynasty with tragic vision and the illegitimate Chance family with comedy is apparent. One motif mostly underlies the Hazard family story and links it to the bastard

Chances, the fiction's parody of *King Lear*. Firstly, the theme of paternal love is twisted by the novel's King Lear marrying his Cordelia. Secondly, the tragic scene of the daughters' betrayal (Imogen and Saskia) is repeated to the suffering mother (Lady Atlanta). Thirdly, Dora's comic narrative subverts the tragic motifs, focusing mainly on the problematic relationship between father and daughter. Dora's narration seems to simply record the two strange coincidences in which both the aging Ranulph and Melchior marry the young Cordelia, played by Estella and Margarine. On a deeper level, the drama between theatrical father and daughter reveals a power relationship in which the patriarch holds the daughter not in the name of filial love only, but with an insatiable desire for domination. The motif of men's hold on power combines thus the erotic drive to the taste for power.

In an article discussing feminist criticism of Shakespeare's family tragedy in *King Lear*, Kathleen Mc Luskie   makes an observation which is relevant to Carter's examination of patriarchal eroticism:

"The misogyny of King Lear, both the play and its hero, is constructed out of an ascetic tradition which presents women as the source of the primal sin of lust, combining with concerns about the threat to the family posed by female insubordination." (1994:106)

While misogyny views female lust as a threat to patriarchal order, Carter's parodic Lear story reverses the feared female lust to that of the father's dominating desire for the daughter, besides confronting the daughter's desire for the father. What is also interesting is that the Ranulph-Melchior-Lear figure is combined with the role of actor-manager, a role equivalent to that of the puppet-master in Carter's fiction, the possessive manipulator in 'The Executioner's Beautiful Daughter' (in *Fireworks*, 1974) for example. The father in this grim story, executing the law, beheads his son for the latter's incestuous offence on the daughter. But, ironically, the father, in his executioner's mask that has long come to replace his natural face, has been engaged in exactly such an offence, but there is no one to cut his head off.   In the Ranulph/Melchior –Lear-Cordelia triangle the incestuous relationships are primarily symbolic, as Melchior married his daughter Saskia's best friend, Margarine, after her impersonation of Cordelia. The sexual implications of the father's grip on the daughter are obvious.

However, the tragic sense that hangs over the Melchior-Lear persona is not just the feared female betrayal but the sense of inadequacy in the father–son relation. Melchior, the father impersonator is also the son symbolically decapitated by his father. In his effort of imitating his father, who was engaged in the same impersonation process, their common goal is

274

to achieve the great patriarchal image of Shakespeare, the god-like figure for their double roles of puppet-masters and players in his plays. While acclaimed, like his father Ranulph, as the greatest living Shakespearean in his life-time, Melchior makes a travesty of the god-father figure when he plays Shakespeare in the comic West End musical *What? You Will?* written by Peregrine. Between his belief in Shakespeare and his patriarchal impersonation there is always a gap, no matter how tiny, which he cannot fill up, for he is "a player to the marrow" who lives in "a permanent stage set" (WC95). He is like a puppet who struggles to become the puppet-master who conceives him, but fails to eliminate the sense of impersonation, which shatters his authority. This sense of tragedy culminates with his playing King Lear, wearing a worn-out paper crown passed from father to son.

How does the daughter respond to the patriarch's calling? "No sacrificial lamb"(WC 15), as Cordelia-Estella fell to his charm, even though she fails to escape his phallic knife in the end. The problem for the daughter is the contradictory longing for the prince-father while she needs to take a subversive stance. It is as if she had to combine Cordelia's devotion with Regan and Goneril's rebellion. If Estella–Cordelia fails to break the old man's grip and dies, the presiding Cordelia, Lady 'Margarine', seems absorbed by the glory of the old patriarch. She plays the supportive daughter-wife, and the only subversive act she brings to the Hazard dynasty is to adapt the theatrical tradition to TV advertising games.

In the problematic father-daughter relationship Dora and Nora's life-long infatuation with their father Melchior appears the most unrequited. Although there is a psychological side to their feelings, the allegorical cultural meaning is more significant. The psychological side is suggested by Dora's name, linked to Freud's case. While Freud's Dora is unwilling to admit to her confused love for her father who, in Freud's analysis, is invoked by Dora to displace her desire for another man, Herr K., Dora Chance openly confesses her filial and erotic love for her father, along with the haunting presence of the father's image in her lovers. She even makes love to two of them in her father's bed. Moreover, Dora's confusion over the erotic and filial aspects of her love undergoes a further twist as her crush on her father is split to her surrogate father Peregrine, for whom she develops a life-long passion. These two father figures represent to the girls powerful charming princes, one dark and noble (Melchior/Hamlet), the other seductive (Peregrine/Falstaff), and their strong male images increase with the passing of time.

The daughters' erotic confusion over fathers and lovers is not just a psychological result of patriarchal rule; it is also a longing for origin. In Dora and Nora's case the maternal origin can be traced from oral female history, such as Grandma Chance's account of their mother Kitty's story, a chambermaid who died in childbirth. What is left is the dominant presence of the father. However, paternal 'authorship', as Dora notes, is a dubious fact, easily forgotten and denied, especially in the case of 'illegitimate' children (WC 174). The daughter's longing for paternal origin parallels her relationship with the culture she is born into. To 'speak' (WC 13), she must borrow the language of that culture, as Irish teaches Dora to write. The daughter develops a longing to belong and identify with the "literary fathers" (WC 123). On the other hand, she is the illegitimate child of the male-centred culture. Her banishment puts her in a subversive position to "fuck the house down"(WC 220), a desire to bring the phallocentric rule down.

The daughter's estrangement from the paternal centre is featured as illegitimacy, which does not entail immunity from the sacrificial role of the lamb. To break free, the daughter has to confront both the tiger preying on her and her desire. For Dora and Nora, not loved by their natural father Melchior, the solution is to face their desire for the father and deconstruct his authority. The first lover Nora has at sixteen is a pantomime goose, old enough to be her father. Dora, speaking for Nora, contradicts the idea that it was "a squalid, furtive, miserable thing", for "He was the one she wanted, warts and all, she *would* have him, by hook or by crook" (WC81).

In Dora's case, the deconstruction of the patriarch's charm starts with her exploitation of a string of lovers. Like Nora, her female 'lust' is like a cat's, so she has numerous lovers, mostly connected to her daughterly complex. Her first love affair with a young man takes place in Melchior's bed, so it can be seen as an act of mocking at the father's authority. The second significant affair is with the modernist Hollywood artist Irish, as old as her father, but his father-lover image is enhanced by his proximity to Peregrine, who introduces him to Dora as "*mon frere,* my collaborator", igniting her lust for a "first old man" (WC67). On her seventy— fifth birthday she makes love to Peregrine, again in Melchior's bed. This time the forbidden desire is illustrated by the image of the lions "roaring their hearts out"(WC 219). Dora admits that she loved him more than she loved any young kid and that he is a 'kaleidoscope' of all the loves of her life, while in Perry's eyes she is still his thirteen-year-old daughter-love (WC221). Interestingly enough, in their filial-erotic complex each has a shadow love overlapped with the one they were making love to. For Dora, it is Melchior behind Peregrine on the former's bed, for Peregrine, Saskia behind Dora, with Dora lying on Saskia's mink coat and Perry wiping them both off with Saskia's scarf.

As the subversive forces within and without the Hazard dynasty, Peregrine and Dora's love–making mirrors the family tradition of patriarchal power over the body of the daughter. The difference between their act and that of Melchior/Cordelia lies in their belief system. For Melchior it is a tragic act of the beheaded son trying to wear the crown of the father and become him (WC224), for Margarine-Cordelia, an act of the sacrificial daughter. Melchior's other twins, Imogen and Saskia, play the roles of Goneril and Regan, turning their bitterness not only to their father. Saskia seduces Tristram (Melchior's son by Margarine) and tortures her mother Lady Atlanta. The evil sisters are trapped in their compulsion to become their parents and remain crippled by sense of guilt over the unnatural act of assuming their parents' roles.

In the case of Dora and Peregrine, however, patriarchal tragedy is no longer the model they follow. Their act is an embrace of forbidden desires, of an old hag and an older trickster who play lovers to one another without becoming sacrificial lambs. Facing the desires in themselves they take control of their roles.

"Life is a carnival" states Perregrine in their transgressive love-making, but Dora limits the power of carnival, "The carnival's got to stop, some time, Perry" (WC 222). Here we can find one difference between the two carnivalesque disrupters. For Peregrine the illusionist, life is a parade of illusions, a confidence game, in which "all the terms of every contract"(WC 222) can be destroyed by the laughter he hears through the theatrical illusions. But for Dora, a realistic illusionist, even the carnivalesque disruption of life's illusion can be an illusion, and there are tragedies that cannot be laughed away. The cautioning against an unconditional belief in the transgressive power of carnival is expressed by Carter herself:

"the carnival has to stop. The whole point of the feast of fools is that things went on as they did before, after it stopped." (Sage, 1994:254)

The paradoxical strategy of both conjuring up and undermining the carnival power needs further consideration. Such a strategy, also used in postmodern fiction, can be problematic, because its play is subject to the same logic of self-subversion.

Dora's narrative practice in relation to the carnivalesque is conducted on two levels, the carnival texture of the text and the content itself. In Lorna Sage's discussion, the textual carnival of *Wise Children* is seen as a spinning of "illegitimate histories, left-handed genealogies, a whole carnival of the dispossessed" (1994:54) but in using it for its 'ideal

277

openness', Carter understands it "as having necessary limits"; moreover, as Sage observes, "If carnival represents the promiscuous and horizontal axis of narrative relations, then at carnival's end we return to verticality – the line, the family, history's determinings, time's irreversibility" (1994:55).

Laughter and utopian vision, crucial elements of the grotesque, are brought forth through the lives of the twins Nora and Dora Chance. Carter focuses on figures whose lives, we might presume, belong primarily to the past. However, Dora's narration reveals that these lives exist in the present and the future, as well. The past and the present are not discrete, they merge in the end with the future. This is how Carter dramatises a potential reality depending on the reality of the present, not as an idealistic dream of the future. Dora mixes past, present and future to emphasise the energetic heterotopic spirit of the novel:

> "Sometimes I think, if I look hard enough, I can see back into the past. There goes the wind, again. Crash. Over goes the dustbin, all the trash spills out...empty food-cans, cornflakes packets, ..., tea-leaves... I am at present working on my memoirs and researching family history – see the word processor, the filing cabinet... What a wind!... the kind of wind that blows everything topsy-turvy. Seventy-five, today, and a topsy-turvy day of wind and sunshine. The kind of wind that gets into the blood and drives you wild. Wild! And I give a little shiver because suddenly I know, I know in my ancient water, that something will happen today. Something exciting. Something nice, something nasty, I don't give a monkey's. Just as long as something happens to remind us we're still in the land of the living." (WC 4)

The term "tessellation" (Grant, 1999:39) seems appropriate in the description of the effects of this 'Sterneian' double time-scheme. The time of telling the story overlaps with the time of the story, just as the tiles laid on a roof support one another:

> "The narrative is always looping back in recapitulation, and also looking forward ("proleptically") in anticipation. The effect is to bring a depth of field to the present moment, creating an impression of simultaneity and temporal suspension - as the fluid present, the elusive now, is always pressed on by the past and foreshadowed, drawn forward into the future."

As Dora recalls Nora's and her own past, her narration does not travel far from the narrative present - this day of their upcoming birthday party – and finally, she tosses the reader into a laughing future. The passage also shows Dora's power as storyteller. We feel that she both gazes into the past and foresees the future. As with Fevvers in *Nights at the Circus*, Carter has Dora insist that as long as there is movement, life exists as a dynamic process. There is

278

responsibility implied in the necessity to change the present through both reason and imagination. Carter's utopic vision incorporates reason to confront the here and now, with the words of Grandma Chance "Hope for the best, expect the worst". Expecting the worst, paradoxically prepares the way to defeat the worst, and implies the idea that the best is only potentiality, not certainty. When Dora recalls her support for the necessity of lying in a past instance involving paternity and the shocked reaction of an American woman, she declares,

> "We lived in an ethical twilight, a cockroach world of compromise, lies, emotional sleight of hand... We called it 'Life'. It's the American tragedy in a nutshell. They look around the world and think: 'There must be something better!' But there isn't. sorry, chum. This is it. What you see is what you get. Only the here and now." (WC 144)

Dora understands the necessity of staying alert to the construction of our lives; any utopia depends on both reason and imagination to shape the best lives in the here and now, because the future is embedded in the present. Bakhtin stresses this idea as he theorises the grotesque. Both the dystopic vision and its contrasting utopic vision denounce the dehumanization of the modern world. While the dystopic offers only a valid warning, the utopic offers a vision of transformation by constructing a liveable present. This gift of the utopic vision is rooted in the desire to change and celebrate. Dora later reflects on the present moment and its relation to the future:

> "When I was young I'd wanted to be ephemeral, I'd wanted the moment, to live just the glorious moment, the rush of blood, the applause. Pluck the day. Eat the peach. Tomorrow never comes. But, oh, yes, tomorrow does come all right, and when it comes it lasts a bloody long time, I can tell you". (WC 125)

As a wise child, she has come to understand that the present contains all the past and the future, and that the time frames used to delimit them are cultural conveniences.

In both *Nights at the Circus* and *Wise Children* a strange clock defies the tracking of conventional time, since none functions accurately. In *Nights at the Circus* Fevvers and Lizzie are proud of a gilded ornate French clock carried from the whorehouse. Its distinctive feature is that it only strikes midnight. In *Wise Children* Dora and Nora own a grandfather clock uncle Perry sent them from one of his journeys:

> "We boast the only castrato grandfather clock in London. The plaque on the dial ...says it was made in Inverness in 1846... Great, tall, butch, horny mahogany thing, but it gives the hours in a

funny little falsetto ping and always the wrong hour, always out by one" (WC 36).

The clock stands as a parodic reminder of the masculine heroic past that inhabits the present. On their 75th birthday, as Dora begins her memoirs, the clock strikes correctly for the first time, signalling the moment of the narrative blend of past, present and future. The reader thus moves into a narrative time zone that mingles all time frames, giving rise to grotesque contradictions, excess, repetitions in the narrative.

Nora and Dora's home takes on the function of the chronotope, the flesh and blood of the novel. 49 Bard Road, Brixton, London is the place saturated with Dora's personal history, a domestic space associated with woman's role outside history. This chronotope takes on more meanings as we learn that it served as a boarding house during the turn-of-the-century, providing a link to public culture. Furthermore, Brixton, located on the south side of the Thames, is historically the "wrong side of the tracks", as opposed to the 'upper class' North side, where Melchior lives with his legitimate family. As Dora declares "me and Nora... we've always lived on...the side the tourist rarely sees, the *bastard* side of Old Father Thames" (WC 1). Brixton is presented as a shared space of public culture

"hub of a wheel of theatres, music halls, Empires, Royalties, what have you.... The streets of tall, narrow houses were stuffed to the brim with stand-up comics; adagio dancers; soubrettes; conjurers; fiddlers; speciality acts with dogs, doves, goats, you name it; dancing dwarves; tenors, sopranos, baritones and basses, both solo artistes and doubled up in any of the permutations of the above as duets, trios etc." (WC 23)

Bakhtin writes of the chronotope of carnival-time as that of the street's activity as "animated and illuminated by the ancient public square's spirit of carnival and mystery" (1982:249). Historical Brixton, as a chronotope, provides carnival-time, suggesting the subversive possibilities inherent in carnival. The literary history of Brixton traces back to Shakespeare's Globe Theatre, which was built on the South side of London when a land dispute prevented its erection on the North side. Back to the present, the narrator Dora tells us that "you can't trust things to stay the same. There's been a diaspora of the affluent, they jumped into their diesel Saabs and dispersed throughout the city" (WC 1). This is how the spatial location accumulates a flow of time spanning four hundred years. Another doubling occurs with the opening sentences of the novel – a question and an answer – "Q. Why is London like Budapest?

280

A. Because it is two cities divided by a river" (WC 1). Everything is doubled, from the city to the family, the space, and the characters, all part of the comic grotesque.

Dora hails comedy as narrative strategy, declaring that

"Only untimely death is a tragedy. And war, which, before we knew it, would be upon us; replace the comic mask with the one whose mouth turns down and close the theatre, because I refuse point-blank to play in tragedy" (WC 153).

The heterotopic vision of the novel acknowledges the existence of the destructive forces at work in the world, so Dora admits that comedy and laughter cannot annihilate horror: "There are limits to the power of laughter and though I may hint at them from time to time, I do not propose to step over them" (WC 220). She includes references to the realities of the wars in her history. Remembering a day in her childhood when Uncle Perry, a flyer in World War I, spread joy and "saved us all from gloom the day the war to end all wars ended, just twenty years before the next one started," she then addresses her thoughts to him:

"And wars are facts we cannot fuck away, Perry; nor laugh away, either" (WC221). Despite Dora's insistence on the joy and energy marking the day of her birth, she makes sure her listener remembers she was born during the war:

"You must remember that there was a war on. If we made her [Grandma] happy, then we didn't add much to the collective sum of happiness of South London. First of all, the neighbours' sons went marching off, sent to their deaths, God help them. Then the husbands, the brothers, the cousins, until, in the end, all the men went except the ones with one foot in the grave and those still in the cradle, so there was a female city, red-eyed, dressed in black, outside the door." (WC 28)

Grandma Chance has an explanation for the occurrence of wars.

"Grandma said it then, she said it again in 1939: "Every twenty years, it's bound to happen. It's to do with generations. The old men get so they can't stand the competition and they kill off all the young men they can lay their hands on. They daren't be seen to do it themselves, that would give the game away, the mothers wouldn't stand for it, so all the men all over the world get together and make a deal: you kill off our boys and we'll kill off yours. So that's that. Soon done. Then the old men can sleep easy in their beds, again." (WC 28)

In the opening sentence of Chapter Four, the penultimate one focusing on the past

281

memories, before the birthday party in the following chapter, Dora reminds us that the war "was no carnival" (WC 163). Although the chapter recounts the black days of World War II, with Grandma Chance's being killed by a bomb as she goes out to buy ale during a blackout, laughter and love support the story, defeating the tragic moment. As the sisters are getting ready for the party, thinking of Grandma as they search her closet for something to wear, suddenly her "hat, ...gloves, ...corsets, ...stockings...cascaded out of the wardrobe" (WC 190). Dora can even hear her voice "clear as a bell" telling them "Come off it, girls! Pluck the day! You ain't dead, yet! You've got a party to go to!" (WC 190). Dora and Nora are touched by the spirit of war, but their spirit celebrates the joy of dancing and singing. Carter's emphasis on humour, hope and vitality is similar to the spirit of Shakespeare's comedies. Although the novel parodically indicates the impossibility of sustaining the stage comedy in the age of the movie and television industry, it appropriates comic theatre as an aesthetic model.

The laughter that seeps out of the comic novel corresponds to the one defined by Bakhtin:

"We have in mind here laughter not as a biological or psycho-physiological act, but rather conceived as an objectivised, sociohistorical cultural phenomenon, which is most often present in verbal expression. For it is in the word that laughter manifests itself most variously. There is a continual passing beyond the boundaries of the given, sealed-off verbal whole" (1982:237)

The narration, inhabited by the utopian spirit and comic familiarity of Dora, relies on Carter's moulding the conventional story. She defies the constraints of linear time, first of all. Secondly, the 'dizzying accumulation' and 'excessiveness' of story that Susan Rubin Suleiman sees in *The Passion of New Eve* and we have noticed in *Nights at the Circus* are present in *Wise Children* as well, contributing to understanding the prevalence of the grotesque. Family matters are complicated, origins are a mystery and constantly generating uncertainties, as is the case of the twins' real mother. Grandma Chance resembles Lizzie in *Nights at the Circus* in her witty comments and aphorisms. Her response to Dora's beaming face at 17 is "Whoever he is, ... he's not worth it" (WC 88).

A further twist in the story is that Grandma Chance might actually be Lizzie, last seen on New Year's Day 1900 at the end of *Nights at the Circus*. Dora notes:

"I don't think for a moment that 'Chance' was her real name, either. All that I know about her is: she'd arrived at 49 Bard Road on New Year's Day, 1900, with a banker's draft ... and the air of a woman making a new start in a new place, a new century and, or so the evidence points, a new name.' (WC26-7)

Lizzie's age is given as between 30 and 50 in 1899, and Dora tells that Grandma must have been at least 50 when she and Nora were born in 1914. Both women "took to children like a duck to water" (WC 28), and their history remains a mystery. Literary history and the story of popular culture intersect with a section of the novel taking place during a movie adaptation of *A Midsummer Night's Dream*, twisting the destinies of the families, whose members are as grotesque as the royal families of Britain, who are mentioned in the novel, with Dora's dance with the Prince of Wales in the 1930s.

Carter's inclusion of a *Dramatis Personae* provides a self-reflexive comment on the confusing narrative, satisfying the reader's need for clarification. The Hazard's genealogical mystery moves into the future with Tiffany's pregnancy. We see how excess works to give rise to a grotesque rather than ordered vision of genealogy. In an early passage Dora comments on her intricate roots:

> "our paternal grandmother, the one fixed point in our father's genealogy. Indeed, the one fixed point in our entire genealogy; our maternal side founders in a wilderness of unknowability and our other grandmother, Grandma Chance, the grandma whose name we carry, she was no blood relation at all, to make confusion more confounded." (WC 12)

Pretty Kitty is assumed to be their mother due to Grandma's accounts, but the girls speculate that Grandma is, encouraged by Perry's assertion that "Mother is as mother does" (WC 223). Genealogy is thus given legitimate and illegitimate dimensions, expanding the notion of the family. Dora poses a question that compels her to tell her story:

> "But the urge has come upon me before I drop to seek out an answer to the question that always teased me, as if the answer were hidden, somewhere, behind a curtain: whence came we? Whither goeth we?" She immediately gives the answer to the second "bound for oblivion, nor leave a wrack behind" (WC 11).

It is the first that proves elusive. Dora will offer no definite answer because certainties do not exist. She can answer partially, but the conclusion she draws is that parentage is open to discoveries and possibilities. The four sets of twins provide an excess of possible parents, and a fifth set of infant twins appears out of the blue at the end of the novel, along with Tiffany's forthcoming child.

Dora's family history is confusing because of its multiple twins and generations, but the narrative twists she adds further complicate the story. While the narrative method resembles

Nights at the Circus in its shifting multiplicity, *Wise Children* is different in its first-person narration. Whereas *Nights at the Circus* uses unidentified narrators in addition to Fevvers or other characters telling stories to one another, *Wise Children* employs one first-person narrator, Dora, who recounts her story to an unnamed figure, the familiar 'you' whom Dora addresses frequently as the implied reader of her memoirs.

A first-person narration opens the possibility of a clear point of view or consistent guide for the story that unfolds. This novel, however, deliberately upsets clarity of reference and insinuates the impossibility of such a task. Early in the novel, Dora addresses the 'you' as if s/he were the guest in her home, pointing to the word processor or filing cabinet as she speaks or writes her memoirs. This leads us to the assumption that her physical location as narrator is in her home. Despite the narrative turns in time almost one hundred years back, the opening of the story in Dora's room stays clear in our minds. A narrative occurs near the end, following the story of the birthday party, the novel's climatic event. For most of the narration the party exists as an upcoming event, but after it has become the past, Dora takes us by surprise by declaring "Well, you might have known what you were about to let yourself in for when you let Dora Chance in her ratty old fur and poster paint, ...reeking with liquor, accost you in the Coach and Horses and tell you a tale" (WC 227).

She places herself in a tavern, giving rise to the postmodern questions "Where have we been? Where are we? What is going on?" derived from Dora's early thoughts on origins and destinations. The impossibility of any certainty of genealogy is paralleled by Dora's shifting spatial position. Perhaps she has been in a tavern all along, constructing for her listeners a place in her home. Or she may have been in her home placing herself imaginatively in a tavern. The story frame remains open in either case. Another narrative tricks she employs is the cinematic "freeze-frame. Let us pause a while in the unfolding story of Tristram and Tiffany so that I can fill you in on the background" (WC 11); "I'll tell you all about it in my own good time" (WC 13); and "There I go again! Can't keep a story going in a straight line, can I? Drunk in charge of a narrative" (WC 158). A few pages later. Dora positions herself in the home as she speaks of the loneliness after Grandma's death: "Nora and I sat down right here, in the breakfast room, in these very leather armchairs, and listened to the silence" (WC164). Whether she has shifted dwellings or not, she has clearly moved to another room, for earlier she was in her room in the attic.

The narrator's uncertain spatial position as personal historian parallels the complexity of the history she relates. It is itself a story about stories. A linear timetable shows that Dora's history begins "some time in or around the year 1870" (WC 13), the year of Estella's birth, extends through the two World Wars, moves into the present, 1989, and tosses us into the future. But the time frames of the story are also fused and jumbled, often in relation to Dora's memory associations. As she connects today's weather with that of the day of her birth in 1914, she associates the blue sky with another event at a time in history currently unknown to the reader, a story we will be told later: "I knew a boy, once, with eyes that colour, years ago. Bare as a rose, not a hair on him; he was too young for body hair. And sky-blue eyes" (WC 2-3). Dora sometimes admits to memory problems: "It was a strange night...and stranger still because I always misremember. It never seems the same, twice, each time that I remember it. I distort" (WC 157); we are reminded that even 'eyewitness' records of history are filtered through a unique consciousness. Dora's memory associations incorporate a broader history as well. Her birthday, as well as Melchior's and Perry's, coincides with that of Shakespeare, but also with the early days of the World War I, which she connects with the present day of the narrative: "Cold, windy, spring weather, just like the day we were born, when the Zeppelins were falling. Lovely blue sky, a birthday present in itself" (WC 2). The novel is combining literary, political, social, and personal history, and exploiting to the maximum the narrative's potential for excess and temporal layering.

As both narrator and protagonist, Dora's identity and desires are crucial to the story which relies on her memory and the notes of her files. We hear the family history along with learning how Dora's identity has been shaped, so that the two threads complete one another. When the story moves into the future birthday party in the final chapter of the novel, Uncle Perry, presumed dead for several years, returns suddenly on his 100th birthday. Before his entrance, Dora recalls "Something unscripted is about to happen" (WC 206), reminding us of the feeling of anticipation she experienced on another occasion. Perry arrives as a Shakespearean tempest and surrounded by a cloud of butterflies (WC 207). Dora and Perry make love that evening, an incestuous act filled with laughter and joy, not before Dora lets us know that

> "he really, truly loved us... He saw the girls we always would be under the scrawny, wizened carapace that time had forced on us for, although promiscuous, he was also faithful, and, where he loved, he never altered, nor saw any alteration. And then I wondered...Did I see the soul of the one I loved when I saw Perry, not his body? And was his fleshly envelope, perhaps, in

reality in much the same sorry shape as those of his nieces outside the magic circle of my desire?" (WC 208).

Bakhtin's image of the grotesque laughing hags in invoked here. Their aged bodies both contain and conceal their own identities as girls. These grotesque bodies with their vivid fleshly materiality can be viewed as a type of personal chronotope in their spatial encompassing of time's passage. The 'magic circle' of Dora's desire indicates a progressive movement toward the day when all the major figures are drawn together in a single room for a magnificent celebration on the legitimate side of the Thames; even television crews are present to record the celebration of Melchior Hazard, the great Shakespearean actor. Dora wonders "if our mother's ghost was somewhere here, too, mingling with Melchior's three wives and the other guests" (WC 209).

The magic circle of Dora's desire originates before her birth, in the complicated family history she has set out to tell. It shapes her narration, but on a different level, the creation of Dora as narrator illustrates Carter's desire. We have seen Dora express desire for comedy and joy; we have seen this desire shape a narrative dominated by the distortions of a comic grotesque. Dora reveals to us how her desire was shaped. Historically it begins with her paternal grandmother Estella who passes on to Perry the capacity to derive pleasure in life. Perry's stories of his mother are filled with joy, as Dora retells Perry's worlds of his mother:
"She took my hand and we danced, right there, on the pavement...Then everybody started dancing, they all took hold of the hand of the next perfect stranger...She made them happy." (WC 18)
It is here that Dora's desire to dance is rooted, but Perry's influence has left its mark, as well:
"Always the lucky one, our Peregrine, even in his memories, which were full of laughter and dancing. Peregrine Hazard, adventurer, magician, seducer, explorer, scriptwriter, rich man, poor man" (WC19).
The link between Peregrine 'wandering' as storyteller and Dora as storyteller is strong. He has shaped her, for Dora's memories focus on the good times and her comic spirit infuses the bad ones. Perry's stories are similar to Dora's in their openness, in the questions they leave unanswered:
"Over the years, Peregrine offered us a Chinese banquet of options as to what happened to him next. He gave us all his histories, we could choose which ones we wanted – but they kept on

286

changing, so. That was the trouble....I know for a fact he'd worked in circuses. Unless it was on the halls. Or else he'd perfected his stage magic, his juggling and conjuring tricks, to entertain his fellow prospectors during the long winter evenings in Alaska. Above all, how did he grow so rich?" (WC 31-2)

Perry acts as the magician who stirs Dora's curiosity and colours her imagination with laughter. When she first meets him she is about four, and he arrives at the end of the first World War, catching Dora and Nora naked, playing pirates in the house. As Dora remembers, "The knocker got a shock. A naked child greeted the stranger. Not a scrap on but for the big, blue bow in my brown hair, and a black eye-patch" (WC 30). Perry's first reaction to the cold stares of the girls is to laugh, but he stifles his laughter when he realizes he is hurting their feelings: "Ceremoniously he unknotted his handkerchief and, lo, and behold! A white dove flew out" (WC 33). With their nakedness and vulnerability as children exposed, Perry begins to place his imprint of laughter and magic on them. His laughter continues on the following visits, as Dora says when she is 18 and uncle Perry shows up again: "Our uncle Peregrine was rich, again, and always laughing. It made a noise in his belly like barrels rolling around a cellar" (WC 92).

On their seventh birthday he does not visit them but sends them a toy theatre, which becomes the sacred symbol of the girls' lives, providing another chronotopic reference point: "We treasured the theatre. We played with it as if we were in church, always on Sunday afternoons" (WC 58). Chapter three relates in detail the filming of *A Midsummer Night's Dream* in the Hollywood's glory days of the 1930s, and the entire Hazard clan takes part in this comic project. Art turns to kitsch, and for Melchior the project becomes a personal and financial disaster.

Perry is not solely responsible for shaping Dora's desire; Grandma Chance is even more central. On his first visit Perry brings a phonograph to the girls. As the chosen record is played – "I can't give you anything but love, baby' – their uninhibited instincts respond to the music with jumping and clapping: '"we couldn't help it, it was as if a voice told us to do it, we were impelled, ...we got up and danced" (WC 33). As Perry starts dancing with Grandma Chance, Dora tells us that "the way she danced was the only clue to her past she ever gave" (WC 33). As Dora recalls, "Then we were all dancing, right there, in the breakfast room, and, as for us, we haven't stopped dancing yet, have we, Nora? We'll go on dancing till we drop... What a joy it is to dance and sing!" (WC 34)

Grandma, Perry, the past, the here-and-now of the breakfast room, and the future blend in this scene to point out the shaping of Dora's voice. Love and laughter keep her desires untainted by fear and free to explore, in accordance with Bakhtin's idea that laughter annihilates fear. Desire, memory and history come together near the end of the novel when Dora quotes Nora on the subject of Melchior, a man who, despite his refusal to recognize them as legitimate daughters, has remained for them a figure of admiration:

"D'you know, I sometimes wonder if we haven't been making him up all along...If he isn't just a collection of our hopes and dreams and wishful thinking in the afternoons. Something to set our lives by" (WC 230).

He represents for the girls a yearning for fatherly love, deepened by his rejection of them. Much earlier in the novel, Dora has told of her and Nora's alleged first vision as newborns, a story repeated at least three times in the novel:

"The sky was blue, that morning, said Mrs. Chance, and there was a wind that made the washing on the clothes line dance...So there was dancing and singing all along Bard Road and Ms. Chance picked us up, one in each arm, and took us to the window so the first thing we saw with our swimming baby eyes was sunshine and dancing. Then a seagull swooped up, past the window, up and away. Grandma told us about the seagull so often that although I cannot really remember it, being just hatched out, all the same, I do believe I saw that seagull fly up into the sky." (WC 26)

Grandma's repeated story of the sunshine, the dancing, and the seagull is essential in memory, not the actual event. Later Dora brings up the story again, and says,

"All the little children in Bard Road were singing a hymn to Charlie Chaplin the day we were born and Grandma Chance took us to the window to look at the shirts and bloomers dancing on the washing-lines all over Lambeth. That made a difference, you know. We were doomed to sing and dance." (WC 193)

The story of that day dooms them to sing and dance; the choice of the word 'doomed' speaks of the imposing power of story to construct our desires and passions. The story of singing and dancing exists as part of Carter's effort to revise the Freudian oedipal story of loss and fear of loss that shape the Western world's desire for certainty and finality – the death desire. Carter is aware that the story of the past not only builds it but also becomes its known reality. The story of Dora's first sight as told by Grandma Chance, combined with others and her own memories, contributes to her spinning of the family history.

The laughter of the grotesque plays a crucial role in Carter's repudiation of seriousness and tradition. Female desire revealed through laughter in the novel is twofold: desire for transformation through rebellion, and desire for shared joy and connection. Carter defies tradition by giving voice to a woman whose feminine vision is responsible for the large picture of events and human relations. Dora and Nora's exuberant sexuality is a means of expression for this defiance. The two women have cultivated it through a sense of being free to twist, parody and enlarge notions of femininity. Dora and Nora stand for both sameness and difference, and they enjoy replacing one another in their escapades. As Dora confesses, "I did what Nora wanted because I loved her best"(WC150). Their femininity radiates an eroticism that totally disregards conventional notions of love.

Grandma Chance first provides a moment when Bakhtin's laughing hags are invoked. Grandma usually walked around the house nude, but she "kept her clothes on more and more" as she got older. Dora tells of an incident when she caught sight of Grandma without her clothes on:

> "She came into the bathroom, once, she hadn't got a stitch on. Me neither, o was just drying off after my bath. There we were, captured in the mirror, me young and slim and trim and tender, she vast, sagging, wrinkled, quivering. I couldn't but giggle. I shouldn't have. I could have slapped myself afterwards. "That's all very well, Dora," she said, "but one fine day, you'll wake up and find you're old and ugly, just like me." Then she cackled...She cackled and she cackled." (WC 94)

The figure of the seventy-five-year-old Dora is also grotesque in its parody of herself as a young woman, given early in the novel:

> "We always make an effort. We paint an inch thick. We put on our faces our faces before we come down to breakfast, the Max Factor Pan-Stick, the false eyelashes with three coats of mascara, everything....our fingernails match our toenails match our lipstick match our rouge. Revlon, Fire and Ice. The habit of applying war-paint outlasts the battle" (WC 6).

Although they are "long and lean with good cheekbones", their appearance is comic. They have created their bodies as Fevvers, according to their own inventions. We are told of changing hair colours, make-up tricks and clothing. Before the party starts, Dora catches a glimpse of herself and Nora in the mirror and recognises the parody:

"I suffered the customary nasty shock when I spotted us both in the big gilt mirror at the top –

289

two funny old girls, paint an inch thick, clothes sixty years too young, stars on their stockings and little we skirts skimming their buttocks. Parodies." (WC 197)

The two women's reaction to their own reflections is laughter, "we had to laugh at the spectacle we'd made of ourselves and, fortified by sisterly affection, strutted our stuff boldly into the ballroom. We could still show them a thing or two, even if they couldn't stand the sight" (WC 198).

The grotesque juxtaposition of age, death, with youth and potentiality is magnified since Dora, at the time she relates the incident, has become the hag that Grandma, the grotesque laughing figure, predicted. Life and death become thus interactive processes. The connections to female abundance are responsible for much of the joy in the novel. Perry's connection to his mother as a child parallels the way Dora's desire was shaped by him and Grandma Chance. Melchior is the opposite figure, whose connection is to his father, the manic-depressive Ranulph. When they were young, Ranulph killed his wife Estella in a jealous rage and killed himself after, replaying his performance as Othello. Melchior adopts his father's temper and engages in a constant contest with his father's memory. He matches Ranulph's success as a Shakespearean actor, but is doomed to repeat the unhappy history of his parent, namely unhappy wives and children; fortunately, he is not drawn into the murder-suicide circle.

With Dora's narration, we hear the feminine voice expressing a feminine vision of family links and desires, a voice that displaces the masculine world structured around death and conquest. Dora and Nora live surrounded by women all their lives so the novel's point of view is saturated with woman's experiences.

Carter gives her last novel a conventional happy-ending. Dora and Nora are publicly recognised by Melchior as his daughters: "We'd finally wormed our way into the heart of the family we'd always wanted to be part of" (WC 226). Dora sees the past as crucial to the family reunion: "There was a house we all had in common and it was called the past, even though we'd lived in different rooms" (WC 226). The fluidity of time materialises in this one room where future exists as evidence alongside the past, when Perry takes two baby twins out of his pockets: "So it turned out the Hazard dynasty wasn't at its last gasp at all but was bursting out in every direction" (WC 227).

Nora and Dora become foster mothers at 75, which gives Nora great delight, as she compresses the entire confused genealogy in her statement: "We're both of us mothers and both of us fathers...They'll be wise children, all right" (WC 229). The proverb says 'It's a wise child that knows its own father', but the irony of the novel lies the uncertainty of biological fatherhood. Mother and father are constructs, Carter suggests, and parenthood is configured by love and care. The twins, a boy and a girl, imply movement into the future. As she and Nora walk the children home one day, a comment from a neighbour ' "Drunk in charge of a baby carriage, at your age"' (WC231) echoes Dora's statement early in the novel that she was 'Drunk in charge of a narrative' (WC158).

The novel's conclusion presents the aged figures of Dora and Nora laughing, in charge of the twins:

> "we went on dancing and singing…Besides, it was our birthday, wasn't it, we'd got to sing them the silly old song about Charlie Chaplin and his comedy boots all the little kids were singing and dancing in the street the day we were born. There was singing and dancing all along Bard Road that day and we'll go on singing and dancing until we drop in our tracks, won't we, kids. What a joy it is to dance and sing!" (WC 231-232)

Whereas in *Nights at the Circus* Walser has to learn to see Fevvers differently, Dora and Nora in will become aware of their own contribution to the construction of Melchior's figure as their father: "And tonight, he had an imitation look, even when he was crying, especially when he was crying, like one of those great, big, papier-mâché heads they have in the Noting Hill parade, larger than life, but not life-like" (WC 230).

Carter has Dora explain the narrative strategy of giving each story a happy-ending: "These glorious pauses do, sometimes, occur in the discordant but complementary narratives of our lives and if you choose to stop the story there, at such a pause, and refuse to take it any further, then you call it a happy ending." (WC 227)

Carter's choice to stop at a happy moment and call it a 'happy ending' indicates the arbitrariness of all endings. The stop is only a pause, not an ending, so the reader moves into an unknown future. We recall Cixous' words: "A feminine text goes on and on and at a certain moment the volume comes to an end but the writing continues and for the reader this means being thrust into the void" (1990:489). This movement describes the incompleteness of the grotesque with its present potential. Dora and Nora have become the laughing hags to the baby twins, just as Grandma Chance has been to them. The term 'cackle' unites them as they approach the end of their lives. They are now responsible for the birth of the future through the lives of the infants, an image that concludes the heterotopian vision of the novel.

5.3. CINEMATIC SPINNERS

One function of heterotopia refers to its openness. Two otherwise unrelated spaces are connected and we are granted entry into what may be called a tangible utopia, a space that is not so perfect as to prevent us from experiencing it. Foucault uses the example of a movie theatre, where our physical space combines with the visual and virtual space onscreen to create an amalgam of two experiences: "a very odd rectangular room, at the end of which, on a two-dimensional screen, one sees the projection of a three-dimensional space" (1986: 25).

In the cinema we venture into heterochrony, another characteristic of heterotopia; we step into another world for two hours or so, experiencing a disjunction and removal from the real world, without reaching the actual setting of the movie. Yet, as the ending credits roll, we feel as if we had. The importance of cinema in the topography of Angela Carter's work is evident if we pay attention to her interviews, in which she asserts her fascination with

" [..] the tension between inside and outside, between the unappeasable appetite for the unexpected, the gorgeous, the gimcrack, the fantastic, the free play of the imagination and harmony, order. Abstraction. [...]The cinema with its mix of the real and the false [...] public and private at the same time." (Evans and Carter, 1992:8-9)

She criticizes the way Hollywood sells illusions and perpetuates dreams, but she also celebrates cinema as a creative medium: "It seemed to me, when I first started going to the cinema intensively in the late Fifties, that Hollywood had colonized the imagination of the entire world and was turning us all into Americans. I resented it, it fascinated me" (1992:5). Carter's taste for the cinema is easily discernible in her narrative style, which is indebted to the grammar of the medium, in the characters' cinematic experiences or their dreams of populating the world of celluloid:

"I'm perfectly conscious of using all kinds of narrative techniques that I've taken from the cinema. Our experience of watching narrative in the cinema has completely altered the way that we approach narrative on the page, that we even read nineteenth-century novels differently" (1989: Radio 4).

All her novels are filled with cinematic allusions and her indebtedness to film has influenced her highly visual representation of action on page and the two subsequent transpositions on screen.

Adrienne Rich talks about 'writing as re-vision' in her essay 'When We the Dead Awaken':

> "Re-vision – the act of looking back, of seeing with fresh eyes, of entering an old text from a new critical direction – is for women more than a chapter in cultural history; it is an act of survival. Until we understand the assumptions in which we are drenched, we cannot know ourselves... A radical critique of literature, feminist in its impulse would take the work first of all as a clue to how we live, how we have been led to imagine ourselves, how our language has trapped as well as liberated us, how the very act of naming has been till now a male prerogative, and how we can begin to see and name – and therefore live afresh... We need to know the writing of the past, and know it differently than we have ever known it, not to pass on a tradition but to break its hold over us" (1980:35).

The multiple texts and the degree of collaboration involved in their realization gives rise to complex questions about authorial control and responsibility, making it difficult to identify the relationship between author and text. These questions must be addressed, outdated as they may seem in an era of 'the death of the author'. Lorna Sage (1994:58) notes that Carter "had a position on the politics of sexuality. She went in for the proliferation, rather than the death, of the author." Carter's mediated texts perform this 'proliferation' both in terms of the multiple adaptations of texts and the collaborative relationships between her as author/scriptwriter and the directors she worked with. She paid attention to both the aesthetic and the technologies of the medium, in the process of adapting her work

The challenge of dealing with mediated texts has encouraged me to embrace a multiplicity of theoretical perspectives, outside the usual scope of literary studies, such as feminist film theory, rather than employ any single theoretical framework. This goes in line with Douglas Kellner's 'multi-perspectival approach' which "draws on a wide range of textual and critical strategies to interpret, criticize, and deconstruct the artifact under scrutiny" (1995:98). Kellner argues that "the more perspectives one brings to bear on a phenomenon, the better one's potential grasp or understanding of it could be" (1995:26). I also embrace his related notion of a 'transdisciplinary' approach, crossing the borders of literary, film, media and cultural studies (1995:27).

In her analysis of Carter's style, Mulvey notes the prevalence of a "magic cinematic attribute even when the cinema itself is not present on the page" (1994:230). In he essay 'Visual Pleasure and Narrative Cinema', she operates a division of looking, typical of classical cinema, into passive and active, namely into female 'to-be-looked-at-ness' and male gaze. In traditional narrative film, there are two ways for the male unconscious to 'escape from this castration anxiety': voyeurism, which is located in a "preoccupation with the re-enactment of the original trauma (investigating the woman, demystifying her mystery)" and 'fetishistic scopophilia', which entails "the substitution of a fetish object or turning the repressed figure itself into a fetish so that it becomes reassuring rather than dangerous" (1989:21)

The filmic image has taken a central place in *The Passion of New Eve*. As the bodyscape is displayed on the cinematic screen we are left with the impression that it is subjected to the human gaze. Angela Carter underlines the spectacular character of the ensuing image, and how it can be changed at will. The fictional historical time, set in the 1960s dreamland of America, is referred back to the late 1940s when there was a vogue in the Hollywood film industry for 'romanticism'. There was a real trend of cinema in that period to produce movies later labelled as 'woman's film'. Laura Mulvey observes that these films position women as the object of the gaze and men as spectators. Carter's fiction parallels Mulvey's (1989) analysis of the cinematic male gaze in terms of voyeurism and fetishism, stressing also the auto-eroticism of the male spectator. In gazing at the desired object on the screen, namely Tristessa, promoted as the female beauty consummate in suffering, the male spectator defines his sexual identity in relation to an illusion.

Tristessa's act of self-creation does not require plastic surgery, as Eve/lyn's. Make-up, clothes, and cinema magic serve as the ingredients of androgyny, nothing but a celluloid shadow. Tristessa is the femme fatal for Evelyn and Zero, who have been lured by the effects she has created on screen. The boundary between dream and flesh is eliminated despite the fact that Evelyn is well aware of his own position as an audience, and that Tristessa is an image that dwells in his mind:

> "I thought I was bidding a last goodbye to the iconography of adolescence; tomorrow, I would fly to a new place, another country, and never imagined I might find her there, waiting for revivication, for a kiss of a lover who would rouse her from her perpetual reverie, she, fleshy synthesis of the dream, both dreamed and dreamer." (PNE 8-9)

Tristessa is a cinematic lie, a product of Tristessa himself as a sculptor of the image of men's desire and sadistic pleasure. In the creation of Tristessa, Angela Carter plays with myth once again. Tristessa may be seen as both Pygmalion, the sculptor, and the statue, the object of his desire. If the original myth turns the statue into one man's object of desire, Tristessa becomes a public figure, the woman many male screen viewers want. Contrary to the artistic pleasures the statue offers its creator in the myth, Tristessa turns into Zero's object of hatred, women's object of identification, as well as Evelyn's secret passion. Furthermore, the material for the statue in the original myth is the female body, while Tristessa uses his own body disguised as a female one. The feminine appearance is completed by the fabricated emotional state, suffering, to allow gender transgression: "She suffered exquisitely until suffering became demoded" (PNE 8).

Tristessa is also a collage of ideals of femininity. All her/his performances are derived from texts that reiterate the ideal of the suffering woman who is either sacrificed or destroyed: Catherine Earnshaw in *Wuthering Heights*, Emma Bovary. S/he is incapable of keeping her life separate from the fictions s/he performs. They invade her perception of reality, so that s/he cites 'memories' of a fictitious past, events s/he has never experienced. The common theme of them all is female degradation, having as a result the pain. Repetition and citation of pain make her incapable of distinguishing between reality and fiction. When Zero breaks into her world of glass s/he performs as if s/he were on the screen:

> "Zero cracked his whip over her head and, though the lash did not touch her, her body convulsed in a gigantic wince, though not immediately; after she heard the crack of the whip, she turned slowly to look at Zero and his instrument and *then*, lavishly histrionic, convulsed, although by now he'd coiled his whip away". (PNE 127)

Tristessa has turned himself into a perfect, immortal woman, beyond the grasp of time and space. Tristessa's existence as a woman is a result of Tristessa's desire as a man to appear feminine and satisfy the expectations of the audience. Off-screen, Tristessa is an extension of the image on screen, and in his off-screen hermaphroditic life, Tristessa appears pathetic, having replaced his past with artificial data borrowed from Marilyn Monroe's biography.

Zero, the 'poet' of masculinity to whom Eve/lyn is sexually enslaved in the desert, illustrates most vividly the false construction of male identity set in opposition to Tristessa's screen image. He is convinced that the loss of his manhood is a result of watching Tristessa in 'revival of *Emma Bovary*':

> "Tristessa had magicked away his reproductive capacity via the medium of the cinema screen...Tristesa's eyes...fixed directly upon his and held them...With visionary certainty he'd known the cause of his sterility. He was like a man who could not cast a shadow, and that was because Tristessa had sucked his shadow clean away." (PNE 104)

Zero's feeling is caused by the tremendous male image Tristessa's screen image entails for a real man to live up to. Defined against the helpless femininity projected on the screen, Zero's masculine identity is hallowed by the mirror image of Tristessa's mournful eyes. His sexual desire is a sadistic one, derived from inflicting pain on women. The cinema screen, focused on Tristessa's eyes, represents the mirror on which he contemplates his sexual image and object. The romantic film genre perfected by Tristessa's performance also highlights the display of femininity, apart from representing its archetypal pain. The essence of femininity appears in the heavenly face of Tristessa, where Eve/lyn finds "our external symbols must always express the life within us with absolute precision" (PNE 5-6).

Cinema seems to be Tristessa's alchemical theatre, the space where she continuously resurrects herself, but it is an illusion, a sterile reanimation:

> "it was as if all Tristessa's movies were being projected all at once on that pale, reclining figure so I saw her walking, speaking, dying, over and over again in all the attitudes that remained in this world, frozen in the amber of innumerable spools of celluloid from which her being could be extracted and endlessly recycled in a technological eternity, a perpetual resurrection of the spirit." (PNE 119)

Having "no function in this world except as an idea of himself; no ontological status, only an iconographic one" (PNE 129), Tristessa is empty:

> "That time should not act upon me, that I should not die. So I was seduced by the notion of a woman's being, which is negativity. Passivity, the absence of being. To be everything and nothing. To be a pane the sun shines through" (PNE 137).

Tristessa has aspired to womanhood as a transcendent essence, wanting immortality through cinema, which would record and preserve it. She resurrects herself through cinema but her transformation is hardly positive, because she adheres to a stereotypical idea of femininity.

Tristessa has inhabited the male for so long that it is no longer possible to determine what is real and what is acting: "Even her terror had a curiously stylized quality; she acted it out with absolute conviction but I cannot tell whether or not she experienced it" (PNE 123).

S/he becomes a ghost in her glass mausoleum (PNE 112), as illusory as her image projected by the celluloid. Her transparent mausoleum stands as a metaphor of Hollywood film industry and its fabrication of desirable icons; but these movie icons are shown to be the work of humans, just as the waxworks of "all the unfortunate dead of Hollywood" in "The Hall of Immortals" (PNE 117-9).

As noted by Peach (1998:2), Sage (1994: 15-16), Bacchilega (1998:50-70) and Warner (1994: 244-247), Angela Carter had a deep and abiding interest in the fairy tale, observable in her short story collection *The Bloody Chamber,* and her editing of fairy tales in *The Virago Book of Fairy Tales* and translation of *The Fairy-tales of Charles Perrault.*

The 'Snow Child' is Angela Carter's most self-reflexive short story, very different from the rest in the volume *The Bloody Chamber* in terms of brevity and narrative voice. The self-reflexive dimension of the story foregrounds the appeal of passive stereotypes of femininity. The omnipotent narrator reduces the plot to key fairy-tale elements, scattered in opposition to one another in the Present tense: ice and blood, animate and inanimate, cold and warmth. The Count and the Countess are presented riding aimlessly until the Count expresses his wish to have a girl "as white as snow", "as red as blood" and "as black as the raven's feathers" (1996:193). The story exposes the violence implied in classical fairy-tales on the one hand and deconstructs the fairy-tale genre on the other hand. The construction and killing of the girl parallel the shaping of a new fairy-tale over the corpse of traditional conventions. The Snow child is stark naked, as the story is reduced to its constitutive elements in its initial stage. The girl is conjured up with the help of words: "As soon as he completed her description, there she stood, beside the road, white skin, red mouth, black hair and stark naked; she was the child of his desire" (1996:193), but remains silent, subordinated to her creator, deprived of her own story. This short story captures in a nutshell Carter's habit of interrogating frozen beliefs, by breaking the structural frame of narrative tradition, and I will turn to her cinematic adaptations to investigate the notes of her narrative echoes across media.

The Magic Toyshop is Carter's first novel assigning the female character agency and a voice to tell the story of coping with patriarchal rule and with her blooming sexuality. The same

297

themes resurface in the closing short story of the volume *The Bloody Chamber*, 'The Company of Wolves', where narrative layers bridge the animality of humans to the humanity of animals. The director of *The Magic Toyshop*, David Wheatley, was drawn to Carter's writings because of the cinematic quality of her work: "I thought that her book was influenced by films" (1996:327)).

Neil Jordan, the director of *The Company of Wolves*, remembers about his collaboration with Angela Carter in the process of adapting her short story, that "she was thrilled with the process, because she loved films, and had never actually been involved in one" (Carter, 1996:506)

When she decided to adapt her writing to the cinema, Angela Carter experienced a different type of excitement:

"the quite unhealthy sense of power with which you feel that you're actually beaming the figments of your imagination across the city, across the century, across the world, is actually quite extraordinary. [...] It's quite different to a novel which is very much a one to one, you know, blasting all these cinema screens with these images of unrepressed libido is really a very exhilarating thing to do." (Mars-Jones, 1984)

Carter's stated in an interview, "I've always written with visual images first and no adaptor could crack it" (Baron, 1987:27). *The Magic Toyshop* (1967), Carter's second novel, proved too difficult to turn into a movie script, according to Baron: "there have been some fifteen attempts to turn it into a successful film script" (1987:27). Carter identifies the reason in an interview with Stephanie Bunbury:

"when I read it again I realized it didn't have a plot. It had a vague beginning and an end but not much middle. And one of the things this particular kind of film needed was a coherent narrative structure, so one had to reassemble the novel in that form" (1987:38)

It was turned into a magical movie in 1987 by David Wheatley, who found the cinematic quality of the novel appealing, and worked very closely with Angela Carter in the process of adaptation:

"I felt the book was filmic, I felt there were images that were referred to in the book, and when she told me she was a film reviewer and also fascinated by film, I just became fascinated by the notion of what films she might have been looking at when she wrote the book and if they'd had any influence." (1996:243)

298

Melanie, the main character in *The Magic Toyshop*, envisages uncle Philip as a character in an Orson Welles movie, and herself acting in a new-wave British film. She also dreams of her brother Jonathon, and he begins "to flicker; as in a faulty projected film" (1967:175).

David Wheatley interprets the abundance of visual elements in Carter's novel as a marked influence of popular culture on the collective imagination:

> "If you look at Garcia Marques at you look at Borges, or you look at other Latin American writers, I think you find the magical realism they talk about, the magic somehow has transcended itself, it's gone from books into films and then come back again, and I think it's actually percolated into the way that people think about story-telling." (1996:237)

The opening sequence of the movie brings before our eyes the main themes of the novel, namely puppetry, the female gaze and cinematic illusion. Laura Mulvey discusses three cinematic looks: "that of the camera as it records the pro-filmic event, that of the audience as it watches the final product, and that of the characters at each other within the screen illusion" (1989:25), and Paul Willemen mentions a fourth, 'the look at the viewer', where "the subject of the look is an imaginary other" (1994:108).

Melanie's active gaze subverts the voyeuristic gaze of the camera lens, for Carter conferred upon the heroine the power to invert the relationship between the image and the viewer. Caroline Milmoe, the actress playing the main heroine, played her part to this end: "I was keen for Melanie not to be passive – I wanted to catch the camera with my eye and make the audience conscious of her voyeurism of them." (Hill, 1987:12)

Traditional structures of looking are broken with Melanie's appropriation of the voyeuristic pleasure, despite the constant threat of Uncle Philip. Carter does not allow her to succumb to the role of the victim, as Doane suggests was the rule of classical cinema: "the woman's exercise of an active investigating gaze can only be simultaneous with her own victimization" (1994: 72).

One sequence that combines Melanie's active looking with the uncanny atmosphere created by grotesque animation presents her spying on Finn and Francie through the peephole she has discovered earlier in the wall dividing her room from that of her cousins'. The hole frames her eye that looks straight into the camera. While Francie is playing the fiddle, Finn's inert body is animated by unseen strings, in a transposition of the script indications: he "shudders convulsively jerking and twisting. The candle flames shiver, creating grotesque shadows" (Carter, 1996:274).

In the magical opening sequence, the slow, vertical tilt of the camera links the main settings and establishes their atmosphere. On the dark street outside the toyshop, a kiss hints at the incestuous relationship between Aunt Margaret and one of her step brothers, Francie. The spinning toys in the window shop parallel the whirl of the camera, as the line between fantasy and reality is blurred. In the gloomy basement of the toyshop, Aunt Margaret, Francie and Finn complete the crew and audience for Uncle Philip's private shows. This second setting constitutes a heterotopia as it combines freedom of expression with control of the puppet master, while alluding, self-reflexively, to our position as spectators. The image of the puppet dancer spinning clumsily dissolves to the third setting, Melanie's contemporary bedroom, a place of secrets preserved in the mirror and the nude paintings that establish the theme of the girl's blooming sexuality.

Melanie's reverie on her first night in the strange house of Uncle Phillip is initiated by her stare at the wallpaper. The scene is a literalization of a paragraph in the novel:

"Now, who has planted this thick hedge of crimson roses in all this dark, green, luxuriant foliage with, oh, what cruel thorns? Melanie opened her eyes and saw thorns among roses, as if she woke from a hundred years' night […] But it was only her new wallpaper, which was printed with roses, though she had not before noticed the thorns." (TMT 53)

The slow editing technique, called **dissolve**, is employed to mark the border between reality and dream, while the luxuriant garden Melanie dreams about is flattened to the drawings on the walls of her room. The same techniques transpose Jonathon from his dark room, presented in low-key lighting, to a beach of freedom, animated by an energetic non-diegetic tune.

The movie overwhelms us with instances conveying the potential of animation for expressing the uncanny. Carter declares that the novel reflects her timely passion for the trope of animation: "I had a passion for automata at one stage; I think it's the simulations of human beings that I'm interested in" (Bunbury, 1987:37).

"I'm very interested in the idea of simulacra, of invented people, of imitation human beings, because, you know, the big question that we have to ask ourselves is how do we know we're not imitation human beings?" (Evans and Carter,1992:24)

The animated beings can be aligned with the capacity of cinema to create the illusion of life, as Mulvey suggests:

"the cinema, too, is inanimate, consisting of still frames which the projector's movement brings to life" (1994:233).

In one of her writing stages Angela Carter focused on famous fairy-tales. Her modern interpretations were aimed at subverting traditional values and patterns that she viewed as constraints. The stories were collected in a volume, *The Bloody Chamber* (1979), in which she "produced her own haunting, mocking, sometimes tender variations on some of the classic motifs of the fairy-tale genre [...] drawing them out of their set shapes [...] into the world of change" (Sage,1994: 39).

The short story 'The Company of Wolves' is a feminist rewrite of *Little Red Riding Hood*. It combines elements of fairy-tale and myth for the taste of the modern reader. Charles Perrault's story is modernised by Carter, as she adds pieces which existed in the original eighteenth century folklore version but which Perrault gave up, considering them too rough for the reading public of his times. In that variant the villain was the werewolf.

The movie based on the short story has the same title and was directed by Neil Jordan and co-scripted by Jordan and Carter herself in 1984. Mark Bell, the editor of Carter's dramatic writings, recalls that she first approached Neil Jordan with the idea of turning the radio play *The Company of Wolves* into a movie (Carter, *SL*), but he considered the play too short, and decided to develop it into a "Chinese box structure, using the dream of Rosaleen, and the thread of Granny's storytelling as the connecting points, thereby enabling us to integrate other stories and themes of Angela's own" (Carter, *SL* 507)

In the movie there are elements from two other stories from the same volume, which revolve around werewolf myths, namely 'The Werewolf' and 'Wolf Alice'. Adolescence and the process of growing up, viewed as danger and passion, are explained in both the story and the movie through a twisted re-enactment of the fairy-tale. Neil Jordan and Angela Carter "mapped out an outline of proposed scenes, which she then wrote up" (*SL* 507). The director mentions that "the writing seemed to flow quite naturally, since it gave free rein to Angela's own taste for narrative subversions" (*SL* :56).

The movie is frightening in its violence and peopled by ambiguous characters living in a dangerous world. It is about a twentieth century teenage girl named Rosaleen who dreams of living in a nineteenth century village, together with her family. The narrative is built with an alternation of layers – reality, dream, tale – whose boundaries become increasingly more difficult to discern for both the main character and the viewer.

The movie represents a heterotopia woven out of overlapping discourses on metamorphosis viewed as adaptation from page to screen, as bodily transformation from human into animal, or transition from childhood to adolescence. The movie remakes Carter's texts, which in turn re-write the original fairy-tale of Red Riding Hood, while pointing intertextually to the conventions of the horror-genre. Carter's choice of the horror genre for the adaptation multiplies the possibilities of preserving the qualities of her narrative style, such as intertextuality, parody, doubling, humour, the same features Philip Brophy attributes to contemporary horror movies (1986).

Kristeva's theory of abjection is concerned with figures that are in a state of transition. The abject is located in a liminal state that is on the margins of two positions. Kristeva defines the abject in connection with bodily functions that "mark the boundary between clean and proper symbolic order and abyssal, impure abject" (Vice (ed.), 1996:153). When we enter the world of the abject, our imaginary borders disintegrate and the abject becomes a tangible threat because our identity system and conception of order have been disrupted. There are violent transformation scenes in the movie that can be read as examples of 'body horror', a subgenre of fantasy films dealing with "crisis of identity through a concentration on processes of bodily disintegration and transformation" (Jancovich:112). Lind Ruth Williams (1994) also maintains that body horror stands for fantasies of interiority, as the boundaries between inside and outside are transgressed and the abject is rendered visible.

In the short story the tension between the visible and the invisible forces accumulates through a series of opening tales reminding the reader of the werewolf superstitions through the voice of the narrator whose role is taken up in the movie by the sometimes witch-like figure of the grandmother or by Rosaleen.

Rosaleen is driven by instincts and guided by two voices. One is the voice of her grandmother, expressing the superstitions centred around werewolves and her theories are supported by tales: "never trust a man whose eyebrows meet in the middle". The other is the voice of reason, expressed by the mother whose interpretations are grounded in reality: "if there is a devil in men there's a woman to match it". In the short story the narrator is the one presenting the tales and superstitions, setting the background for the re-telling of *Little Red Riding Hood* and some lines appear in the movie unchanged: "Before he can become a wolf, the lycanthrope strips stark naked. If you spy a naked man among the pines, you must run as if the devil were after you" (1996:113).

One technique used in the short story to keep up the suspense is that of tense switching. The writer mixes the use of the present and the past tenses. The traditional function of the latter is to establish a psychological distance between reader and events, while the use of the former involves the reader more. Tense switching also signals the alternation between reality and the archetypal world of the fairy-tale: "One beast and only one howls in the woods by night. The wolf is carnivore incarnate and he's as cunning as he is ferocious; [...] There was a hunter once, near here, that trapped a wolf in a pit" (BB 111).

The use of **direct speech** is a second technique that increases the degree of reader involvement and causes the reader's alternating roles, that of witness and that of interlocutor: "it is winter and cold weather. In this region of the mountain and forest, there is now nothing for the wolves to eat.[...] Fear and flee the wolf; for, worst of all, the wolf may be more than he seems" (BB 111).

Barbara Creed (1993:14) considers the horror movie an equivalent of the rites of defilement in its attempt to purify the abject and "redraw the boundaries between the human and the non-human". The most violent transformations appear framed by Granny's tales of aggressive sexuality. In one of them, the runaway husband comes back years later to find the wife he has left on their wedding night, married to another man and mother to his children. He turns into a werewolf under the horrified gaze of the woman. The scene is rendered with the use of close-ups and extreme close-ups, jump cuts and slow motion, filmic techniques that deepen the emotional impact of a scene on the viewer. The husband peels off his skin, revealing the tissue and muscles beneath, before becoming a werewolf. The difference between the surface of the skin and the flesh under it is no longer apparent.

Rosaleen's two stories, on the other hand, situate the women in a position of agency when it comes to the metamorphoses of the others. The first story expands a short tale from the short story, about a pregnant woman who turns 'an entire wedding party into wolves because the groom had settled on another girl' (BB111). The woman's laughter is reminiscent of that of Cixous' (1997:357) Medusa, ready "to smash everything, to shatter the framework of institutions, to blow up the law, to break up the 'truth' with laughter". The metamorphosis of the greedy guests into famished wolves is displayed in slow motion, with carnivalesque non-diegetic music as background, relating the tilt shots smoothly and inter-cutting to extreme close-ups of the woman's face. The climatic moments of transformation occur in the mirror, the heterotopia where everything is distorted by the power of the woman's words.

In the movie, the alternation between relaxed attention and involvement is achieved through the cuts between long shots and point of view shots. The horror genre has taught us to be afraid of wolves and the woods, and the suggestion of danger is conveyed through the technique of the point of view shot. For example, the opening of the movie is presented by the camera eye identified to that of the family's dog, or the woods seem explored by the hungry eyes of a wolf. A second technique employed in the movie is that of repetition. Actions take place twice, or even three times, once in the real world with no hidden meaning, and the second time either in the characters' dreams or in the tales they hear. For example, there are two cars in the movie; the first is driven by Rosaleen 's parents at the beginning of the movie when they come home, the second is driven by Rosaleen in a tale of superstition, where she is the chauffer of the Devil who corrupts young boys into an instinctual adulthood.

The abject is foregrounded through the position of the heroine animated by the innocence of a childlike curiosity, and the shock realisation caused by the confrontation with the abject. The conventional view of adolescence as an easy period is challenged. Growing up is seen as estrangement, as suggested in Rosaleen's dream, which starts with the shock produced by her sister's death, who suggestively is killed by the wolves in the forest. After the funeral Rosaleen has to spend some time away from home in order to let her mother recover from the shock. Rosaleen's first menstruation, alluded to in the short story as well, indicates the girl's transition to a woman, a natural transition marked by a natural process, while Rosaleen's friend, the village boy, needs a ritual of initiation. He wants to guide her through the woods but he stumbles and has his path blocked by a carriage, being thus unable to follow the girl. Rosaleen is active, very determined and full of initiative in disobeying her mother and grandmother's advice not to stray away from the path. The short story points to the lack of patriarchal authority: "she is a closed system; she does not know how to shiver. She has her knife and she is afraid of nothing. Her father might forbid her, if he were home, but he is away in the forest, gathering wood, and her mother cannot deny her" (BB 114).

In order to mature, she has to become aware of the changes within her. The development of her awareness is marked in the movie by symbols that have the short story as starting point. Rosaleen is no longer a child, not yet a woman, so that her in-between status alligns her with the figure of the werewolf. Her developing sexuality is represented in a

304

sequence that uses the symbols of the short story, tha mirror, the lipstick and the miniature eggs. The opening shot of the movie presents Rosaleen asleep holding a mirror and wearing her sister's lipstick. Later on, as she strays from the path she finds both objects in the woods and carries them with her all the time from then on. On meeting the hunter she tries on his hat and admires herself in the mirror, but she gives up the mirror as soon as she realises the power of her beauty. Having his admiring gaze as reinforcement, she no longer needs the mirror. In the short story she is ready to face danger and temptation: "He went through the undergrowth and took her basket with him but she forgot to be afraid of the beasts, although the moon was rising, for she wanted to dawdle on her way to make sure the handsome gentleman would win his wager" (BB 115).

Red is the symbol of passion, the moon turns red when the world of dreams opens up, Rosaleen's shawl is "as soft as a kitten" as it ensures protection or "as red as blood" when it restrains her movements. In the seduction scene the girl has to give it up and throw it into the fire along with the clothes of the wolf/hunter. The short story warns of the effect of burning the clothes "Seven years is a werewolf's natural span but if you burn his human clothing you condemn him to wolfishness for the rest of his life"(BB 113), but "the flaxen-haired girl" is ready to accept her sexuality.

Rosaleen's second tale, the one ending the movie, reconciles the animal and the human worlds, as the girl has found a voice to break the rigid frame of werewolf lore and its damaging superstitions. The well links all the layers in the movie. It is outside Rosaleen's house, it is the centre of the village she inhabits in her dream and the passage to the world of the instincts where the wolf-girl in her last story comes from. After the seduction scene she tells the wolf the story of a wolf-girl who comes in the world of the humans as a wounded wolf to heal her physical and spiritual wounds and leaves it as a naked woman. The story is inspired from the short story *Wolf Alice* which is about the search for subjectivity. The wolf-girl in Rosaleen's tale has no voice and no identity, and is a stranger in both worlds because her shape is never the appropriate one. She will be marked for a while, as the priest in the story tells her: "It will heal. . . in time…". The narrator's voice, in fact Rosaleen's voice, tells the wolf/hunter her story of her becoming a woman, helped by the metaphor of the red rose presented in close-ups:

"ROSALEEN (voice) And the wound did heal. . . .. . for she was just a girl after all. . .
CLOSEUP of a white rose in full bloom.
ROSALEEN (vo) . . . who had strayed from the path in the forest. . .

CLOSEUP Slowly the rose opens and turns deep red.

CLOSEUP of the WOLF GIRL weeping.

ROSALEEN (vo) . . . and remembered what she'd found there". (TMT 1984: script)

Toys represent stereotypes of childhood and innocence. In Rosaleen's dream her older sister is running through the forest and the toys are threatening her. At the end of the movie wolves invade real life and break through the window in Rosaleen's room. The first thing they destroy and the only thing the viewer sees destroyed are the toys. Rosaleen's scream is ambiguous, as she is not attacked. She might scream on realising what she loses in the process of growing up. The short story on the other hand places the girl in the dominant position. The seduction scene shatters the traditional mentality that regards the woman as property "What big teeth you have![…] All the better to eat you with. The girl burst out laughing; she knew she was nobody's meat. She laughed at him full in the face, she ripped off his shirt for him and flung it into the fire, in the fiery wake of her own discarded clothing" (BB 118).

The short story ends with a direct address from the narrator to the reader, pointing out the way she has upset the traditional ending of the fairy-tale:

"Midnight; and the clock strikes. It is Christmas Day, the werewolves' birthday, the door of the solstice stands wide open; let them all sink through. See! Sweet and sound she sleeps in granny's bed, between the paws of the tender wolf" (BB 118).

In the ending of the movie the narrator's voice takes over, a voice that is neither that of the grandmother nor that of Rosaleen . The moral of the movie is told overlapping with the closing credits and warns of the risk involved in letting adulthood corrupt innocence:

"Little girls, this seems to say:

Never stop upon your way;

Never trust a stranger friend

No one knows how it will end.

As you're pretty, so be wise

Wolves may lurk in every guise

Now, as then, 'tis simple truth:

The sweetest tongue hides the sharpest tooth".(TMT, 1984:script)

John Collick (1989) describes three types of dream films: those which present the viewer with dream imagery and cast the viewer as an analyst who will interpret the hidden meanings; those which replicate the experience of dreaming, unsettling the viewer's expectations about narrative coherence, and those that throw the viewer's own position into question. *The Company of Wolves* and *The Magic Toyshop* belong to the third because they challenge the viewer to interpret their endings. The dream framework serves a double purpose: it enlarges the space for the assertion of Rosaleen and Melaie's subjectivity, and draws the viewer into a fantastic territory balanced at times by flashbacks to the contemporary bedrooms and sleeping girls.

The convoluted narrative lines in the novel and in the short story are mirrored in the movie adaptations by the full range of editing techniques, from fades to irises and jump cuts. Angela Carter has her heroines stray away from the path they have traditionally followed, that of victims, to become a generic "she" who can expose the flaws of Western culture.

***

The third principle of heterotopias refers to the combination of several separated spaces into one space and Carter's fiction and cinema mingle different places before our very eyes. "Everybody always assumes because I'm a writer I don't know what cinema is. I do, I do, I do" (Carter in O'Brien, 1987). Making movies is all about inducing a heterotopia, about finding the juxtaposition and intersection where we can simultaneously experience an imaginary and real concept of space. We give in to the enchanting voice of Carter's storytellers in her fiction and her cinematic adaptations, just as the author observes that "Dora, the heroine of *Wise Children*, is perfectly aware that when they go to Hollywood they're taking leave of their senses" (Evans and Carter, 1992 32)

The movies based on her work represent a heterotopia woven out of overlapping discourses on metamorphosis, viewed as adaptation from page to screen, as bodily transformation from human into animal, or transition from childhood to adolescence. In *Cinematic Spinners* I have focused on the critical edge of cinematic illusion, abundant in *The Passion of New Eve*, and I have pinpointed tense switching, direct address, smooth and abrupt editing and non-diegetic sound as the main techniques used in the two cinematic adaptations, in view of breaking the frames separating fiction from reality.

In the *Omnibus* documentary made shortly before her death, *Angela Carter's Curious Room*, she asserts her belief that "there is something sacred about the cinema, which is to do with it being public, to do with people going together, with the intention of visualizing, experiencing the same experience, having the same revelation" (Evans, 1992:7)

The question asked in relation to Fevvers, "is she fact or is she fiction?" (NC 7), is a challenge posed by both *Nights at the Circus* and *Wise Children*. In The 'Confidence Trick' and V.2. Embroidering Genealogies I addressed the craft of reader manipulation and the extension of fictional planes beyond the closed books. What is the difference between fact and fiction, since both are mediated by language and narrative, thus equally unreliable? The writer brings to light the kinship between the serious and the comic, the legitimate and the illegitimate. The link of low comedy with popular culture in *Wise Children* is indicative of the carnival power that popular culture possesses in shifting the perspective on the edifice of Shakespeare, and shaping the narrator's voice and identity. Posing offers room for self-creation through telling stories, that is, fictional play.

The narration is multiple in both novels, leaping from heterodiegetic accounts to those of various diegetic narrators. Fevvers declares on the first page of *Nights at the Circus*: "I never docked via what you might call the normal channels, sir" (NC 7); neither does Carter. She rolls out a thick fabric of events that not only dazes her characters, but also confuses us, readers. We conspire with the author to believe in Fevvers' 'flight' and Dora's objectivity. Magic makes Fevvers desirable to some, disbelief turns her into a challenge for others. Her identity shifts according to whether she is the narrator or Walser or Lizzie, Carter or the reader, but no answer is satisfactory as long as the questions concern her ontological status. She preserves her subject position which started with her youth in "a wholly female world" (NC 38), by exploiting her grotesque physicality and intricate autobiography. Walser, like Evelyn in *The Passion of New Eve*, participates in the same carnivalesque downward movement that reverses the roles by placing the subject in the object position.

The storyteller in Carter's fiction and cinematic adaptations never falls short of her subversive aims, as the textual discourses deemed authoritative are challenged. She turns the tables on the male gaze by exposing the artificial nature of its object. Telling stories proves the best solution in fighting the confining power of the male gaze. The voices of the storytellers ring after the novels end and the credits roll, they resist closure, celebrating the potential for the reconstruction of the world. By animating her written work with the dialogism and polyphony of the spoken word, Carter's texts become plural and resistant to categorisation, spiralling between fantasy and realism, history and tall tale. Angela Carter makes us understand that different discourses mould our perception of what is real. Intertextuality is a form of play to her, one that fulfils a double function: that of keeping the narrative spool rolling, and that of constructing interpretation. This clashing of languages takes the form of dialogic exchanges between narrators and reader, with the formal and thematical issue of storytelling lying at the heart of the warp and weft of Carter's heteroglossia.

CONCLUSION

Angela Carter is one of those writers who enjoy co-forging, rather than borrowing, literary devices spanning across centuries and conflicting discourses. Her style is marked by her critical hostility towards realistic writing techniques, along with her movement towards fantasy and dream, that is, other spaces, heterotopia. Her re-creation of popular fairy-tales, re-working of myths and re-cycling of literary themes serve as an antidote to a contemporary mythology built on Western democracy and its values. Carter probes their petrified versions, unveils their ambiguity and adds alternative meanings.

In the first chapter of my study I have pointed out the loudest echoes of the critical reception Angela Carter's work has enjoyed, in view of justifying my argument and my approach. Postmodernism and feminism are the two relevant directions which have generated heated debates in terms of points of difference and intersection, in relation to Angela Carter's fiction and non-fiction. The overview of her main thematic concerns, that have led critics to label her writings as Gothic, magical realist, feminist, science fiction, has served my purpose of introducing the key term of my argumentation, **heterotopia**, and the ensuing revision of its definitions. The meanings assigned to the term range from medical to geographical and cultural and I have analysed her work as a locus where clashing discourses meet and real topographies juxtapose with oneiric trajectories, bringing into focus social, cultural or political systems that contribute to the formation of identity. The term heterotopia takes on new layers of meaning in each chapter and, hopefully, underscores my perception of Angela Carter's work as kinetic and fluid, animated by opposing forces.

The second chapter of my study has relied on the division of spaces in Angela Carter's novels and short stories, into outer and inner, and the illustration of the subversive methods the writer employs in shaping them. I have used the term heterotopia in relation to subdivisions of space, with reference to features such as ambiguity and elusive nature. The protagonists embark on mentally and physically exhausting journeys to liminal zones defined by paradoxical fluctuations of time, areas born from the **juxtaposition, superimposition, interpenetration** and **misattribution** (McHale, 1987) of spaces with neither margins nor centres. These magical spaces of transformation breathe an air of irony, stemming from the author's subversive mode. The centre of the maze, once uncovered, brings about the awareness that there is no secret hidden there. The topos of the journey leads the way to exotic settings, depicted as routes of alienation for both characters and readers. The three types of inner zones I have focused on, variations on the motif of the labyrinth, escape definition due to their shifting nature. Carter deconstructs the puzzle of the labyrinth by approaching it from various perspectives, an empirical space and a psychological one.

The **castles** mirror the victimization of women and become heterotopia where myths stop functioning, as the dismal buildings collapse. The claustrophobic atmosphere and hollow echoes of the castle appear as snares in the characters' path to self-knowledge. Its significance hovers between a geographical structure of circumscribed, but boundless possibilities, on the one hand, and a surrealist representation of the human mind as reason loses the battle with superstition, on the other hand.

Constant surveillance defines the site of terror illustrative of incarceration and mental paralysis, **the prison**. Oppression is configured spatially and takes the shape of confining interiors, designed to house and control women as potential disrupters of the established order. The spatial variations of panopticism turn it into heterotopia, as Gothic terror is disrupted by carnivalesque and comic elements Carter places in the hands of the women prisoners. The powerful voice of female communities on the margins, coupled with the desire to withstand the gaze of the established male or female power, provide the necessary means to melt down the structure of the panopticon.

The **cave/womb** is another heterotopian space, founded on abjection as recurring, threatening sensation of an instability of the self. Fear and desire animate the wandering subject, as identity issues buried in the unconscious rise to the surface. Time and space annihilate and generate one another, while the reader slides along with the characters from the realm of mythology to the borders of biology. The hybrid character of this resulting zone, uncanny in its familiarity, hovers, first of all, between the womb as a mythological repository of motherhood, which Carter views as a way of suppressing the complexity of women's bodies and desires. Secondly, the womb is seen as an aggressive and nurturing organ, a fleshy space of birth and death which affects the subject's sanity. Carter's message is that the successful completion of this rite of passage entails giving up the complex mythology constructed around the womb, as well as women's desire for maternal power.

Turning to zones on the outside, the space of **the forest** is equally double-faced, as I have demonstrated in my examination of short stories. The woods exercise an irresistible lure

311

upon the nostalgic wanderer drawn deeper into a nightmarish world of confusion which paradoxically seduces and threatens the accompanying reader, at the same time. One moment there is the intricate leafy labyrinth, delimited by countless paths where characters find pieces of subjectivity, and the next moment protagonists struggle to breathe while the claustrophobic bowers are shrinking upon them. The combination of mutability and inescapability operating within the woods supports the foucauldian concept of the ubiquity of power. Not only does the traveler appear simultaneously outside and inside the space of power which cannot be transgressed physically, but the reader also struggles to make sense of the voices destabilizing the narrative space. The journey into the dangerous but appealing forest becomes a magical one, into a world that is other, heterotopia of self-discovery.

The **desert** is figured in Carter's work as an emblem of emptiness, a space of memory, cryptic and puzzling in its provision of exile and escape. Movement towards the heart of the desert equals loss of subjectivity for Carter's protagonists, marking the transition to the slippery realm of chaos and hallucination. Its heterotopian character derives from the fusion of a sphere of alienation, generated by the characters' failing memory, and a luring mirage with false centres which collapse under the pressure of vertigos of time.

The **city** is forged as a product of masculine reason and order, which decomposes as the feminine, Gothic forces erode its very structure. Streets become routes of confusion, metaphoric projections of the characters' sense of isolation, or cardboard puzzles forming a carnivalesque zone. Dichotomies such as high and low, legitimate, illegitimate, chaos and order no longer operate at the dreamtime structuring heterotopia. A low-key atmosphere complements the cities' lack of colour, and characters cross a topography of nightmare, assembled from conflicting elements that may be detached and re-arranged to provide an appropriate setting for the characters' circular journeys.

Throughout her fiction Carter presents a world polarised by sex, a battlefield of male and female principles reflected in the literary past and present. She regards the past as a shop with old decorations which she freely moulds to compose her subversive work. In the third chapter of my study I have turned to disruptive spaces, populated by women, places of otherness, following Hetherington's definition of heterotopia as framed by antagonistic relations and power roles. The hybrid character of these spaces is sustained with the women's struggle to forge an identity, by transgressing the boundaries drawn by patriarchal surveillance. Women's exclusion is asserted as unsettling otherness. I have selected four roles in which female characters act out their difference and convert monstrosity into a stage of their metamorphosis into free agents.

Duplicitous Dolls, the first section, follows Carter's use of fetishism as a metaphor of exploitation, and her Gothic treatment of the artificiality of woman as automaton. The grotesque arises from the comic treatment of the subject matter, as well as the combination of the horrific and the ludicrous in the representation of gender stereotypes. I have argued that the female subject is able to subvert the patriarchal discourse from an object position by participating in a complicated visual exchange. Male fetishism turns woman into a living doll, appreciated in terms of her exchange value, but puppetry extends beyond a manifestation of entrapment, and signals the role of fantasy into the creation of fiction and shaping of characters.

The stories under scrutiny in the second section, **Innocent Predators,** are populated with both human and non-human characters, placed in a borderland between human consciousness and the consciousness of other species, the realm of the almost/not quite human. I have shown that Angela Carter's rebellious characters are allied with the semiotic, and employ strategies such as citation and repetition to tilt the balance of power. The gaps in the performance of power roles become visible, and differences are re-negotiated in new spaces of in-betweenness.

Thirdly, in **Cannibals,** I have traced Carter's development of what she regards an extreme form of aggression, the act of turning the other into a comestible. The consummation of the other results from the aggressors' insatiable longing for wholeness, and takes the form of seduction meals, narcissistic outbursts or literal consumption of human flesh. Eating as a form of colonialism, explored within the confinements of the household, is reduced to the losing side of heterotopic relations, for social eating emerges as the effective alternative to perversion.

Desired Others, the fourth section of my approach, tackles the inner struggle between reason and desire, and Carter's way of subverting the long held demarcation between the two concepts, mainly through the mixture of literary genres. Her fantastic style proves an intellectual exploration of what has culturally been kept unsaid. The characters are plunged in a fantasy-like world, in which their desires represent a re-play of what has been inscribed on them as lack in their existence. The woman as desired other is defined as excessively fluid and enigmatic, but she strengthens her ontological status, forcing both characters and readers to find clues to the interpretation of her desire. In the end, the antithetical struggle between reason and

313

desire reveals the disappearance of a clear boundary between seemingly opposed perspectives. Acts and sites of performance reflect the idea of a space that transcends gender, in chapter four, with my focus on acting as socially transgressive practice. The notion of selfhood becomes fragmented, as underscored by the subversive figure of the androgyne, making identity confusing and defined by dissonant selves.

In **Scenes of Dissemblance** the theatre is used as a mimetic device that undermines patriarchal psychoanalysis through imitation and gender performance. In the encounter between the self and the alien other, anxiety about the magnetic lure of the unknown is rendered through the creation of grotesque bodies, as Carter joins science, myth and allegory. Magic and performance become a means of deconstructing gender. The hybrid figures and doubles are the essential component of the writer's alchemical symbolism, advancing the idea of becoming and multiplicity. The hybrid overtakes the androgyne in Carter's work, it is made up not of masculine and feminine, but of elements such as human and animal, which deconstruct not only gender but also anthropocentrism. Erotic relationships entail an exchange of desire and sexual identity, mediated by the heterotopia of the mirror which no longer reflects woman's entrapment in the male gaze.

Womanhood under construction in a theatrical site animated by theatrical horror is the topic of the second section, **Twists of Passion**. The monstrous woman learns to enjoy her artificial sexuality through the power to play and move beyond the masculine representation of 'woman' as a collage of metaphor and flesh. I have dwelled on the effectiveness of femininity as masquerade and the possibilities and limitations of feminine transgressions. If performance replaces nature, the bloody process of becoming a woman still torments the performing woman, whereas the doubling of disguises renders gender distinctions unnecessary.

In **Songs and Dances** I have interpreted theatre as a site where clashing discourses resonate and the illegitimate engages in competition with the legitimate, filtered through the legacy of Shakespearian theatre. The merging of fictional space and real space, punctuated by ritual activity turns theatre into a heterotopia. Located simultaneously in the world of the performance and in the real world, the stage can be one of the border crossings to a hybrid world. The figure of Shakespeare as the supreme metaphor for English culture is used to illustrate the tragicomic game of attraction and oppression played by daughters and sons. The blurring of the self is mediated by confusing twists of the plot, or illegitimate vantage points the narrators adopt, resulting in the hybridization of high cultural forms with the popular ones.

314

In chapter five I have addressed the polyphonic facet of Carter's novels *Nights at the Circus, Wise Children, The Passion of New Eve* and her two cinematic adaptations, *The Magic Toyshop* and *The Company of Wolves*, illustrating the creation of a heteroglossic space. Angela Carter's entire work breathes the author's delight at entering into dialogue with the literary and cultural past in order to expose its ornamental function. She draws attention to the arbitrariness of language and its artificial nature by weaving a net of words and imagery. Storytelling mediates the transformation of fiction into film, and the resulting narrative worlds are defined by anachronism and dynamic meanings.

Spinning stories brings about textual innovations in **The Confidence Trick** and **Embroidering Genealogies**, as differing discourses and conflicting categories are interweaved to challenge the traditional appropriation of women's lives in Western male-centred culture. Given Carter's disobedience of language taboos and stylistic restrictions, the result is an overabundance of coarse and graceful vocabulary, employed with sensual inventiveness. Self-reflexive comments destabilize the boundary between fact and fiction, in line with the fluid identities female characters' fabricate for themselves. They are figures in a state of transition, whose voices take over the narrative thread, leading to the contamination of categories and the disintegration of spatiotemporal dimensions. The reader is entangled into a narrative weaved from the tessellation of time frames, in the hands of narrators who cross diegetic levels. I have dwelled upon the subversive potential of the grotesque in the novels and picked out excessiveness, dissonance, and cinematic techniques as key tactics Carter uses in order to engage the reader in a seductive fictional game, similar to the one her female characters play.

In **Cinematic Spinners** I have approached Carter's cinematic adaptations as examples of heterotopia defined by heterochrony and the overlapping of physical space with virtual reality. In turning her written works into film, Carter stresses the dialogism and polyphony of the spoken story on screen, involving the reader-turned-viewer into a debate about the role of the camera lens as the link which empowers the object of the gaze. Both movies are illustrations of heterotopia woven out of self-reflexive allusions to adaptation from page to screen, discourses on the false dichotomy human-animal, or on the transition from childhood to adolescence. The movie screen is no longer a flat surface, but a site of alterity which transforms Carter's characters from letters on the page to voices and entities, who have stepped outside the frame of the text.

My excursion into the spaces of Angela Carter's fiction has come to an end. I have

315

condensed her rich patchwork of stories, characters and techniques into a term extricated from its medical and geographical roots, befitting the rich intertextuality of her themes, her interest in boundaries between fact and fiction, margins and centres, or the interplay between sacred and profane. The concept of heterotopia emphasizes the ambiguity, as well as the dialogic interaction of Carter's often discordant discourses. The spectacular and the pragmatic threads of her texts, framed by extreme seriousness and witty humour, have delighted and offended readers, consequently maintaining Carter's literary and cinematic montage at the top of the literary canon. Her untimely death has, unfortunately, left too many stories untold, too many journeys not made.

"We travel along the thread of narrative like high-wire artistes. That is our life" (Carter, *ED* 2).

I would like to think that readers feel compelled to boldly tackle Carter's journalistic writings or audio drama into further studies, so I pass the narrative thread to them and conclude my study with a new beginning.

BIBLIOGRAPHY

Adăscăliței, Mirela. 1998. 'Mirrors that Strike Back: A Narratological View of Baudrillard and Angela Carter', in *Uniwersytet Slaski Review*.

Altevers, Nanette. 1994. 'Gender Matters in *The Sadeian Woman*' in *The Review of Contemporary Fiction*. 14.3: 20.

Anderson, Linda. 1997. 'Virginia Woolf: "In the Shadow of the Letter I '"' in *Women and Autobiography in the Twentieth Century. Remembered Futures*. London: Prentice Hall 42-75.

Appignanesi, Lisa. 1987. *Angela Carter in Conversation*. London: ICA Video my transcription.

Armitt, Lucie. 1996. *Theorising the Fantastic*. London: Arnold Arts Journal.

Atwood, Margaret. 1992. 'Magic Token through the dark forest', *The Observer* (23 February), 61.

Bakhtin, Mikhail. 1973/1984. *Problems of Dostoevsky 's Poetics*. Caryl Emerson (ed. and trans.). Minneapolis:University of Minnesota Press.

Bakhtin, Mikhail. 1982. 'Forms of Time and of the Chronotope in the Novel: Notes toward a Historical Poetics.' 1937-38. *The Dialogic Imagination*. Kenneth Brostrom (trans.). Michael. Holquist (ed.). Austin: U of Texas P. 84-254.

Bakhtin, Mikhail.1982. 'Discourse in the novel.' *The Dialogic Imagination*. Kenneth Brostrom (trans.). Michael. Holquist (ed.). Austin: U of Texas P. 259-422.

Bakhtin, Mikhail. 1984. *Rabelais and His World*. Helene Iswolsky (trans.). Bloomington.

Bakhtin, Mikhail. 1986. 'From Notes Made in 1970-71'. *Speech Genres and Other Late Essays*. Vern W. Mc Gee (trans.). Caryl Emerson and Michael Holquist (eds.). Austin: Univ. of Texas Press. 132-158.

Bakhtin, Mikhail. 1994. 'Problems of Dostoevsky's Poetics' in *The Bakhtin Reader: Selected Writings of Bakhtin, Medvedev and Voloshinov*. Pam Morris (ed.). London: Edward Arnold.

Bataille Georges.1985. *Visions of Excess: Selected Writings 1927-1939.* (trans). Allan Stoekl, Carl R. Lovitt, and Donald M. Leslie, Jr. University of Minnesota Press.

Baron, Saskia. 1987. 'Toying with Fantasies' in *Independent*. 31st July. 26.

Bataille, 1989. Georges. *The Tears of Eros.* (trans.) Peter Connor. City Lights Books

Baudrillard, Jean. (1986) 1988. *America* trans. Chris Turner. London/New York: Verso.

Baudrillard, Jean. 1988. 'Ecstasy of Communication'. (trans.) Schutze Bernard, Schutze Caroline. New York: Semiotext(e).

Bălănescu, Olivia. 2004. 'Angela Carter: The Revenge of the Puppet' in *Annals of the University of Craiova, Series Philology-English*, Year V, No. 1. Craiova: Universitaria. 23-33.

Belsey, Catherine. 2002. 'Constructing the Subject, Deconstructing the Text' in *Feminisms.* (eds.) R.R. Warhol, D. P. Herndl. New Jersey: Rutgers University Press. 657-674.

Belsey, Catherine. 2002. *Critical Practice*. London: Routledge.

Belsey, Catherine.1994. *Desire: Love Stories in Western Culture*. Oxford: Blackwell Publishers.

Bhabha, H. K. 1994. *The location of culture*. London: Routledge.

Bloom, Harold. 1963. Blake's *Apocalypse: A Study in Poetic Argument*. Ithaca/ New York: Cornell University Press.

Borges, Jorge Luis. 1999. 'John Wilkins' Analytical Language'. *Selected Non-Fictions.* (trans.) Eliot Weinberger. (ed.) Eliot Weinberger. New York: Penguin Putnam. 229-32.

Botescu Sireteanu, Ileana. 2007. *The Fiction of Angela Carter and Jeanette Winterson.* Iaşi: Lumen.

Bristow, Joseph and Trev Lynn Broughton (eds).1997. *The Infernal Desires of Angela Carter: Fiction, Femininity, Feminism*. Harlow: Addison Wesley Longman.

Britzolakis, Christina. 1995. 'Angela Carter's Fetishism' in *Textual Practice*. 9:3. 459-76.

Brînzeu, Pia. 1995. *Armura de Sticlă*. Timişoara: Excelsior.

Brooks, Peter. 1984. *Reading for the Plot: Design and Intention in Narrative.* New York: Vintage.

Brophy, Philip. 1986. 'Horrality – The Textuality of Contemporary Horror Films' in *Screen* 27:1. Jan-Febr. 2-13.

Bunbury Stephanie. 2000. 'The Write Stuff' in *Cinema Papers.* September. 37-8.

Butler, Judith. 1990. *Gender Trouble: Feminism and the Subversion of Identity.* New York: Routledge.

Cagney Watts, Helen. 1985.'An Interview with Angela Carter.' *Bête Noir* 8 :161–76.

Camus, Albert. 1991.*The Myth of Sisyphus and Other Essays.* (trans.) Justin O'Brien. New York: Vintage.

Carr, Helen. 1989. *From My Guy to Sci-Fi,* London: Pandora Press.

Carroll, Rachel. 2000. 'Return of the Century: Time, Modernity, and the End of History in Angela Carter's *Nights at the Circus.*' *The Yearbook of English Studies* 30: 187-201.

Carter, Angela.1972. *Heroes and Villains* (1969). London: Picador.

Carter, Angela.1981. *The Magic Toyshop* (1967). London: Virago Press.

Carter, Angela. 1982. *The Passion of New Eve* (1977). London: Virago Press.

Carter, Angela. 1982. *Nothing Sacred: Selected Writings.* London: Virago.

Carter, Angela. 1984. *Nights at the Circus* London: Vintage.

Carter, Angela 1989: Radio 4 *Britannia – The Film 7:Fantasy by Gaslight,* 12th August.

Carter, Angela. 1992. *Expletives Deleted: Selected Writings.* London: Chatto and Windus.

Carter, Angela. 1992. *Wise Children* (1991). London: Vintage.

Carter, Angela. 1994. *The Infernal Desire Machines of Doctor Hoffman* (1972). New York: Penguin Books.

Carter, Angela.1994. *Shadow Dance* (1966). London: Virago Press.

Carter, Angela.1995. *Several Perceptions* (1968). London: Virago Press.

319

Carter, Angela. 1996. *The Curious Room: Collected Dramatic Works*. (ed.) Mark Bell. London: Chatto& Windus.

Carter, Angela. 1996. *Burning Your Boats: Collected Short Stories*. London: Vintage.

Carter, Angela. 'Overture and Incidental Music' (1985) in *Burning Your Boats: The Collected Short Stories*. 1996. London: Vintage. pp. 273-283.

Carter, Angela 'The Lady of the House of Love.' (1979) in *Burning Your Boats: The Collected Short Stories*. 1996. London: Vintage. Pp. 195-209.

Carter, Angela 'The Loves of Lady Purple' (1974) in *Burning Your Boats: The Collected Short Stories*. 1996. London: Vintage.pp. 41-52.

Carter, Angela ' Master' (1974) in *Burning Your Boats: The Collected Short Stories*. 1996. London: Vintage.pp.75-81.

Carter, Angela 'The Erl-King' (1979) in *Burning Your Boats: The Collected Short Stories*. 1996. London: Vintage.pp. 186-193.

Carter, Angela 'The Company of Wolves' (1979) in *Burning Your Boats: The Collected Short Stories*. 1996. London: Vintage.pp. 212-221.

Carter, Angela. 'Penetrating to the Heart of the Forest' (1974) in *Burning Your Boats*, pp. 58-67.

Carter, Angela. 'Peter and the Wolf' (1982), in *Burning Your Boats*, pp. 284-91.

Carter, Angela. 'The Mother Lode' (1976), in *Shaking A Leg*, pp. 2-15.

Carter, Angela. 1997. *Shaking A Leg: Collected Journalism and Writings*. (ed.) Jenny Uglow. London: Chatto & Windus.

Carter, Angela. 1997. 'Notes from the Front Line' in *Shaking a Leg: Collected Journalism and Writings*. (ed.) Jenny Uglow. London: Chatto & Windus.

Carter, Angela.1997. *Love* (1971). London: Vintage.

Carter, Angela. 2000. *The Sadeian Woman: An Exercise in Cultural History* (1979). London: Virago Press.

Chadwick, Whitney. 1985. *Women Artists and the Surrealist Movement.* Boston: Little, Brown & Co.

Chatman, Seymour. 1983. *Story and Discourse: Narrative Structure in Fiction and Film.* Ithaca: Cornell UP.

Cheetham, Mark A., Linda Hutcheon. 1991. *Remembering Postmodernism.* Toronto: Oxford University Press.

Cixous, Hélène, Susan Sellers.1993. *Three Steps on the Ladder of Writing.* New York: Columbia University Press.

Cixous, Hélène, Catherine Clement. 1986 (1976). 'Sorties' in *The Newly Born Woman.* (trans.) Betsy Wing. Minneapolis: University of Minnesota Press.

Cixous, Hélène. 1990. "Castration or Decapitation?" in *Out There: Marginalization and Contemporary Cultures,* (ed.) Russell Ferguson, et al. New York & Cambridge: MIT Press.

Cixous, Hélène. 1997(1975). 'The Laugh of the Medusa' (trans.) Keith and Paula Cohen, in Robin R. Warhol and Diane Price Herndl (eds.) *Feminisms: An Anthology of Literary Theory and Criticism,* pp. 347–62. New Brunswick, NJ: Rutgers University Press.

Clark, Robert. , 1987. 'Angela Carter's Desire Machine.' *Women's Studies, 14*:147-61.

Clément, Catherine and Julia Kristeva. 2001. (1998). *The Feminine and the Sacred.* (trans.) Jane Marie Todd . New York: Columbia University Press.

Collick, John.1989. *Shakespeare, Cinema and Society.* Manchester: MUP.

Creed, Barbara. 1993. *Horror And The Monstrous Feminine : An Imaginary Abjection .* London Routledge.

Cummings, Katherine.1991.*Telling Tales: The Hysteric's Seduction in Fiction and Theory.* Stanford Univ. Press.

Danow, David. 1995. *The Spirit of Carnival: Magic Realism and the Grotesque.* Lexington, KY: University Press of Kentucky.

Davis, Lennard. 1987. *Resisting Novels: Ideology and fiction.* NY: Methuen.

De Beauvoir, Simone. 1989. *The Second Sex.* (trans.) H. Parshley. New York: Vintage Books.

de Lauretis, Teresa.1991. 'Film and the Visible', pp. 223–64 in *How Do I Look?: Queer Film and Video*. Bad Object Choices (ed.). Seattle: Bay Press.

de Lauretis, Teresa. 1994. *The Practice of Love: Lesbian Sexuality and Perverse Desire*. Bloomington: Indiana University Press.

de Lauretis, Teresa. 1984. *Alice Doesn't: Feminism, Semiotics, Cinema*. Bloomington: Indiana UP.

de Lauretis, Teresa. 1987. *Technologies of Gender: Essays on Theory, Film and Fiction*. Bloomington: Indiana U.P.

De Sade, 1990. *One Hundred and Twenty Days of Sodom* London: Arrow Books.

Deleuze Gilles and Felix Guatari. 1977. *Anti-Oedipus: Capitalism and Schizophrenia*. Trans. R. Hurley, Mark Seem and Helen Lane. New York: Viking.

Deleuze Gilles and Felix Guattari. 1988. *A Thousand Plateaus: Capitalism and Schizophrenia*. Trans. Brian Massumi. London: Athlone Press.

Dentith, Simon.1995. *Parody*. London: Routledge.

Doane, Mary Ann. 1987. *The Desire to Desire: The Woman's Film of the 1940s*. Bloomington: Indiana UP.

Duncker. Patricia. 1984. 'Re-imagining the Fairy Tales: Angela Carter's Bloody Chambers', *Literature and History*, Spring. Vol. 10, No. 1 pp. 7, 11.

Dworkin, Andrea.1974. *Woman Hating*. Available online

www.nostatusquo.com/ACLU/dworkin/WomanHating.html

Erlemann, Christiane. "What is Feminist Architecture?" in *Feminist Aesthetics* ed Gisela Ecker. Boston: Beacon Press.

Evans, Kim and Angela Carter. 1992. Post-production script of *Angela Carter's Curious Room. Omnibus*, BBC Music and Arts Department archive, part published as 'The Granada, Tooting', in Carter, *Shaking A Leg: Collected Journalism and Writings*, 1997:400.

Faris, Wendy. 1995. 'Scheherazade's Children: Magical Realism and Post-modern Fiction', in *Magical Realism: Theory, History, Community*, (ed.) Lois Parkinson Zamora and Wendy B. Faris. Durham, NY and London: Duke UP.

Finney, Brian H. 1998. 'Tall Tales and Brief Lives: Angela Carter's *Nights at the Circus.*' *The Journal of Narrative Technique* 28.2 (Spring): 161-185.

Flieger, Jerry Aline. 1991. *The Purloined Punchline: Freud's Comic Theory and the Postmodern Text.* Baltimore and London: The Johns Hopkins University Press.

Forster. E.M. 1974. *Aspects of the Novel and Related Writings.* London: Edward Arnold.

Foucault, Michel. 1966. *Les Mots et les choses.* Paris: Editions Gallimard.

Foucault, Michel. 1966b. *Utopie et littérature* [Utopia and Literature], recorded document, 7 December. Centre Michel Foucault, Bibliothèque du Saulchoir, reference C116.

Foucault Michel. 1979. 'What is an author?' in Josue Harari (ed.) *Textual Strategies: Perspectives in Post-Structuralist Criticism*, Ithaca: Cornell University Press.

Foucault, Michel. 1984. *Des espaces autres.* Lecture given by M. Foucault in 1967. (trans.) Jay Miskowiec. English title: *Of Other Spaces (1967) Heterotopias.* Available online http://foucault.info/documents.hetertopia/foucault.heterotopia.en.html [30/12/05].

Foucault, Michel. 1986. *Of other spaces. Diacritics,* Spring. pp.22-27.

Foucault, Michel. 1989. 'The Eye of Power', in S. Lotringer (ed.) *Foucault Live: Collected Interviews, 1961–1984.* New York: Semiotext(e), pp. 226–40.

Foucault, Michel. 1975/1977. *Discipline and Punish: the Birth of the Prison*, (trans.) Alan Sheridan. London, Penguin.

Foucault, Michel. 1979. *Discipline and Punish.* (trans.) Alan Sheridan. New York: Vintage.

Foucault, Michel. 1988. *Madness and Civilization: A History of Insanity in the Age of Reason.* New York:Vintage.

Foucault, Michel. 1991. *The Order of Things: An Archaeology of the Human Sciences* (1970). London: Routledge.

Foucault, Michel.1983. 'This Is Not A Pipe'. (trans. and ed.) James Harkness .Berkeley: U of California P, Quantum Books.

Foucault, Michel. 1998. *The Will to Knowledge: The History of Sexuality.* Vol. 1. (trans.) Robert Hurley. London: Penguin.

Freud, Sigmund. 1998. Extract from 'The Uncanny.' in *Gothic Horror: A Reader's Guide from Poe to King and Beyond*. Ed. Clive Bloom. Basingstoke: Macmillan.

Gamble, Sarah. 1997. *Angela Carter: Writing From the Front Line*. Edinburgh: Edinburgh UP

Gasiorek, Andrzej. 1995. *Post-War British Fiction: Realism and After*. London: Edward Arnold.

Gass, Joanne M. 1994. 'Panopticism in *Nights at the Circus*.' *Review of Contemporary Fiction* 14: 71-76.

Genette, Gerard. 1988. *Narrative Discourse Revisited*. (trans.) Jane Lewin. New York: Cornell UP.

Genocchio, Benjamin. 1995. 'Discourse, Discontinuity, Difference: the Question of 'Other' Spaces', in Sophie Watson and Katherine Gibson, (eds.) *Postmodern Cities and Spaces*. Oxford:Blackwell.

Gilbert, Sandra and Gubar, Susan. 1979. *The Madwoman in the Attic: The Woman Writer and the Nineteenth Century Literary Imagination*. New Haven: Yale UP.

Grant, Damian. 1999. *Salman Rushdie*. Plymouth: Northcote House.

Grigore, Gabriela (trans). 2008. *Nopţi la Circ*. Bucureşti: Leda.

Grosz, Elizabeth. 1989. *Sexual Subversions: Three French Feminists*. Sydney: Allen and Unwin.

Haffenden, John. 1985. *Novelists in Interview*. London:Methuen. 76-96.

Hall, L. and Huyskens, M. 2002. 'Finding joy: An exploration of the necessity of leisure in the Resettlement process of two refugee women.' *Mots Pluriels*, No.21. Online http://www.arts.uwa.edu.au/MotsPluriel/MP2102hh.html [3/12/02].

Hand, Sean. 1990. 'Missing you: Intertextuality, Transference and the Language of love' in *Intertextuality: Theories and Practices*. (ed.) Michael Worton & Judith Still. Manchester:MUP.

Hanţiu, Ecaterina. 2006. '"Déjà – LU"? : Angela Carter and The Postmodern Fairy Tale', *Lucrările simpozionului « Cultură, educaţie, societate*. Arad: Editura Universităţii "Aurel Vlaicu".

Hanţiu, Ecaterina. 1999. 'Exploring the Archetype of the Monstrous Woman- Angela Carter's *Lady of the House of Love'*. in *B.A.S.* Timişoara:Hestia.

Haraway, Donna. 1996. 'A Cyborg Manifesto: Science, Technology and Socialist –Feminism in the Late Twentieth Century' in *Simians, Cyborgs and Women: The Reinvention of Nature.* New York: Routledge. 149-181.

Harvey, David. 1996. *Justice, Nature and the Geography of Difference.* Oxford, Blackwell.

Harvey, David. 1989. *The Condition of Postmodernity.* Oxford: Basil Blackwell.

Hayman, Ronald, 1977. *Artaud and After.* New York: Oxford University Press.

Hetherington, Kevin. 1998. *The Badlands of Modernity: Heterotopia and Social Ordering.* London:Routledge

Higonnet, Margaret. (ed.). 1994. *Reconfigured Exploration of Literary Space.* Amherst:University of Massachusetts Press.

Hill, Joanne. 1987. 'Dream Machines' in *City Life*, 9-23 October, 12.

Holland, Norman. 1973. *Poems in Persons.* New York: Norton.

Hutcheon, Linda. 1985. *A Theory of Parody: The Teachings of Twentieth Century Art Forms.* London : Methuen.

Hutcheon, Linda. 1988. *A Poetics of Postmodernism: History, Theory, Fiction.* New York: Routledge.

Hutcheon, Linda. 1989. *The Politics of Postmodernism.* New York: Routledge.

Hutcheon, Linda. 1994. *Irony's edge- the Theory and Politics of Irony.* New York: Routledge.

Huxley, Aldous. 1987. *Brave New World.* London: Chatto &Windus.

Irigary, Luce. 1985. *Speculum of the Other Woman.* Trans. G.C. Gill. NewYork: Cornell UP.

Jackson, Rosemary. 1995. *Fantasy: The Literature of Subversion.* London and New York: Routledge.

Jancovich, Mark. 1992. *Horror.* London: Batsford.

Jardine, Alice, 1985. *Gynesis: Configurations of Woman and Modernity.* Ithaa: Cornell UP.

Johnson, Heather L. 1997. 'Unexpected geometries: transgressive symbolism and the transsexual subject in Angela Carter's *The Passion of New Eve*', in Bristow and Broughton *The Infernal Desires of Angela Carter: Fiction, Femininity, Feminism*. Harlow: Addison Wesley Longman.

Jordan, Elaine. 1990. 'Enthrallment: Angela Carter's Speculative Fictions' in *Plotting Change: Contemporary Women's Fiction. (ed.)* Linda Anderson. London: Edward Arnold. 19-40.

Jordan, Elaine. 1992. 'Down the Road, or History Rehearsed' in *Postmodernism and the Reading of Modernity*. (eds.) Francis Barker, Peter Hulme, Margaret Iversen. Manchester:MUP.

Jordan, Elaine. 1992. 'The Dangers of Angela Carter' in *New Feminist Discourse*. Ed. Isobel Armstrong. New York: Routledge. 119-132.

Jordan, Elaine. 1994. 'The Dangerous Edge' in *Flesh and the Mirror: Essays on the Art of Angela Carter*. London: Virago.

Jung, Carl Gustav. *The Collected Works*. Vol.13. trans. R.F.C. Hull. Princeton: Princeton UP.

Kafka, Franz. 1998. *The Castle*. (trans.) Harman, Mark. Schocken Books.

Kahn, Miriam. 1995. 'Heterotopic Dissonance in the Museum Representation of Pacific Island Cultures', in *American Anthropologist*, 97(2):324-338.

Katsavos, Anna. 1994. 'An Interview with Angela Carter' in *The Review of Contemporary Literary Fiction*. 14:3. Autumn. 11-17.

Kaveney, Roz. 1994. 'New New World Dreams: Angela Carter and Science Fiction', in Sage (ed). *Flesh and the Mirror*. London:Virago.

Keller, Catherine. 1986. *From a Broken Web: Separation, Sexism, and Self*. Boston: Beacon Press.

Kellner, Douglas. 1995. *Media Culture: Cultural Studies, Identity and the Politics Between the Modern and the Postmedern*. London and New York: Routledge.

Kent, Leonard and Elizabeth Knight (trans). 1972. *Tales of E.T.A. Hoffmann*. Chicago and London: University of Chicago Press.

King, Nicola. 2000. *Memory, Narrative, Identity*. Edinburgh: Edinburgh UP.

Kirkegaard, Soren. (1843). *Repetition d*, trans. by H. Hong and E. Hong. 1983. Princeton: Princeton University Press.

Komar, Kathleen L. 1994. 'Feminist Curves in Contemporary Literary Space' in Higonnet (ed.). *Reconfigured Exploration of Literary Space.* University of Massachusetts Press. 89-107.

Kristeva, Julia. (1977). 'Women's Time' in *The Kristeva Reader.* 1986. (ed.) Toril Moi. Oxford: Blackwell.

Kristeva, Julia. 1982. *Powers of Horror. An Essay on Abjection.* (trans.) Leon S. Roudiez. New York: Columbia University Press.

Kristeva, Julia . 1991. *Strangers to Ourselves*, (trans.) Leon S. Roudiez .New York: Columbia University Press. 29-30.

Lee, Alison. 1990. *Realism and Power. Postmodern British Fiction.* London, New York: Routledge.

Lefebvre, Henri. (1974).1991. *The production of space*, (trans.) by Donald Nicholson-Smith. Oxford:Blackwell.

Manlove, Colin. 1992. 'In the Demythologising Business: Angela Carter's *The Infernal Desire Machines of Doctor Hoffman*' in *Twentieth-Century Fantasists.* (ed.) Kath Filmer. London: Macmillan.

Marin, Louis. 1984. *Utopics: The Semiological Play of Textual Spaces.* New York: Humanity Books.

Marin, Louis. 1993. 'Frontiers of Utopia: Past and Present', *Critical Inquiry* 19: 397–420.

Mars-Jones, Adam. 1984. *Writers in Conversation.* London:ICA Video.

Massey, Doreen. 1998. 'Spatial disruptions', in Sue Golding, (ed.) *The Eight Technologies of Otherness.* London:Routledge.

Mayne, Judith. 1991. 'A Parallax View of Lesbian Authorship' in Diana Fuss (ed.) *Inside/Out: Lesbian Theories, Gay Theories.* 173–84 . New York: Routledge.

Mayne, Judith. 2000. *Framed: Lesbians, Feminist and Media Culture.* Minneapolis:University of Minnesota Press.

McHale, Brian. 1987. *Postmodernist Fiction*. London and New York:Routledge.

McLuhan, Marshall.1965. *Understanding Media*. New York: McGraw-Hill.

McLuskie, Kathleen. 1994 'The Patriarchal Bard: Feminist Criticism and Shakespeare: *King Lear* and *Measure for Measure*,' in Jonathan Dollimore, Alan Sinfield (eds.), *Political Shakespeares: New Essays in Cultural Materialism*. Manchester: MUP 88-108.

Michael, Magali Cornier. 1996. *Feminism and the Postmodern Impulse: Post-World War II Fiction*. New York: State University of New York Press.

Moi, Toril. 1985. (ed.). *Sexual/Textual Politics: Feminist Literary Theory*. London: Methuen.

More, Thomas. 1997 (1516). *Utopia*. New York: Dover Publications.

Mulvey, Laura. 1989. *Visual and other Pleasures*. Bloomington: Indiana UP.

Mulvey, Laura. 1994. 'Cinema Magic and the Old Monsters: Angela Carter's Cinema' in Sage (ed.), 230-242.

Norris, Christopher. 1988. *Derrida*. Cambridge: Harvard University Press.

O'Brien, Geraldine. 1987. 'Putting Pen to Celluloid' in *Sydney Morning Herald*, 29th September.

Orenstein, Gloria, Feman.1975. *The Theatre of the Marvellous: Surrealism and the Contemporary Stage*. New York: New York UP.

Owens, Craig. 'The Allegorical Impulse: Towards a Theory of Postmodernism' in *Beyond Recognition: Representation, Power, and Culture*. (eds.) S. Bryson, B. Kruger, L. Tillman, and J. Weinstock Berkeley. Los Angeles-Oxford: U of California Press. 52-70.

Owens, Craig. 1983. 'The Discourse of Others: Feminists and Postmodernism' in *The Anti-Aesthetic, Essays on Postmodern Culture*. (ed.) Hal Foster. Port Townsend WA: Bay Press.

Owens, Craig. 1992. 'Posing.' in *Beyond Recognition: Representation, Power, and Culture*. (eds.) S. Bryson, B. Kruger, L. Tillman, and J. Weinstock Berkeley. Los Angeles-Oxford: U of California Press. 201-217.

Palmer, Paulina 1987, 'From 'Coded Mannequin' to Bird Woman: Angela Carter's Magic Flight', in Sue Roe (ed.), *Women Reading Women's Writing*. Brighton, Sussex: Harvester Press. 179-205.

Peach, Linden. 1998. *Angela Carter.* Basingstoke: Macmillan.

Pitchford, Nicola. 2002. *Tactical Readings: Feminist Postmodernism in the Novels of Kathy Acker and Angela Carter.* Lewisburg: Bucknell UP.

Pearson, Jaqueline. 1999. ' "These Tags of Literature": Some Uses of Allusion in the Early Novels of Angela Carter.' *Critique: Studies in Contemporary Fiction.* 40.3. March. 248-256.

Punter, David. 1998. *Gothic Pathologies: The Text, the Body and the Law.* Basingstoke: Macmillan.

Ratiu Adina & Ratiu Gabriel (trans). 2007. *Magazinul Magic de Jucarii.* Bucureşti: Leda.

Relph, Edward. 1991. 'Post-modern geography', in *The Canadian Geographer/Le Geographe canadien*, 35(1):98-105.

Rentmeister, Cillie. 'The Squaring of the Circle: The Male Takeover of Power in Architectural Shapes' in Higonnet, Margaret (ed.).*Reconfigured Exploration of Literary Space.* University of Massachusetts Press.

Rich, Adrienne.1980. *On Lies, Secrets, and Silence: Selected Prose 1966-1978.* London: Virago

available online www.nbu.bg/webs/amb/american/5/rich/writing.htm

Rimmon-Kenan, Shlomith. 1983. *Narrative Theory: Contemporary Poetics.* Routledge: London.

Rob Shields 1991. *Places on the Margin: Alternative Geographies of Modernity*, London: Routledge.

Robinson, Sally. 1991. *Engendering the Subject: Gender and Self-Representation in Contemporary Women's Fiction.* Albany: State University of New York Press.

Rose, Gillian. 1993. *Feminism and Geography: The Limits of Geographical Knowledge* Cambridge: Polity.

Rubin-Suleiman, Susan. 1994. 'The Fate of the Surrealist Imagination in the Society of the Spectacle,' in *Flesh and the Mirror: Essays on the Art of Angela Carter.* (ed.) Lorna Sage. London: Virago.

Rubin-Suleiman, Susan. 1990. *Subversive Intent. Gender, Politics, and the Avant-Garde.* Cambridge: Harvard UP.

Rushdie, Salman. 1992. 'Angela Carter, 1940-92: A Very Good Wizard, a Very Dear Friend'. Online [http://www.network54.com/Forum/253130/thread/1082444436/last-1082444436/quick+deady]

Russ, Joanna. 1978. 'Science Fiction and Technology as Mystification.' in *SFS* 16:250-60, #16, November.

Russo, Mary. 1994. 'Revamping Spectacle: Angela Carter's *Nights at the Circus*' in *The Female Grotesque: Risk , Excess and Modernity.* New York: Routledge. 159-181.

Saldanha Arun. 2000. *Structuralism And The Heterotopic* 'Thinking Projects' 5/Nov. Online www.homepages.vub.ac.be/~ncarpent/koccc/Publications/thinking5.doc

Sage, Lorna. 1992. 'Interview with Angela Carter' in *New Writing.* Ed. M. Bradbury and J. Cooke. London: British Council. 185-194.

Sage, Lorna. 1994. *Angela Carter.* Plymouth: Northcote House.

Sage, Lorna. (ed.). 1994. *Flesh and the Mirror: Essays on the Art of Angela Carter.* London: Virago.

Sanders, Julie. 2002. *Novel Shakespeares – Twentieth Century Women Novelists and Appropriation.* Manchester: Manchester University Press.

Schmidt, Ricarda. 1990. 'The Journey of the Subject in Angela Carter's Fiction' in *Textual Practice* 3.1: 56-75

Sceats, Sarah. 2000. *Food, Consumption and the Body in Contemporary Women's Fiction.* Cambridge: CUP.

Selden, Raman. 1988. *A Reader's Guide to Contemporary Literary Theory.* Brighton, Sussex: Harvester Press 17-18.

Showalter, Elaine. 1985. 'Feminist Criticism in the Wilderness' in Elaine Showalter (ed.) *The New Feminist Criticism: Essays on Women, Literature and Theory.* New York: Pantheon.

Simon, Julia. 2005. *Rewriting The Body: Desire, Gender and Power in Selected Novels by Angela Carter.* Frankfurt: Peter Lang Publishing.

Soja, Edward S. 1989. *Postmodern Geographies: the Reassertion of Space in Critical Social Theory.* London, Verso.

Soja, Edward. 1995. 'Heterotopologies: a remembrance of Other spaces in the Citadel-LA', in Sophie Watson and Katherine Gibson, (eds.), *Postmodern cities and spaces.* Oxford:Blackwell.

Soja, Edward. 1996. *Thirdspace: Journeys to Los Angeles and Other Real and Imagined Places.* Blackwell:Oxford.

Stam, Robert. 1989. *Subversive Pleasures: Bakhtin, Cultural Criticism, and Film.* Johns Hopkins University Press.

Stamm, Robert. 1982. 'On the Carnivalesque', *Wedge*, I, 47-55.

Tamboukou, Maria . 2000. 'Of other spaces: women's colleges at the turn of the nineteenth century in the UK', in *Gender, Place and Culture*, 7(3):247-263.

Todorov, Tzvetan. 1973. *The Fantastic: A Structural Approach to a Literary Genre.* (trans.) Richard Howard. Cleveland: Press of Case Western Reserve University.

Turner, Victor. 1974. *Dramas, fields, and metaphors: Symbolic action in human society.* Ithaca, NY: Cornell University Press.

Turner, Victor. 1982. *From ritual to theatre: The human seriousness of play.* NewYork: Performing Arts Journal Publications.

van Gennep, Arnold. 1960. *The rites of* passage. M. B. Vizedom & G. L. Caffee (trans.). Chicago: University of Chicago Press.

Vice, Sue (ed.).1996. *Psychoanalytic Criticism: A Reader.* Cambridge: Polity Press.

Ward, Barbara. 1976. *The Home of Man.* in Vallorani, 1994.

Vallorani, Nicoletta. 1994. 'The Body of the City' in *Science Fiction Studies*. No. 64. vol 21. part 3.

Warner, Marina. 1994. 'Angela Carter: Bottle Blonde, Double Drag', in *Flesh and the Mirror: Essays on the Art of Angela Carter*. Ed. Sage Lorna. London: Virago. 243-257.

Wearing, Betsy. 1998. *Leisure and Feminist Theory*. London: Sage Publications.

Webb, Darren. 2005 'Bakhtin at the Seaside', *Theory, Culture & Society* 22: 121–38.

Webb, Kate. 1994. 'Seriously funny: *Wise Children*' in *Flesh and the Mirror: Essays on the Art of Angela Carter*. Ed. Sage Lorna. London: Virago. 279-308.

Wheatley, David. 1996. Interview with Angela Carter. London. 5th April.

Whitford, Margaret (ed). 1992. *The Irigary Reader*. Cambridge: Blackwell.

Willemen, Paul. 1994. *Looks and Frictions: Essays in Cultural Studies and Film Theory*. London: British Film Institute.

Williams, Linda Ruth. 1995. *Critical Desire: Psychoanalysis and the Literary Subject*. London & New York: Edward Arnold.

Wilson, Elizabeth. 1991 *The Sphinx in the City. Urban Life, the Control of Disorder and Woman*. London:Virago.

Wolf, Christa. 1998. *Cassandra. A Novel and Four Essays*. New York: Farrar, Straus and Giroux.

***

UNIVERSITY OF WINCHESTER
LIBRARY

Lightning Source UK Ltd.
Milton Keynes UK
UKOW04f0315210214

226885UK00002B/15/P